SECOND EDITION

FORCES OF DEVIANCE

SECOND EDITION

FORCES OF DEVIANCE

Understanding the Dark Side of Policing

VICTOR E. KAPPELER
Eastern Kentucky University

RICHARD D. SLUDER
Central Missouri State University

GEOFFREY P. ALPERT
University of South Carolina

3/04

WAVELAND
PRESS, INC.
Prospect Heights, Illinois

For information about this book, write or call:
  Waveland Press, Inc.
  P.O. Box 400
  Prospect Heights, Illinois 60070
  (847) 634-0081

Photo Credits
P. 27, Bettmann Archive; p. 59, *Chicago Tribune*; p. 83, *Chicago Tribune*; p. 109, Armando F. Mola; p. 149, *Milwaukee Sentinel*; p. 165, Armando F. Mola; p. 187, Architect of the Capitol; p. 253, *Chicago Tribune*.

CONTENTS

11 Prospects for Controlling Deviance
Forging the Boundaries of Police Behavior   253

FOREWORD

From the Baltimore election frauds of 1875 to the beating of Abner Louima in 1997, Americans have followed the misdeeds of their police with a complex mixture of disgust, fear, and prurient pleasure. From the Lexow Committee of 1894 to the Mollen Commission of 1993, scholars, administrators, and concerned citizens have produced suggestions for understanding, detecting, punishing, and preventing police misconduct. Given the sheer tonnage of government reports, newspaper articles and academic publications on this topic, is there really any room for another volume on police deviance?

Well—yes, there is. *Forces of Deviance: The Dark Side of Policing* not only brings together a great deal of previously scattered information, it adds some substantial insights of its own.

One of the book's earliest and most original contributions is an increased understanding of *why* Americans find the topic of police misconduct so fascinating. It is difficult, after all, to imagine a similar, century-old market for reports and analyses (not to mention novels, films, and movies of the week) devoted to the moral frailties of school teachers, doctors, plumbers, bankers, and air traffic controllers. Yet each of these occupations has a major effect on our daily well-being and surely members of each have, at one time or another, neglected their duties, accepted gratuities, or murdered their spouses. But news of such derelictions produces neither the interest nor the disquiet that accompanies news of misbehavior on the part of the police.

Forces of Deviance reminds us that the police occupy a uniquely complex place in our civic lives. Police are the most visible component of the branch of government meant to control harmful behavior and to protect the civil liberties of the population. We expect them not only to enforce the law but to act as moral exemplars—to provide by their own behavior a model for the law-abiding citizen. When police disappoint these expectations, we respond with the same mixture of hurt, anger, and naughty glee that accompanies the discovery of the preacher committing adultery.

But the police also have a degree of temporal power denied to the preacher. To support them in their mission of protecting civil peace, society permits them to use a degree of force far greater than is permitted to other citizens. This delegation of force is acceptable only when we are convinced that the police use that force solely in a lawful and legitimate manner. When the behavior of some officers causes us to doubt that conviction, we have the right to fear that the police are at least as dangerous as the criminals from whom they are supposed to protect us.

We also need the police to do their work effectively and efficiently. Misconduct is corrosive, as the need to cover up one illegal act produces another and another. Misconduct is expensive, as agencies need to use tax money to protect themselves from lawsuits and find themselves liable to extensive damage awards. And misconduct is dangerous, when corrupt police allow criminal activity to flourish or when substance abuse affects an officer's judgment.

Finally, we need the police to do their work fairly and equitably, but officers are drawn from a society that is neither fair nor equitable. Part of our fascination with police misconduct is the fact that it often reflects the biases and prejudices of society—prejudices that some of us try to justify, and others try to deny.

This volume also shows clearly how policing structures misconduct. Police are, of course, capable of committing crimes that are intrinsically unrelated to their status as police officers. An officer who assaults a spouse or robs a liquor store while off-duty is certainly guilty of a crime, as is anyone else who performs the same acts. But the occupation of policing provides additional opportunities for misconduct, opportunities that are unique to policing.

Some of these opportunities facilitate crimes that could also be performed by anyone else. The officer who investigates a burglarized jewelry shop and pockets a watch which is then included in the report of missing items is guilty of larceny. But the most distinctive feature of policing—perhaps the defining feature—is its authority and its monopoly on the legitimate use of force or threat of force. Abuse of subjects, coercion of sexual favors, misappropriation of impounded property or the manufacture of evidence all depend on the abuse of police authority. And, of course, when authority is abused in the pursuit of personal gain, it becomes corruption.

Forces of Deviance not only makes these distinctions clear, it shows how the development of American law enforcement, with its insistence on police authority being subject to local political control, has fostered a climate in which misconduct is allowed to flourish. This is illustrated with gripping descriptions of some of the more egregious cases of contemporary police deviance. The roles of training, organization, and administration are carefully explored; the history of police reform and its ambivalent results thoughtfully described. Finally, there is an annotated catalogue of recommendations for improvement.

This is an informative, disturbing, and challenging book, one that forces the reader to confront both the extent and the consequences of police deviance. It is a valuable addition to the bookshelf of any student of American policing.

Dorothy H. Bracey
John Jay College of Criminal Justice

PREFACE

Misdeeds of police officers have a remarkable ability to spark media interest and to capture public attention. Abner Louima, Rodney King, Laurence Powell, Stacey Kuhn, and Justin Volpe have all become household names. Many other activities of the police have come under public scrutiny; most of these cases involve some form of "deviance."

Two white Detroit police officers were convicted of second-degree murder for bludgeoning Malice Green, a black motorist, to death with metal flashlights. A government report criticized the Bureau of Alcohol, Tobacco, and Firearms for its incompetence in handling the David Koresh case in Waco, Texas. Federal Bureau of Investigation Director William Sessions was forced to resign his office because he allegedly misused government funds for personal use. The U.S. Marshals Service and the FBI have come under fire for their use of deadly force at Ruby Ridge, and Congress has begun an investigation into practices at the FBI's crime laboratory. The "king" of corrupt cops, New York City Police Department officer Michael Dowd, testified publicly before the Mollen Commission that he: accepted thousands of dollars a week for protecting drug dealers; regularly stole from crime victims and suspects; routinely drank on duty; and snorted lines of cocaine off the dashboard of his patrol cruiser. In addition to these "celebrated" cases, citizens are bombarded with reports of police misdeeds on a regional or local level.

With the images of police violence and corruption palpably fixed in their minds, citizens are less willing to tolerate police misbehavior. Feeling pressure from constituents, public officials have taken a more active role in curtailing police corruption and deviance. These actions are highly publicized. With policing under the microscope, there have been significant shifts in the social acceptability of police violence, corruption, and other forms of deviance.

These circumstances form the backdrop for writing this book. Aware that police deviance is a complex, multifaceted topic, we do more than simply provide students with a "cookbook" text. The text relies on both theory and description. Our goal is to enhance the student's conceptual understanding of "deviance" and the special significance of the term in the unique environment of policing. After providing the student with a theoretical framework, we then dissect several noteworthy cases. The often grim realities of police deviance provide a graphic illustration of theories and principles. The book concludes with a discussion of the means and prospects for controlling police deviance and corruption.

Throughout the text we endeavor to address police deviance analytically, conceptually and integratively. To do this we have drawn heavily from the contributions of several leading scholars in the areas of policing, criminology, and sociology. Their theories, ideas, and opinions are woven throughout the text. The contributions of these scholars to our understanding of both deviance and policing made this work possible. While mention of each scholar would be impractical, several have contributed to the intellectual filter through which this book was created and deserve recognition. They include: Peter K. Manning, Jerome H. Skolnick, Egon Bittner, Victor G. Strecher, William J. Chambliss, John Van Maanen, Lawrence Sherman, Dorothy Bracey, David Carter, Thomas Barker and Sidney Harring. Crafting a text that is theoretically informed, analytically oriented, and practically relevant is a tall order. If readers discern the presence of these elements as they work their way through the book, at least one of our goals will have been accomplished.

Victor E. Kappeler
Eastern Kentucky University
Richard Sluder
Central Missouri State University
Geoffrey P. Alpert
University of South Carolina

ACKNOWLEDGMENTS

Writing a book, like any worthwhile endeavor, is a major undertaking that requires the assistance of many people. A final manuscript is seldom the sole product of those fortunate enough to claim its authorship. We owe a debt of collective gratitude to the many people who took part in bringing this work together. Larry K. Gaines, Richard N. Holden, Michael S.Vaughn, and Allen D. Sapp deserve acknowledgment for their contributions. They provided us with institutional support, advice, or literature during the writing of this book. Several of our colleagues were especially generous with their time. Gary W. Potter, Victor G. Strecher, and Peter B. Kraska acted as sounding boards improving on many of the ideas that eventually appeared in this book. Dorothy Bracey deserves special thanks. She was not only kind enough to write the foreword to this book, but she introduced the principal author to the wonderful world of cultural anthropology. We remain in her debt.

A larger collection of academicians, scholars, and practitioners contributed to our development in the early years. To all of them, we express our appreciation. Rolando V. del Carmen, Frank P. Williams, James Short, Dennis Longmire, Margaret Farnworth, Jane Williams, Robert Shearer, Rudolph C. Ortquist, and Matt Eichor, among others, have played especially important roles in our careers.

We are in debt to the kind people at Waveland Press, Inc. Neil Rowe has been a formidable force in moving many of our projects from conception to publication. His considerable talents, energies, and resources made it possible for our books to appear in classrooms across the country. Without his talents, our work would have remained merely a good idea. Carol Rowe's contribution to our work is immeasurable. She made what can be a laborious and frustrating undertaking a joy. It is doubtful that this work would have been completed had she not made it so enjoyable. Besides holding our hands through the entire project, Carol's marvelous conceptual and editorial skills vastly improved the quality of this manuscript. We ramble less, say more, and say it better because of Carol. Gayle McSemek-Zawilla did an excellent job of proofing our final manuscript; her eye for detail did not go unnoticed.

Finally, we dedicate this book to our families who have always been a source of encouragement and more than a little tolerant of the work that keeps us apart.

Chapter One

THE IDEA OF POLICE DEVIANCE

Definitions, Perceptions and Concerns

> We enjoy the luxury of opinion without the difficulty of thought.
> John F. Kennedy   (1917–1963)

The criminal justice system—composed of components including police, courts, and corrections—plays an intimate and integral role in ensuring social tranquility, order, justice, and freedom. Our lives are constantly affected by the decisions and actions of criminal justice agencies and their personnel.

The police are the most likely component of the system of criminal justice to have an influence on our daily lives. There are about 1.8 million public employees in the justice system; more than 800,000 serve in a law enforcement capacity (Maguire, Pastore, & Flanagan, 1996). The police are both the most numerous and the most visible component of criminal justice. The vast majority of commissioned personnel in police agencies are uniformed, making them readily identifiable to the public. In addition, the majority of commissioned personnel in police agencies are assigned to patrol duties, and most work out of marked patrol vehicles.

The influence of the police over citizens' lives cannot be explained simply on the basis of numbers or visibility. In a democratic society striving for freedom, the police are vested with both powers and responsibilities accorded few others. For example, the police have been given the power to detain and arrest persons, to search and seize property, and to apply various levels of force—up to and including deadly force—in carrying out legal mandates. The authority inherent in such powers distinguishes law enforcement officials from employees in other government agencies. Another differentiating factor is that the police have been given the responsibility of responding to citizens' requests for services. While other agencies may deal with citizens from time to time, the police have been delegated this responsibility on a continuous basis. Citizens frequently call the police for assistance regardless of whether the matter requires a traditional law enforcement response.

As an institutional force (Bittner, 1995a), the police are intricately intertwined in the social fabric of American democracy. Law enforcement officials have been charged with a complex mission and accorded extraordinary powers. Society has done so with the expectation that officers will fulfill their responsibilities in a fair, impartial, ethical, and legal manner. In essence, this means police hold positions of public trust and are expected to carry out their mission in a fashion consistent with the fundamental principles underlying a democratic society.

For some segments of society, the police represent what has been termed the "thin blue line" that separates anarchy from order. Seen in this light, the police represent a governmental body whose ultimate mission is to protect the civil liberties of citizens. The police are confronted with serving in what are often competing and contradictory roles in their responsibilities to enforce the law while keeping the public peace and doing justice (Skolnick, 1994). It is often necessary for the police to restrict or to take away the freedoms of some to protect the liberties of others. Adding to the paradox is the fact that the police themselves represent one of the greatest threats to civil liberties. Police who violate the public trust by engaging in inappropriate work-related activities—such as making illegal arrests, conducting unwarranted searches, or using excessive force—are one of the greatest threats to the protections extended to citizens in a free and democratic society.

Because of both the onerous mission and the powers accorded the police, the public has always had a deep fascination with law enforcement personnel and their activities. Public scrutiny of the police function, however, has traditionally been most intense whenever police become involved in high-profile activities and work-related misconduct. Misconduct involves not only a violation of the public trust but also a threat to the right to be free from unjust and unwarranted governmental restrictions and intrusions.

PUBLIC PERCEPTION OF POLICE MISCONDUCT

One of the by-products of holding a position of public trust is the necessity to guard against even a suspicion of violating one's duties. The public is exposed to various reports of police misconduct as well as to stories that suggest impropriety. Police officers and police executives have an obligation to avoid the appearance of impropriety. As the former chief of police in Houston, Texas and former commissioner of NYPD Lee Brown (1997) has remarked, "it is critical that police leaders judge their own behavior on the following basis: 'Do my actions have the appearance of impropriety' rather than 'have I violated the law?'" (p. 26).

To study police deviance objectively, one must first be able to distinguish between actual misconduct and the mere appearance of wrongdoing. Students of policing have an obligation to guard against the sensationalism and distortion often present in media accounts of police activities. All too often, the media leave uncritical readers with the impression that an obvious and intentional wrong has taken place. These accounts seldom provide a context from which to understand the reported actions. A few media reports on the police that appeared in a national newspaper serve to illustrate the point.

- Deputy U.S. Marshal Karen Davis, assigned to the Louisville, Kentucky, office, brought charges of sexual harassment against U.S. Marshal Charles Logsdon. A lawsuit alleges that her employers failed to take action on her complaint. [*USA Today*, 6/11/97, p. 7A]
- Federal Bureau of Investigation agents in Augusta, Georgia, lost or misappropriated a $20,000 ring and $6,000 in cash seized during the search of a gambler's home. [*USA Today*, 7/14/92, p. 4A]
- Shelton, Connecticut, Police Chief William Pitman was suspended from the force for failure to comply with the city's requirements for awarding contracts. The chief apparently awarded a $7,800 contract without proper bidding. [*USA Today*, 9/11/92, p. 12A]
- Emery County, Utah, Sheriff LaMar Guymon and a county attorney were ordered to surrender $100,900 seized from a motorist who was never charged with a crime. [*USA Today*, 6/5/92, p. 7A]
- In Syracuse, New York, employees discovered 11 bags of cocaine under the seat of a police vehicle. The patrol unit had been assigned to other municipal employees who found the drugs while adjusting the seats. [*USA Today*, 6/2/92, p. 8A]

In each of these media accounts, there is a tendency to infer that the police engaged in an intentional act of wrongdoing. However, close inspection of these items shows that reaching such a conclusion requires a leap beyond the presented facts. In the account of the Federal Bureau of Investigation (FBI) agents, readers are left to choose between whether agents lost or stole the cash and jewelry. In the case of the police chief, the audience is left to draw its own conclusion whether the chief intentionally violated the city's bidding requirements and whether he received personal gain from the alleged impropriety. In the matter of the sheriff, the reader is not told whether the money was seized according to forfeiture laws. The uncovering of drugs by municipal employees leaves to one's imagination how the drugs got into the police vehicle. The deputy marshall's charges have not yet been verified.

Many media accounts of police misconduct offer limited information. There is also a tendency to generalize from limited evidence to the entire police system. Such generalizations lead some of the public to estimate the extent and frequency of police misconduct as far greater than what actually occurs. While reports of wrongdoing should raise concern, popular media accounts must be judiciously, objectively, and circumspectly assessed before any conclusions can be drawn about alleged acts of police misconduct and the larger police institution.

One undeniable conclusion about media accounts of police misconduct is that they generate substantial public interest. Consider, for example, some additional reports presented by the media. While these reports are based on factual events and show the extent to which police in select departments engage in misconduct they are, nevertheless, limited evidence of misconduct across the police system and provide no context for understanding the significance of the actions reported.

- Investigation into evidence tampering, false testimony, and the planting of evidence at crime scenes by Philadelphia Police officers has led to the overturn of over 100 criminal convictions since 1995. Departmental officials insist that corruption in the department is limited to a few officers. [*New York Times*, 5/13/97, p. A8]

- During a 2-year period residents of Cincinnati, Ohio, brought 1,400 allegations of brutality against officers in the department. Of the 1,400 complaints alleging that police officers used excessive or unnecessary force, only 1 case resulted in a finding that an officer used improper force. [*USA Today*, 6/23/97, p. 10A]

- In the first six months of 1992, 29 police officers in the Washington, D.C. Police Department were indicted on criminal charges. The department has a 4,800 officer force. [*USA Today*, 7/1/92, p. 9A]

- In 1992, New York City began one of the largest police corruption probes in the history of the department. Federal investigators and a board appointed by Mayor David Dinkins probed corruption and lawlessness in 10 of the department's 75 precincts. They investigated claims that New York City police officers distributed drugs, accepted bribes, extorted merchants, and committed murders. [*USA Today*, 6/19/92, p. 3A]

- A 6-month long investigation of excessive force and brutality in the Los Angeles Sheriff's Department found that abuses were widespread and that there was "disturbing evidence of excessive force and lax discipline." [Kolts, 1992, p. 169]

- Over 61 percent of the 3,440 citizen complaints filed against members of the Boston Police Department in the 1980s were levied against 11 percent of the 3,200 officers. The 5 officers receiving the most complaints are still employed by the department and were cleared in 90 of the 100 citizen complaints they received. [*USA Today*, 10/15/92, p. 12A]

Each of these accounts of police wrongdoing was accompanied by intense media speculation and public attention. The next two sections look at both varying perceptions and the common concerns about police conduct that transcend those differences in order to understand why there is such a high level of public interest in the "dark side" of policing.

Diversity of Public Perceptions

For the most part, citizens view the police positively. Nearly all of the research on public attitudes reports that the majority of the general public are supportive toward their local police (Flanagan & Vaughn, 1995). Even though the majority of citizens have a positive view of the police, this support is not uniform across all segments of society and in all social settings.

Scott Decker (1981) argued that an attitude-effectiveness link is critical to the proper functioning of the police. That is, where citizens hold positive attitudes toward police, police actions will be more effective. This idea was discussed earlier in the *Task Force Report: The Police* (1967):

> Poor police-community relations adversely affect the ability of the police to prevent crime and apprehend criminals. People hostile to the police are not so likely to report violations of the law, even when they are the victims. They are even less likely to report suspicious people or incidents, to testify as witnesses voluntarily, or to come forward and provide information. . . . Yet citizen assistance is crucial to law enforcement agencies if the police are to solve an appreciable portion of crimes that are committed. (p. 144)

Since research findings indicate citizens generally hold positive attitudes toward police, they should be receiving sufficient assistance from citizens. However, many citizens refuse to report crimes, provide information to police, or testify when it would seem in their best interest to do so.

The consensus among researchers is that older citizens tend to view the police more positively than do younger citizens (Waddington & Braddock, 1991). There are several possible explanations for this disparity in views. First, younger persons are resistant to and less respectful of authority. Younger persons tend to value their freedom and to resent control. When police inquire into their activities or stop them for violations, many young people see this as an infringement on their personal freedom. Second, younger persons tend to have more frequent and negative contacts with the police (Snyder & Sickmund, 1996). This is especially true with regard to minor offenses. Youths may feel that the police target them for control to a greater extent than older persons are targeted. Finally, as people become older they tend to become more conservative. The police represent an institution which is held in high regard by more conservative individuals, and the institution is a tool by which society upholds conservative values (Gaines, Kappeler & Vaughn, 1997).

Research also suggests that white citizens tend to view the police more positively than do minority citizens (Nasser, 1993; Waddington & Braddock, 1991). In a study by Herbert Jacob (1971), African Americans tended to believe that the police were more corrupt, more unfair, harsher, tougher, less friendly, and crueler than did whites. Jacob also found that African Americans generally were more dissatisfied with police service in comparison to the white population. David Bordua and Larry Tift (1971) found that African Americans were more angry, unhappy, and upset about encounters with the police. A national poll of citizens conducted by Gallup found that 74 percent of whites rated their local police as good whereas only 48 percent of African-American citizens gave police this favorable rating. Likewise when white citizens were asked if they thought police gave truthful testimony in court, 76 percent said yes, whereas only 52 percent of African-American citizens agreed (Nasser, 1993).

There are multiple explanations for these attitudes toward and perceptions of the police. First, minorities have a higher number of negative contacts with the police relative to non-minorities (Erez, 1984; Skogan, 1991). Minorities tend to have a higher representation in arrest statistics (FBI, 1997). Second, minorities tend to be victimized at higher rates than non-minorities (Maguire et al., 1996). Victimization adversely affects views of the police, especially when the police fail to apprehend the perpetrator. Third, as the research suggests, police do in fact treat minority citizens differently than they treat white citizens (Gaines et al., 1997), and minority citizens recognize this fact (Nasser, 1993).

The complex relationship grew out of urban violence and the turbulent racial history of the United States. A 1995 U.S. Justice Department survey found that only 31 percent of blacks nationwide—compared with 65 percent of whites—expressed "a great deal or quite a lot" of confidence in the police. Most whites surveyed believed the police could protect them from violent crime; most blacks did not. A report on Chicago's community-policing program released in November 1996 also found that blacks were less satisfied with police performance than were either whites or Hispanics (White, 1997). Finally attitudes toward the police are affected by the racial composition of both a city's political leadership and its police force. James Frank, Steven G. Brandl, Francis T. Cullen, and Amy Stichman (1996) found that "negative attitudes toward the police are part of a larger belief system that includes negative attitudes toward authority exercised by a government composed of individuals who belong to a different racial or ethnic group" (p. 332).

Citizens from a lower socioeconomic background are more likely to view the police negatively. Stan Albrecht and Miles Green (1977) found that minorities from poor urban areas held the least favorable attitude toward the police; urban middle-class whites held the most positive attitudes. The reasons for negative perceptions include perceived injustice, lack of concern and attention on the part of the police, and ineffectiveness—especially in comparison to the level of services provided wealthy citizens. Lower socioeconomic areas within most urban cities experience the greatest crime rates, generally contain a higher number of minorities, and receive fewer social services from the police.

Peggy Sullivan, Roger Dunham, and Geoffrey Alpert (1987) found significant differences in how Cubans, African Americans, and whites *structure* their attitudes. The police are perceived not by a single public but by multiple publics. Each has differing views of the police, their conduct, and the services provided. The publics' attitudes are not unidimensional and are structured differentially for different population samples.

One of the most important factors affecting opinions of police misconduct is the differential contacts citizens have with the police. While

> dissatisfaction seems to be limited to a minority, that minority has significance beyond its size because those who comprise it tend also to be those most likely to come into contact with the police, much of that contact being confrontational. (Waddington & Braddock, 1991, p. 31)

Those most supportive of the police often experience little actual contact. To them, misconduct may appear to be an aberration that represents little more than one "rotten apple" in an otherwise clean barrel. Media depictions of police misconduct often reinforce this conception of policing with excusing language. Following a televised investigative report into police sexual violence against women, Tom Jarriel (1997) closed the segment which appeared on *20/20* with "Again, most cops are extremely good and law abiding. And our safety depends upon them" (p. 10). The concluding remark was made despite the investigation's finding that "too many trusting women end up betrayed by the badge" (p. 1). Those groups less supportive of the police, often having more experience and contact, may view incidents of police misconduct as corroborating their unfavorable experiences. In later chapters, we will resume the discussion of different publics and how the police respond differentially to them.

Common Public Concerns

Public concern with the misconduct of the police is not always affected by differences in age, class, gender, or experience. There are several plausible explanations for the intense scrutiny that often accompanies accounts of police misconduct that transcend these differences. One obvious explanation is the journalistic adage that bad news is good news. Stories centering around suffering, tragedy and venality sell newspapers and attract viewer attention (Kappeler, Blumberg, & Potter, 1996).

While this is one explanation for the massive attention given accounts of police misconduct, there are other important reasons for intense public interest. First, the police hold *symbolic positions* in society. That is, they are the most visible component of a system empowered to control harmful and criminal behaviors (Kraska & Kappeler, 1988). The public assumes the police will obey the laws they are charged with enforcing; beyond that, it expects the police to exhibit model behavior. The police are "role models and parental figures" for the public (Marx, 1992, p. 167). Clearly, when the police engage in the behaviors they are mandated to control, they are deficient law enforcers, poor role models, inappropriate parental figures and incompetent teachers. Thus, a critical problem with police misconduct is the hypocrisy of the behavior.

When the police engage in deviant acts, their behavior is not only hypocritical, it is a precondition for further and perhaps more serious forms of police misconduct. This means, in essence, that some deviant behaviors may have a *corrupting influence* on the police (Kraska & Kappeler, 1988). For example, a police officer who uses excessive force while effecting an arrest may "doctor" his or her report adding additional criminal charges to justify the initial impropriety. If called to testify in an administrative hearing, criminal proceeding, or civil lawsuit, the officer must then perjure him/herself to cover for the first two crimes. A similar corrupting influence can be seen in the hypothetical case where a rookie officer accepts payoff money in exchange for allowing an illegal enterprise to operate. Unless the officer is willing to report the initial indiscretion to a superior and to accept the consequences, the officer will be forced to tolerate further criminal acts by the briber even if the officer decides not to accept future payoff money (McAlary, 1987). Once the officer's integrity has been compromised, the briber can use the threat of disclosure to control the officer. Both of these hypotheticals illustrate the corrupting influence of an initial act of police deviancy. Following a deviant act, an avalanche of further misconduct may be necessary to cover the initial indiscretion. If the public learns about progressive corruption, it may assume any report of police wrongdoing is only the "tip of the iceberg"—exacerbating the tendency to view police misconduct as widespread.

A third reason why the public is highly sensitized to police wrongdoing is that police perform an *unparalleled function*. Unlike other public organizations, the police are charged with an important social function: to promote and to preserve civil order and to protect constitutional guarantees (ABA, 1976). To accomplish this, police have been granted highly privileged powers. Egon Bittner (1995a) has argued that at the core of this power is the police prerogative to use violence and deadly force, if necessary, to carry out their responsibilities. This unparalleled function of the police is not taken lightly by the public. Hence, when charges are made alleging police misconduct, the public, as should be expected, reacts with alarm and is vitally interested in resolving the matter.

The public also has an *economic interest* in controlling police misconduct. From a legal perspective, a major concern for public officials over the past few decades has been the increasing number of civil lawsuits filed by citizens (del Carmen, 1991; Kappeler, 1997). When police use excessive force, for example, the result is likely to be a civil suit filed by the injured citizen. At a minimum, the agency, and perhaps the officer, will incur legal expenses in defending the lawsuit. The far larger concern is when plaintiffs are awarded damages that can amount to millions of dollars (del Carmen, 1991). Ultimately, the public bears the financial burden in such cases, either through increased taxes or higher insurance fees (Kappeler, 1997).

Other forms of misconduct also carry financial costs to citizens. From a management perspective, some forms of police misconduct result in the inefficient or ineffective delivery of police services in addition to the unlawful or unethical behavior. For example, police so involved in graft or corrupt practices that a significant portion of their work time is consumed cannot fulfill the responsibilities of the job for which they were hired. If businesses do not feel they are receiving sufficient protection, they may hire private security or price their product higher to cover losses that result from crime. The consumer ultimately pays the costs. In sum, these and other types of cases involving police improprieties amount to significant financial costs to citizens.

Finally, there is an especially high level of interest in several varieties of police deviance because they represent a *safety hazard* to the general well-being of societal members (Kraska & Kappeler, 1988). While officers who use excessive force present obvious dangers to the public, officers who engage in other forms of police misconduct threaten the public's safety and sense of order. Police who use illicit drugs or who consume alcohol on the job are potential threats. Substance abuse affects reaction time, the ability to think clearly, and the capacity to make decisions. Other forms of police deviance may also indirectly threaten citizen safety. When criminal enterprises receive police protection, for example, citizen safety is endangered because some forms of crime are permitted to flourish. Clearly, many forms of police misconduct have public safety ramifications that extend beyond the initial deviant act committed by the officer.

In summary, when police improprieties become known, they generate a considerable amount of public attention. Most of the concern focuses on the violation of public trust. As mentioned earlier, the police have been given tremendous powers and responsibilities. When police abuse those powers by engaging in inappropriate work-related activities, the public views this as a violation of the trust they have placed in the police. This factor alone suggests that there is ample justification for the intense public scrutiny that often accompanies reports of police misconduct. The public, however, must guard against making unwarranted generalizations or accepting excusing language based on the limited information often provided in popular media accounts of police misconduct. While there is great public interest in the topic, citizens have the obligation to assess reports candidly and fairly before reaching conclusions about the nature and extent of misconduct in the police system.

DEVIANCE AS A THEORETICAL CONSTRUCT

To study the topic of police deviance objectively, it is essential to define what is meant by the term *deviance* and then to develop an analytical framework to examine forms of police deviance. Sociology has a rich tradition in the study of deviant behavior. However, as with other behaviors, defining police deviance has proven problematic.

Defining what is deviant is akin to defining other socially unacceptable behavior. That is, the task of reaching a definition is often vexing and bewildering to those attempting to articulate what is, as opposed to what is not, deviant. Supreme Court Justice Potter Stewart once remarked about obscenity that, "I know it when I see it." Similarly, most of us would admit that we know deviance when we see it. Using illegal drugs, cheating in school, and stealing are typical examples of what is considered deviant. Conceptualized this way, determining what is deviant is inherently subjective—it is whatever one says it is. The problem with a subjective conceptualization of deviance is its variability and imprecision. While one person might consider smoking marijuana to be deviant, another might regard the behavior as normal. Hence, subjective or individualistic conceptions of deviance are riddled with uncertainty and are often based on personal prejudice.

To circumvent the obvious difficulties associated with using subjective conceptions, we can examine previous attempts to reach a uniform definition of the term "deviance." Definitions are often expressed in quite general terms. For example, "deviance refers to differentness" (Meier, 1989, p. 204). Providing a nominal definition, David Matza (1969) suggested that "to deviate is to stray, as from a path or standard" (p. 10). Criminology texts typically define deviance in a Durkheimian (1938/1982) tradition as any behavior that members of a social group define as violating their norms. Finally, if one were to consult a dictionary, deviance would be defined as behavior which departs from an accepted norm.

While serving as a beginning point, these definitions have some problems. At best, they sketch the outer limits of the term by noting that to deviate is to be "different" and that deviant behavior departs from accepted "norms." These definitions are still too imprecise to understand fully what is meant by deviant behavior. *Difference*, for example, is a matter of degree and depends on context. To be different would include acts from wearing shorts in the winter to committing multiple murders. While the *norms* of one group may condone certain behaviors, other groups' norms may be in conflict with the norms of the first group. To illustrate, certain religious groups approve of animal sacrifice, but the practice would be considered highly inappropriate by the majority of mainstream religious groups practicing in the United States today. Clearly then, behaviors that some would classify as deviant, others would consider acceptable and appropriate. Because of the vast differences in determining what is deviant by using these simple definitions, we will look at deviance within the context of four sociological paradigms: the statistical paradigm, the absolutist or violation of values paradigm, the reactivist paradigm, and deviance in the context of normative systems.

Statistical Definition of Deviance

The statistical definition of deviance is perhaps the easiest to understand. Using the statistical definition, deviance is any behavior that departs from the average (Becker, 1963). On the one hand, some behaviors are common and occur with some regularity. These "common" behaviors, would be considered "normal." On the other hand, behaviors which are rare or that occur fairly infrequently would be considered deviant. However, simple use of this definition presents many difficulties. Since the statistical definition requires the use of an average, many persons who may not ordinarily be thought of as deviant would be classified as such using this conception. Marshall B. Clinard and Robert F. Meier (1995) have noted, for example, that if one were to use this definition, those who have never stolen, never smoked marijuana, or never had premarital sex would all be classified as deviant. Thus, behavior which significantly departs from the average even in a "positive" direction is classified as deviant. To illustrate, police who use excessive force to make an exceptional number of arrests would be classified as deviant, as would those who have received an inordinate number of commendations for performance beyond the call of duty. Thus, use of the statistical definition is problematic for the study of police deviance.

Absolutist Definition of Deviance

Up until the 1950s, many social scientists viewed the concept of deviance as an "absolute." For the most part, it was implicitly understood (at least by many social scientists) that some behaviors were inherently and intrinsically deviant. Behaviors typically falling into the category of "deviant" were those involving a violation of criminal law—especially those crimes committed by persons with little social influence or power. Interestingly, ethical and legal infractions committed by business persons, corporations, and professionals were often not considered as "absolutely" deviant (Clinard & Meier, 1995).

The absolutist perspective on deviance is premised on a few important assumptions. First, it is assumed that members of society agree that certain behaviors should be proscribed. Second, it is assumed that people are both acquainted with and understand the rules prohibiting certain acts. In short, the absolutist perspective suggests that there is a consensus in society that some acts are repugnant. To control these behaviors, certain rules have been adopted, endorsed, clearly articulated, and made known to all societal members.

Although the absolutist perspective on deviance continues to be supported by some, it has come under attack by others. The absolutist perspective has been criticized for supposing that there is universal agreement among societal members that certain behaviors should be prohibited. In contrast, some have argued that the values held by Americans are pluralistic rather than absolutist (Douglas, 1970). This criticism points to substantial disagreement in society over which behaviors should be considered deviant. In a similar vein, it has been suggested that those acts considered by absolutists as deviant most often reflect the values and morals of the middle class. Hence, acts defined as deviant may actually represent a violation of the value positions of only certain segments or classes of society.

The absolutist conception of deviance can also be criticized for its assumption that the vast majority of citizens are aware that certain acts are deviant and that this has been clearly communicated. Statutes, regulations, rules, and social norms proscribe many behaviors. However, not all these prohibitions are universally known. Even if known, they may not be completely understood because of their complex nature. Finally, in some settings certain acts are prohibited, while in others, they are considered appropriate. Murder for example is ordinarily prohibited, but in the case of societies at war, killing becomes expected and even rewarded behavior. Thus, on several accounts, the absolutist definition of deviance is problematic for the study of police deviance.

Reactivist Definition of Deviance

Often referred to as the labeling, societal reaction, or interactionist perspective (Kitsuse, 1972), the reactivist conception of deviance was developed by Durkheim in the late 1800s but became popular in the 1950s and 1960s. The reactivist perspective represents an important alternative way to conceptualize and to understand deviance. In contrast to the absolutist definition, the reactivist paradigm proposes that no act is inherently deviant (Durkheim, 1938/1982; Erikson, 1962). Instead, this school of thought notes that members of society routinely engage in various rule-breaking behaviors. However, some of those who break rules are labeled deviant while many others are not.

Whether an act is labeled deviant depends on the response of others to the particular act. Expressed in its simplest form, deviance

> ... is *not* a quality of the act the person commits, but rather the consequence of the application by others of the rules and sanctions to an "offender." The deviant is one to whom that label has successfully been applied; deviant behavior is behavior that people so label. (Becker, 1963, p. 9)

In brief, reactivists propose that the key factor in determining whether an act is deviant is how others react to it. Being labeled deviant is contingent on many factors. These include the status of the person violating the rule, the status of those who feel harmed by the behavior, and the context in which the behavior occurs.

The reactivist conception of deviance is important because it illustrates the relative nature of deviance. That is, what may be classified as deviant in one setting may be considered socially acceptable behavior in another. As an illustration, corrupt police working on a squad together would likely label deviant any newly assigned officer who refused to participate in corrupt activities. It would be unlikely that the same officer would be labeled deviant if assigned to work with a group of officers who were not engaged in corrupt activities. These illustrations are consistent with the reactivist proposition that not all criminal behavior is deviant, and not all deviant behavior is criminal.

The reactivist definition has also received criticism. First, many have challenged the contention that no act is intrinsically deviant. Charles Wellford (1975), for example, has argued strongly that there is almost universal agreement that some acts—such as homicide and rape—are deviant. Yet, both homicide and rape have been permitted throughout history by many societies and, in some cases, even encouraged. One need only consider two societies at war for a context in which these behaviors can become acceptable. A second criticism with the definition is its failure to define specifically what deviance is and, conversely, what it is not. The pure reactivist approach to deviance, while enlightening and necessary for developing a complete understanding of police deviance, is problematic as it does not provide a multidimensional framework from which to judge the appropriateness of conduct.

Normative Definition of Deviance

The normative definition suggests that deviance is the violation of a norm. Simply stated, norms may be defined as social expectations or guidelines for conduct (Durkheim, 1938/1982). When people violate the norms governing a particular setting, they would be considered deviant. Yet, as noted in the previous section, it is important to understand that what is considered deviant behavior in one society or social setting may not be seen as deviant in another. Deviance is relative not only to behavior but to the social context in which behavior occurs. Therefore, the normative definition of deviance includes an interactive process between social actors, settings, and norms. In other words, people who are labeled deviant must engage in behavior that is viewed as departing from the bounds of acceptable conduct that governs a particular social group or setting. The process of detecting and labeling behavior deviant, then, depends on behavior, the social context in which behavior occurs, the formal and informal rules of conduct, and the perception of the behavior as violating existing social norms. Therefore, deviance is based as much on the perception of social control agents and social interpretation as it is on actual behavior. "It is the audience which eventually decides whether or not any given action or actions become a visible case of deviation" (Erikson, 1962, p. 308).

We will use a normative definition to sketch some of the parameters of police deviance. To understand some of the fundamental elements of police deviance more thoroughly, it is most useful to discuss the topic within a normative "systems" framework. A *systems* framework includes multiple levels and sources of both formal and informal norms that influence our conception of deviance. The framework allows us to examine the conflict among normative levels and to assess the appropriateness of police conduct, while retaining the insight of the reactivist approach. In essence, the normative systems approach acknowledges the existence of different sources and levels of norms that influence both behavior and the social reaction to behavior. From this perspective, deviance can be seen as the consequence of adhering to different norms and the application of those norms to different behaviors. Thus, deviance can be understood as a product of both conformity and conflict.

NORMATIVE SYSTEMS

Norms and values of social and occupational groups differ. As in social settings, what is considered deviant behavior in one occupation may be viewed as perfectly acceptable conduct in another. This makes the study of "police deviance" an especially difficult task. Police conduct occurs within a unique occupational and normative context. The police occupational group often subscribes to values that depart drastically from those found in many segments of the larger society. This means that behavior unacceptable to the public may not be seen as constituting anything particularly wrong by the police as an occupational group. Since police officers have special powers, authority, and a unique culture, their attitudes, values, and beliefs sometimes conflict with those of private citizens. Often these sentiments directly conflict with the formal rules of social interaction.

Another complication is that norms and values tend to differ within and between police groups. Collective experience or cultural differences in police organizations contribute to the development of different values and norms. Members of one police organization may condemn the use of physically aggressive measures to control crime, while another organization may have a history of rewarding its members for aggressive practices. Similarly, different groups within a single police organization may adhere to values and expectations different from other groups or cliques. Police assigned to patrol a "violent, crime-ridden" neighborhood might view aggressive practices as necessary police behavior, whereas another group of police assigned to a middle-class neighborhood might be less likely to subscribe to violence as normal police behavior. Given the complexity and diversity of the norms and values that affect the police, the study of deviance necessarily entails an understanding of the differences in norms as they are expressed at the legal, organizational, and subcultural levels.

Identification of police deviance would be a virtually impossible task if not for some generally accepted standards that can be applied to assess whether a particular behavior is socially acceptable. As discussed, this depends upon the rules used to determine deviance. There are two sets of rules or standards that apply to police conduct. There are standards developed externally from the police occupation and standards developed internally by the police occupation. Standards of conduct developed external to the police occupation include: constitutional, criminal, common, and civil law. Ideally, these legal standards should apply to citizens and police alike. Internal standards include departmental policies, procedures, practices, and regulations. While some agencies still rely on an informal system of regulation, most have adopted formal policies and standardized operating procedures (Gaines et al., 1997; Smith & Alpert, 1993). In developing these limits on behavior, the agency defines its values and establishes expected norms of conduct for its members.

Another important element in the normative system of deviance is the threat of a negative social sanction. Several theorists have argued that for a behavior to be considered deviant, it must both violate an existing social norm *and* the violation must potentially result in a formal negative social sanction (Black & Reiss, 1970; Schur, 1971). This element of deviance means that behavior is relative to real social responses and consequences (Becker, 1963; Kitsuse, 1962). Social responses, however, can vary greatly in application and intensity. The observation that deviance requires a negative social response has unique ramifications for the study of police deviance. When police deviate, there exists a continuum of negative responses. Social responses to police deviant behaviors depend on who discovers the deviance, the perception of the severity of the deviation, the restraints placed on social control agents, and the effect of sanctioning of police deviance.

For example, a police supervisor who discovers that several subordinate officers have been sleeping on duty may not view the behavior as deviant even if there is a departmental policy against such behavior. In this case, the supervisor's perception of the behavior is the determining factor in whether or not a negative sanction is applied. Even if the behavior is perceived as deviant, the supervisor may not feel that it warrants a formal negative sanction. To sanction the behavior might call attention to the unit from the agency's administration or the public. The decision to ignore behavior serves the agency ". . . to develop a smooth-work processing system, to maintain community demand for, and support of, its policies and programs, and to operate in relation to other organizations and additional outside forces, including especially sources of funding and legitimation" (Schur, 1980, p. 20). If the supervisor feels the behavior is deviant and should be penalized, the range of available sanctions is limited to those permissible under departmental regulations (internal standards), since sleeping on duty is not a violation of law (external standard).

The same behavior, however, uncovered by a journalist and exposed to the public may receive a much different social response—to both the individual officer and to the supervisor and the agency. The officer may be counseled or suspended, and the agency may suffer diminished public support (or funding). All of this may result, even if the supervisor's initial perception was that the behavior did not warrant an official response. A totally different set of negative sanctions may occur where someone uncovers police criminality.

There exists a less formal set of guidelines or codes that drive police behavior. Deviation from the *customs* and *practices* of the police culture can result in sanctions by members of the police agency. Police who fail to conform to the customs of the police culture may find themselves sanctioned not by any formal system of social control but by their coworkers. Police who step beyond the bounds of acceptable conduct may be isolated by their peers and, in some cases, may even be placed in life-threatening situations. This informal system of sanctions can either prevent or promote police deviance. In a police organization where sleeping on duty becomes normal and accepted practice (informal norm), an officer who refuses to engage in the behavior, or alerts sanctioning authorities to the behavior, might be subject to negative treatment by coworkers. Similarly, in a police culture that does not tolerate this type of conduct, an officer found sleeping on duty might be shunned by peers. Depending on the values, norms, and customs of a police organization, informal sanctions can serve either to control or to contribute to police deviance.

These external and internal standards, as well as informal norms of conduct in the police culture, cause problems of perception. The general public may be aware of external standards of police conduct because many of them apply to the typical citizen. Criminal laws prohibiting murder, robbery, rape, arson, assault, and other behaviors are generally known to both the police and public. The public, however, may not be aware of the informal codes of police conduct and the actual customs and practices that exist within the police occupational group. These different standards of conduct may conflict with one another. A law enforcement officer may behave within the accepted bounds of police custom, but when that behavior comes to the attention of the public and is viewed from the public's understanding of external standards of conduct or from an individualistic conception of misconduct, it may be seen as deviant. Police conduct often differs drastically from external societal standards of conduct and from formal, internal statements of police policy and practice. For example, a police department may routinely engage in the practice of stopping and harassing juveniles in a particular area of town. To the police, this behavior is an accepted practice thought to help prevent crime and to reduce juvenile delinquency. When the same behavior becomes public knowledge, however, it may be perceived as an abuse of authority and power. Since they are conforming to the normative standards of their occupational group, the police may resent citizens who express their disapproval.

The process of being labeled as a deviant is composed of several stages and elements. Table 1.1 illustrates the arrangement of the basic features of deviance as it applies to the police. Police behavior may not be viewed as deviant by the officer engaged in a particular form of conduct—depending upon the source of the norms the officer is observing.

Table 1.1

Normative System of Police Deviance

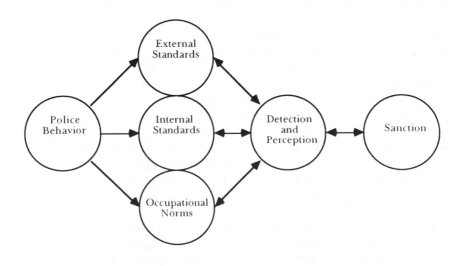

Someone who perceives the police behavior may interpret the behavior based on another normative structure and judge it differently from the original actor. The sanctioning authority depends on detection and interpretation of the behavior as deviant. Still, sanctioning authorities are differentially limited in their course of actions by the normative source, the actual behavior, the personal and organizational interests of control agents, and the limitations of available sanctions associated with the normative violation. Finally, in the mix of actual conduct, detection, ascription, interpretation, and organizational interests, sanctioning often depends on "a kind of negative reciprocity in which one person is deterred from aggressing socially against another by awareness of the immediate power to retaliate with unpleasant or costly consequences" (Lemert, 1997, pp. 71–72). Many members of the media, for example, have learned about the power of the police to control information or to restrict access to information as a sanction for exposing police misconduct. Table 1.2 shows some of the many factors that influence the sanctioning of police deviance.

To summarize, police deviance may be best understood in the context of a multi-faceted system that includes external, internal, and informal norms from which social actors independently choose to decide courses of action and which the public uses—equally independently—to pass judgments on the appropriateness of those choices.

Table 1.2

Factors Affecting the Sanctioning of Police Deviance

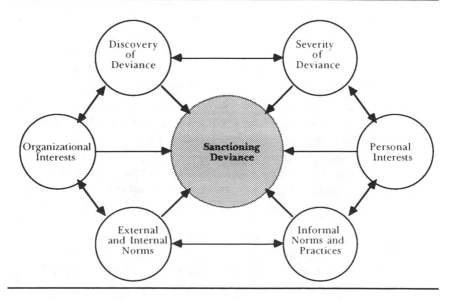

VARIANTS OF POLICE DEVIANCE

Given the complexity of deviance and the unique characteristics of the police occupation, scholars struggle to distinguish types of police deviance. To describe police behaviors and the special circumstances and contexts in which these behaviors occur, scholars have taken two approaches. First, broad definitions have been developed to designate police conduct as deviant. These inclusive definitions attempt to capture the motivational and behavioral aspects of various forms of police deviance. Second, terms and concepts associated with police deviance are grouped into behavioral classifications to allow for more specific definitions. Both approaches have contributed to a better understanding of the dark side of policing.

Police Crime

At the simplest level, according to the *Model Penal Code*, a crime may be defined as an "act or omission prohibited by law for the protection of the public, the violation of which is prosecuted by the state in its own name and punishable by incarceration" (Sec. 1.1014[1]). The most serious forms of police deviance—such as using excessive force or illegal drugs—involve acts that are clearly in violation of existing criminal statutes. Not all crime committed by persons employed as police officers should be categorized as *police crime* (Sherman, 1978). The police officer who assaults a spouse during an argument is guilty of a crime; the cop who commits a burglary while off-duty has engaged in crime; the officer who purchases the favors of a prostitute has committed a criminal act; an off-duty officer who uses an illegal drug is engaged in crime, but these acts do not amount to police crime. The following are examples where police engaged in criminal activity that had little to do with their employment.

- A Fairfax, Virginia police officer, Jeffery Hand, a 23-year veteran on the force, was charged with robbery. He is charged with forcibly taking $71,782 from a bank. [*USA Today*, 6/6/97, p. 10A]
- A Carlisle, Kentucky police officer, Daryl McFarland, was convicted of several burglaries. The charges stemmed from the burglary of a Foodtown grocery store and a car wash. Officials claimed that the officer acted as a lookout for others who stole $300 in change from the store. [*Carlisle Mercury*, 8/20/92, p. 1]
- A Glendale, California police officer, Victor Felix, broke into his ex-wife's residence. He shot and killed her and her boyfriend in front of the woman's three children. The officer later killed himself. [*USA Today*, 5/14/91, p. 4A]

- A Broward County, Florida sheriff's deputy was charged with aiding his wife in prostitution. [*USA Today*, 7/31/91, p. 3A]

The factor which distinguishes police crime is the commission of the crime while on the job or by using some aspect of the occupational position to carry out the illegality. Here are some cases where the police engaged in crimes while performing their duties as law enforcement officers.

- On-duty Chicago Sergeant Kathleen Wit was killed when her police cruiser struck a utility pole. The 10-year veteran of the force was found to have a blood-alcohol level of .25, which is more than three times the legal limit in Illinois. [*USA Today*, 7/16/97, p. 7A]
- Tennessee State Trooper Rodney McCarty faces termination from the force over a missing kilo of cocaine. The cocaine was confiscated from a car, and the trooper allegedly never returned the evidence after he checked it out from the crime lab. [*USA Today*, 7/3/97, p. 20A]
- An 11-year veteran of the New Jersey State Police was arrested for stealing 11 ounces of crack cocaine from an evidence locker and then attempting to sell the drug. [*USA Today*, 1/21/93, p. 9A)]
- A Norman, Oklahoma police officer was charged with the murder of two people. Both of the bodies were discovered in the trunk of a car on the officer's beat. [*USA Today*, 6/3/91, p. 5A]
- Jack Dicklin, 34, 10-year veteran of the Lakemoor, Illinois police department, was fired March 6, 1997 for falsifying reports and withholding information about the firing of a handgun by a village trustee before a charity golf outing. Dicklin was later sentenced to 30 months probation after pleading guilty to official misconduct for trying to help a McHenry auto dealer repossess a Jeep illegally. Dicklin drove 30 minutes outside his jurisdiction while on duty to the home where the Jeep was housed. He was in his police uniform, armed with his revolver, and in a squad car. He did not have a court order for repossession and no theft report had been filed. He made a second visit to the home while off duty but still in uniform with his revolver and displayed his badge. [*Chicago Tribune*, 10/22/97, p. 1]
- FBI Agent Mark Putnam confessed to strangling a 27-year-old eastern Kentucky woman. The woman had served as an informant for the FBI. The agent killed her after she became pregnant and threatened to expose their affair to the agent's wife and the FBI. Putnam is the first FBI agent to be found guilty of murder. [*Courier-Journal*, 8/20/92, p. B4]

In each of these cases, law enforcement officers committed traditional crimes in their capacity as police officers.

Occupational Deviance

In an article published in 1940, criminologist Edwin Sutherland discussed the criminal activities of upper-class business and professional persons. Although Sutherland referred to his work as a study of white-collar criminals, his study represents one of the first efforts to address occupational deviance. In essence, Sutherland noted that many persons employed in business enterprises and in political positions routinely engaged in job-related criminal activities during the course of their work. The crimes committed by these professionals were made possible because of the very nature of their work.

Police *occupational deviance* refers to inappropriate work-related activities in which police may participate. More specifically, police occupational deviance may be defined as "behavior—criminal and noncriminal—. . . committed under the guise of the police officer's authority" (Barker & Carter, 1994, p. 6). It is important to note that the distinguishing factor here is that occupational deviance is possible because of the position held by the officer. Consider a few examples where police abused the power of their office to engage in occupational deviance.

- North Salt Lake City, Utah police received severe criticism after it was learned that they had lied to the public about a murder investigation. In an attempt to apprehend a murder suspect, police created a fictitious couple who they said witnessed the crime. [*USA Today*, 7/14/97, p. 12A]

- Fairfield County, South Carolina Sheriff Leroy Montgomery resigned from office after being charged with illegally taking citizens' vehicles which the department had impounded. [*USA Today*, 9/17/92, p. 6A]

- Five Harris County, Texas deputies were fired following allegations that they abused boot camp inmates and pitted the inmates against each other for sport and the enjoyment of the camp's instructors. [*USA Today*, 6/11/92, p. 3A]

- A Baton Rouge police legal advisor was suspended from the force following a charge of malfeasance. The charge alleged the officer asked women seeking exotic dancing and modeling licenses to show him their breasts while at police headquarters. [*USA Today*, 9/18/92, p. 10A]

- During a protest, members of the Honolulu police subjected 11 female protesters to strip searches. A jury awarded $10,000 to each of the women, noting that the officer did not strip search a single male protester in the incident. [*USA Today*, 9/21/92, p. 12A]

It is doubtful that any of these incidents could have occurred without the officers having been vested with the authority of their position.

Corruption

While many consider any crime committed by the police as evidence of *corruption*, there is considerable disagreement among police experts as to which behaviors should be termed corrupt (see Hale, 1989). For some, corruption would include any wrongful act—from taking a gratuity to committing a homicide. Others may define it very narrowly, excluding a good deal of criminal behavior. McMullan (1961) defined public officials as corrupt if they accept "money or money's worth for doing something that [they are] under a duty to do anyway, . . . under a duty not to do, or to exercise a legitimate discretion for improper reasons" (p. 182). Lawrence Sherman (1978) defined corruption as "an illegal use of organizational power for personal gain" (p. 30). Similarly, Herman Goldstein (1977) notes that for activities to be considered evidence of corruption, they must involve the abuse of a police officer's power or authority for personal gain.

Consider a few cases that are normally considered acts of police corruption because they are economically-based, job-related, and driven by personal gain.

- A federal grand jury handed down a 21-count indictment against seven Chicago police officers. The indictment charges that members of the department's tactical unit extorted tens of thousands of dollars from federal agents posing as drug dealers. Several of the officers were members of street gangs, and officials are investigating the extent to which Chicago police officers are affiliated with street gangs. [*New York Times*, 12/31/96, p. 11; *Chicago Tribune*, 12/31/96, p. 1]

- Detroit, Michigan's Police Chief William Hart was sentenced to 10 years in federal prison for embezzling $2.6 million from a secret police drug enforcement fund. Charges alleged the chief diverted agency funds for personal use and evaded taxes. [*USA Today*, 6/18/91, p. 11A]

- The sheriff of Newton County, Mississippi, Bud Miles, pled guilty to charges of failure to perform his duties and possession of a gambling table. The charges were brought following an investigation into the sheriff's alleged protection of a bootlegging operation. In exchange for his guilty plea, the state dropped felony charges of accepting bribes while in office. [*USA Today*, 6/24/91, p. 10A].

- Oregon State Police Major Robert Moine was convicted of taking bribes. The conviction involved the acceptance of money in return for preferential treatment in awarding contracts. Contracts involved the lease or purchase of building space used by the state police. [*USA Today*, 6/3/92, p. 8A]

According to most scholars, corruption involves the potential for personal gain and the use of police power and authority to further that gain.

Abuse of Authority

David Carter (1985) defined police abuse of authority as "any action by a police officer without regard to motive, intent, or malice that tends to injure, insult, tread on human dignity, manifest feelings of inferiority, and/or violate an inherent legal right of a member of the police constituency" (p. 322). This sweeping definition covers three general forms of abuse of police authority. First, officers may physically abuse others through the use of excessive force. Second, police may psychologically abuse citizens through the use of verbal assault, harassment, or ridicule. A third type of abuse is legal abuse, where officers violate a citizen's constitutional, federal, or state rights. Each of these types of abuses is made possible by the power and authority of the police but do not necessarily involve personal economic gain. In fact, a great deal of the police abuse of authority is a result of attempts to achieve organizational objectives rather than to secure personal economic gain. Consider the following cases.

- Over 12 Philadelphia police officers were charged or were sentenced to prison for planting evidence and committing perjury. Because of the officers' conduct, over 283 criminal cases have been overturned or dismissed by the courts. One case involved the 3-year imprisonment of a 54-year-old grandmother who had drugs planted in her home by a police officer. Hundreds of other cases are being investigated or are under review. [*New York Times* 12/21/96, p. 11; 3/15/97, p. 6]

- Boston Police Detective Carlos Luna was convicted of perjury. The perjury charge stemmed from a drug raid in which the detective's partner was killed. The detective fabricated the existence of an informant which allowed police to secure the warrant and conduct the drug raid that led to his partner's death. [*USA Today*, 6/6/91, p. 8A]

- A New York state trooper was charged with 11 counts of perjury and tampering with evidence. A judge ordered the investigator to be held in jail after reviewing audio tapes in which the trooper admitted placing evidence at the scene of a robbery. [*USA Today*, 7/8/92, p. 12A]

- Two Missouri State Highway Patrol commanders were demoted because of their roles in an illegal telephone tap. [*USA Today*, 7/24/92, p. 5A]

- In defiance of an order of the city manager of Key West, Florida, Police Chief Ray Peterson said that he will be returning to work. The chief was relieved of duty based on charges that he abused officers in the department. [*USA Today*, 6/23/97, p. 10A]

SUMMARY

The police have always been responsible for performing an important function in society. Because the police have been vested with incredible powers to carry out their mission, public scrutiny intensifies whenever there are reports of police misconduct. There are multiple reasons for public interest in police misconduct: the police hold symbolic positions in society; some deviant behaviors may have a corrupting influence and actually encourage further wrongdoing; the police perform an unparalleled function; society has an economic interest in controlling police deviance; and, some forms of police deviance may present a public safety hazard. In addition to understanding why there is a high level of interest in police deviance, students must grasp what the term deviance means and how it applies to the complex world of policing. It is also important to understand terminology associated with police deviance. The various labels associated with police misconduct do more than merely describe the nature of a particular form of deviance. The terms have implications for police motivation, normative systems, and the context in which the behavior occurred.

Chapter Two

A HISTORY OF
POLICE DEVIANCE

The Forging of an Occupation

> To observe the past is to take warning for the future.
>
> Lope de Vega (1562–1635)

P olice deviance is not a phenomenon peculiar to the late twentieth century. Since the creation of the first law enforcement agencies, police have engaged in misconduct. Police corruption was particularly pronounced in the nineteenth and early twentieth centuries (Simpson, 1977). However, "for as long as there have been police, there has been corruption" (Sherman, 1974, p. 1). To study the history of police is to study police deviance, corruption and misconduct.

In this chapter, we briefly examine the history of policing, highlighting some of the deviance problems experienced by agencies and their officers. Comprehension of the present is possible only through the study of the past. In the words of Victor G. Strecher (1995), our understanding of the present "is little more than an elusive knife-edge between the past and future—or in a practical sense, a thin, recent slice of the past" (p. 69). Understanding and responding to police deviance necessitates reviewing major dilemmas police have confronted in their relatively short, but complex, history.

A complete and exhaustive review of the evolvution of policing would be impossible to accomplish in a single chapter. We will review major events in the growth and change of policing, primarily in the United States. Police agencies, as we currently know them, have not evolved from a simple linear series of historical events (Kappeler, 1996). Instead, contemporary police agencies—whether considered at the local, state, or federal levels—are the products of innumerable complex, and often conflicting, social forces.

To comprehend the complexities of police deviance from a historical perspective requires consideration of the nature of police work and the social conditions of the time, as well as modern sensibilities that guide our interpretation of history (Kappeler, 1996). As we noted in chapter 1, police "deviance" is a relative concept. What is deemed deviant depends on the social context of the behavior. Acts that would clearly be considered deviant today might not have been so at the time they were committed. For example, it would be considered highly improper today for a uniformed officer to spend time sitting in a bar during working hours. Yet in the early 1900s, it was fairly common practice for some police to spend part of their shift in saloons. The lengthy hours police were required to work offer one explanation for the practice; many forces placed officers on 12-hour or longer shifts. In St. Louis, Missouri, for example, it was not until 1854 that police officers worked the standard 8-hour shift (Kappeler, 1989). Philadelphia police were required to work a 108-hour week until 1912 (Walker, 1977). Hence, "Sitting in a saloon during working hours may have been an honest effort to survive a [long] working day" (Hernandez, 1989, p. 36).

Since police behaviors cannot be understood apart from the social, political, and economic contexts in which they occur, this chapter will sketch the history of police misconduct in terms of the accompanying social conditions. We begin with a general review of the police function in ancient times, then discuss the emergence of policing in England, and finally trace the historical development of the police in the United States.

THE HISTORICAL ROOTS OF POLICING

A common theme in the evolution of any society has been the creation of some method of enforcing social regulations. In primitive societies social control mechanisms were the responsibility of community members. Under early forms of government, policing responsibilities were largely within the province of the military. As social, economic, and governmental structures became more complex, specialized police agencies were created. Cyril D. Robinson, Richard Scaglion, and J. Michael Olivero (1994) have argued that, "specialized police agencies are generally characteristic only of societies politically organized as states" (p. 6). The same authors go on to point out that

> in a period of transition, the crucial factor in delineating the modern specialized police function is an ongoing attempt at conversion of the social control (policing) mechanism from an integral part of the community structure to an agent of an emerging dominant class. (p. 7)

During ancient times, clans and groups controlled their own members, primarily through the use of a "kin" police system. Under kin policing, transgressors were punished by the injured party or his/her family members. Punishments included banishment or death. As societies developed, more formalized and less primitive mechanisms evolved to ensure conformity.

Although formal social control mechanisms were developed in Sumerian, Babylonian, Egyptian, and Hebrew societies (Holden, 1992), the Greeks were one of the first societies to develop a rudimentary form of city police (Hernandez, 1989). In fact, the term "police" is derived from the Greek word *polis*, which refers to the "exercise of civic or collective authority" (Manning, 1997, p. 48). Under the Greek ruler Peisistratus, a guard system was established to protect him, the tower, and highways (Germann, Day, & Gallati, 1985). Loosely structured, this bodyguard system was ineffectual in protecting the ruling elite, ultimately leading to the downfall of the government.

Social order in the early Roman Empire was also maintained by military force. Augustus created the Praetorian Guard to protect the life and property of the emperor. Others, including the *praefectus urbi* (prefect of the city), *curatores urbi* (each responsible for sections of the city), and *vigiles* and *lictores* (who patrolled the streets acting as enforcement officers), were assigned public order responsibilities. Eventually, the Praetorian Guard was conscripted into regular military service, ultimately leading to social disorder (Kelly, 1988) and the Empire's eventual collapse.

POLICING IN ENGLAND

Much of contemporary policing in this country can be traced to practices and beliefs in England. As Craig Uchida (1997) notes, many of our ideas about such concepts as community policing, crime prevention, and the role of sheriffs were conceived from English law enforcement practices. In many ways, police wrongdoing in these early years set the stage for police deviant activities in contemporary times.

Historians note that by the 1500s England was characterized by general lawlessness and the proliferation of criminals. A visitor to the country in the sixteenth century remarked, for instance, "There is no country in the world where there are more robbers and thieves than in England" (Samaha, 1974, p. 11). At the same time, however, Britain also had one of the harshest criminal codes in the world. Children as young as seven years old could be sentenced to death for the theft of something as minor as a pocket handkerchief (Pringle, n.d.). Between the years of 1530 and 1630 some 75,000 people were hanged for crimes; by 1800, 225 offenses were punishable by death (Clear & Cole, 1997; Jenkins, 1987). As a punitive country with a major crime problem, how did England first provide law enforcement services?

Constables and Other Early Law Enforcement Officials

In early Anglo-Saxon England between A.D. 700 and 900, English villages were primarily self-governed, with each assuming responsibility for administering justice and establishing defenses against attackers. Law enforcement was a local responsibility with citizens enjoying a collective social obligation for maintaining order. England was primarily a rural and agrarian society; however, systems were established and officials appointed to maintain order and to deal with criminals. Borrowing from the "frankpledge" system in France, the English developed a "tithing" system as a social control mechanism. Under this system, each male above the age of twelve was required to form a group with nine neighbors into a "tithing." Ten tithings were grouped into a "hundred." Hundreds were supervised by a constable, who was appointed by the local nobility. Ten hundreds, in turn, were grouped into a "shire," which was supervised by a "reeve" (Uchida, 1997). This system worked fairly well in rural settings in early times. As people began to migrate and urban society developed, the system was no longer sufficient to maintain peace or order.

In 1066, William, the Duke of Normandy, invaded and conquered England. The changes in government structure were dramatic.

> The philosophy of law enforcement . . . was that of a highly repressive police state. Collective security was deemed far more important than individual freedom, so William proceeded to militarize the existing civil arrangement of the Anglo-Saxons. He divided England into fifty-five separate military areas and placed an officer of his own selection into each shire to take charge. In this way the *state* assumed the responsibility for keeping the peace, and set the stage for *the diminution of community responsibility* as had been required by the tithing system. Martial law was in effect. (Germann et al., 1985, p. 52)

William centralized government functions and created systems that separated enforcement and judicial responsibilities. Judges, known as "vice comes," assumed traveling juridical responsibilities. Sheriffs (the "shire reeves" mentioned earlier) maintained order, collected taxes, and quelled political upheavals. Constables assumed greater importance since these officials were recognized by the Crown as having the responsibility of keeping the King's peace (Critchley, 1985).

Throughout the next few centuries enforcement responsibilities established by the Norman Conquest continued to evolve. By the late 1100s, sheriffs became responsible for controlling vagabonds (Robinson et al., 1994). Sheriffs, constables, and town bailiffs were responsible for enforcing labor laws (Gaines et al., 1991). Regardless of the changes implemented, social control mechanisms continued to augment the power of the ruling elite and propertied classes.

In 1285, the Statute of Winchester was enacted by King Edward I. Among other provisions, the Statute created a watch and ward system to ensure social order at night. The watch and ward was comprised of all males between the ages of sixteen and fifty. They were required to maintain a weapon in their homes as a means of keeping the peace. The Statute of Winchester also created the parish constable system, which remained the primary policing system in England for the next six hundred years (Berg, 1992).

In the beginning, constables' positions were viewed as prestigious; most were filled by prominent community members. T. A. Critchley (1985) has noted that the office of the constable continued to be an esteemed public position throughout the fifteenth and most of the sixteenth centuries. By the eighteenth century, however, the office of the constable was notoriously corrupt. With the beginning of the Industrial Revolution, the population of many towns grew rapidly. With this growth came increases in crime and general disorder. Because of the increased workload of the constable's office and because the wealthiest segment of society enjoyed growing prosperity, many prominent citizens became unwilling to serve as constables. The office came to be seen as a burden, rather than a public service obligation. Many constables began to pay others to do their work. In the end, only those who could not afford to pay a substitute assumed the responsibility of the constable's office. As a result, the least qualified often provided law enforcement services. It was common for the illiterate, elderly, infirm, lazy, or simply corrupt to be working as constables (Johnson, 1981).

There were many opportunities for constables to engage in corrupt practices. Since they received no formal salary, they were permitted to collect certain fees and gratuities. Constables were given, for example, a percentage of fines levied against offenders whom they brought into the court system for formal processing. Patrick Pringle (n.d.) notes that in theory this practice should have encouraged constables to enforce the law. In reality, however, the constables performed "shakedowns" of citizens by accepting payment to keep criminal matters out of court. When England experienced a problem with gin houses and public drunkenness in the 1700s, laws were passed requiring gin sellers and makers to purchase prohibitively expensive licenses. In response to these toughened laws, constables were bribed to forego law enforcement so that gin shops could remain open (Rubinstein, 1973). Early links between the merchant class and corrupt constables were forged by developing economic relationships.

Others responsible for law enforcement services at this time were also engaged in various corrupt activities. Magistrates accepted bribes, forced innocent persons to pay for release from custody, and provided protection for illegal businesses. Watchmen participated in burglary rings and would overlook offenses for a fee. Given the structure of the "justice system" and its corrupt nature,

> One of . . . [its] . . . most striking features . . . was that no one concerned in the enforcement of the law had any incentive to prevent crime. On the contrary, the police force —if one could call it that—had a direct incentive to encourage it. (Pringle, n.d., p. 48).

It is important to note that in eighteenth-century England, the political system and government were also rife with corruption. In the House of Commons, for example, it was common for votes to be sold and for members to buy their seats. Positions in the civil service system, the army, the navy, and the church were also commonly sold. Thus, the corruption of the early law enforcement system was in many ways simply a reflection of the corruption occurring in many segments of British government.

Early police systems in England were the responsibilities of local politicians. Those working as constables or in other law enforcement capacities were often inept and corrupt—more interested in collecting a bribe than controlling crime. They were largely unpaid amateurs whose efforts to address a growing crime problem were either ineffective or nonexistent. As the Industrial Revolution approached and the country's population began to grow, new crime problems and social issues compelled England to create its first "professional" police force.

The London Metropolitan Police

During the eighteenth century, Britain's population grew from about six to twelve million persons (Critchley, 1985). With the Industrial Revolution, thousands of people were drawn away from an agrarian existence to urban centers in search of better paying jobs. Ironically, increasing mechanization meant that manufacturers needed fewer and fewer workers. Many job seekers found themselves unemployed and impoverished. Resentment developed that often pitted the industrialists against labor—a condition which drastically changed the nature of policing (Manning, 1997). Another factor leading to the collapse of previous enforcement practices was the introduction of gin to English society in the early 1700s. Before then, true drunkenness was primarily the domain of the wealthiest segment of society; only they could afford brandy—the sole hard liquor available (Tobias, 1979). With the invention of gin, hard liquor became available to the masses. The result was described by Rubinstein (1973):

> Within a few decades, London was awash in an orgy of drinking which has probably not been matched in history. By 1725, there were more than seven thousand gin shops in London and drink was sold as a sideline by numerous shopkeepers and peddlers. For a penny anyone could drink all day in any "flash house" and get a straw pallet in a back room to sleep it off. (p. 6)

With the breakdown of informal social control mechanisms, social conditions in the eighteenth century worsened for most citizens. While the rich isolated themselves in enclaves with private security forces, others faced more difficult times. Evidence of disorder could be found everywhere. Riots occurred throughout Europe over food shortages, high prices, the introduction of machinery, and religious prejudice (Richardson, 1974). Public drunkenness became a common sight, and intoxicated mobs often engaged in unpredictable and violent activities (Rubinstein, 1973)—many of which were directed at the industrialists and their factories. Urbanization was accompanied by homelessness, sewage, and air pollution (Hernandez, 1989). Thieves were emboldened, often knocking down and robbing people in broad daylight. Working in groups, burglars often pillaged homes. Fences, pickpockets, and counterfeiters plied their trades with reckless abandon. The number of prostitutes grew rapidly. At one point, it was estimated that there were twenty-five thousand prostitutes working in London alone (Berg, 1992).

Well-to-do and middle-class citizens cried out for the restoration of order. Law enforcement measures that had been in place for nearly 500 years were ineffectual to address a broad range of public order and crime problems—many of which were new. The previous system relied on the notion that each citizen shared a collective responsibility to prevent crime and disorder. In an increasingly complex society, this simple notion was inadequate and failed to serve the interests of the new industrial-based economy; nor did it provide social elites any relief from the growing cost of obtaining private security.

Attempts were made to adjust the system in place. One adjustment was to expand the number of constables (Emsley, 1987). In London, for example, some citizens were sworn in as special constables to assist when needed. Since most of these volunteers had neither the training nor the skills to deal with the problems of disorder and crime, this adjustment failed. Another adjustment was to use the military to control mob riots. However, military personnel often employed brutal tactics, and their effectiveness was questioned (Miller, 1977). Also, "wealthy citizens who controlled the constables in their wards did not want to relinquish their perquisites to a central authority who might use this extension of power to alter the traditional character of English government" (Rubinstein, 1973, p. 9). A third type of approach involved the use of the militia (comprised of local landowners), the yeomanry (organizations of cavalry volunteers), or private volunteer groups. While ineffective in minimizing crime or controlling disorder (Richardson, 1974), these groups helped to ensure that the interests of the propertied classes were protected.

Despite the fact that the law enforcement system in place was incapable of dealing with riots or crime, English citizens were reluctant to abandon the constable-watchmen system and to replace it with a full-time, centralized, preventive police force. The propertied classes, however, demanded a return to order and normalcy. Conditions had so deteriorated that "the choices by 1829 seemed fairly limited: a standing police force or martial law" (Hernandez, 1989, p. 15). Largely due to the efforts of Sir Robert Peel, the Metropolitan Police Act was passed by Parliament in 1829, creating the first professional police force for the city of London.

The structure of this police force differed from what was to evolve in the United States. Perhaps most importantly, British policing was highly centralized. Centralization in this case meant the police force was an extension of the national government. This organizational approach was specifically calculated by Peel to remove police from the direct influence of local political leaders (Bopp & Schultz, 1972). This structural difference was an important factor in explaining the variability of police deviancy between the countries. Centralization was in line with practices in business and government to improve efficiency and to minimize costs. It is also important to note that Peel's police force was intended to serve in a preventive role. Prior to this time, police services had been provided primarily on a reactive basis. The new force, however, was expected to prevent crime through proactive patrol (Lynch & Groves, 1989).

Understanding that a segment of English citizenry would be distrustful of the police, Peel was very concerned about the quality and type of persons selected for the new police force. The minimum expectations for those applying for police positions were good physical condition, above-average intelligence, and a scrupulous moral character (Miller, 1977). Peel carefully selected the first two police commissioners to run the department, and he personally participated in the interviewing of twelve thousand applicants for the first one thousand police positions (Berg, 1992).

Despite the care taken to select the officers, there were still problems with police misbehavior. Substance abuse was evident from the beginning. During the inaugural parade-ground ceremony, "Quite a few [officers] were unable to stand at attention because they had been celebrating the historic occasion by getting drunk" (Rubinstein, 1973, p. 11). Strict discipline was instituted; officers who could not, or would not, comply with police rules were discharged (Emsley, 1987). "During the first three years of operation, there were 5,000 dismissals and 6,000 required resignations—the largest police turnover rate in history" (Germann et al., 1985, p. 63). Many of these dismissals were for drunkenness on duty (Paley, 1989). The quest for professionalism moved policing away from social control by neighbor to social control by stranger.

Because Peel sought to construct a force that was professional, impartial, and removed from local interference, one of the criteria was that candidates should have no close ties to the residents they would be serving. It was believed that these types of relationships might impair impartiality. Accordingly, many of the first officers came from cities and towns outside of London (Richardson, 1974).

Despite all of the measures taken to minimize police misbehavior, reports of corrupt activities surfaced. There were incidents of police receiving payoffs from illegal gambling houses, and they received both bribe money and services from brothels. Police received rewards for making some arrests. There were charges that officers did not prevent thefts because they were more interested in receiving the reward after the crime was committed than in preventing the crime from occurring. Corruption among London police officers in the mid-1800s, however, was not nearly as extensive as it was in some cities in the United States during the same period (Richardson, 1974).

There are several reasons why the early English police system was not as mired in corruption as the American system. First, as mentioned above, English policing was centralized both structurally and operationally. A nationally supervised force resulted in more uniformity and accountability. A second explanation was the emphasis placed on institutional authority by police administrators. Police officers were clearly instructed "that their power was grounded in the English Constitution and that their behavior was determined by the rules of law" (Uchida, 1997, p. 22). Historian Wilbur Miller (1973) notes that, "To help bobbies carry out their role as impartial agents of the legal system, the commissioners stressed procedural regularity, confinement of police power to legally sanctioned duties, and limitation of patrolmen's personal discretion in exercising their authority" (p. 15). In contrast, American police officers enjoyed greater personal power attained through an exceptional amount of discretion—factors which become important in explaining contemporary police involvement in various forms of corruption.

A third explanation for the comparative lack of corruption was that English police administrators did not seek out and hire persons who were "well connected" in the communities they would be serving. Instead, Peel sought polite, aloof, self-disciplined persons who would view policing as a professional civil service career (Uchida, 1997). Fourth, there were strong informal social control mechanisms that governed off-duty police behavior. Unmarried police officers, for example, lived together in "section houses" under the watchful eyes of a police supervisor. Married police were required to live within their divisions and also had to submit to inspections of their lodgings (Richardson, 1974). Officers were required to wear their uniforms both on- and off-duty. This visibility subjected officers to continuous scrutiny from the public (Paley, 1989; Stead, 1985). Police supervisors kept a close watch on their employees—not only to avoid conflicts with a hostile public but to keep them from associating with questionable members of society. The English policing system attempted to divorce itself from its political and community publics by selecting police officers with few ties to the public and by controlling police-citizen interactions.

Excerpts of 1882 General Instructions to
Constables of Manchester, England

It is not possible to frame rules for your guidance under all circumstances. Something must be left to your intelligence and discretion. . . .

You must bear in mind that, to be thoroughly efficient, your character as a Police Officer as well as in private life should be above reproach. You must, therefore, be particular in the choice of your companions and avoid the practice of taking any intoxicating drink when on duty. If you resolutely decline it when offered you will become respected for your sobriety and decision of character. Experience has proved that coffee is better adapted for keeping the body warm and comfortable in cold and wet weather than spirits or beer.

Entering public or beerhouses when in uniform is positively forbidden, unless by the special instruction of a superior officer, or for the purpose of apprehending a felon, or by the express desire of the landlord to assist in removing drunken or disorderly persons. . . .

Do not loiter on your beat unnecessarily, and abstain from idle gossiping with other constables or any other persons. Never leave your beat except under absolute necessity, nor quit the front or outside of your beat to take refreshment in the night time; and remember that neglect of duty in any way not only brings disgrace upon the force of which you are a member, but also that it gives thieves the opportunity of committing their depredations. . . .

Let your conduct towards all persons, of whatever rank or class, be marked by kindness and civility. Be careful not to handle prisoners more roughly than is absolutely necessary for their security. Endeavor under all circumstances to keep your temper under control. You will more readily obtain assistance when you require it from bystanders if you perform your duty quietly and with good humour than by adopting an opposite course. Never use your staff or strike any person unless in self-defense.

Be very reserved, particularly with strangers and women of the town on all points connected with your own duties and the arrangements of the Police Force. . . .

You must be cautious not to interfere with anyone unnecessarily. When required to act you must do so with discretion and firmness, and never push or lay hands upon a person unless to take him into custody.

You are on no account to ask for or even hint at remuneration for a service you may have performed. . . . Any property which you may find, or have handed over to you, must be reported without delay and delivered to the officer on duty at the station.

Excerpted From: Kleinig, J., & Zhang, Y. (1993). *Professional law enforcement codes: A documentary collection.* Westport, CT: Greenwood Press.

POLICING IN THE UNITED STATES

Encapsulating the history of policing and police deviance in the United States is much more difficult than doing the same for England. Remember that policing in the United States was premised on a decentralized model as opposed to the British centralized system. Decentralization has meant that there is no national police force responsible for providing routine local law enforcement services. The provision of law enforcement services has been left to the states and localities through the separation of powers provision of the Constitution. One of the effects of decentralization was that early police operations were largely controlled by local political leaders who often rewarded loyal supporters with police positions. Another result was that a patchwork collection of police agencies developed across the United States.

Before 1800, the vast majority of the country's citizens came from England, and the law enforcement agencies that emerged in the United States had English undertones. In the larger industrial cities in the East and Northeast, a watch system was adopted. Because the South was more rural and agriculturally based, a county system of government emerged with the office of the sheriff providing law enforcement services. As the Midwest and West began to develop, citizens preferred law enforcement services provided by constables and sheriffs—both of whom were elected officials. As the country continued to grow, these borrowed means of providing law enforcement services were no longer adequate. This was especially true for municipalities. In the remainder of this chapter, we examine the history of police misconduct occurring in two general time frames: before 1920 and from 1920 to the present.

Policing and Police Deviance Before 1920

Before the early 1800s, there were simple mechanisms for the provision of law enforcement services in most municipalities. Since most of the nation was rural until 1790, there were only six cities with a population of more than eight thousand. Towns such as New York, Philadelphia, and St. Louis used a night watch to ensure order and security. In St. Louis, citizens were selected for service on the night watch by conscription. The city developed a list of citizens which excluded the elderly, disabled, females, and slaves; people were selected from this list for service (Kappeler, 1989). Much like the early English system, the wealthiest segment of society was excluded from service or could employ a replacement. Also like the English counterpart, the watch system was riddled with problems. For one, most watchmen were lazy and incompetent; many citizens referred to them as "leather heads" (Louis, 1989). In cities where the watch was a paid position, most secured their positions through political contacts so that they could work a regular job during the day and then sleep at night during the watch. Ironically, in some communities a punishment for minor offenders was a sentence to serve on the watch.

In the early 1800s, the United States began to experience many social changes that dictated the development of a new style of law enforcement. The population of many cities increased greatly. New York City, for example, grew from 33,000 in 1790 to 150,000 in 1830 (Uchida, 1997); by 1845 the city had grown to 250,000, and by 1855 the population had skyrocketed to 620,000 (Hernandez, 1989). Much of this growth was due to massive immigration. Immigrants brought with them cultural values, beliefs, and practices that were at odds with those of many settled urban residents (Johnson, 1988). Richardson (1974) described some of the strains, noting, "Many newcomers were poor, unwashed, whiskey drinking, and Catholic, a devastating combination in a society that tended to judge a man's worth by his wealth and regarded decency and respectability as synonymous with Protestantism" (p. 20).

Those who were established residents saw immigrants as threats both to the established social order and as competitors for jobs and other economic advantages. There was also tension in both the South and North over slavery. Nonslave black and white abolitionists who spoke out against slavery were subjected to verbal and physical abuse. In fact, police in the United States were involved in the slavery controversy from the beginning (Williams & Murphy, 1995). In 1704, the colony of Carolina implemented the nation's first slave patrol (Reichel, 1992). "Slave patrols helped to maintain the economic order and to assist the wealthy landowners to recover and punish slaves who essentially were considered their property" (Gaines et al., 1997, p. 47). The St. Louis night watch was developed primarily to control the behavior of slaves. The watch was started following the passage of city curfew ordinances that prohibited slaves from being out at night (Kappeler, 1989). In the early 1800s, slaves accounted for approximately 25 percent of the population of St. Louis.

These types of social issues contributed to riots, mob violence, and civil disorder in nearly every major American city beginning in the 1830s. Walker (1977) describes a sequence of riots in St. Louis, Missouri:

> On election day, 1844, groups of Catholic Irish-Americans battled Protestant native-born Americans in the streets. . . . Five years later, volunteer fire companies representing the Irish and native-born communities fought each other in the streets. The next year, 1850, a mob ransacked the brothels in the city in another attempt to enforce standards of public decency through group violence. Election day in 1852 featured a riot between German-Americans and the native born, while both in 1853 and 1854 there were more riots involving Irish-Americans. (p. 5)

Similar episodes of mass violence took place in most other major cities. In New York, for example, 1834 was christened the "year of the riots" following repeated outbreaks of civil disorder (Miller, 1977). Since there were no full-time police forces, cities had to resort to calling out the militia to restore order. Given problems of civil disorder, coupled with an increase in citizens' fear of crime, many cities had few options other than to create full-time, organized police forces. As a result, police forces were formed in New York City in 1845, New Orleans and Cincinnati in 1852, Boston and Philadelphia in 1854, Chicago in 1855, Baltimore in 1857, and St. Louis in 1861. By the mid-1860s, police forces had been created in virtually every major city and several smaller ones in the United States (Johnson, 1981).

From its inception, policing in the United States had several unique features which eventually contributed to police deviance. One key factor was that policing was closely linked with local political systems (Bopp & Schultz, 1972). In most major cities, city councilmen, aldermen, and ward bosses had a great deal of power. To a large extent, these political leaders controlled police departments. Most police officers, for example, were recruited and selected by ward or precinct politicians. This meant the police were more of a political tool than an independent professional law enforcement service. Police officers were generally recruited from the same ethnic groups as the neighborhoods they were serving. In New York City, a residency stipulation required persons to have lived in the wards they would be policing for five years. The effect of this type of rule was that police officers were intimately connected to the persons they were policing (Miller, 1973). More importantly, however, this practice ensured that the police were tied to the local political order. David R. Johnson (1981) notes that politicians thought little about intervening in such matters as disciplining officers and creating police policies. Since police positions were based on political patronage, it was common for masses of officers to be replaced when new politicians were elected. Given the political nature of the occupation, it was also common for officers to be heavily involved in political campaigns—even to the point of rigging elections.

Another unique feature of early policing in this country was the provision of a variety of social service functions. Many departments provided overnight lodging for indigents. In the 1880s, the Philadelphia police furnished overnight lodging to about 127,000 persons (Walker, 1977). Between 1861 and 1869, the New York police provided lodging to 880,161 persons—about equal to the number of persons arrested (Gaines et al., 1997). Departments ran soup lines and helped ward leaders find work for unemployed immigrants (Kelling & Moore, 1995). In 1915, the Los Angeles police established an "anti-cigarette" clinic that treated 2,300 people in its first month of operation; in the same year, the New York City police raised money for destitute men (Walker, 1977). During these early years the police performed both law enforcement and social service functions. In most cities, police were probably the most important social welfare agency.

Finally, an important aspect of policing during this time frame was the exceptional amount of discretion enjoyed by individual police officers in performing their jobs. Police in the United States generally had much greater discretionary powers than did police in Britain. Miller (1973) raises an interesting question by asking why, if most people in the United States were anti-authoritarian, they were willing to tolerate authoritarian discretion on the part of the police. He notes that people entrusted public officials with broad discretionary power because politicians were held accountable through the popular vote. Since the police were largely controlled by local elected officials, they could be trusted with these broad discretionary powers. Because police did not have a strong source of centralized authority from which to draw (in comparison to the English) and because the police were not restricted by many institutional or legal restraints, each officer established individual authority among citizens. Many citizens had only vague ideas about what the police should or could do, and the police were given wide leeway to define their role and how it was to be carried out (Fogelson, 1977). Police most often used questionable discretionary authority when dealing with immigrants and the poor—those with the least power in society. Since the police had few institutional or legal restraints, they were relatively free to do their jobs and enforce their rules and laws as they saw fit.

Uchida (1997) notes that if there is a common theme that can be used to characterize the police in the nineteenth century, it is the large-scale corruption that occurred in most departments across the United States. Corrupt activities that started in this era became accepted and ingrained patterns of behavior in many departments. By today's standards, police were engaged in a host of wrongful acts. Some of the more notable forms of police misconduct are discussed under two broad categories: (1) police corruption and graft and (2) police violence and abuse of force.

Police Corruption and Graft. In the nineteenth century, "the 'crime' problem was largely one of vice laws" (Walker, 1977, p. 24). In many large cities, the police virtually ignored laws against drinking, prostitution, and gambling. Nonenforcement of the law, in many cases, was tied directly to systematic payoffs made to the police (Bopp & Schultz, 1972). Corruption in many departments was controlled at the precinct level but often involved officers throughout a department. St. Louis, for example, had repeated incidents of top-ranking police officials notifying the operators of gambling operations that a police raid was about to take place.

Statement of Police Practice and Procedures in New York City

Be loyal. The success of a squad, precinct or district depends greatly on the even teamwork of all its members. You should be for and not against the accomplishment of the functions of the Department, giving your most earnest and hearty support to those in authority. You cannot be loyal and be a knocker, a grumbler or a shirker. Just one man of this type in a command is a nuisance and a centre of dissatisfaction. . . .

Do not criticize the actions or orders of those placed in authority over you. You must assume that they are responsible, that they understand what they are trying to accomplish and have reasons for wanting things done in the way they prescribe. You must not assume that because you know of another way by which the same results might be obtained that they are wrong and you are right. . . .

The Police Department itself is often gauged by acts of its individual members. If you favorably impress persons, they will judge the entire Department by that impression. Every officer, whether on or off duty, on patrol, in reserve, or at home, should, therefore, conduct himself in an exemplary manner. When in uniform, whether on or off duty, you are a target for the eyes of the public and if you do not conduct yourself in a gentlemanly manner, you will be quickly observed. . . .

Do not do anything that is not gentlemanly. Do not spit on the sidewalk, cough in anyone's face, chew tobacco or gum, talk loudly or too much, or make unnecessary noise. Mind your own affairs and do not meddle with or criticize business people or other persons passing over your post. Refrain from influencing the business of any person. . . .

Idle gossip concerning yourself, the Department, or citizens, should not be indulged in, as a blasted reputation is seldom recovered and a gossipy man seldom makes a good policeman. . . .

Do not shirk your duty. Leaving post unnecessarily and conversing are habits. Do not make appointments to meet persons on post; make them for times when you are excused from duty. Be particular about conversing unnecessarily with women while on duty. . . .

From the first tour of duty you perform, it should be your aim to prepare for the competitive examinations for promotion. Men who are ambitious for promotion make good policemen; they are attentive to the duty, jealous of their character and reputation, and as a result of the study of the rules and regulations, usages and customs of the Department, and the laws and ordinances, are mentally well equipped. . . .

Excepted From: Kleinig, J., & Zhang, Y. (1993). *Professional law enforcement codes: A documentary collection.* Westport, CT: Greenwood Press.

At the lowest level in the system, patrol officers might receive favors or money from brothel owners or barkeeps for taking care of unruly guests or looking the other way. Many saloons also offered officers free drinks, and officers obligingly overlooked liquor laws (Kappeler, 1989). At the precinct level, corruption was more systematic and organized. In New York City, for example, precinct captains often controlled systematic pay-offs from illegal businesses. Once each month, one of the captain's "bag-men" collected protection fees from illegal businesses. Johnson (1981) notes that around 1900, standard monthly payoffs were $100–$300 for poolrooms, $50–$150 for brothels, and $50–$300 for gambling houses. In order to circumvent Sunday closings and other regulations, it is esti-mated that saloons in New York City paid $50,000–$60,000 each month to police and politicians (Johnson, 1981). Bagmen, for their part in the scheme, usually received 20 percent of the payoff moneys.

Perhaps one of the most notoriously corrupt precinct captains of the times was Alexander S. Williams. Appointed a captain in the New York City Police Department in 1871, Williams reportedly became rich from payoff moneys. By the 1890s, he owned a fashionable house in the city, a country estate, and a fifty-three-foot luxury steam yacht—in addition to having considerable cash holdings (Richardson, 1974).

Because of the money to be made, some precinct positions were highly sought after. Johnson (1981) notes that by the 1900s, standard fees were established by politicians in New York City for various police positions. An appointment as a patrol officer in that city was $300; $1,600 was the going price for a sergeant's position; while captain's positions were sold for $12,000–$15,000. At the time, an average captain's annual salary was around $3,000, suggesting strongly that the appointee would have to benefit from illegal payoffs to make the promotion worthwhile (Richardson, 1974).

Detectives were also involved in graft. In some cases, they permitted pickpockets or confidence men to ply their trade in exchange for a per-centage of the stolen earnings. Some detectives also manipulated investi-gations so that theft victims either paid rewards for the return of their property or criminals paid bribes to avoid arrest. One New York City detective was able, for instance, to earn more than double his salary from the payment of rewards (Richardson, 1974).

Police Violence and Abuse of Force. Few historians would argue with the idea that police brutality and violence, at least defined by today's standards, was widespread during this period. In an important article, Mark Haller (1992) provides three reasons for the widespread use of vio-lence by early police. First, many police believed they had a responsibility to punish certain wrongdoers. Instead of arresting a neighborhood youth for theft, an officer might, for instance, deliver a good beating to deter the youth from future indiscretions. Before the advent of the patrol wagon in 1881, making an arrest was often a cumbersome process. Officers would have to walk the arrestee, or tote offenders in a wheelbarrow in the case of drunks, to the station house. Thus, arrests were typically reserved for serious offenders, while minor offenders were given a good measure of "streetside justice." It is important to note that arrestees did not escape physical violence simply because they were formally taken into custody. Instead, it was common for an offender to be beaten either immediately before or after the arrest. The second reason for police violence during this period was to carry out interrogations (Skolnick & Fyfe, 1993). Police used physical violence to obtain confessions and to force suspects to reveal the names of accomplices—a tactic that became known as the "third degree." Police in some jurisdictions developed crude, but effective, means of torturing suspects. These tactics were used to extract information from both adult and juvenile offenders. In some instances, violence was accompanied by prolonged questioning, sometimes extending for hours and days on end. The third reason for violence could be attributed to the police subculture. The subculture, in this case, sanctioned and even encouraged violence to uphold the personal "dignity" of the policeman and police work.

There was also a considerable amount of violence between police and strikers. In the latter part of the 1800s there were literally hundreds of strikes in most major cities in the United States. Sidney Harring (1981) notes, for instance, that there were 5,090 strikes in New York City between 1880 and 1890; Chicago had 1,737 strikes; St. Louis had 256 strikes; and Cleveland experienced 207 strikes. Workers protested what they saw as economic exploitation by factory owners—poor working conditions and insufficient wages were two grievances. In some cities, police commissioners and police chiefs were intimately linked to factory owners and other business leaders (Harring & McMullin, 1992). It was a natural extension for the police to be used as strike breakers.

Harring (1981) cites instances where police in many cities—including Cleveland, St. Louis, Buffalo, Duluth, Houston, Columbus, Indianapolis, Chicago, Brooklyn, Philadelphia, and San Francisco—used brutal and excessive force. In some cases, women and children who were supporting the strikers were also beaten by the police. Police broke up union workers' meetings, refused to allow pickets, and arrested suspected labor leaders (Harring & McMullin, 1992). The relationship between the police and industrialists was particularly well developed in St. Louis, Missouri, with police chiefs deputizing factory owners and their nonstriking employees. When a riot or strike would emerge, these deputized officers would be deployed to break the strike violently.

Although the police of this era were involved in many different corrupt and violent activities, this did not mean that the public simply ignored police wrongdoings. Instead, there were several attempts to reform police operations. As early as 1853, for example, New York City created a Board of Police Commissioners. Primarily designed to remove the police from partisan political influence, the New York board was given authority to oversee police operations, including the personnel function. Comprised of three elected officials—the mayor, the recorder, and the city judge—it was believed that such a board would bring greater stability and improve professionalism, while still retaining the essence of democratic control. Although similar schemes were subsequently adopted by several other major cities like St. Louis and Kansas City, "control of the police merely shifted from one political faction to another: the fact of the police as a partisan instrument remained constant" (Walker, 1977, p. 28).

Haller (1992) has noted that early police operations in this country can be understood better when we examine facets of their relationship to broader society. First, policing was decentralized to the community level. The operation of the departments reflected the values of local politicians. Second, police operations were not just affected by politics, they were an integral part of the political system. Policing was, in a sense, a part of the "rackets" since it provided officers and other officials with a means of earning extra income. Police officers developed informal ways of performing their jobs that only remotely mirrored their official mandate (Fosdick, 1920). Finally, the police were tied to the merchants and industrialists and were more likely to support those interests than to restrict themselves to enforcing the law.

By the late 1800s, the neighborhood model for providing police and other governmental services seemed doomed to failure. Rapidly expanding populations and the accompanying increased demand for services extended beyond the abilities of local politicians. When agencies were decentralized, the result was a duplication of effort and increased corruption. The increasing demands on police services, unintended results of decentralization, and other factors encouraged agencies to professionalize their officers and administrators.

Many business and community leaders followed the lead of the private sector during the industrial revolution and transferred lessons learned in industry to government. In particular, it was felt that many principles from the emerging field of management science could be put to use to reform the political "boss" system. The idea was to "alter the structure of local government to achieve the same rationality, centralization, and uniformity which were the hallmarks of a well-run business" (Johnson, 1981, p. 65). To do this, leaders drew from the works of management theorists such as Frederick Taylor and Henry Fayol to divide and coordinate work, to improve efficiency, and to increase productivity.

Another factor contributing to police reform during this era was the attention given to the police actions from the media. The newspaper business was expanding rapidly during this time. Sensationalism sold newspapers; crime and police activities were often featured (Kappeler et al., 1996). One effect of this coverage was to increase citizen awareness of crime problems—not only in their own cities but in others across the country. As citizen awareness of police problems increased, so did their desire to reform law enforcement.

One group of reformers, known as the "Progressives," began to press for changes in both police operations and government as a whole. Movement members were particularly concerned with what they considered the growing disorder and the decline of morals in parts of cities where police had stopped enforcing vice laws (Moore & Kelling, 1976). Consisting primarily of white, upper-middle class, educated Protestants, the Progressives fought against the political machine that had corrupted government and police operations (Uchida, 1997).

In terms of law enforcement, the Progressives had several reform interests. For one, they believed that the police function should be narrowed and that law enforcement officers should not be engaged in activities such as operating homeless shelters, performing building inspections, and supervising elections. Second, the Progressives advocated that police operations should be centrally organized. Where possible, precincts should be consolidated under a central command authority so that police operations would no longer be so easily susceptible to local political manipulation. The Progressives also argued for specialization to improve police efficiency. Under the principle of specialization, specific divisions or units—such as vice, internal affairs, records, etc.—would be created to handle particular tasks. To the Progressives, centralization also meant that police chiefs should be able to perform their duties free from the threat of losing their jobs because of the interference of local political leaders. Thus, it was proposed that chiefs should be provided with contracts or other means to insulate them from external threats. Finally, the Progressives recognized the importance of upgrading the quality of law enforcement personnel. This meant that police should be selected, deployed, and promoted on the basis of personal ability, rather than partisan politics (Fogelson, 1977).

The advent of civil service systems was an important factor contributing to a change in police operations (Strecher, 1995). The Pendleton Civil Service Act was passed by Congress in 1883 following the assassination of President Garfield by a frustrated job seeker. This federal law was designed to ensure that workers were managed on the basis of merit rather than political connections. Several cities were inspired to create their own civil service systems (Bopp & Schultz, 1972). By 1915, 204 local police departments in the country had developed some form of civil service system (Johnson, 1981). In theory, civil service meant that police personnel decisions had to be based on merit. While some early civil service systems were manipulated by both the police and politicians, the move to establish merit-based personnel systems was an important ideological statement signaling a move away from badly corrupted employment practices of the past.

The movements toward reform noted above met with varying degrees of success. Corruption that had been widespread in the 1890s was apparently reduced in a few cities. Despite calls for reforms by groups like the Progressives, little substantive change occurred in many police agencies. For the most part, the police resisted demands made by outsiders. From the perspective of the police, outside reform groups were unable to understand the complexities and the uniqueness of law enforcement work. Thus, outsiders were often viewed as meddlers whose ideas were ill conceived.

Although some reforms did occur in government and policing, they were not nearly as pervasive as those sought by the Progressives. David Johnson (1981) has noted, however, that reform efforts of this era did have an impact:

> . . . progressivism seriously weakened the national dominance of the decentralized model for policing by introducing changes in the structure of politics and by organizing the various ideas about police reform into a fairly consistent intellectual position. The latter achievement was perhaps the more important in the long run. By weaving together various proposals the progressives eventually handed the police a valuable tool for asserting control over their own affairs after 1920. (p. 68)

Policing and Police Deviance After 1920

Eventually, many police executives acknowledged the need for reform in law enforcement. Many of the ideas championed by police administrators echoed those of progressive reformers. Included among them was the police need to minimize political interference and the need to improve personnel through selection and training (Uchida, 1997). Recommendations for change in this case, however, came from within policing. Thus, the police could no longer claim that reforms were suggested by outsiders having little understanding of police work.

"Professional" Model Policing. An overarching goal of reform emphasized by police administrators was to narrow the police role to that of crime fighting. The extraneous functions traditionally handled by the police should be eliminated, administrators argued, so that the police could concentrate their energies on their primary mission—combating crime. "Henceforth, virtually every policy . . . and every innovation, from juvenile officers to police athletic leagues, would have to be rationalized in terms of crime prevention" (Fogelson, 1977). This mode of policing has often been referred to as the "professional model" of policing.

Before the 1920s, few police agencies expressed much enthusiasm about the new professional model. The virtues of the crime fighting model were, however, soon endorsed by police leaders such as August Vollmer and his student, O. W. Wilson. Vollmer, Wilson and their protégés published articles and spoke at professional meetings about the benefits of the professional model in policing (Fogelson, 1977). As a result, the new model was subsequently sanctioned and adopted by most agencies in the country.

While the advent of the professional model of policing can be traced to the 1920s, many of the innovations that characterize it occurred over the course of several decades both before and after 1920. George Kelling and Mark Moore (1995) have identified several characteristics of policing under the professional model. It is important to review a few of these characteristics since many police agencies today continue to base their operations on these features. It is also important to examine ingredients of this model because of the role they play in the production and continuation of police deviance.

- *Source of Police Legitimacy and Authority*—Kelling and Moore noted that before the professional model era, police derived much of their authority from local political leaders. Under the professional model, however, this idea was flatly rejected, and it was suggested that police authority was derived from those laws they were charged with enforcing. Thus, if citizens questioned why a situation was handled in a particular way, they were informed that the police were merely enforcing the law.
- *The Role of the Police*—Under the professional model, the police themselves stated that their primary function was to control crime through the apprehension of offenders. The police denied that they had a responsibility to perform social service functions, suggesting that non-crime-fighting activities were not "real" police work.
- *Police Relationships with Citizens*—Police were encouraged to interact with citizens in a neutral and detached manner. The role of citizens in the fight against crime was to be passive; if citizens observed criminal infractions, they were to take no actions themselves. Instead, citizens were to call the true "professionals" in handling crime—the police.
- *Use of Technology*—The police applied several technological innovations in this era that tremendously affected the way that they performed their jobs. Foot patrol, for example, was declared inefficient and virtually all beat officers were assigned to motorized patrol. New police communications technologies revolutionized the way that police performed their jobs. Two-way police radios, for example, were a significant improvement over the call-box system. Both vehicular patrol and police radios dramatically

affected the way police officers related to citizens and superiors—and, ultimately, the way they performed their jobs.

• *Gauging Police Effectiveness*—Police administrators suggested that the effectiveness of their operations could be determined by examining "objective" measures. First, the Uniform Crime Reports could be used to track criminal activity and the police response to this activity. Second, police efficiency could be determined in part by examining response times to calls for service. (pp. 10–14)

The professional model reforms had important ramifications for various types of police deviance. In chapter 3, for example, we discuss why officers in specialized units have unique opportunities for engaging in deviant activities and why it is often quite difficult for administrators to address this deviance. In chapter 4, we discuss how civil service provisions, although premised on equitable treatment, limit the diversity of police personnel and how this contributes to a police culture that may be inclined to exploit certain segments of society.

Although several reforms were instituted under the professional model with the objectives to maximize "crime fighting" and to minimize police corruption, policing continued to be plagued by numerous accounts of wrongdoing. John Crank (1998) has remarked that "The twentieth century witnessed broad police reform under the banner of the police professionalism movement. . . . However, the movement had little effect on black Americans . . ." (p. 209). According to Sherman (1974) every police agency has probably witnessed some form of organized corruption or major scandal since the 1920s. The next sections briefly review, by decade, some examples of police misconduct, along with some of the social issues that surrounded them. The listing illustrates continuing themes of police wrongdoing and indicates that many contemporary forms of police misconduct are neither new nor particularly unique.

Police Misconduct in the 1920s. Prior to the beginning of the decade, several cities experienced major problems with racial violence. The police response to these incidents revealed a pattern of discriminatory practices that continued for decades. In 1917, for example, the buildup of racial tensions in East St. Louis culminated in massive rioting. The facts of the St. Louis case parallel the outbreak of racial violence in other cities around the same period of time. Angered over the use of African Americans to strike-break in East St. Louis, a carload of whites drove through an African-American area of the city indiscriminately discharging firearms into homes. A large crowd of African Americans gathered afterwards and, upon seeing a police car containing several officers, opened fire. Two policemen subsequently died. The local media published inflammatory accounts of the incident and the police placed the bullet-ridden cruiser on public display at the station house. The results were predictable; there was massive retaliation by whites. Crowds of white men, women, and children beat, stabbed, clubbed, and shot minorities. Several citizens were chased into their homes, which were subsequently burned by white rioters. In all, thirty-nine African Americans and eight whites were killed. In a congressional investigation of the incident, the police were chastised for their part in the tragedy. The police had failed to take action in the early stages to prevent the incident from developing into a full-scale retaliatory riot. The investigators noted that, in many instances, the police passively stood by as whites victimized African Americans. The police were also active participants in some of the mob violence; they clubbed African Americans who had committed no offense and fired into crowds who were not resisting. Interestingly, the police also attacked newspaper reporters who had taken pictures during the riot, smashing cameras and destroying film (Walker, 1977).

Race-related incidents occurred in other cities as well. A race riot was touched off in 1919 in Chicago, for instance, when an African-American youth crossed into a white area at the beach. In the riots that occurred during the next six days, thirty-eight people were killed, more than five hundred were injured, and one thousand persons were left homeless. Once again, the police were criticized in the investigation that followed for failing to take appropriate action when necessary and for engaging in racially discriminatory behavior.

Samuel Walker (1977) found that although investigations suggested the presence of police discrimination, little or nothing was done to rectify the situation. He pointed out that the pattern of racial discrimination could be seen as the continuation of a pattern of police support for the most powerful segments in society. Historically, the police were used to control riots and strikes that negatively affected the interests of the propertied classes. When the powerful white majority resorted to rioting and violence, police merely looked the other way. There was no call from the broader society for police reform to eliminate the discrimination or for police training programs to teach cultural sensitivity.

The 1920s were transition years for many police agencies. Following on the heels of the Progressive movement, many agencies moved toward the professional model of policing. It was during these same years that Prohibition took its toll on attempts to reform policing. Since Prohibition was not supported by a majority of the population, there was great demand for illegal alcohol. Thus, extensive black markets sprung up to satisfy this demand. These illegal markets were able to survive and operate only because police overlooked flagrant violations of the law. Johnson (1981) notes that the effect of Prohibition was to raise the level of corruption to new heights in many police departments. In Chicago in the mid-1920s, a reporter told the director of the Chicago Crime Commission that he believed only 1 percent of the Chicago police force was honest. In

Los Angeles, a bootlegger who had been paying members of the police department nearly $100,000 a year complained that he was forced out of business when police raised the amount he had been paying for protection (Fogelson, 1977).

Police Misconduct in the 1930s. In 1931, the National Commission on Law Enforcement and Observance—popularly known as the Wickersham Commission—released its report on the criminal justice system in the United States. The commission, which had been put together by President Herbert Hoover, published a fourteen-volume set on several aspects of the country's justice system. Two of these volumes were devoted specifically to the police. One of the volumes discussed the need to upgrade the police and contained suggestions in line with tenets of the professional model of policing, including: the need for training and education programs for police officers; the need to provide police chiefs with protections from political manipulation; and relief from the burdensome volume of duties placed on each patrol officer.

The Wickersham Report's other volume on the police was a condemnation of police brutality and misconduct. In this volume, the commission chastised the police for their use of the "third degree." In an extensive report on the topic, the commission provided detailed information on the practice. The third degree was most commonly used against citizens in order to secure confessions from them, to get information on other suspects, or to get other evidence. The commission noted that there were several forms of the third degree, including: prolonged questioning for hours or days; depriving persons of sleep or food; placing a suspect in close proximity to a corpse; subjecting suspects to a blinding light during questioning; the use of threats; and the beating of suspects with fists, feet, and rubber hoses. The commission cited several instances where police had tortured suspects, noting that in one case, "a police surgeon was present . . . [to take] the victim's pulse during a beating so that he could tell the police how much the man could stand" (Chafee, Pollak, & Stern, 1969, p. 172).

The commission noted that the police presented several arguments in support of their use of the third degree. As we shall see in later chapters, many of the justifications for the use of the third degree were similar to reasons used by contemporary police to justify their involvement in other types of deviant activities. Police arguments for the use of the third degree included:

- It is necessary to get all of the facts from criminals.
- The third degree is used only against those who are guilty.
- The police face so many obstacles in performing their jobs that it is almost impossible to get convictions except by third degree methods.

• Police brutality is an inevitable and therefore an excusable reaction to the brutality of criminals.

• If restrictions are placed on the use of the third degree, it will seriously impair police morale.

• The growth and existence of organized gangs in large cities creates an unprecedented situation; thus, constitutional and legal guarantees created for other times and simpler conditions are no longer applicable. (Chafee et al., 1969, pp. 174–180)

The commission's report seemed to shock the public, placing the police on the defensive. The International Association of Chiefs of Police, for example, vehemently attacked the report and formed a special committee to refute the commission's findings (Fogelson, 1977). Perhaps most importantly, however, the public reaction that followed the report was an important signal that the people were no longer willing to tolerate unchecked brutality on the part of the police.

Police Misconduct in the 1940s. During the first part of this decade, the public's attention was understandably riveted on World War II. Police wrongdoing, nonetheless, continued to be reported in incidents across the country. A grand jury investigation in Los Angeles revealed that police were protecting hundreds of prostitutes for about $100 per week per woman. Police in that city were also doing other favors for underworld figures (Fogelson, 1977). Similar reports of police wrongdoings surfaced in other cities across the country.

Racial violence once again became an issue in this decade. The incongruity between the rhetoric of equality and the reality of racism increased the frustration of African Americans. The worst incident occurred in Detroit in 1943. Rioting in that city led to 34 deaths and more than $2 million in property damage. Again, the police were criticized for their failure to handle incidents of racial violence properly.

The public response to outbreaks of racial violence was, however, much different than it was for the incidents nearly two decades earlier. At a time when the public had been shocked by reports of Nazi racism, "A broad coalition of civic leaders emerged and united to encourage improved race relations" (Walker, 1992a, p. 818). With the public interest in reforming race relations, the first police-community relations programs were started. Manuals and texts on the topic began to appear; simultaneously, many departments began to train their officers in race relations.

Police Misconduct in the 1950s. After millions of people watched the televised hearings of the Kefauver Committee in 1950–51, U.S. citizens became sensitized to the problem of extensive corruption in government. Partly as a result of this new awareness, public response to reports of police corruption in some cities was more serious than it had been in the past. In Oakland, California, for example, a grand jury was convened to investigate a case where police allegedly attempted to extort money from a store owner. During the investigation, it was also revealed that detectives had taken gifts from burglars who were in jail awaiting trial. A new police chief was subsequently appointed who was apparently successful in rooting out most forms of corruption within the department (Sherman, 1974).

Reports of police wrongdoing were taken seriously by the public in other cities as well. A grand jury was convened to look into reports of police misconduct in Philadelphia in 1951. They found evidence that each precinct was overlooking prostitution, gambling, and other forms of vice for about $3,000 to $4,000 per month. In Chicago, the Emergency Crime Committee was established by the city council to investigate whether police were protecting racketeers (Fogelson, 1977). The chief of police in that city was suspended after the media published the chief's "little red book" which listed taverns and bars making payoffs to the police (Bell, 1960).

Police Misconduct in the 1960s. Several police scandals were publicized in the 1960s. In Denver, Colorado, for example, about thirty police officers working the night shift were found to be involved in an extensive burglary ring. In that case, officers burglarized stores and restaurants, using their police cruisers to carry away stolen goods. The Chicago police department was rocked by the Summerdale Scandal, where police officers served as lookouts and planners for a burglar who split proceeds from the thefts with the police (Bopp & Schultz, 1972).

Perhaps most important were incidents of mass civil disobedience that occurred across the country. Inner-city riots occurred in New York, the Watts section of Los Angeles, Detroit, and other cities. At the same time, protests occurred at many colleges and universities over U.S. involvement in Vietnam. In response, President Johnson appointed the National Advisory Commission on Civil Disorders (popularly known as the Kerner Commission). The report issued by the commission cited several factors that contributed to urban disorder. The professional model of policing emphasized such approaches as vehicular patrol, impersonal professionalized contacts with members of the public, and aggressive preventive patrol. These approaches tended to isolate the police from the public and had the effect of exacerbating existing racial tensions. The commission pointed to other police practices, noting that police brutality, harassment, verbal abuse, and general discourtesies toward African Americans were factors that also contributed to civil disturbances. The commission also noted the need to provide citizens with effective complaint procedures and to hire and promote more African Americans within police agencies.

Police Misconduct in the 1970s. During the 1970s, society continued to question the social role of the police. One of the most noteworthy cases of police corruption reported during this decade had to do with the New York City Police Department. In the latter part of the 1960s, New York police officer Frank Serpico tried for more than two years to get authorities to investigate his allegations of corruption within the department. Partly as a result of the attention Serpico eventually drew to the issue, Mayor John V. Lindsay appointed a commission in 1970 (which became known as the Knapp Commission) to investigate corruption in the New York City Police Department. Two years later, the commission released its report, finding that corruption was widespread throughout the department (Knapp Commission, 1972). The report noted that the police had an organized system wherein they collected payoffs from gambling and narcotics violators. In other instances, the police received payoffs from construction firms and bar owners to ignore ordinance violations; routinely accepted gratuities from business owners; and accepted money and narcotics from drug traffickers in exchange for the offenders' freedom. In all, it was estimated that more than one-half of the city's 29,600 officers had taken part in corrupt practices.

The death of Arthur McDuffie at the hands of police officers in Miami, Florida, also marked the decade of the 1970s. On December 17, 1979, Arthur McDuffie, an African American, was riding his motorcycle on the streets of Miami, Florida. According to accounts by the police, he "popped a wheelie," accelerated the motorcycle, and gave the finger to a near-by police officer. The police officer gave chase and was eventually joined by more than a dozen Miami patrol cars. Following a brief pursuit that allegedly reached speeds over one hundred miles per hour, McDuffie stopped his motorcycle. Officers converged on the scene, and at least six white officers jumped McDuffie. In a matter of minutes McDuffie lay motionless on the ground with his head split open. He died four days later as a result of police-inflicted injuries.

Initial reports by the officers involved in the beating indicated that McDuffie was injured while falling off his motorcycle, but it was later learned that police fabricated the explanation and contrived evidence to support it. As a result of inconsistencies uncovered by a departmental investigation, the officers were indicted for manslaughter and tried in Tampa. An all-white jury was selected to hear the charges. In May of 1980, the jury acquitted all of the officers; the jury spent only two hours and forty-five minutes to reach its decision.

As a result of the jury's verdict "one of the ugliest incidents of racial violence in the United States rocked Miami and sent shock waves across the whole country. As a consequence of the three days of rioting, eighteen deaths, and extensive property damage, promises were made concerning the revitalization of the inner city, enhancement of the economic development of the affected areas, and a variety of other social, economic, and political improvements for blacks" (Alpert, Smith, & Watters, 1992, p. 472). Police officials also made pledges for changes in police recruitment, selection, training, complaint management, supervision, and other areas. The local police were thus induced to develop several alternative approaches to policing, including a precursor to problem-oriented policing and a strategy for combating civil disorders.

Police Misconduct in the 1980s. The 1980s were marked by highly publicized incidents of police misconduct. The New York City Police Department was rocked by intense media scrutiny over the activities of the "Buddy Boys," an organized group of rogue officers who stole money and drugs from dealers and other residents in the city's 77th precinct. The Buddy Boys case is analyzed in chapter 8.

The 1980s were marked by intensified law enforcement efforts to combat illicit drugs in the country. Beginning in about 1981, substantial police resources began to be allocated to fight the "war" on drugs (Reuter & Kleiman, 1991). These efforts resulted in thousands of arrests and prison sentences for drug offenders. At the same time, police in agencies throughout the country have been sanctioned for illegal activities associated with the illicit drug market.

One of the most notable cases of drug-related police corruption occurred in the "River Cops" case in Miami, Florida, in the mid-1980s. In this case, an organized group of police officers from the Miami Police Department became involved in large-scale cocaine thefts from illicit drug distributors. Inquiry into the thefts began in May of 1985 when drug smugglers informed Miami police that they had been transporting hundreds more pounds of cocaine at the time of their arrests than had been logged into evidence. Miami police officers had skimmed and subsequently sold drugs amounting to hundreds of thousands of dollars. In late July of the same year, several Miami police raided a boat, intending to steal the 350 kilograms of cocaine on board. Six smugglers jumped into the water; three of them drowned. In the investigation that followed, 19 Miami River Cops were indicted, tried, and sentenced for various offenses. When one of the accused officers began cooperating with investigators, a fellow officer used a machine gun in an unsuccessful murder attempt (Salopek, 1997). Three of the officers were convicted of murder, and several of the officers were sentenced to prison terms of 20 years or longer (Sechrest & Burns, 1992). Further scrutiny of police activities led to the dismissal of more than 70 officers by 1988, with some estimates suggesting that as many as 200 of the 1,060 officers in the Department faced investigation for corruption-related matters (Dombrink, 1988).

The Miami River Cops case was not the last debacle involving corruption in the Miami Police Department. In 1987, $150,000 was stolen from a safe from the Department's Special Investigation Section (Dorschner, 1993). In another case, 500 pounds of marijuana was stolen from a secure area of the Department's Compound (Dombrink, 1988). Investigations in both cases implied that police were responsible for the thefts.

Police departments in other cities experienced widely publicized cases of wrongdoing during the decade of the 1980s. More than 30 officers from the Philadelphia Police Department were convicted of criminal offenses stemming from gambling-related protection and payoff schemes. Among the officers sanctioned were a deputy commissioner, four lieutenants, an inspector, and a chief inspector. The Philadelphia case revealed that the Department had a long-standing, sophisticated, institutionalized system of corruption that spanned the rank structure (Dombrink, 1988).

In 1980 several officers in Medford, Massachusetts, burglarized the safety deposit boxes in a bank (Clemente & Stevens, 1987). In 1986 the media relayed reports of widespread corruption in the Boston Police Department. Several bar owners reported having been threatened that they would be issued liquor license violations if cash payoffs were not made to police officers. In other instances, both criminal and liquor license violations were overlooked by police in exchange for payoffs. A contribution factor in the Boston police corruption scandal was that officers were empowered to inspect bars for compliance with liquor regulations. "Eventually, seven Boston police officers were indicted under the RICO statute for obtaining kickbacks from Boston restaurants and nightclubs" (Dombrink, 1988, pp. 77–78). In 1987 a scheme to sell police promotion examinations was discovered; it had been operating for about fifteen years throughout Massachusetts (Berg, 1992).

In 1985, several San Francisco police officers participated in an incident where, following a recruit graduation dinner, a paid prostitute performed oral sex on a bashful recruit who had been handcuffed to a chair by his colleagues (Dombrink, 1988). The incident culminated in the firing of two recruits, two veterans, and two sergeants.

Police Misconduct in the 1990s. Police wrongdoing in the 1990s is a reflection of misconduct occurring in previous decades. The latter part of this text is devoted to case studies critically assessing incidents occurring in the decade of the 1990s. These case studies include use of force in the Rodney King case, police discrimination in the Jeffrey Dahmer investigation, drug-related misconduct in the Buddy Boys case, and apparent institutionalized corruption in the Washington D.C. Police Department. There have been numerous incidents in addition to those chosen for the case studies. We will mention several of the most egregious.

In New Orleans, 40 police officers were arrested between 1992 and 1996 on charges of bank robbery, auto theft, narcotics trafficking, rape, and aggravated assaults. About 200 officers were eventually fired, retired, or reprimanded (Salopek, 1997). A vice squad was disbanded after a deputy supervisor was convicted of robbing bars and strip clubs. Len Davis, an officer known as "Robocop" to public housing residents, arranged the murder of a woman who had filed a brutality complaint against him (Kirby, 1996). On March 4, 1995, Antoinette Frank entered a Vietnamese restaurant to commit robbery. She killed the security guard, an off-duty police offer, Ronald Williams, who had occasionally been her partner. She then murdered two restaurant employees. Both Frank and Davis face the death penalty.

A Justice Department investigation found patterns of excessive use of force, false arrest, improper stops and bogus searches and seizures in Pittsburgh in 1997. A consent decree was signed in April that leaves the Bureau of Police in Pittsburgh under scrutiny for five years. The department must create a computer database that tracks every officer and includes detailed descriptions of all citizen complaints, claims filed in civil court, incidents involving use of force, and the race of everyone arrested, searched without a warrant, or stopped for traffic violations (Zorn, 1997).

SUMMARY

This brief history of policing and police corruption highlights two important points. First, police wrongdoing is not peculiar to contemporary policing. Police deviancy has existed for as long as there have been police. Second, forces both within and outside of policing play an important role in the production of police wrongdoing. When we look at the history of policing, it is clear that external factors—the economic, political, and social structure of society—and internal factors—the organizational arrangement, management style, and stated role of a police agency—all play intricate and important roles in police wrongdoing.

Chapter Three

THE WORKING ENVIRONMENT
Organizing and Structuring Police Deviance

> I urge you to learn the harsh facts that lurk behind the
> mask of official illusion with which we have concealed
> our true circumstances, even from ourselves.
> Robert Kennedy (1925–1968)

D eviance and crime can be found within almost every occupation and profession. Although there are no statistics collected on a national level that allow us to estimate the extent of police deviance, it is safe to conclude that virtually every law enforcement agency in the United States has witnessed both organized corruption and some form of police scandal (Bracey, 1989). Criminological and sociological theories can be applied to explain work-related deviance—whether it involves police or citizens. It is important to recognize that many police officers are honest citizens (as are many doctors, stock brokers, or college professors). However, it is important to study those who deviate as well as those who conform. While the level of misconduct may be similar among all occupations, the opportunities for deviance are greater in some professions than in others.

Policing is an occupation with unique features, many of which contribute to deviant behavior. When society accords police the power to deal with law-violating members of the public, it also provides them with many opportunities to engage in similar behaviors. Deviant police are unlikely to be detected for many reasons—one of which is the loose supervision that characterizes most police organizations.

When social conditions are organized in such a manner that they promote deviance, these conditions can be referred to as *structurally* induced deviance. Police deviance can be conceptualized as a manifestation of the structure of the police and society, the organization of the police as an institution of social control, the development of a unique police role and function, and the creation of situational opportunities that facilitate police deviation. Considered together, these structural facets create an occupation that is inherently prone to deviance in the forms of corruption, exploitation, and abuse of the public.

This chapter explores determinants of police deviance and discusses how police deviance is internally and externally affected by structural and organizational factors. Consideration is given to the role of law and police authority as legitimizing forces for police deviance. In some instances, the law itself contributes to the victimization of certain segments of society.

DEVIANCE OPPORTUNITY STRUCTURE

Many scholars have noted that policing creates a unique opportunity for deviance (Barker, 1994; Reiss, 1971). Some have even characterized the opportunity as "unlimited," particularly in comparison with other occupations (Rubinstein, 1973). The structure of police organizations "provides the police officer with more than ample opportunity for a wide range of deviant activities" (Barker, 1994, p. 48). Some of the most important structural and organizational factors contributing to an opportunity for police deviance include: legitimizing police deviance with the authority of law; creating operational justifications and rationalizations for police deviance which color public perceptions; isolating police-citizen encounters; and limiting and subverting police supervision.

Legitimizing Police Deviance

Some police conduct would raise suspicion if ordinary citizens engaged in similar activities. Many routine behaviors of the police would indeed be considered criminal for ordinary citizens. Police can exceed posted speed limits while responding to citizens' calls for service. They can encroach on private property to investigate suspicious people and activities. They can use their authority to confiscate property, to detain and arrest, and even to take citizens' lives. Police can access confidential information, possess illegal substances, and control official records all with the benefit of legal authority. The police enjoy the legal authority and the operational justification to engage in forms of conduct that would be deemed criminal for others. Thus, the special legal privileges accorded the police provide unprecedented opportunities to engage in deviance without arousing suspicion.

Table 3.1 shows that many of the forms of conduct ordinarily considered criminal are actually quite commonplace for the police and are legitimized by the law. For example, while murder is prohibited by criminal law, police are allowed under certain conditions to use deadly force to accomplish their crime control objective. The authority to use deadly force may, however, mask the intention to use that authority for deviant purposes. Police have killed citizens for personal gain or to satisfy a sense of justice. Police have also contrived situations that would allow them to use deadly force when lesser means of force could have accomplished the same legal objective. The police also have the legal authority to seize property if it is deemed evidence of crime. The seizure of property by the police, however, sometimes results in the unlawful conversion of that property from individuals to police officials or their organizations. The drug forfeiture laws—a legally granted authority—create opportunities to commit deviant acts (Holden, 1993). Because the police hold a unique position in the law—one that allows certain actions that would be illegal for other citizens—the police are presented the means for deviance as part of their occupational obligations.

Table 3.1

Criminal Law, Police Legal Authority, and Deviance

Criminal Law	Police Legal Authority	Police Deviance
Murder	Deadly Force	Police Executions
Kidnapping	Detention and Arrest	False Arrest
Rape and Sexual Assault	Strip and Body Cavity Searches	Sexual Exploitation
Robbery	Use of Force to Seize	Extortion/Accepting Bribes
Assault and Battery	Reasonable Force	Brutality/Coercion
Burglary	Search and Seizure	Theft
Drug Offenses	Possess and Seize Evidence	Use and Sale of Drugs
Theft	Seizures	Unlawful Conversion
Forgery	Reporting Crime	False Reporting

Based on Brodeur, J. (1981). Legitimizing police deviance. In C. D. Shearing (Ed.), *Organizational police deviance*. Toronto, Canada: Butterworth.

If an ordinary citizen were to exceed the speed limit or wander onto private property, he or she would be hard pressed to explain these actions. Police officers, however, have ready explanations for such activities that are grounded in legitimate police functions. For example, the police were exceeding the posted speed limit while responding to a citizen's call for service—not to avoid rush-hour traffic. They were on private property to check out suspicious activities—not to peer into someone's window. They stopped female motorists because of safety concerns or traffic violations—not to "check them out." They use force to subdue a violent suspect—not to inflict punishment for defiance. The authority vested in the police and the tasks performed offer both the opportunity for deviance and plausible, operationally based justifications if the behavior is questioned.

The placement of police in a unique legal position is not the only source of legitimization that invites deviance. The law is often written and can be interpreted in ways that give the police sufficient latitude to deviate in their pursuit of legitimate goals. Richard Ericson (1981) has noted that

> substantive laws are written broadly enough, and with sufficient ambiguity, that they can be applied across a range of circumstances. Causing a disturbance, a breach of the peace, obstructing police, and many others serve as a pretext for making the arrest. (p. 91)

Because of the ambiguity in criminal law, the police interpret legal mandates according to the demands of a particular situation. Thus, the law itself contributes to police deviance. Ericson's discussion illustrates how the police can use the law as a tool to facilitate achievement of enforcement objectives.

Not only do the police use the law selectively to maintain or create social order, they also use it as an instrument of coercion to achieve organizational and personal objectives. Some of these methods have been referred to by police as making "chump" arrests and "stacking" or "jacking-up" charges against citizens. These practices entail the use of the law to detain or arrest citizens on relatively minor infractions with the intent of extracting information or building more serious cases against them. For example, identical legal infractions—such as two traffic violations—can result in different outcomes depending on the motives of the police and their interpretation and application of the law.

First, police can merely release the citizen with no more than a verbal warning—there is no legal mandate that the police enforce minor infractions of the law. Second, the police can choose to employ the force of law by issuing a citation or summons for the violation. Third, if police feel that the citizen fits the "mold" or "profile" of one who is likely to have engaged in other criminal behavior, such as the possession of a weapon or controlled substance, the citizen may be arrested for the sole purpose of searching the vehicle for evidence. This may occur even though the police do not have legal cause to believe the citizen was in violation of a weapons or drug law. The traffic arrest provides justification and serves as a pretext for conducting a vehicular search.

The law insulates officers from civil repercussions because of the initial "good" arrest. Whether evidence of a weapons or drug violation is uncovered is of little concern to the police; this escalating technique is often approved by supervisors. Police organizations often reward their members for this form of behavior—which in other contexts would be considered deviant. Consider the example just given. If the officer uncovers a cache of controlled substances, the tactic is considered "good" police work. The officer might be rewarded for being so observant. Police often use minor violations of the law to justify searches, collect information, interrogate citizens, and to build more serious criminal cases. As we shall see in later chapters, deviant police often use their powers of detention to abuse citizens.

In addition to arrests based on minor infractions ("chump" arrests), police often stack or jack-up charges against citizens. If the police arrest an offender who has committed a burglary, they may "stack" offenses by charging the offender with a variety of crimes subsumed under the legal definition of burglary. The burglar may be charged with criminal trespass, theft, and/or vandalism. Motivated by an occupationally developed

Criminal Law, Police Authority, and Deviance

[On December 23, 1984, Barbara Bielevicz and David Tumpa were arrested by Officers Johnson Dubinon and Virginia Beck of the Pittsburgh Police Department. They were jailed for several hours and then released with no formal charges filed. Bielevicz sued the police department. Chief Moore, a station commander in 1984, testified at the trial.]

"At trial, Moore described customary police conduct in making public intoxication arrests. He testified that everyone in the police department generally understood that the charge of public intoxication could be used to arrest someone . . . without probable cause to believe that they were intoxicated. Moore also maintained that it was common knowledge among police officers that the charge could be used with impunity to remove someone from the street whose responses or attitude infuriated the officer. He further stated that the discretion to confine the person in the Public Safety Building belonged exclusively to the arresting officer. If incarcerated for public intoxication, the individual was detained for a period of up to four hours and then released. At no time prior to confinement or subsequent to release did anyone other than the arresting officer evaluate the condition of the allegedly intoxicated person.

"Moore's account of common police practice is consistent with the testimony of Officer Dubinon. Dubinon stated that when he arrested and incarcerated Tumpa and Bielevicz for public intoxication, he did not intend to prosecute them for this charge and knew that there would not be a hearing. In fact, Dubinon had made countless such arrests in the past and had not once appeared at a hearing. Dubinon further conceded that it was his understanding from his experience as a police officer, that anyone arrested for public intoxication was incarcerated in the Public Safety Building for a maximum of four hours. As a general practice, the individual was then simply released, and the charge of public intoxication was never pursued.

"Ralph Pampena, chief of police since June, 1987, similarly described police custom. Pampena stated that when someone was placed in lock-up for public intoxication, the arresting officer was the only person to review that individual's condition beforehand. Pampena also acknowledged that, in his thirty-one years as a police officer, he had made numerous arrests for public intoxication and, like Dubinon, had never appeared at a hearing. . . .

"In our view, the foregoing testimony constitutes sufficient evidence . . . there was a long-established custom in the Pittsburgh Police Department of arresting and detaining people on charges of public intoxication without probable cause and with no intention of prosecuting them or of holding a hearing. Such well-established custom exists only with the approval or, at the very least, with the sufferance of policymakers.

"In short, . . . Bielevicz and Tumpa were arrested and incarcerated not because of alcohol, but because of personal animus. Scattered throughout the record are indications that the relationship between the officers and the plaintiffs at some point degenerated to a less than cordial state. On two occasions, for example, the officers used profanity in addressing Bielevicz and Tumpa. But perhaps most probative of the officers' hostility toward plaintiffs was Beck's 'Merry Christmas' remark when she locked Bielevicz in her jail cell."

Source: *Bielevicz v. Dubinon*, 915 F.2d 845 (3rd Cir. 1990).

sense of just punishment and a mistrust of the court system, police often elevate the seriousness or increase the number of criminal charges to influence the outcome of the judicial process.

In many jurisdictions, identical conduct can be charged either as a misdemeanor or a felony. One example is a charge of possession of a fictitious or altered driver's license versus possession of a forged instrument. Many juveniles obtain false drivers' licenses in order to frequent nightclubs and to purchase alcoholic beverages. Police who run across these licenses when making traffic stops will often jack-up the charge against the juvenile, hoping that he or she will "turn" or provide information on where the fake license was purchased. In many jurisdictions, stacking and jacking-up charges allow police to accomplish their goal of law enforcement. Police may charge or threaten to charge a citizen with a more serious offense or with several offenses if he or she fails to cooperate with the real police objective. This is often the case in drug enforcement activities. Police will charge a minor violator to obtain information on a major drug distributor.

Police who have violated the rights of a citizen or even committed an outright criminal act may charge the abused citizen in hopes that the number or severity of charges will induce a guilty plea so the incident will never be aired in the court room.

> [O]fficers know that the operation of the criminal justice system itself usually protects them from having to commit testimonial perjury before a grand jury or at trial. The vast majority of charges for narcotics or weapons possession crimes result in pleas without the necessity of grand jury or trial testimony, thus obviating officers' concerns about the risk of detection and possible exposure to criminal charges of perjury. (Mollen Commission, 1994, p. 37)

The distinction between the use of law to achieve organizational objectives and the use of the law to achieve personal objectives is often blurred.

The court system contributes to the deviance of stacking charges. Often, defense attorneys and prosecutors bargain with offenders concerning criminal charges. Defense attorneys offer prosecutors a guilty plea in exchange for a reduction in charges and a recommendation for a light sentence. Police, well aware of this practice, charge citizens with the most serious crime available, knowing that other criminal justice officials will negotiate the outcome of the case.

For deviant police officers, the law serves not as a control on practice but rather as a device for securing enforcement objectives. The law is often used in a selective fashion because "a wide range of rules can be used to justify any particular disposition an official deems appropriate for his organizational interests" (Ericson, 1981, p. 86). In addition to taking advantage of the discretion and ambiguity afforded by the law, some officers are guilty of outright violation of the law to advance the objectives of the police organization. The Mollen Commission's (1994) investigation into corruption in the NYPD found, for example, that

> When officers genuinely believe that nothing is wrong with fabricating the basis of an arrest, a search, or other police action and that civil rights are merely an obstacle to aggressive law enforcement, the Department's top commanders must share the blame. Indeed, we found that for years the Department was content to address allegations of perjury on a case-by-case basis, rather than pursuing the potential for a broader-based investigation. For example, supervisors were rarely, if ever, held accountable for the falsifications of their subordinates. We are not aware of a single instance in which a supervisor or commander has been sanctioned for permitting perjury or falsification on their watch. (p. 38)

Lawrence Sherman (1978) has noted that, "police failure to observe due process requirements in arresting suspects is an illegal practice, but such practices are usually viewed as supportive of the formal goal of police organizations" (p. 13). Similarly, when the law does not serve to advance the organizational objective of the police, police are likely to resort to deviant behavior to secure objectives. Many authors have noted that while the exclusionary rule was constructed to prevent police abuses of citizens' constitutional rights through the exclusion of evidence obtained illegally by the police, its use has resulted in an increase in police perjury (Burger, 1964; Oaks, 1970).

Public Perception of Police Deviance

Detecting police deviance is much more difficult than detecting the deviance of ordinary citizens. Police are the primary formal social institution charged with the detection and control of crime. This greatly reduces the chances that police will focus on themselves as potential deviants or that citizens will perceive the police as engaged in a significant amount of deviance. Generally, public attitudes toward the police suggest that they are perceived as honest, hard working, and free from corruption (Marx, 1992). This public perception creates an intellectual bias and assumption that those charged with controlling deviance will not themselves indulge in such behavior.

Peter K. Manning has provided invaluable insight into the police manipulation of public appearances. According to Manning (1997), police are not passive actors in the construction of the police public image. In fact, they cultivate their appearances by "selective systematic presentation of their activities" and by taking "special care to manage or control access to knowledge. . . . This protects that which they conceal, such as organizational secrets, plans, and the less-than-laudatory features of organizational life" (p. 43). Police, in fact, cultivate the appearance of full and impartial enforcement of the law and are generally unwilling to admit publicly that they have broad discretionary power to interpret the law situationally in their own best interests.

One of the most powerful constructions about the police is the administrative and political promotion of the myth of the "rotten apple" (Sherman, 1974). This myth—the deviant police officer operating alone and in isolation from the social environment without organizational and peer support—further cultivates the public assumption that police do not engage in significant systematic deviance. The public perceives the police as a legally controlled institution, bound by the letter of the law, and working only within the confines of legally articulated procedures. This conception of the law is also promoted by members of the legal profession who view law as built on a foundation of precedent that has resulted in a distinct set of doctrines that determines the outcome of cases. This cultivated image of clearly delineated law furthers the general assumption that police will not deviate; their behaviors are thought to be subject to the same review and sanction as the behaviors of ordinary citizens. When an incident of misconduct publicly surfaces, police administrators are quick to point out that the officer involved was a single rotten apple in an otherwise clean barrel—the officer's behavior was an aberration that is not acceptable under existing law nor is it condoned by the police organization. The police thus maintain the public appearance of a profession governed by the rule of law and free from organizational interests.

The police management of appearances and the rotten-apple myth have taken on increasing complexity in recent years. The rise of community policing has been accompanied by a reframing of police imagery. Police have begun reconstituting themselves as scientific problem solvers and community caretakers (Kelling & Moore, 1995; Moore & Trojanowicz, 1988), transforming their public image from crime fighters to service providers. The police characterize themselves as striving to be accountable to their "clients," "consumers," or "customers" and producing a "quality product" (Kappeler & Kraska, 1998). This new public construction of policing plays down incidents of police deviance and violence (and moves the police further away from legal accountability). Meanwhile, overt police violence appears in the increasing use of police paramilitary units (see Kraska & Kappeler, 1997). These events are sanitized for public consumption by emphasizing the services they provide—ridding neighborhoods of drug dealers and using a show of force to signal that unacceptable behavior will not be tolerated.

The rotten-apple myth is now woven through the image of the police as service providers. Incidents of police brutality and corruption are excused as singular aberrations from the enormous benefits of the community policing movement and the declining crime rates attributed to it (see Kelling, 1997). While the police tout the new community image, evidence suggests that policing is becoming more aggressive. There is no dearth of police deviance even in community-oriented police departments. As Victor Kappeler and Peter Kraska (1998) have noted, "police violence is as a whole thus more effectively implemented and public resistance is more proficiently regulated through the mixing of community rhetoric, the circulation of overt violence, and the realignment of the constellation of various social control agencies" (in press). The rotten-apple explanation for police deviance seems even more palatable in an age where community policing is said to be the dominant philosophy of the police institution.

Police Deviance and Isolation

Many citizen encounters with the police are conducted in isolation from public observation. As a result, police deviance often goes undetected by the public. Since many forms of police deviance are unobtrusive, citizens victimized by police are often unaware that they are the targets of deviance (Sapp, 1994). Female motorists may not even know when police run computer checks on their license plates just to get their addresses. Motorists stopped by the police are unlikely to question police motives, especially if they are not given a citation for some traffic violation. The same holds true for other types of selective and highly discretionary law enforcement. A young adult caught by the police with illegal drugs or other contraband is unlikely to question how the police dispose of the substance—especially if he or she is not charged with a crime. The police officer who retains the drugs for personal use or later sale is unlikely to be detected because of a citizen's complaint. Even when enforcement action is taken, citizens may be unaware of their legal rights, and the police may take advantage of such ignorance in the course of their work.

If deviance is detected and an inquiry is made concerning motive, police often avail themselves of an abundance of plausible explanations to justify conduct—a traffic stop for a defective taillight; the encounter never took place; or the drugs were destroyed. These justifications and rationalizations for behavior are grounded in a combination of police legal authority, the police role and function, the structure of citizen-police encounters, and the public's desire to believe the police.

Police often encounter lone motorists in isolated locations, they enter people's homes, or they work late at night when relatively few people are on the streets. Each of these conditions reduces the likelihood of witnesses to police actions and activities. Deviant police are aware of the need to carry out their misconduct far from the sight of the public. They stop vehicles when out of the public eye, or they wait until late at night to question citizens in isolated locations (see Kappeler & Vaughn, 1997).

Because the police can choose the settings in which encounters occur, there is only a small chance that police deviance will be witnessed and reported or even detected by the public. In addition to choosing locations, the police can select weak victims for particular types of deviance.

Many forms of police deviance result from the opportunities the police have to select their victims. In this selection process, police are likely to choose victims who have limited credibility in the eyes of the public (Kappeler & Potter, 1993). Citizens who live on the margin of society are particularly vulnerable to victimization by the police. A police officer may decide to violate a person's rights knowing the victim will not report the crime or will not make a credible witness if it is reported (Kraska & Kappeler, 1995). Prostitutes and teenage runaways are susceptible to this type of police violation and exploitation (Sapp, 1994).

Citizens engaged in criminal behavior are caught in a double bind. They can be arrested for violating the law and/or are powerless to protect themselves from police deviance and exploitation. Drug traffickers, for example, are not in positions to report their victimization by the police. This was clearly the situation in the "Buddy Boys" case in New York City (discussed in chapter 8). These police officers routinely watched for drug dealers who were holding either large quantities of cash or drugs. Rather than arrest the drug offenders, the police would steal the money and later sell the drugs they had confiscated (McAlary, 1987)—confident that their victims were not in a position to report the theft. In other situations, police have underreported the amount of confiscated drugs—leaving them with the remainder to use or sell (Murphy & Pate, 1977).

Police Deviance and Supervision

The opportunity for deviance is greatly enhanced by the relative lack of supervision of the police. Unlike many other occupations, police are relatively free to come and go with little oversight by superiors. While variations among departments exist, it is not unusual for a police sergeant to be charged with supervising five to ten officers. In addition, subordinates are often dispersed across large geographic areas. In many cases, police supervisors might see their officers only at the beginning and end of their tours of duty. It is common for police to work entire shifts without ever having any meaningful contact with their supervisor. As one commentator has noted, police supervision

> is sporadic, for it is impossible to maintain for long periods of time. The police officer[s] on patrol or on many special assignments are away from the supervisor's eye for considerable periods of time. The expectation is that the disciplines of the job will pervade the apparently independent and autonomous decisions of the individual officer. (Bahn, 1984, pp. 390–391)

Police Sexual Deviance and Isolated Citizen Contacts

A sergeant on the Village of Briarcliff Manor police force "was convicted of stopping and detaining five female drivers, one of them on two occasions. Each stop took place late at night on a deserted stretch of the Taconic State Parkway in Westchester County under the pretense of enforcing intoxication/driving laws. Although the Parkway passes through Briarcliff Manor, it is not a road on which the village's police force maintains patrol responsibility. Rather, the state police are responsible for patrolling the Parkway. After pulling his victims over and detaining them, he accused each of them—uniformly—of committing traffic violations such as swerving and speeding on the Parkway. He interrogated them as to any drinking they may have engaged in that evening. He did not issue a single ticket to any of his victims. The women whom appellant stopped were detained for various periods of time—from ten to fifteen minutes to more than an hour.

"All but one of the victims testified at appellant's subsequent trial that they were afraid for their safety during their detentions. The only victim who failed to mention that the experience frightened her was an off-duty New York City police officer. The officer, Fran Calderone, was coming home from work at approximately 3:00 A.M. when appellant pulled her over. Calderone produced her police identification and asked if there was a problem. Appellant, who insisted on calling Calderone by her first name, told her that she was 'doing fine' on the 'straightaways' but that he was 'worried about her' around the turns. Calderone testified that she had not been swerving and that in fact the road was straight. Appellant asked her if she had been drinking and repeatedly inquired whether she was able to drive but did not ask her to get out of her car. After about ten to fifteen minutes of conversation, appellant let her proceed.

"Another of the crimes for which appellant was convicted involved a nineteen-year old-victim. On February 28, 1987, at approximately 3:00 A.M., Jennifer Hummel was heading southbound on the Taconic Parkway, near Campfire Road, when she was stopped by appellant. Despite Hummel's insistence that she had just passed a state police breathalyzer test, appellant refused to permit her to proceed. He insisted on taking Hummel for a ride in his patrol car in order to 'sober [her] up.' After driving around for some time, appellant pulled his patrol car into a deserted spot overlooking the Croton Reservoir. Hummel testified that, after talking for a brief period, appellant told her that she was 'a really good listener and [she] was very understanding and he thought [she] was very attractive . . . [and] he [wanted] to take [her] out.' After Hummel declined, stating that she had a boyfriend, appellant persisted in questioning her about her relationship with her boyfriend. Then Hummel requested that appellant return her to her car. He declined, telling her that he did not feel as though she was ready to drive yet. Hummel testified that appellant insisted on taking her to a diner for coffee, even though she told him, 'I don't want coffee. I don't like coffee and I really . . . don't think I need it.' Once at the diner, Hummel told appellant, 'I can drink the coffee in my car. Please take me back to my car.' He again rejected her request. Eventually, after Hummel drank her coffee, appellant acquiesced and drove Hummel to her car. She testified that, once back at her car, 'I thanked him for taking me for the ride and he said, "Well, why don't we make it an even exchange. Why don't you give me your phone number?" I again reiterated I have a boyfriend, like I said at the lake, but he was insistent. So, I gave him my telephone number. He walked me to my car and I took my keys and I opened the lock, and [appellant] opened up my car door for me, and when I turned around to get into the car, [he] grabbed me by the shoulders and pushed me against the car with his body and kissed me.' Hummel further testified that, after this incident, she pulled away and threw herself into her car and locked the car and she drove away. The entire incident lasted over an hour. Appellant subsequently called Hummel several times and left messages on her answering machine. Eventually, Hummel returned appellant's calls and told him not to call her again.

"Our careful review of the record satisfies us that appellant clearly was guilty of stopping and detaining these young women in violation of §242. . . . In our view, unlawfully stopping female drivers on a deserted stretch of highway, in the early hours of the morning, under color of law, clearly is 'constitutionally significant' conduct. Appellant's falsely accusing his victims of drinking and driving served to compound the anxiety he inflicted. Our decision today is intended as a sharp warning that the Courts of the United States are not powerless to punish egregious conduct of lawless police officers who violate the civil rights of citizens under the color of state law."

Source: *U.S. v. Langer*, 958 F.2d 522 (2nd Cir. 1992).

While the tasks of police work and the manner in which these tasks are carried out limit supervision, it is also undermined by the informal working practices and arrangements that develop within police organizations. Police place a high value on professional and personal autonomy (Reiss, 1971). Supervisors who infringe on that autonomy by micromangement will have personnel conflicts.

Police administrators and supervisors alike cannot require subordinates to make a specific number of arrests or even require them to issue a certain number of traffic citations. Any attempt to prescribe police productivity in law enforcement would be met with public outrage. Therefore, there are both formal restrictions from the public and informal pressure from officers for supervisors to "stay out of the way" of their subordinates unless their presence or assistance is requested—translating again to opportunities for work-related misconduct.

Failure to supervise can be linked to a lack of training. Often, promotions merely add stripes to a uniform and more authority. The promotion frequently does not include the training necessary to supervise effectively. If acclimation to the new position is left solely to informal learning exchanges without the balancing ingredient of formal training for the new responsibilities, the supervisor has an insufficient basis for approaching the complex problems—deviance, being one—of the new position. His or her occupational self-perception will continue to be shaped by the social bonds established as a line officer rather than being adjusted or mediated by the new roles and responsibilities. Training should provide a transition and acclimation to the new duties.

Besides reducing potential conflict with subordinates, lax supervision serves the interests of police supervisors. Unless they are directly involved in deviance or have firsthand knowledge of deviance, it is unlikely that supervisors will be held accountable for the actions of subordinates. Ignorance of subordinates' activities therefore benefits police supervisors. It is common to hear supervisors tell their subordinates "just keep me out of it," or "I don't want to hear about it." Organizational and supervisory ignorance of police deviance insulates supervisors and the police organization. Hubert Williams (1997) has remarked that police supervisors "fail due to an ignorance of what is occurring in their own department" (p. 33). When incidents of deviance are detected, this ignorance provides the organization and its ranking officials with the cover necessary to support the "rotten apple myth"—again supporting the public perception of limited organized deviance.

Finally, police supervisors are not free from the corruption and deviance associated with their subordinates. Obviously, the corruption of police supervisors affects the quality of supervision and administration of the police organization. As Herman Goldstein (1975) observed:

> The effect on administrative control is especially devastating if supervisory personnel are corrupt. A large-city precinct commander who routinely accepts bribes may lose control over subordinates. In order to carry on illegal commitments it may be necessary to do or refrain from doing things that would eventually make activities known to subordinates. If the commander shares profits with officers or openly tolerates their own corrupt practices, he [or she] will still continue to exercise reasonably effective supervision. If not, the knowledge subordinates have about the illegal activities renders the commander impotent and gives the officers license to operate without regard for departmental regulations and procedures. (p. 11)

From Goldstein's perspective, corrupt police supervisors undermine their ability to regulate the actions of subordinates. Essentially, if a police supervisor is corrupt and this fact becomes known, the supervisor has compromised the ability to command and can no longer regulate even the most basic behaviors of subordinates. By way of example, how could a corrupt police supervisor sanction an officer for sleeping on duty when that officer knows of the corrupt practices of the supervisor?

Corrupt police supervisors are faced with the dilemma of either concealing their corrupt practices to maintain supervisory control or attempting to draw subordinates into corruption to prevent exposure. Goldstein's comments are predicated on the assumption that corruption can exist without substantial support from other operatives in the police organization. While there are cases of police supervisory personnel engaging in corrupt acts on a lone or individual basis, most forms of corruption require a significant level of support if they are going to be viable enterprises. Any significant level of corruption cannot occur without the support of numerous individuals, both within and outside the police organization. As Lawrence Sherman (1977) has noted, many forms of police corruption "consist of well-organized institutional arrangements involving the cooperation of many people" (p. 3). Thus, certain forms of corruption and deviance at the supervisory level may be indicative of corruption and deviance at other levels of the police organization.

ORGANIZATIONAL STRUCTURE

Police organizations have long been characterized as classic bureaucratic institutions. As bureaucracies, nearly all police agencies have common features. There are, for example, superior-subordinate relationships that compose the chain of command. As bureaucracies, police agencies are also "rulified"—a system of rules and regulations defines worker responsibilities and attempts to ensure conformity and uniformity. In addition, police agencies make personnel decisions based on merit; that is, hiring and promotion decisions are theoretically driven by the abilities of workers (Alpert & Dunham, 1997). As with any administrative approach, however, bureaucracy has both strengths and weaknesses. There are many features of bureaucratic organizations that promote deviance.

Division of Labor

As police organizations grow, they have a tendency to create areas of specialization. A detective's position is often created to handle follow-up investigations so that patrol officers can remain on the street and respond to citizens' calls for service (Gaines et al., 1997). Large departments develop multiple areas of specialization. Some common specialized units include: sex crimes, stake-out squads, drug enforcement units, felony patrols, and vice units. Most recently researchers have uncovered a growing specialization in police use of force (Kraska & Kappeler, 1997). The division of labor among police and the departmentalization that characterizes most police agencies present problems and contribute to structurally induced deviance.

Creating divisions that specialize in selected forms of crime control makes the supervision of police personnel more difficult than in departments without specialized units. Specialized drug units often request "special funds" to carry out their unique missions and require great autonomy/secrecy in the use of these funds. Because the functions of specialized units are so varied, it is easy for supervisors to argue that they should have discretion in the assignment and supervision of personnel, the use of resources, and the control of information. Supervisors of specialized units have access to information that may not be available to members of the larger organization (Williams, Redlinger, & Manning, 1979). Information from these units is often restricted to a "need to know basis"—the need to know being determined by the members of the specialized unit. Members of a specialized unit tend to develop a sense of group identification and goal orientation toward the unit to the exclusion of the larger organization. Solidarity is likely to develop among police officers assigned to a specialized unit; collectively these groups can develop values that deviate from those found in the larger organization. This situation is conducive to deviance since goal attainment is seen as a means to achieving greater autonomy and enhanced resources for the unit. There is also the possibility that members of such units will identify with informants because of the close working relationships established. Undercover officers, for example, may develop emotional bonds with their informants because of "the strong ties that usually bind together people facing the same risky situations. Such situations favor loss of police identity (either partial or complete) and are conducive to police corruption" (Brodeur, 1992, p. 126).

The creation of specialized units has the effect of focusing and specializing police deviance. Following the creation of a drug enforcement unit, for example, one can expect most of the police corruption associated with drug enforcement to occur within that unit. There is often an incubation effect on deviance. Giacopassi and Sparger (1991) note:

> A different form of police misconduct is probably more common today in vice enforcement than monetary inducements to overlook vice operations. Many are convinced that the only way to get high arrest and conviction rates in the area of vice enforcement is to have the police engage in illegal activities themselves, entrapping individuals and then denying it in the courtroom. (p. 42)

Members of specialized units, drug enforcement units, or vice units have greater opportunities to engage in corruption and deviance than patrol officers. Officers in these units come into contact with a desolate element of society, have limited supervision, control the dissemination of information, and use resources with little or no accountability. "Their position as regulators of vice activities presents the police with the opportunity to 'go on the pad,' collect a "steady note,' or 'collect the rent'" (Barker, 1994, p. 48).

The division of labor in any organization serves to enhance the autonomy of some and threaten the autonomy of others. The division of labor limits their exclusive jurisdiction over decisions by fragmenting the decision-making process and distributing it among various groups in different roles, each of which makes claims to professional competence. . . . The detective division of many police departments, for example, restricts the autonomy of line officers . . . by giving the detective jurisdiction over all subsequent investigation as well as authority to review line officers' decisions. (Reiss, 1971, p. 125)

As specialized units appropriate enforcement jurisdiction from patrol, patrol's enforcement areas will be reduced. Because of their limited scope of enforcement, officers assigned to vice units will be focused on vice crimes and therefore better equipped to engage in vice-driven deviance than their counterparts on patrol. Police who specialize in vice control develop strong contacts with the purveyors of vice-related services; they come into contact with drugs and money more frequently; and they have the ability to control information concerning these contacts and activities. Jean-Paul Brodeur's (1992) observations on this point are most instructive:

I have been a member of a civilian police review committee for more than three years. I was struck by how often police officers whose behaviour was under review tried to justify the fact that they were at the wrong place (*e.g.,* a strip joint), at the wrong time (being on duty) and doing the wrong thing (getting drunk) by alleging that they were "meeting with an informer." These claims being unverifiable, "working an informant" provides a shield for all kinds of misconduct. . . . (p. 127)

Conversely, because the patrol unit's jurisdiction is reduced, so are the opportunities for deviance. Patrol officers will have a reduced set of activities in which to participate and may begin to specialize aggressively in certain forms of deviance—accepting and extorting bribes from motorists or shaking down local merchants. In effect, the division of police labor not only results in a specialization in crime control, it also results in a police specialization in deviance.

Career Mobility

Career mobility in police organizations is limited. Lateral movement of personnel across the criminal justice system is minimal. As Gary Marx (1992) notes, promotion within police departments occurs almost exclusively from the line. This creates a climate in which both line and staff officers are confronted with situations in which deviance is tolerated or solicited.

Police corruption and deviance, from this perspective, is structured by the practices of the organization. Both the limited number of positions available for promotion and the lack of training for those who are promoted (discussed earlier) contribute to the potential for deviance. Herbert Beigel (1978) describes the problem as

> An officer's gradual step-by-step advance breeds not only administrative incompetence but also prevents him from developing new approaches and attitudes to eliminate police corruption. The patrolman carries with him to each new position or rank the same attitudes which he now sees. (p. 3)

Police supervisors "readily overlook practices and violations that are common among patrolmen either because they, themselves, engaged in them when they served as patrolmen or many of their friends did so" (Reiss, 1971, p. 162). The pernicious nature of deviance once established is characterized by Beigel (1978): "The salient fact of police corruption, so often ignored, is that one need only corrupt a patrolman to succeed in corrupting the captain he may one day become" (p. 5).

When so few opportunities for promotion exist, officers may become frustrated. Regardless of merit or performance, a significant number of police officers are cut off from the opportunity to improve their economic and organizational standing. Police personnel who cannot achieve their goals because legitimate means are blocked may seek illegal means to gain their objectives. This deviance may take one of two directions: institutionally driven or extra-institutional. Jean-Paul Brodeur (1981) describes the first direction: "Overzealousness in the pursuit of institutional goals could, in certain cases, be explained by an individual's ambition to be quickly promoted" (p. 128). The limited number of positions available and the competitiveness for them may propel lower ranking officers in the other direction (extra-institutional). They may find it more expedient to seek personal rather than organizational gain. When the means to achieve social and economic goals are structurally blocked, as they are in most police organizations, the potential for police deviance and corruption increases.

INTERNALLY AND EXTERNALLY STRUCTURED DEVIANCE

Thomas Barker and David Carter (1994) developed a typology of police occupational deviance and abuse of authority. These researchers identified two categories of police wrongdoing, one with an internal and one with an external behavioral locus. They theorize that abuse of authority has an external locus "because the behavior is inconsistent with law and/or policy" (p. 9). Police who abuse authority breach the external standards of conduct developed by society. Conversely, occupational deviance has an internal locus because the conduct violates an organizational rule or a trust of office. It is a breach of the internal standards of conduct developed by the police as an organization. These researchers further theorize that " . . . abuse of authority is largely motivated by the officer's intent to accomplish a direct or peripheral police goal; occupational deviance is largely prompted by the personal benefit, gratification, or convenience of the individual officer" (p. 9). Barker and Carter's distinction is important to an understanding of structural determinants of police deviance. It relates police deviance to the normative system of conduct that covers both police behavior and the social reaction to that behavior.

Structuring Opportunities for Internal Deviance

Internal deviance is directed toward the police organization, its members, or the criminal justice system; *external deviance* is directed toward citizens. When deviance is directed internally and is intended for a designated target (usually another member of the organization), deviance is guided by the structure of the organization. Personnel holding positions of power and authority within the police organization have the greatest opportunity to engage in deviance directed toward others at lower levels of the organization. "The organizational placement of police supervisors provides them with the opportunity to get a 'piece of the action' from all their subordinates or 'sell' their occupational prerogatives" (Barker, 1994, p. 49).

Conversely, police at lower levels of the organization have a limited opportunity for internal deviance because they have few supervisory prerogatives, less authority, and fewer subordinates. When they deviate, it is usually directed toward the police organization as an entity rather than at an individual within the organization.

From this framework, internal police deviance by those having the most organizational power can be viewed as *domination* (Quinney, 1977). Higher ranking officers have greater opportunities to engage in behavior such as sexually exploiting workers, using authority to force organizational compliance, reaping the benefits of line officers' deviance, and selling their supervisory prerogatives. For example, police supervisors are responsible for making personnel assignments; they are involved in the promotion of personnel; and they control the process of awarding and sanctioning police conduct. They also control the organizational resources necessary to exert pressure on subordinates.

Those individuals having the least amount of power in the organization are more likely to engage in deviance that represents *resistance* (Quinney, 1977) to organizational domination. Their deviance often takes the form of deception, vandalism, perjury, and falsely reporting. Each of these behaviors can be seen as attempts to undermine the organization or the criminal justice system and its officials. Because lower ranking officers control few organizational resources in terms of administrative power and control over subordinates, their deviance is usually limited in scope.

Middle level police supervisors play pivotal roles in organizations. Lower level supervisors (sergeants for example) perform tasks that more closely resemble those of their subordinates than those of police administrators. This limited power makes it more likely that lower level supervisors will engage in acts of resistance rather than domination, although the potential for acts of domination does exist because they hold authority positions over line officers. Middle level supervisors (captains for example) are more removed from the work of street enforcement officers. Their organizational position and power make it more likely that they will engage in acts of domination. The extent to which middle level supervisors engage in acts of resistance and domination depends on the size of the organization, the role the supervisor is given in the organization, and the extent to which supervisors are ideologically and structurally separated from subordinates.

There is, however, some balance to the relationship between organizational position and assignment. A sergeant assigned to supervise a group of patrol officers is in more direct contact with line officers than is a sergeant assigned to the records division of the organization. Therefore, the patrol sergeant has a greater opportunity to engage in acts of domination but is also more likely to identify with the values and norms of subordinates. The sergeant assigned to the records division is more removed from the norms and values of patrol officers and is therefore more inclined to dominate subordinates. However, the position in the organization provides less opportunity for direct domination.

Many acts of police deviance that involve citizens are the products of internally motivated deviance. Although citizens are affected by these behaviors, often they are no more than the conduit through which deviance directed at the police organization or the criminal justice system flows. Many scholars have noted the police dissatisfaction with the judicial system (Balch, 1972; Bittner, 1995; McNamara, 1967; Niederhoffer, 1967; Westley, 1970). While dissatisfaction is not uniform across all police groups (Crawford & Crawford, 1983) and stems from a number of problems, we have seen how police sometimes stack charges. When courts fail to find defendants guilty, police often feel that the judiciary is undermining their authority and professional judgment. Stacking charges is one means of resisting this perceived behavior of the courts. Therefore, the recipient of police abuse is not always the target of police deviance. Citizens often become unknowing pawns in the internal struggles of resistance and domination that occur within the police organization or the larger justice system.

Structuring the Opportunity for External Deviance

Police deviance does not exist within a political, economic, or social vacuum. Legal, economic, and social structures external to the police contribute to the occurrence of deviance. The behavior of law (Black, 1976), the process by which enforcement policies are developed, and the manner in which both law and policy are executed by the police all contribute to a differential victimization of various segments of society. The law is created in a political forum with its character and effect being determined by power differences that exist in society. Different segments of society can alter the character of law and thus shape its effect on citizens. Law serves as a tool that supports existing social arrangements and relations and preserves the distribution of power in society (Chambliss & Seidman, 1971; Turk, 1976). Therefore, the law serves the interests of those most likely to influence its creation. It regulates behavior, economic arrangements, and social relations to the benefit of the dominant segments of society.

The law in itself, however, only serves a symbolic function in society; it must be turned into action to be effective as social control. The law must be interpreted through the development of enforcement policy and put into action by the operationalization of that policy through police practice. Not unlike the creation of law, different segments of society can influence the development of enforcement policy. Certain segments of society are in better positions to contribute to the development of crime control policy and law enforcement practices than others. This results in differential attention by the police to certain segments of society. This is largely determined by a group's placement in the social structure and that group's ability to direct and control the course of law enforcement policy and police activity.

Many scholars have characterized the criminal law as being disproportionally directed at the least powerful members of society (Turk, 1969). Consider Peter K. Manning's (1995b) remarks concerning the nature and construction of criminal law.

- As activities either slip away from popularity, or drift downward to the lower classes, they are defined as criminal and subject to arrest and prosecution.
- Certain "deviant" lifestyles are stigmatized and defined as "criminal." Activities publicly associated with lower class, native peoples, or immigrant pastimes and lifestyles . . . are subject to criminal sanction.
- Space is regulated to maintain control of symbolically valued property and places. Changes in the uses and control of space marginalize certain powerless groups and place them at risk from public and private policing.
- Shared activities are differentially sanctioned. When leisure patterns are shared by middle and lower middle classes, such as sport gambling, the

middle class form is legalized while the lower class form(s) are made subject to the criminal sanction and police-initiated control.

- As . . . activities gain respectability they are de-criminalized and are diffused widely e.g., marijuana and alcohol use.
- Lifestyle conflicts or "cultural wars" between cultural segments . . . may lead to a movement to redefine some behavior or lifestyles as criminal. The targets of control shift from providers to those demanding the goods or services.
- Dissent such as flag burning, public demonstrations and draft evasion, when carried out by members of the dominant coalition, is treated *sub rosa*, and with discretion within the criminal justice system, while marginal groups are given the full benefit and force of the law. (pp. 359–360)

Likewise, the behavior of the police in enforcing law has been characterized as placing an inordinate amount of attention on those having the least power in society (see Wacholz & Mullaly, 1993). While this is a natural extension of the process by which law is created and crime control policy developed, some point to extra-legal factors that ensure differential application of the law and a differential effect on certain segments of society. Carl Klockars (1995), for example, has remarked that law enforcement is directed

> disproportionately on the activities of the poor and ignores for the most part the crimes and delicts of corporate and white collar criminals . . . the evidence for it is empirically overwhelming, and anyone with even passing familiarity with the routine activities of a patrol officer or detective in any contemporary American city would be obliged to agree with it. (p. 350)

The disproportionate resources argument is based on the training and orientation of the police. In other words, police are directed by the law and are trained to target the criminality of those who have the least power in society and are the least likely to complain or be heard.

Manning (1995b) analyzed the interrelationship between the development of law, the structuring of society, and police action.

> To claim that contemporary Anglo-American police employ violence against the poor because the poor behave in ways that demand such overlooks the historic use of the criminal law as a tool, or means of ordering and regulating often large and contentious marginal populations. Policing has attended primarily to the political control of the poor and the disorderly as these matters have been defined by the dominant societal coalition and the government of the nation state. Historically, it is not true that intrinsically the poor require ordering. Rather, the criminal law, with other legal sanctions and regulatory actions, is used by the police to restrict the movements and activities of the poor and marginal and to protect property. . . . Sometimes iron-

ically, since it involves controlling population segments from similar class and ethnic origins, the police are actively engaged in dramatic marking and arranging of the vertical and horizontal order, and in defending, in a variety of ways, the status quo. (pp. 358–359)

Members of society with the least power are more likely to bear the brunt of certain forms of police deviance. This is especially true of the varieties of police deviance associated with street enforcement activities. Some scholars, however, have attributed this difference not only to the nature of the law and its application but to an extra-legal criterion used by the police to identify and attempt to control "problem" or "marginal" populations (Manning, 1995b; Quinney, 1977; Spitzer, 1975). Although the law serves the interests of the most powerful in society, the police enhance that effect by developing their own criteria for applying laws differentially against the poor and powerless. As we mentioned earlier, police select their victims carefully. This selection, however, is not merely the product of individual officer choice. The structuring of power in society is another contributing factor.

Police victimization of select segments of society is not limited in enforcement actions; it is also evident in the distribution of services. Frank Williams and Carl Wagner (1995) emphasize this point in their discussion about the prospects for a proactive police institution. They note certain segments of the public make distinct demands of the police and, accordingly, the police respond differently to certain segments of the population. "The elite demand requires a non-specific response by the police. . . . Such responses can be profound and far-reaching, but will tend to produce new enforcement strategies and/or directions of activity aimed at particular segments of society" (p. 367–368). The intense and disproportionate focus of the police on "problem populations" can be seen as the provision of service to the most powerful members of society. Members of the subordinate segments of society experience more police deviance that is a product of law enforcement and its accompanying violence than do their counterparts in the dominant segments of society, while members of the elite segment of society receive more of the desirable services the police provide—the protection of people and property and the control of populations deemed to threaten both.

While the poor and powerless in society are frequently victimized by the police; other segments of society present unique opportunities for police victimization. Merchants and other moderately "well-to-do" citizens will not experience the brutality and violence associated with the enforcement directed at the least powerful segments of society, but they may encounter the economic crimes of the police. Their economic status makes them vulnerable to police corruption rather than violence.

Extortion, blackmail, bribery, and other forms of economically based police corruption require the victim to control resources in order for police deviance to be a viable venture. This type of victimization often takes the form of an exchange relationship, with the police providing enforcement services or overlooking certain practices in exchange for economic considerations. The forms of these arrangements can range from providing police with free meals to direct cash incentives for overlooking code requirements, to participating in the criminal activities of the merchant class.

Certain segments of society are able to buy the cooperation of the police, whereas others are unable to control the forms of police deviance they experience. Only one segment of society does not experience significant victimization at the hands of the police. This very small, elite segment of the population can afford to insulate itself from police deviance, has considerable resources to buy private police service, and can direct the activities of the public police by determining the character of the law, enforcement policy, and police activities.

SUMMARY

Police deviance can result from a number of factors structured into the social conditions surrounding the police and their work. These structural factors include the way that law is created, emphasized, and enforced; the unique opportunities that the police have to engage in work-related deviance; the organizational setting in which police work occurs; and the unique features of the police working environment itself. Considered together, these structural factors provide a framework to analyze police deviance.

Police deviance is not the product of individual pathology residing in aberrant law enforcement officers. The suggestion that police deviance is primarily due to a few "rotten apples" is too simplistic and fails to consider the multitude of possible determinants of police deviance. The extent to which police deviance can be viewed as a pathology is limited to any pathology that exists in the structuring of society, the organizing of the police institution, and the opportunities inherent in the police role and function. In short, if pathology exists, it is best reflected by the existing social order. This social order not only facilitates police deviance but legitimizes police violation of legal, organizational, and ethical norms.

Chapter Four

BREEDING DEVIANT
CONFORMITY
The Ideology and Culture of Police

> Man is not just an individual, he belongs to the whole; we must always
> take heed of the whole, for we are completely dependent on it.
>   Theodor Fontane (1819–1898)

W hile it is important to understand the structural and organizational
explanations of police deviance, it is equally important to consider
the processes that shape the character of police. Police are selected based
on demonstrated conformity to dominant social norms and values. Those
who become police officers bring to the occupation the perceptual baggage
and moral standards common to the working middle class. Police learn a
distinct orientation to their occupational role through formal and informal
learning exchanges. In essence, police are selected, socialized, and placed
into a working environment that instills within them an ideology and
shared culture that breeds unprecedented conformity to the traditional
police norms and values.

In this chapter, police ideology is examined by focusing on the processes that shape the cultural and cognitive properties of police officers.
The chapter illustrates that police selection techniques, while premised on
equity of treatment, limit the diversity of the police and contribute to an
occupational culture and working ideology conducive to the exploitation of
certain segments of society. Similarly, the methods by which police are
trained reinforce the ideology and its application in the performance of
police tasks. The occupational culture of policing is given extensive treatment to develop an understanding of how police internalize norms and values in adjusting to the profession.

PERSPECTIVES ON THE DEVELOPMENT OF POLICE CHARACTER

Before exploring the ideological and cultural attributes of the police,
it is instructive to examine some of the different perspectives theorists and
researchers have used to gain a better understanding of the character and
behavior of the police as an occupational group. At the risk of oversimplifi-
cation, one of three general perspectives or paradigms are commonly
selected: psychological, sociological, or anthropological. In the sections that
follow, the psychological and sociological perspectives of police character
are discussed first to demonstrate the difference between researchers' perspectives on the police and to show the complexity of understanding police
character. The anthropological perspective of police character is then given
extensive treatment because it allows for the integration of research find-

ings from the other areas and provides a broad framework for understanding both police character and behavior.

The Psychological Paradigm of Police Character

Many researchers adopt a psychological orientation to the study of police character. At one extreme, theorists taking this perspective limit their examination of the police to individual officers and attempt to understand how individual personality shapes behavior. According to this view, each person has a core personality that remains static throughout life (Adlam, 1982). Although events, experiences, and social situations change, an individual's basic personality is thought to stay the same. Behavior is structured by preexisting personality traits that are fixed early in life and remain intact.

When this fixed perspective of personality is applied to the police, researchers tend to focus on the personality characteristics exhibited by people who are attracted to the police occupation. Persons with certain personalities enter law enforcement and behave in distinct ways (Rokeach, Miller, & Snyder, 1971). Often this approach is limited to an examination of the personality structures of police recruits (see Burbeck & Furnham, 1985; Hannewicz, 1978). Theorists adopting this perspective think that people with certain personality characteristics are attracted to careers in law enforcement; those with other personality characteristics choose alternative career paths. From this perspective, researchers are inclined to examine the theorized "police personality." This perspective and research orientation has been referred to as a *predispositional model* of police behavior (Alpert & Dunham, 1997).

The predispositional model has led some to conclude that police recruits are more authoritarian than people who enter other professions. The *authoritarian personality* is characterized by conservative, aggressive, cynical, and rigid behaviors. People with this personality have a limited view of the world and see issues in terms of black and white. For the authoritarian personality, there is little room for the shades of gray that exist in most aspects of social life. People are either good or bad, likable or unlikable, friends or enemies. People with this psychological make-up are said to be conservative, often having "knee jerk" reactions to social issues. Some have labeled these people as "reactionary conservatives" because they seem to react instinctively in a conservative manner regardless of the merit of their position and often without reflecting on the consequences of their acts. It is thought that people with these personality traits have a dislike of liberal values, sentiments, and ideals. The authoritarian personality is also characterized by a rigid view of the world that is not easily changed; they are, in essence, defenders of the *status quo*. People with an authoritarian personality are thought to be submissive to superiors but are intolerant toward those who do not submit to their own authority (Adorno, 1950). John J. Broderick (1987) has done an excellent job of capturing how the term authoritarian is used in discussions of the police.

> Those who . . . use it are usually referring to a person who has great respect for power and authority and strongly adheres to the demands of his or her own group. This person is also submissive to higher authority and hostile toward outsiders who do not conform to conventional standards of behavior. The characteristics of willingness to follow orders and respect for authority might seem to be virtues when possessed by police officers, but in the sense used here, the term authoritarian means an extreme, unquestioning willingness to do what one is told and an extremely hostile attitude toward people who are different than oneself. (p. 31)

While Broderick rejected the notion that police are more authoritarian than people who go into other occupations, there is research to support the authoritarian police character. Recently, research from this perspective has focused on positive personality characteristics of the police, but it still captures the basic idea that police are conformists with personalities that more closely resemble the characteristics of military personnel than those from other occupations. Carpenter and Raza (1987) found that police applicants differ from other occupational groups in several significant ways. First, these researchers found that police applicants, as a group, are psychologically healthy, "less depressed and anxious, and more assertive in making and maintaining social contacts" (p. 16). Second, their findings indicated that police are a more homogeneous group of people and that this "greater homogeneity is probably due to the sharing of personality characteristics which lead one to desire becoming a police officer" (p. 16). Finally, they found that police were more like military personnel in their conformance to authority.

The psychological perspective of police and its conclusion that people attracted to law enforcement are more authoritarian than their counterparts who go into other occupations have been called into question by researchers who adopt a different perspective of police behavior (Bayley & Mendelsohn, 1969). Researchers who take a more social psychological perspective see personality as developmental and, therefore, subject to change given differential socialization and experience (Adlam, 1982). Instead of assuming that personality is fixed, these researchers see personality as dynamic and changing with an individual's life experience. Essentially, researchers adopting this alternative orientation feel that personality cannot be divorced from the experience that shapes it. Researchers like Bahn (1984) and Putti, Aryee and Kang (1988) often focus on the role police perform in society and how training influences personality. From this perspective, researchers study the effects of police training, peer group support, and the unique working environment—all of which are thought to influence and shape police character and behavior. Many of these researchers, however, still view behavior from an individualistic level focusing on a single officer's unique experiences and the development of individual personalities. This limited view of the police character has been questioned by researchers adopting a sociological perspective.

The Sociological Paradigm of Police Character

Several studies have rejected the concept of an individualistic socialization process in favor of a group socialization model (Stoddard, 1995). Arthur Niederhoffer (1967), David H. Bayley and Harold Mendelsohn (1969), as well as other social scientists, have rejected the notion that police have certain personality characteristics that might predetermine their behavioral patterns. Instead, they and others adopt the perspective that behavior is based on group socialization and professionalization. *Professionalization* is the process by which norms and values are internalized as workers learn their occupation (Alpert & Dunham, 1997; Gaines et al., 1997). It is maintained that just as lawyers and physicians learn their ethics and values through training and by practicing their craft, so do the police. Exposure to a police training academy, regular in-service training, and field experience all shape occupational character. Police learn how to behave and what to think from their shared experiences with other police officers.

From this perspective, many researchers find that rookie police officers just beginning their careers are no more authoritarian than members of other professions who come from similar backgrounds (Broderick, 1987). This proposition, however, does not conflict with the notion that citizens who are selected to become police officers are very conservative and homogenous. This perspective of police behavior assumes police learn their occupational personality from training and through exposure to the unique demands of police work (Skolnick, 1994). If officers become authoritarian, cynical, hard, and conservative, it is not necessarily because of their existing personalities or because of their pre-occupational experiences. Rather, the demands of the occupation and shared experiences as law enforcement officers shape their development.

Research findings support the position that recruit and probationary officers are profoundly affected by their training and socialization. The socialization process experienced by the police affects their attitudes and values. Richard R. Bennett (1984) studied police officers from several departments and found that while recruit and probationary officers' values are affected by the training process, there was little support for the idea that police personalities were shaped by their peers in the department. This however, may be explained by the fact that new officers often do not become true members of the department until they are accepted by their peers and granted membership and acceptance into the police occupational culture. Others maintain that the full effect of the police socialization process is not felt during this initial "setting in" phase and may not develop until later in a police career (Bahn, 1984). Similarly, Joseph Putti and his colleagues (1988) stated their findings on police values "could be interpreted to mean that complete socialization into an occupational subculture is a function of time" (p. 253). While it is not known to what extent other reference groups shape personality in older officers, it seems that—at least initially—new police officers' values are shaped as they are trained for the demands of law enforcement and as they become accepted into the occupation.

The Anthropological Paradigm

The most dramatic change in the police social character occurs when officers become part of the occupational culture. The term *culture* is often used to describe differences among large social groups. Social groups differ in many aspects, and people from different cultures have unique beliefs, laws, morals, customs, and other characteristics that set them apart from other groups. These attitudes, values, and beliefs are transmitted from one generation to the next in a learning process known as socialization. Cultural distinctions are easy to see when one compares, for example, cultures of Japan and the U.S. Both of these countries have laws, language, customs, religions, and art forms that are different from the other. These differences provide each group with unique cultural identities.

There can also be cultural differences among people who form a single culture or social group. People who form a unique group within a given culture are called members of a *subculture*. The difference between a culture and a subculture is that members of a subculture, while sharing many values and beliefs of the larger culture, also have a separate and distinct set of values that set them apart. Clearly, police share cultural heritage with others in the United States—they speak the same language, operate under the same laws, and share many of the same values. There are, however, certain aspects of the police occupational subculture that distinguish the police from other members of society. The police are set apart from other occupational groups and members of society by their unique role and social status. Therefore, some scholars have adopted a *culturalization* perspective of the police as a unique occupational subculture.

THE POLICE WORLDVIEW

The concept of *worldview* refers to the manner in which a culture sees the world and its own role and relationship to the world (Benedict,

1934; Redfield, 1952, 1953). This means that various social groups, including the police, perceive situations differently from other social or occupational groups. For example, lawyers may view the world and its events as a source of conflict and potential litigation. Physicians may view the world as a place of disease and illness. For the physician, people may become defined by their illness rather than their social character. The police process events with similar cognitive distortion. The police worldview has been described as a working personality. According to Jerome H. Skolnick (1994), the police develop cognitive lenses through which to see situations and events—distinctive ways to view the world.

The way the police view the world can be described as a "we/they" or "us/them" orientation. The world is seen as composed of insiders and outsiders—police and citizens. Persons who are not police officers are considered outsiders and are viewed with suspicion. This "we/they" police worldview is created for a variety of reasons: the techniques used to select citizens for police service; the normative orientation police bring to the profession; an exaggeration of occupational danger; the special legal position police hold in society; and the occupational self-perception that is internalized by people who become police officers.

Before citizens can become police officers they must pass through an elaborate employment selection process. In order to be selected for employment, police applicants must demonstrate that they conform to a select set of middle-class norms and values. Police selection practices, such as the use of physical agility tests, background investigations, polygraph examinations, psychological tests, and oral interviews, are all tools to screen-out applicants who have not demonstrated their conformity to middle-class norms and values. Many of the selection techniques that are used to determine the "adequacy" of police applicants have little to do with their ability to perform the real duties associated with police work (Cox, Crabtree, Joslin, & Millet, 1987; Gaines et al., 1997; Holden, 1984; Maher, 1988; Paynes & Bernardin, 1992). Often, these tests are designed merely to determine applicants' physical prowess, sexual orientation, gender identification, financial stability, employment history, and abstinence from drug and alcohol abuse.

If police applicants demonstrate conformity to a middle-class life style, they are more likely to be considered adequate for police service. The uniform interpretation of psychological tests, based on middle-class bias, tends to produce a homogeneous cohort. As one researcher has noted "the usefulness of psychological testing for police officer selection is, at best, questionable . . . no test has been found that discriminates consistently and clearly between individuals who will and who will not make good police officers" (Alpert, 1993, p. 100).

In part due to the traditional police selection process, the vast majority of people in policing have been (Kuykendall & Burns, 1980; Sullivan,

1989) and are today (Maguire et al., 1996), middle-class white males. The data in Table 4.1 show that even in cities where minority citizens are the majority, few municipal police departments employ personnel representative of the communities they serve in terms of race or gender.

Table 4.1

Minority Citizens and Police in Select Cities and Departments*

| City | Citizens | | Police | | |
	Population	Minorities	Employees	Minorities	Females
Compton, CA	90,454	98.5%	126	75.4%	7.1%
Laredo, TX	122,899	94.4%	188	98.4%	5.9%
East Orange, NJ	73,552	93.8%	245	56.7%	3.3%
Inglewood, CA	109,602	91.5%	206	35.5%	5.8%
Brownsville, TX	98,962	90.7%	144	41.1%	5.6%
Hialeah, FL	188,004	89.1%	315	40.0%	9.2%
Miami, FL	358,548	87.8%	1,110	64.7%	12.1%
Gary, IN	116,646	85.9%	208	74.0%	12.5%
Camden, NJ	87,492	85.6%	291	11.0%	2.4%
El Monte, CA	106,209	84.8%	113	24.0%	8.8%
Newark, NJ	275,221	83.5%	1,260	42.0%	3.0%
Detroit, MI	1,027,974	79.3%	4,595	53.5%	20.0%
McAllen, TX	84,021	78.1%	162	87.0%	4.3%
Santa Ana, CA	293,742	76.9%	382	29.6%	3.9%
Paterson, NJ	140,891	75.5%	352	27.0%	3.1%
Honolulu, HI	365,272	74.5%	1,781	80.4%	8.3%
El Paso, TX	515,342	73.6%	738	63.8%	6.4%
Washington, D.C.	606,900	72.6%	4,506	67.9%	18.5%
Pomona, CA	131,723	71.8%	172	13.9%	2.9%
Oakland, CA	372,242	71.7%	661	44.6%	7.0%
Atlanta, GA	394,017	69.7%	1,560	54.2%	12.9%
Hartford, CT	139,739	69.5%	443	30.1%	7.0%
Richmond, CA	87,425	69.4%	179	45.2%	5.0%
Oxnard, CA	142,216	67.7%	145	25.6%	4.1%
New Orleans, LA	496,938	66.9%	1,397	40.1%	12.0%
Birmingham, AL	265,968	64.2%	706	36.0%	18.0%
Mount Vernon, NY	67,153	64.2%	176	22.2%	6.3%
San Antonio, TX	935,933	63.8%	1,576	43.8%	5.7%
Jersey City, NJ	228,537	63.4%	918	13.4%	2.8%
Los Angeles, CA	3,485,398	62.7%	8,295	37.5%	12.5%
Trenton, NJ	88,675	62.5%	358	16.8%	2.2%
Chicago, IL	2,783,726	62.1%	11,837	30.4%	13.0%
Baltimore, MD	736,014	61.4%	1,540	27.7%	10.9%
Salinas, CA	108,777	61.2%	132	19.0%	3.0%
Elizabeth, NJ	110,002	60.3%	296	13.5%	4.7%
West Covina, CA	96,086	59.6%	109	14.7%	5.5%
Wilmington, DE	71,529	59.5%	259	34.3%	6.95
Houston, TX	1,630,553	59.4%	4,104	26.3%	9.6%
Harrisburg, PA	52,376	59.3%	154	29.8%	11.7%
Monroe, LA	54,909	57.1%	125	21.6%	10.4%
Richmond, VA	203,056	57.0%	646	27.4%	9.4%
New York, NY	7,322,564	56.8%	25,655	23.8%	12.8%
Jackson, MS	196,637	56.6%	350	37.1%	5.4%
Stockton, CA	210,943	56.4%	242	10.3%	16.9%
Memphis, TN	610,337	56.3%	1,382	32.2%	14.6%
Albany, GA	78,122	56.2%	189	41.9%	12.7%
Corpus Christi, TX	257,453	56.2%	367	46.0%	6.0%
Port Arthur, TX	58,724	54.9%	108	17.6%	2.8%
Pinebluff, AR	57,140	54.5%	111	18.0%	4.5%

*Cities with populations greater than 50,000 where minorities are the majority. Municipal police employing 100 or more sworn officers. Compiled by authors from: US Census, 1990; Bureau of Justice Statistics (1992). *Law Enforcement Management and Administrative Statistics, 1990: Data for Individual State and Local Agencies with 100 or More Officers.* Washington, D.C.: US Department of Justice.

A consequence of the police personnel system is that it selects officers who are unable to identify with groups on the margins of traditional society. The police process people and events in the world through cognitive filters that overly value conformity in ideology, appearance, and conduct. This conformist view of the world, derived from a shared background, provides police a measuring rod by which to make judgments concerning who is deviant and in need of state control (Matza, 1969) and what is "suspicious" (Skolnick, 1994) and in need of police attention. The shared background of the police provides a common cognitive framework from which police process information and respond to events.

This homogeneous group of police recruits experiences formal socialization when it enters the police academy. The police academy refines the cohort again by weeding out those recruits who do not conform to the demands of paramilitary training. Police recruits soon learn

> that the way to "survive" in the academy . . . is to maintain a "low profile," by being one of the group, acting like the others. Group cohesiveness and mutuality is encouraged by the instructors as well. The early roots of a separation between "the police" and "the public" is evident in many lectures and classroom discussions. In "war stories" and corridor anecdotes, it emerges as a full blown "us-them" mentality. (Bahn, 1984, p. 392)

Some have argued that the paramilitary model of police training and organization is inconsistent with humanistic democratic values. It demands and supports "employees who demonstrate immature personality traits" (Angell, 1977, p. 105) and creates dysfunctional organizations (Argyris, 1957). The encouraged traits closely resemble attributes of the authoritarian personality. In short, police are further differentiated from the public and become more homogeneous in their worldview through formal training.

As Skolnick (1994) has noted, danger is one of the most important facets in the development of a police working personality. The relationship between the "real" dangers associated with police work and the police perception of the job as hazardous is complex. While police officers perceive their work as dangerous, they realize that the chances of being injured are not as great as their preoccupation with the idea of danger. Francis T. Cullen, Bruce G. Link, Lawrence F. Travis, and Terrence Lemming (1983) have referred to this situation as a paradox in policing. Their research in five police departments found that

> even though the officers surveyed did not perceive physical injury as an everyday happening, this does not mean that they were fully insulated against feelings of danger. Hence . . . it can be seen that nearly four-fifths of the sample believed that they worked at a dangerous job,

and that two-thirds thought that policing was more dangerous than other kinds of employment. (p. 460)

The disjuncture between the potential for injury and the exaggerated sense of danger found among police officers is best explained in the remarks of David Bayley (1976) who observes:

> The possibility of armed confrontation shapes training, patrol preoccupations, and operating procedures. It also shapes the relationship between citizen and policeman by generating mutual apprehension. The policeman can never forget that the individual he contacts may be armed and dangerous; the citizen can never forget that the policeman is armed and may consider the citizen dangerous. (p. 171)

An inordinate amount of attention and misinformation concerning the dangers of police work is disseminated to police recruits at police academies. Police instructors are generally former street enforcement officers; their occupational experiences and worldview have been filtered through the cognitive framework described earlier. Thus, much of the material presented to new police officers serves to reinforce the existing police view of the world rather than to educate police recruits or to provide appropriate attitudes, values, and beliefs (Cohen & Feldberg, 1991; Delattre, 1989; Murphy & Caplan, 1993).

Even though well intended, police instructors' ability to educate is restricted because most police training curricula overemphasize the potential for death and injury and further reinforce the danger notion by spending an inordinate amount of time on firearms skills, dangerous calls, and "officer survival." The training orientation often resembles preparation for being dropped behind enemy lines on a combat mission. This is not to dismiss the possibility of danger in police work. Certainly, police are killed and injured in the line of duty, but these figures remain relatively small (FBI, 1997; Kappeler et al., 1996) in comparison to the time spent indoctrinating recruits with the notion that the world is a dangerous place—especially if you are a police officer.

As Table 4.2 shows, police training is dominated by an attempt to develop the practical rather than the intellectual skills of recruits. In addition to the substantial amount of time spent on the skills associated with officer safety, a large block of time is spent indoctrinating police on the basic elements of criminal law and the techniques to be used to detect criminal behavior. Little time is spent on developing an understanding of constitutional law, civil rights, or ethical considerations in the enforcement of the law. As the table indicates, police instructors evaluate student performance by weighting certain areas more heavily than others. Differential importance is given to the use of firearms, patrol procedures, and how to use force in arresting and restraining citizens. These three areas are seen as the most critical functions by instructors and are given greater emphasis in scoring the performance of recruits in the police academy.

Police vicariously experience, learn, and relearn the potential for danger through "war stories" and field training after graduation from the police academy (see Kraska & Paulsen, 1997). The real and exaggerated sense of danger inherent in police work contributes greatly to the police picture of the world. As a result, the police may see citizens as potential sources of violence or as enemies. Citizens become "symbolic assailants" to the police officer on the street (Skolnick, 1994). The symbolic assailant is further refined in appearance by taking on the characteristics of marginal segments of society (Harris, 1973; Piliavin & Briar, 1964). The image of the symbolic assailant takes on the characteristics of the populations police are directed to control (see Sparger & Giacopassi, 1992).

Table 4.2
Typical Law Enforcement Basic Training Program

Topic	Hours Spent	Percent of Time	Weight
Administration	24.5	6.13	(—)
Introduction to Law Enforcement	20.5	5.00	1.00
Firearms (skills development)	56.5	14.10	2.00
Vehicle Operation (pursuit driving)	25.5	6.40	1.00
First Aid/CPR	16.0	4.00	.50
Accident Investigation	15.0	3.80	.50
Criminal Law (statutes)	55.5	13.80	1.00
Patrol Procedures (crime detection)	50.0	12.50	2.00
Criminal Investigation	19.0	4.80	.50
Specific Investigations (street crime)	31.0	7.80	1.00
Arrest and Restraint/Physical Fitness	67.5	16.90	2.00
Practical Performance Exercises	19.0	4.75	1.00

To the officer in southern Texas, the young Hispanic man becomes the potential assailant; in Atlanta, the poor inner-city black man becomes a source of possible injury; and in Chinatown, the Asian becomes the criminal who may resort to violence against the police.

Symbolic assailants, however, are not limited to those persons who pose a threat to the officer's physical safety, nor are they identified solely in terms of race or ethnicity. Jennifer Hunt's (1985) field study of police practice in one large urban police department found that officers also perceive certain types of citizens' actions as symbolic threats. She remarks that while

> [f]ew officers will hesitate to assault a suspect who physically threatens or attacks them . . . [v]iolations of an officer's property such as his car or hat might signify a more symbolic assault on the officer's authority and self, justifying a forceful response to maintain control. (p. 328)

She also found that some of the female officers she observed resorted to the use of force when their authority was explicitly denied by insults or highly sexualized encounters.

The element of danger and the symbolic assault are recurring themes in police culture. A survey in 1997 documented an enormous increase in the use of police paramilitary units (PPUs). The survey reported that these units were employed routinely in situations where there was the perception of a high potential for assault or danger. Most often these units are deployed in drug raids, street sweeps, or in dense urban areas seen by the police as constituting a high potential for danger. Police perceive these situations as inherently dangerous and have even extended the use of tactical units to serving what once were thought of as routine search and arrest warrants. Likewise many of these units are used precisely for their symbolic or shock value. In urban areas, officers conduct "jump outs"—numerous officers exiting vehicles simultaneously and creating an enormous display of fire power.

Peter Kraska and Derek Paulsen (1997) describe the sense of "hyper-dangerousness" in tactical units and remark that

> the military weapons, tactics, training, and drug-raids generate an intense feeling of "danger" among the officers. There exists of course a universal fear of being victim of violence among regular police officers. . . . However, the preoccupation with danger in this special operations team, and the fear of being a victim of violence, is heightened. All the PPU officers expressed an extreme fear of the worst happening to them, emphasizing the "real possibility" that every call-out could end in tragedy. . . . The perception of danger and death serves to create a military-like camaraderie among PPU officers. Just as the fear of danger involved in the PPU is more intense than in normal policing, the camaraderie formed is also more intense. Officers emphasize that they must rely on fellow officers more, and their close bonding functions to protect each other's "backsides." (p. 263)

Emphasizing danger fosters the "we/they" worldview and focuses police attention on selective behaviors of certain segments of society. Research into the police culture over the course of thirty years has documented the changing nature yet sustained presence of danger and symbolic assailants as central themes in police culture. Perhaps the greatest change in this aspect of police culture is the growing abstraction of who and what constitutes symbolic danger.

Skolnick (1994) has noted the importance of authority vested in the police as another important characteristic in the development of the police working personality. The law shapes and defines interactions between people and grants social status to members of society (Black, 1970, 1976). The police, by virtue of their social role, are granted a unique position in the law. Police have a legal monopoly on the sanctioned use of violence

(Bittner, 1995a; Bordua & Reiss, 1967; Reiss, 1971; Westley, 1995) and coercion (Bittner, 1995a; Westley, 1995) against other members of society. The legal sanctions that prevent citizens from resorting to violence are relaxed for police officers. Police often resort to coercion to accomplish their organizational goals of controlling crime and enforcing the existing social order. This legal distinction between citizens and police sets officers apart from the larger culture and other occupations.

Since the primary tools used by the police are violence and coercion, it was easy for the police to develop a paramilitary model of training and organization (Bittner, 1995b). In this model, likeness of dress, action and thought is promoted; homogeneity of appearance, ideology, and behavior is emphasized. The military model reinforces the "we/they" worldview of the police; it allows officers to see themselves as a close-knit, distinct group and promotes a view of citizens as "outsiders and enemies" (Sherman, 1982; Westley, 1956). The strength of this conditioning is evident in the alienation felt by officers promoted to positions of management or by those who leave the profession. These individuals often feel isolated from their reference group when their organizational or occupational standing changes (Gaines et al., 1997).

Finally, the police worldview is intensified by the perception of policing as the most critical of social functions. As the process of socialization and culturalization continues, police begin to believe and project for the public the image that they are the "thin blue line" that stands between anarchy and order. "Brave police officers patrol mean streets" and are on the front lines of a war for social order and justice. The war for social order is seen by the police as so important that it requires sweeping authority and unlimited discretion to invoke the power of law—through the use of force if necessary.

The police believe in the goodness of maintaining order, the nobility of their occupation, and the fundamental fairness of the law and existing social order. Accordingly, the police are compelled to view disorder, lawbreaking, and lack of respect for police authority as enemies of a civilized society.

> They are thus committed ("because it is right") to maintain their collective face as protectorates of the right and respectable against the wrong and the not-so-respectable. . . . Thus, the moral mandate felt by the police to be their just right at the societal level is translated and transformed into occupational and personal terms and provides both the justification and legitimation for specific acts of street justice. (Van Maanen, 1995, pp. 313–314)

Criticality of Police Function and Abuse of Authority

". . . On January 24, 1991 two inmates of the Coahoma County Jail, Alonzo Wilson and Eddie Wilkins, attempted to escape while leaving church services which were conducted in the conference room on the first floor. They attempted to make their escape by breaking through glass doors at the front of the jail, but were seized by officers while the attempt was in progress. Wilson and Wilkins were shackled hand and foot and were then taken into the conference room where church services had been held. They were at that time fully controlled by the officers, and there were no further escape attempts. All of the other inmates were locked in their cells or secured behind locked doors.

"When the escape attempt occurred, Sheriff Thompson was not at the jail, but was at the courthouse approximately one block away. When he learned of the escape attempt he immediately went to the jail and found Wilson and Wilkins secured in the conference room. . . . An investigation of the escape attempt was promptly begun, and it was learned that plans for the escape had involved at least one other inmate and that the escape plan called for the glass front doors of the jail to be broken with a metal bar which the conspiring inmates had secreted somewhere in the jail. However, the bar was not used by Wilson and Wilkins in their abortive attempt.

"Sheriff Thompson questioned Wilson and Wilkins in the conference room in an effort to obtain information which might lead officers to weapons and implements, including the metal bar. . . . That interrogation was not productive. Accordingly, Sheriff Thompson obtained a length of coaxial cable approximately three to three and one-half feet long. . . . According to Sheriff Thompson he used this length of cable in an attempt to 'coerce' Wilson and Wilkins into revealing where the metal bar was secreted and was thereby able to extract from them the information that it was upstairs in the jail. According to Thompson, in the process of 'coercing' them he struck Wilson and Wilkins on the buttocks with the cable 'a couple of times each.'

". . . Sheriff Thompson had them taken to their third floor cell and there proceeded to interrogate the five occupants of the cell. . . . Thompson asked the occupants of the cell to surrender the metal bar or brace, but they did not respond. He ordered his deputies to search the cell, and that search produced a steel rod and a length of coaxial cable similar to that which Thompson had used to 'coerce' information from Wilson and Wilkins. However, the bar or brace which was the principal object of the search was not found.

"Thompson then required the five inmates in the cell to remove all clothing from the lower parts of their bodies, including trousers and underwear, and 'applied' the cable to their lower bodies. The only substantial evidentiary dispute centers on the number of blows struck and the severity of those blows. Thompson's testimony was that he 'applied' the cable to each of the five inmates 'a couple of times each.' He also testified that at his direction Deputy Sheriff Tony Smith 'applied' the cable to two of the inmates. According to Thompson the force used was not sufficient to injure the inmates or to raise welts. . . . Alonzo Wilson testified that he was struck nine or ten times in the downstairs conference room and was whipped again in the third floor cell, both by Sheriff Thompson and Deputy Smith. He testified that all five of the inmates in the cell were crying after the whipping and that his right hip was bleeding and discolored. A photograph taken the next day, January 25, 1991, shows raised and discolored areas on Wilson's right hip, which he described as welts and sores caused by the whipping. On January 25, Wilson was seen by the jail doctor, who gave him a lotion to apply to his hip.

"The whipping of the five inmates with the coaxial cable led to discovery of the metal bar in the shower of the cell, and to information that a shank, a type of homemade knife, had been passed out of the cell to another inmate. The metal bar was retrieved from the shower, but the shank was never found.

"Sheriff Thompson testified that he has approximately seventeen years experience in law enforcement, eight and one-half years as a deputy sheriff in Coahoma County. He further testified that this was the only occasion on which he had used such a method to elicit information from an inmate. He also testified that under the same circumstances he would do the same thing again, although it would be as a last resort. . . . In the opinion of the sheriff, he [has] the authority to authorize the use of force, including the use of force to obtain information when it is deemed necessary to jail security. He recognized, however, that it is not appropriate to use force to obtain a confession or to solve a crime. Sheriff Thompson emphasized that he used the cable strictly for the purpose of coercing information concerning the location of the metal bar, which he deemed to be a threat to jail security because of its potential for use as a weapon or a tool for escape. In the opinion of Sheriff Thompson, as long as such an item remained in the jail it constituted a threat to the officers, as well as other inmates. While, in the sheriff's view, the presence of the metal bar in the jail constituted a security emergency which justified his use of force, he admitted that he had in the past received other reports of weapons in the jail and had never resorted to such tactics to obtain information concerning those weapons."

Source: *Cohen v. Coahoma County, Miss.*, 805 F.Supp. 398 (N.D.Miss. 1992).

If law, authority, and order were seen as fostering inequity or injustice, the police self-perception would be tainted and the "goodness" of the profession would be questioned by the public. Police could no longer see themselves as partners in justice but rather partners in repression—a role most police neither sought nor would be willing to recognize. Police who begin to question the goodness of the profession, the equity of law, or the criticality of maintaining the existing social order often quit or are forced out of the occupation for other careers, further solidifying the police social character of those who remain.

The Spirit of Police Subculture

The concept of *ethos* encompasses the distinguishing character, sentiments, and guiding beliefs of a person or institution. When this term is applied to the police subculture, three general ideas surface. First, the police value an *ethos of bravery*. Bravery is a central component of the social character of policing. As such, it is related to the perceived and actual dangers of law enforcement. The potential to become the victim of a violent encounter, the need for support by fellow officers during such encounters, and the legitimate use of violence to accomplish the police mandate all contribute to a subculture that stresses the virtue of bravery. The bravery ethos is so strong among police that two authors have remarked,

> Merely talking about pain, guilt or fear has been considered taboo. If an officer has to talk about his/her personal feelings, that officer is seen as not really able to handle them . . . as not having what it takes to be a solid, dependable police officer. (Pogrebin & Poole, 1991, p. 398)

The military trappings of policing, organizational policies such as "never back down" in the face of danger, and informal peer pressure all contribute to fostering a sense of bravery. "Reprimand, gossip and avoidance constitute the primary means by which police try to change or control the behavior of co-workers perceived of as unreliable or cowardly" (Hunt, 1985, p. 322).

It is common for training officers to wait until a new recruit has faced a dangerous situation before recommending the recruit be given full status in the organization. Peer acceptance usually does not come until new officers have proven themselves in a dangerous situation. More than anything else, training officers and others in the police subculture want to know how probationary officers will react to danger—will they show bravery?

The importance of bravery in criminal justice occupational groups was highlighted in James Marquart's participant study of the prison guard subculture. Following a confrontation that required the use of force, Marquart (1986) found that:

> The fact that I had been assaulted and had defended myself in front of other officers and building tenders raised my esteem and established my reputation. The willingness to fight inmates was an important trait rewarded by ranking guards. Due to this "fortunate" event, I earned the necessary credibility to establish rapport with the prison participants and allay their previous suspicions of me. I passed the ultimate test—fighting an inmate even though in self-defense—and was now a trustworthy member of the guard subculture. (p. 20)

An *ethos of autonomy* is also evident in the police subculture. As the first line of the criminal justice process, police officers make very authoritative decisions about whom to arrest, when to arrest, and when to use force. To this extent the police are the "gatekeepers" to the criminal justice system (Alpert & Dunham, 1997). Police officers cling to their autonomy and the freedom to decide when to use force. The desire for autonomy often exists despite departmental, judicial, or community standards designed to limit the discretion of street enforcement officers. Personally defined justice, reinforced by subcultural membership, can lead to abuses of discretion. Any attempt to limit the autonomy of the police is viewed as an attempt to undermine the police authority to control "real" street crime and not as an attempt on the part of citizens to curb police abuses of authority.

A third ethos evident in police subcultures is the *ethos of secrecy*. William Westley (1995, p. 298), a leading scholar on policing, noted that the police "would apply no sanction against a colleague who took the more extreme view of the right to use violence and would openly support some milder form of illegal coercion." Similar conclusions were reached by William J. Chambliss and Robert B. Seidman (1971) in their consideration of police discretion. The police code of secrecy is often the result of a fear of loss of autonomy and authority as external groups try to limit police discretion and decision-making ability. A second factor supporting the development of a code of secrecy is the fact that policing is fraught with the potential for mistakes. Police feel they are often called upon to make split-second decisions that can be reviewed by others not directly involved in policing. This "split-second syndrome" rationalization, however, has been used by the police "to provide after-the-fact justification for unnecessary police violence" (Fyfe, 1997, p. 540). The desire to protect one's coworkers from disciplinary actions and from being accused of making an improper decision can promote the development of a code of secrecy. John Crank (1998) observed that

> the veil of secrecy emerges from the practice of police work from the way in which everyday events conspire against officers. . . . It is a cultural product, formed by an environmental context that holds in high regard issues of democratic process and police lawfulness, and that seeks to punish its cops for errors they make. (p. 226)

The police code of secrecy is also a product of the police perception of the media and their investigative function. Some researchers suggest that police officers are very concerned with the manner in which the media report their actions (Berg, Gertz, & True, 1984). Coupled with a police perception of the media as hostile, biased, and unsupportive, this contributes to friction in police-media relations and to increased police secrecy.

However, it is sometimes mandatory for officers to refrain from making media releases, having public discussion, or commenting on current criminal investigations. Media Information Restrictions (Section 6.9) in Illinois prohibit a police department from releasing the name of an officer under investigation unless there has been a criminal conviction or a decision rendered by the Police Board. Police unions say these restrictions protect innocent officers from bogus claims, but they also provide police with protections not available to other citizens. In addition, they reinforce the wall of silence. By state law, police internal investigations are off-limits to the public and subject to only minimal review by a civilian oversight board. This is often interpreted by the media, citizens, and others as a self-imposed censorship of information. Perceptions of this nature can promote the separation of the public and the police and create the impression of a secret police society.

Cultural Themes in Policing

The concept of *themes* in a culture is related to the "dynamic affirmations" (Opler, 1945) maintained by its members. Themes help to shape the quality and structure of the group's social interactions. Themes are not always complementary to one another; however, they do occasionally balance or interact. This fact becomes readily apparent in studying the police subculture's dominant themes of social isolation and solidarity.

Isolation is an emotional and physical condition that makes it difficult for members of one social group to have relationships and interact with members of another group. This feeling of separateness from the surrounding society is a frequently noted attribute of the police subculture in the United States (Cain, 1973; Harris, 1973; Manning, 1995a; Reiss & Bordua, 1967; Sherman, 1982; Skolnick, 1994; Westley, 1956, 1970, 1995). Social isolation, as a theme of police subculture, is a logical result of the interaction of the police worldview and ethos of secrecy. The self-imposed social isolation of the police from the surrounding community is well documented.

Persons outside the police subculture are viewed somewhat warily as potential threats to the members' physical or emotional well-being, as well as to the officer's authority and autonomy. According to James Baldwin (1962) and Jerome H. Skolnick (1994), police impose social isolation upon themselves as a means of protection against real and perceived dangers, loss of personal and professional autonomy, and social rejection. Rejection by the community stems, in part, from the resentment which sometimes arises when laws are enforced (Clark, 1965). Since no one enjoys receiving a traffic ticket or being arrested and no one enjoys being disliked, the police tend to look inward to their own members for validity and support. Therefore, the police often self-impose restrictions on personal interactions with the community.

Bruce Swanton (1981) examined the topic of police isolation. He pointed out that two primary groups of determinants promote social isolation. Swanton maintained that these determinants were either self-imposed by the police or externally imposed upon the police by the community. Self-imposed police determinants generally concerned work-related requirements of the police profession. These represent structurally induced determinants created by the organization and the police subculture. The most important of these include: administrative structures, work structures, and personality structures.

Swanton found that the traditional view of police work—enforcing the law, detecting, and apprehending criminals—created a sense of suspiciousness in police officers. This suspiciousness led to a false belief that positive community interactions or kindness from citizens were designed to compromise the officer's official position. A further deterrence to the maintenance of relationships with members of the general community outside the police subculture is the ambiguity evident in the police officer's on-duty and off-duty status. Swanton noted that the long and often irregular working hours—a result of shift schedules and possible cancellation of days off or vacations—coupled with the community's perception of police work as socially unattractive contribute to the police officer's sense of isolation. Swanton's (1981) publicly initiated determinants of isolation include:

> suspicion that police compromise their friendships with higher loyalty to their employer; resentment at police-initiated sanctions or the potential thereof; attempts at integration by those wishing to curry favor, which are resented by others; and personality of police perceived as socially unattractive, thereby reducing the motivation of nonpolice to form close relationships with them. (p. 18)

Charles Bahn (1984) summarized the problem using a different perspective of the police.

> Social isolation becomes both a consequence and a stimulus. . . . Police officers find that constraints of schedule, of secrecy, of group mystique, and of growing adaptive suspiciousness and cynicism limit their friendships and relationships in the nonpolice world. (p. 392)

The second theme evident in the police subculture is *solidarity* (Banton, 1964; Harris, 1973; ; Skolnick, 1994; Stoddard, 1995; Westley, 1956, 1970, 1995). Traditionally, the theme of police solidarity and loyalty was seen as the result of a need for insulation from perceived dangers and rejection by the community. Michael Brown (1981) has noted the importance of loyalty and solidarity among the police. Consider his interpretation of one police officer's remarks.

> "I'm for the guys in blue! Anybody criticizes a fellow copper that's like criticizing someone in my family; we have to stick together." The police culture demands of a patrolman unstinting loyalty to his fellow officers, and he receives, in return, protection: a place to assuage real and imagined wrongs inflicted by a (presumably) hostile public; safety from aggressive administrators and supervisors; and the emotional support required to perform a difficult task. The most important question asked by a patrolman about a rookie is whether or not he displays the loyalty demanded by the police subculture. (p. 82)

Theodore N. Ferdinand (1980), however, has noted that solidarity and loyalty change in proportion to an officer's age and rank. He maintained that police cadets have the least amount of solidarity and line officers have the greatest amount of solidarity. Ferdinand noted that until the age of forty, much of a police officer's social life is spent within the confines of the police subculture. However, solidarity declines as police move into higher ranks in the department. Indeed, we saw earlier that members of the police administrative hierarchy are frequently categorized by line officers with nonpolice members of the community as threatening to the welfare of the subculture.

Police solidarity, therefore, may be said to be an effect of the socialization process inherent to the subculture and police work. New members are heavily socialized to increase their solidarity with the group, and those who move away from the subculture, either through age or promotion, are gradually denied the ties of solidarity. This cohesion is based in part on the "sameness" of roles, perceptions, and self-imagery of the members of the police subculture.

Postulates of Police Culture

Postulates are statements which reflect the basic orientations of a group (Opler, 1945). Postulates are the verbal links between a subculture's view of the world and the translation of that view into action. Because postulates and cultural themes may conflict, the degree to which they complement one another and are integrated is said to indicate the homogeneity and complexity of a culture. Postulates, then, are statements—expressions of general truth or principle that guide and direct the actions of subcultural members. These statements reveal the nuances of a subculture to a greater degree than do ethos or themes. Postulates act as oral vehicles for the transmission of culture from one generation to the next and reinforce the subcultural worldview.

Postulates basic to an understanding of the police subculture have been collected and arranged into an informal code of police conduct. Elizabeth Reuss-Ianni (1983), drawing from the research of many others (Manning, 1997; Rubinstein, 1973; Savitz, 1971; Skolnick, 1994; Stoddard, 1995; Westley, 1956, 1995), identified several of these postulates (also see Reuss-Ianni & Ianni, 1983) to demonstrate the conflict between administrators and line officers. Reuss-Ianni's work is important because it illustrates the influence that line officers have on the total organization. Her work shows that despite administrative efforts to produce organizational change, substantive change is difficult to attain without the collective efforts of group members. In the case of the police, Reuss-Ianni recognized the importance of informal work groups and the influence those groups have on structuring social relationships both in- and outside the police subculture. Hence, postulates are important in shaping not only the attitudes, values, and beliefs of police officers but also in shaping a shared understanding of unacceptable behaviors.

Postulates Shaping the Ethos of Secrecy and the Theme of Solidarity. The first group of postulates identified by Reuss-Ianni (1983, pp. 14–16) contribute to the ethos of secrecy that surrounds much of police work. This secrecy has many functions, three of which are especially important to the study of police deviance. First, the public is denied knowledge of many police activities because, in the eyes of the police, they have no "need to know." While it may be prudent to restrict access to certain types of sensitive information in law enforcement, the veil of secrecy that shields police from the public has the effect of minimizing public scrutiny of police activities and behaviors. Secondly, many of the postulates identified by Reuss-Ianni are guideposts which keep officers from relaying too much information to police supervisors. Line officers support these postulates as necessary protections to insulate themselves from punishment or challenges to their autonomy. Because police administrators are perceived as applying sanctions situationally and erratically, line officers develop postulates that bring predictability to their working world. Finally, perhaps the most important function is providing line officers with a sense of solidarity. As the Mollen Commission's (1994) investigation of the New York City Police Department found:

> These aspects of police culture facilitate corruption primarily in two ways. First, they encourage corruption by setting a standard that nothing is more important than the unswerving loyalty of officers to one another—not even stopping the most serious forms of corruption. This emboldens corrupt cops and those susceptible to corruption. Second, these attitudes thwart efforts to control corruption. They lead officers to protect or cover up for others' crimes—even crimes of which they heartily disapprove. (pp. 51–52)

The discussion in chapter 11 of the assault on Abner Louima provides a chilling illustration of the corruption facilitated by these postulates. Some of the postulates reinforcing the ethos of secrecy and the theme of police solidarity include:

- *"Don't give up another cop."* As perhaps one of the most important factors contributing to secrecy and to a sense of solidarity, this postulate admonishes officers to never, regardless of the seriousness or nature of a case, provide information to either superiors or nonpolice that would cause harm to a fellow police officer. Reuss-Ianni notes that this postulate implicitly informs a police officer that abiding by this canon and never giving up another cop means others "won't give you up."

• *"Watch out for your partner first and then the rest of the guys working that tour."* This postulate tells police officers they have an obligation to their partners first, and then to other officers working the same shift. "Watching out," in this context, means that an officer has a duty not only to protect a fellow officer from physical harm, but also to watch out for their interests in other matters. If, for example, an officer learns that another member of his or her squad is under investigation by an internal affairs unit, the officer is obligated to inform the officer of this information. As with the postulate listed above, the implicit assumption here is that if you watch out for fellow police, they will also watch out for you.

• *"If you get caught off base, don't implicate anybody else."* Being caught off base can involve a number of activities, ranging from being out of one's assigned sector to engaging in prohibited activities. This postulate teaches officers that if they are discovered in proscribed activities, they should accept the punishment, not implicate others. This postulate insulates other police officers from punishment and reduces the possibility that organized deviance or corruption will be uncovered.

• *"Make sure the other guys know if another cop is dangerous or "crazy."* Police are caught in a double-bind if they become aware that one of their fellow members is unstable or presents a safety hazard. The secrecy dictum prohibits a line officer from informing police supervisors of another officer's instability; at the same time, an officer has an obligation to watch out for his or her peers. In order to deal with such a contradiction, this rule of behavior tells an officer that there is an obligation to let other police know of potential safety risks but not to take formal action against another officer. This postulate allows "problem" officers to continue to operate within the profession and reduces the chances that they will be detected by the agency administration or the public. It does, however, allow informal sanctions of exclusion to be imposed.

• *"Don't get involved in anything in another cop's sector."* Reuss-Ianni notes that in older, corrupt departments, this dictum advised officers not to try to hedge in on another police officer's illegal activities. In essence, this rule informed police that officers "owned" certain forms of corruption in their sector. Today, this postulate teaches officers that they are to stay out of all matters in other officers' sectors. This rule of territoriality is believed necessary because officers are responsible for activities in their respective beats. This postulate serves to limit the spread of information making it easier for officers to deny knowledge of deviance, which in turn makes deviance appear to be a mere aberration.

• *"Hold up your end of the work; don't leave work for the next tour."* These postulates teach officers that if they neglect their work responsibilities, two results are likely to occur. First, other officers must cover for those who shirk their responsibilities. Second, malingerers call attention to everyone on a shift. Thus, there are pressures for all officers to carry their own weight to avoid being detected for deviance. If, however, an officer fails to follow this edict, other officers are expected to "cover" for the officer and to deflect attention away from the group.

• *"Don't look for favors just for yourself."* This dictum admonishes officers not to "suck up" to superiors. In essence, this rule tells officers that their primary responsibilities are to their peers and that attempts to curry favors with superiors will meet severe disapproval. This postulate prevents line officers from developing relationships with superiors that might threaten the safety of the work group.

Postulates Supporting Police Isolationism. Reuss-Ianni (1983, pp. 14–16) identified several postulates that teach new officers that nonpolice simply do not understand the true nature of police work. These statements reinforce the notion that there are vast differences between police and citizens—who will never be able to understand the unique problems inherent in policing. In John Van Maanen's (1995) typology of how the police characterize outsider views of their occupation, these citizens are classified as "know nothings" (p. 309). This we/they worldview increases police isolation from citizens.

• *"Protect your ass."* As perhaps one of the most important postulates leading to a sense of isolation, this rule teaches police to be wary of everyone including citizens and superiors. At the simplest level, the rule informs police that anyone who wants to cause trouble for an officer probably can; it teaches police that others cannot be trusted. Officers must be vigilant and take all steps necessary to protect themselves from any possible threat. While threats include the possibility of physical harm, they also include the possibility of disciplinary action by superiors and the potential for citizens to complicate the lives of police by filing complaints, making allegations, or uncovering deviance.

• *"Don't trust a new guy until you have him checked out."* Rookie police and officers who are new to a work group are not accorded status automatically. Instead, outsiders are treated cautiously until information about them can be obtained—until they have "proven" themselves. In some cases, rookie officers are "tested" to determine if they can be trusted. Those officers having a history with the department are checked out through the "grapevine" and are often intentionally placed in situations to see if they can be trusted.

• *"Don't talk too little or too much; don't tell anybody more than they have to know."* The themes of "don't talk too much," and "don't reveal more than necessary" inform new police officers that others including citizens and supervisors are not to be trusted. These dictates reinforce the notion that "loose lips sink ships" and that there is no need to provide others with information beyond the minimum required. Information can be distorted or used in other ways that are potentially harmful. At the same time, the dictate "don't talk too little" lets new police officers know that excessive silence or introversion will be seen as suspicious behavior by other officers.

As Reuss-Ianni notes, the extremes of talking too much or too little are both viewed as suspicious behaviors by fellow officers. This postulate directs officers to maintain communications with the work group but to limit their exposure to administrators and citizens.

- *"Don't trust bosses to look out for your interests."* This maxim informs new police officers that when forced to make a choice, managers and administrators will look out for their own best interests rather than those of the officer. Whether true or not, this idea has the effect of further distancing officers from their superiors. Since line officers are taught that they cannot depend on either citizens or superiors, they are forced to align themselves with the only group left for protection—fellow police.

Postulates Indicative of the Ethos of Bravery. David H. Bayley and Egon Bittner (1997) have noted that a crucial part of a police officer's job is to take charge of situations and people. Taking charge, in this sense, involves developing a "presence" to handle incidents. In essence, this means that officers must be poised to take control regardless of the situation. Yet, it is crucial not to appear too ready, since overeagerness can escalate situations. In one officer's words, "Always act . . . as if you were on vacation." At the same time, however, "One must be keyed up but not 'choke'" (p. 28). Reuss-Ianni (1983, p. 16) identified two postulates that strongly suggest new officers must always, above all else, show bravery in the performance of police work.

- *"Show balls."* The police characterize their work as dangerous and fraught with hazards. This postulate counsels police that they are never to back down from a situation; backing down signals weakness. All police are harmed by the cowardice of an individual officer. Officers must have fortitude to control situations. When the authority of a single officer is challenged, the authority of the entire police group is challenged and must be addressed. While this is especially true for incidents that occur in view of the public, it is also important for an officer never to back down from a situation where other officers are present.

- *"Be aggressive when you have to, but don't be too eager."* This postulate reflects the idea that while officers should always be alert, they should not go out of their way to seek trouble. This is partly because overeagerness, or having a "chip" on one's shoulder, will only bring unneeded complications. In a sense, the maxim, "If you look for trouble, it will find you," applies here. Therefore, challenges to authority must be met and dealt with, but they should not be sought out. Police are to avoid acting in ways that cause the group to undergo unnecessary scrutiny. However, this postulate also reminds an officer to meet a challenge or confrontation as aggressively as necessary to handle it effectively.

Through exposure to these and other postulates, new generations of police officers combine their experiences and perceptions of the world—all of which are filtered through the unique perspective of police officers' eyes. With these "truths," officers develop a belief system which dictates acceptable and unacceptable behavior. These postulates serve as reinforcers of the police worldview and act as part of the socialization process for members of the police occupation. Through these postulates, officers are taught the necessity for secrecy and solidarity among the ranks, and the belief that police are different and isolated from larger society. Violations of these canons may lead to immediate sanctions from fellow subculture members, frequently resulting in expulsion from the security of the group. It is ironic that police who violate the precepts of the subculture are doubly isolated—first from the community by nature of the occupation and later by the police subculture for violation of its informal norms of conduct. Police officers who do not conform to the postulates of the work group become outcasts who have been stripped of the benefits of group membership.

SUMMARY

Many approaches have been used to explain the unique character of the police. Scholars who endorse the psychological paradigm suggest that police character may be explained by one of two approaches. Personality theorists suggest that people with certain personality types—such as those who are authoritarian—are attracted to police work. Seen in this light, police character is a reflection of the unique personality characteristics of those who enter and remain in police work. An alternative social-psychological explanation for police character posits that the police working environment shapes the personality, character, and behavior of individual officers. Those who adopt this perspective believe that experiences such as recruit training and relationships with coworkers shape personality and, therefore, the behavior of individual officers.

The sociological paradigm rejects the idea that personality characteristics alone predetermine police character. Instead, this paradigm suggests that police character is molded and shaped by occupational experiences. That is, police character is determined by the police working environment. Socialization experiences—including academy and on-the-job training—are responsible for the development of police values and ethics.

The anthropological paradigm offers perhaps the most complete explanation for the development of police character. The occupational culture provides police with a unique working personality. This working personality includes the development of a worldview that teaches police to distinguish between insiders and outsiders (i.e. police/nonpolice)—in other words, those who are okay versus those who must be watched.

This we/they perspective instills in officers a perpetual concern for the element of danger in their work. The police working personality reinforces the notion of "differentness" in three ways. First, police are taught that they are vested with the unique power to use force and violence in carrying out legal mandates. Second, the paramilitary nature of police work isolates police from others in society. Finally, police are indoctrinated with the idea that they are the "thin blue line" between anarchy and order.

Three guiding beliefs define the police ethos. The social character of policing is shaped by a reverence for bravery, autonomy, and secrecy. The police subculture stresses these sentiments and teaches new officers the value of adopting these attitudes—and the consequences of not conforming.

Cultural themes are also a part of the police culturalization process. In this case, cultural themes are fairly specific rules of behavior that shape police interactions. A dominant cultural theme in policing is the idea that police are socially isolated from the rest of society. A second important cultural theme extols the need for police solidarity.

Finally, several postulates of the police culture were reviewed. Postulates are specific statements that guide and direct the actions of subcultural members. Postulates that reinforce the need for police secrecy and solidarity include instructions never to "give up" another cop and to watch out for other police, especially one's partner. Postulates that support police isolationism instruct police to "protect your ass" by being wary of everyone; not to trust new officers until they have proven themselves; and not to trust supervisors to look out for an officer's best interests. Postulates also instruct officers on the ethos of bravery: never back down and be aggressive but not overeager in handling situations.

Chapter Five

LEARNING TO DEVIATE
Motive and Justification for
Breaking Normative Bonds

Learning can put forth leaves without bearing fruit.
Georg C. Lichtenberg (1742–1799)

T he police subculture and its attendant ideology do more than just provide officers with a shared cognitive framework from which to view
the world, people, and situations. The subculture facilitates deviance by
providing its members with the beliefs, values, definitions, and manners of
expression necessary to depart from acceptable behavior. Police are provided the conceptual tools necessary to develop a unique approach to the
normative system. They view the normative system and its elements as a
set of culturally and situationally relative behavioral concepts. Their
shared culture and ideology allow the police to select from competing elements in each level of the normative system. This allows them to rank the
importance of each level and to interpret the various elements according to
culturally based and situationally derived definitions.

The shared beliefs and values provide officers with the ability to
rationalize, excuse, and justify their deviance while maintaining and pro-
jecting a conformist image to the public. Collectively, these intellectual
tools allow the police to deviate from the norms and values of the larger
society without suffering the dissonance and social stigma normally associated with deviance. In essence, these tools allow a homogeneous group of
conformists to depart from convention by distorting or replacing the values
found in the larger normative system with conformity to a set of subcultural norms and values. This unique orientation to the normative system
guides police response to situations and allows use of after-the-fact justifications for deviance.

This chapter explores techniques police use to break the bonds of
social norms while still maintaining a law-abiding master status and public
image. First, we consider the nature of these techniques by distinguishing
between motive and motivation. Second, we consider the actual techniques
police use to prepare themselves intellectually for departure from the
larger normative system and how the bonds of control of the normative
system are broken. Third, consideration is given to the function of motive
as a neutralizer of negative self-image and social stigma. Finally, the chapter explores the importance of these processes to the larger society by
examining how these techniques work to negotiate the content of the normative system by redefining social expectations to make police deviance
acceptable and even anticipated by a large segment of society.

MOTIVE AND MOTIVATION

Before beginning a discussion of the process by which police break
the bonds of the larger normative order and substitute norms drawn from

the police subculture, it is necessary to draw distinctions between several concepts in the theory of motive. It is important to recognize the differences between motive and motivation. Unlike motivation, a term that means an inner drive or impulse that causes a person to act in a particular way or to engage in a certain behavior, *motive* is a device used to bring structure, organization, and meaning to behavior. Motives are used by members of social groups to "link particular concrete activities to generally available social roles" (Blum & McHugh, 1971, p. 98). The use of force is a good example. When the police use force to arrest someone, the motive is to apprehend a suspect—a lawful action. When citizens use force, one motive could be to kidnap—an unlawful action. The difference comes, in part, from the manner in which the concrete act is linked to social roles and existing expectations of social interactions. Motives are social constructions that "situate" (Mills, 1940) concrete acts and assign meaning within a social and cultural framework. As such, motive has meaning for social actors—those who act, those affected by the act, and those who interpret the act. Motive is the expression of attributes attached to activities that allows society to view an act with an understanding of its social context. Motive depicts the social character of the act rather than the physical properties or the causes of the act (Blum & McHugh, 1971). Motive is the verbal descriptor of a behavior rather than the concrete behavior itself. When a police officer uses force to make an arrest, it is different from a citizen who uses violence to kidnap, because different meanings are attached to the actors' social roles and different ascriptions are associated with their actions.

Motive involves events, reasons for behavior, and justifications for courses of action (Gerth & Mills, 1953; Mills, 1940; Scott & Lyman, 1968; Sykes & Matza, 1957). We can distinguish between event, reason and justification by saying that an *event* is the factual and concrete activity stripped from its social meaning. *Reason* is the communicated and unembellished explanation given for an activity by the social actor. *Justification* is the actor's explanation of the activity designed to excuse behavior, mitigate sanction, or support the correctness of a certain course of action. With deviance, motive involves the behavior of a social actor, the interpretation of the behavior by an audience, the assessment of the social context of the behavior, and the appraisal of social reaction to the behavior. Motives are "those situationally relevant and acceptable terms with which interpretation of conduct by social actors proceeds" (Mills, 1940, p. 904).

While motives do not necessarily refer to the underlying causes of behavior, they can prepare a social actor for alternative courses of action. When behavior is viewed as a social process, motive can vary at different stages. Motive, therefore, has a temporal sequence that is relative to social interaction. Motive can be expressed before, during, and after an act. Motive before an act is a verbal expression of preparation. Since preparation operates within pre-existing social frames of reference, it can be conscious or unconscious. Culture and ideology provide the necessary frames of reference that prepare an actor for future courses of action. Police must first perceive the use of force as a viable response to citizens and as an effective measure for crime control before it can become a course of action. Whether this knowledge is expressed or experienced intuitively, it prepares police to use force in given situations. The motive takes shape when an "event" is incorporated into an actor's collective experience. This event becomes a factor that helps interpret future events and courses of action.

An actor's worldview, background assumptions, and other socially and culturally constructed frames of reference prepare the actor for the future. From this view "to locate motive is . . . to describe the necessary and analytical prior understandings and conventions which *must* be employed in order for a member to even invoke motive as a method for making a social environment orderly and sensible" (Blum & McHugh, 1971, p. 103). Motive draws on one's understanding of the social world to determine a course of action that anticipates social reaction by linking the contemplated act to available social interpretations. When an actor's understanding of the social world is favorable to a certain course of action and when the actor anticipates little or no negative social reaction to the behavior, there is a greater likelihood that the behavior will occur.

When motives are invoked during an act, they are the verbal expressions of the preconceptions the actor has internalized. Present motives are composed of past frames of reference. Present motive, however, is a more reliable indicator of the social construction of the behavior because it has not yet been embellished with new interpretations. Motive in the present is more spontaneous and less reflective than are verbalizations of motive following an act. Verbalization during an act thus expresses the instinctive quality of the behavior and the unconscious preparation of the actor for the behavior.

Motive after the fact is more indicative of the social construction of behavior through excuse, mitigation, and justification. These verbalizations often reflect an actor's desire to situate conduct within a frame of reference that presents action as socially acceptable. As Harold Garfinkel (1967) instructs, "It consists of the possibility that the person defines retrospectively the decisions that have been made . . . in order to give their decisions some order, . . . officialness, or justification" (p. 113). Motive following an act has two basic qualities that distinguish it from motive appearing before and during an act. It interprets the behavior for the actor by providing structure, organization, and meaning. It also provides a social context for others' understanding of the act. Motive is always in a state of progression or a process of transformation. Past frames of reference shape present motive which is then subjected to after-the-fact interpretations—which, in turn, become the most recent refinement of the social actor's understanding of the world.

JUSTIFYING POLICE DEVIANCE

In their classic theory of delinquency, Gresham Sykes and David Matza (1957) argued that deviants employ certain techniques that neutralize the consequences of their actions by insulating offenders from the negative self-image normally associated with the commission of crime. Techniques of neutralization prepare the individual mentally for the initial act of deviance. They also negate or deflect stigmatization by providing deviants with after-the-fact justifications for their conduct. Techniques of neutralization both allow for deviance and attempt to socially situate deviance after it has occurred.

In developing their theory, Sykes and Matza identified five general techniques used by deviants. These techniques include denial of responsibility, denial of injury, denial of the victim, condemnation of the condemners, and appeal to higher loyalties. The five techniques can be expressed as: "They made me do it," "No innocent got hurt," "They deserved it," "They don't know anything," and "Protect your own." Table 5.1 shows the relationship between the techniques of neutralization and their application to various forms of police deviance. These techniques are important in understanding how police draw on their shared culture and ideology to prepare themselves for a deviant act, how they express their deviation when acting, and how they justify their action after it has occurred.

Police Denial of Responsibility

According to Sykes and Matza denial of responsibility prepares the actor for deviance and provides a partial justification following the commission of a deviant act. Denial of responsibility is the pre-act belief or the after-the-fact assertion that the potential or real injury caused by the anticipated or actual deviance is "due to forces outside the individual and beyond his control . . ." (Sykes & Matza, 1957, p. 667). These theorists argued that deviants see themselves as little more than "billiard balls on a pool table" rebounding from external influences. This assertion, however, should not be interpreted as refuting the idea that factors influence, channel, or focus deviance. It means that deviants will often view their acts as predetermined by people, events, and situations that they cannot influence.

Table 5.1
Police Techniques of Neutralizing Deviance

Sykes and Matza's Neutralization Technique	Verbalization	Techniques in the Police Context
1. Denial of Responsibility	"They made me do it."	Police use of excessive force in arresting a citizen who challenges police authority.
2 Denial of Injury	"No innocent got hurt."	Police use of perjury to justify an illegal search.
3. Denial of Victim	"They deserved it."	Failure of police to uncover drugs during an illegal search of a "known" drug dealer is rationalized because he didn't have drugs "this" time.
4. Condemning the Condemners	"They don't know anything."	Police rejection of legal and depart-ment control and sanction of deviant behavior.
5. Appeal to Higher Loyalties	"Protect your own."	Police perjury to protect another officer, destruction of evidence, using punishment for personal justice.

Sources: Sykes, G. M. and Matza, D. (1957). Techniques of neutralization. *American Sociological Review*, 22, 664–670.

This technique of neutralization is particularly useful in understanding some forms of police deviance. The police culture provides law enforcement officers with the necessary ideological or background assumptions for deviance. Since police officers are granted the authority to use violence to accomplish their social control objectives and because they internalize a "we/they" orientation to the world that frames citizens in terms of the "enemy," the use of violence is seen as an appropriate and even necessary response to citizens' defiance of police authority. Defiant citizens are viewed from this neutralization technique as provocateurs in need of police control. When police use violence or choose to use the force of law illegally against citizens, they are merely responding to the provocation of citizens—situations and events that they have little or no control over and for which they are not responsible regardless of their own contributions to the situation or their departure from social expectations.

Jennifer Hunt's (1985) field study found that "acts of force become excusable when they are depicted as the natural outcome of strong, even uncontrollable emotions normally arising in certain routine sorts of police activities." Her study suggested that police frame their accounts of use of force in two distinct ways: situational and abstract.

> In the former the officer represents force as a response in some specific situation needed to restore immediate control or to reestablish the local order of power in the face of a threat to police authority. In contrast, abstract accounts justify force as a morally appropriate response to certain categories of crime and criminals who symbolize a threat to the moral order. (p. 325)

Capitalizing on their occupationally generated conception as protectors of the innocent and their self-perception as law-abiding public servants, police often rationalize their deviance. In his study of policing in Los Angeles, Steve Herbert (1996) highlighted the use of rationalization through denial of responsibility.

> If the "bad guys" are defined as essentially evil, then officers' responses are more easily justified. Even if, say, the use of force was a bit excessive, it was the perpetrator who initiated the encounter and who sought to harm the community. And whatever the officer did, he/she was ultimately motivated by the praiseworthy virtue of protecting the good from the depredations of evil. (pp. 811–812)

Denial of responsibility provides police with an after-the-fact justification for their abuse of authority. Police who engage in brutal assaults on citizens often allege that they were forced into deviance because there was no alternative course of action or that it was expedient—the citizen or situation "forced my hand." By offering these excuses for deviance, police can violate external (law) and internal (policy) norms while maintaining a law-abiding social and self-image. "By learning to view himself as more acted upon than acting," an officer "prepares the way for deviance from the dominant normative system without the necessity of a frontal assault on the norms themselves" (Sykes & Matza, 1957, p. 667). Police are able to sidestep the normative control society places on their use of force by shifting responsibility.

Most police condemn domestic violence, stranger assaults, and other physical abuses committed by citizens. Police often have strong emotional responses to the physical abuse of children, but they are more than prepared to view their own violence as an inevitable and even necessary aspect of policing and crime control. Consider the remarks of the president of the St. Louis Police Officer's Association (SLPOA).

> I think part of the problem with police work today is that the *bad guys* aren't *afraid* of us anymore. Years ago when a *scum-bag* knew he'd get his *head split*, you didn't get half the *crap* that you do now [italics added]. (Oldani, 1992, p. 2)

Invoking the Criminal Law for Citizen Defiance

Two Douglas, Arizona police officers were dispatched to a downtown hotel in response to a bartender's complaints about an unruly patron. Officer Aguilar "arrived to find Duran intoxicated and threatening the bartender. Aguilar and Duran exchanged a few heated words, following which Aguilar escorted Duran out. Duran left the bar in an automobile driven by his wife Alice. . . .

"Soon thereafter, while out on patrol, Aguilar observed a car with a passenger who was directing an obscene gesture toward him through an open window. Aguilar did not know the passenger's identity at that time because the car had darkly-tinted glass. . . . It was, however, the car driven by Alice Duran. . . .

"Aguilar and backup Officer Rudy Salazar followed the Durans' car into a mobile home park, where it stopped in front of what turned out to be their residence. Aguilar does not contend that Duran was yelling or otherwise causing a disturbance when the car drove into the park. Nevertheless, Aguilar initiated a traffic stop by turning on his emergency lights. Aguilar ordered Duran to step away from the car to which Duran replied 'I don't have to.' Aguilar then told Duran that the reason for the traffic stop was to find out why Duran had yelled profanities and made an obscene gesture toward him. Duran responded with further profanities in both Spanish and English. In response, Aguilar decided to arrest Duran for disorderly conduct. A scuffle ensued, during which Aguilar and Duran were injured before Duran was subdued and shackled. . . .

"According to the court's review of the evidence, missing from the record here is any legitimate, articulate reason for Aguilar to have detained Duran. There was no evidence of a danger to public safety, and Aguilar was not executing a warrant. Nor is there any evidence that Duran was in possession of a controlled substance or had been or was about to be engaged in criminal activity. To be sure, Duran was intoxicated, but defendant does not contend that any law or ordinance prohibited Duran from riding as a passenger in an automobile while drunk. Nor can Aguilar claim that he detained Duran due to what had happened earlier in the evening at the bar. Aguilar had already confronted Duran regarding the incident and had let him go; there is no indication that Aguilar learned new facts to justify detaining Duran for further investigation of the earlier incident.

"What then is left? Defendant relies heavily on the fact that Duran was making obscene gestures toward him and yelling profanities in Spanish while traveling along a rural Arizona highway. . . . We don't see how Duran's boisterous conduct, tasteless though it may have been, gave Aguilar any cause to detain him. Absent such cause, the stop and detention was illegal. . . . Inarticulate and crude as Duran's conduct may have been, it represented an expression of disapproval toward a police officer with whom he had just had a run-in. As such, it fell squarely within the protective umbrella of the First Amendment and any action to punish or deter such speech such as stopping or hassling the speaker is categorically prohibited by the Constitution. Aguilar admits that he stopped Duran because he made an obscene gesture and yelled profanities toward him."

Source: *Duran v. City of Douglas, Arizona*, 904 F.2d 1372 (9th Cir. 1990).

Denying responsibility helps prepare police for deviance by providing the necessary cognitive foundation, lessening adherence to external norms in favor of subcultural norms, and providing justifications that are grounded in the police view of the world and their interpretations of effective means of crime control.

Police Denial of Injury

Sykes and Matza (1957) note that, in the eyes of the deviant, "wrongfulness may turn on the question of whether or not anyone has clearly been hurt by his deviance, and this matter is open to a variety of interpretations" (p. 667). There are numerous examples of police deviations accompanied by a denial of injury: theft of evidence from suspects for personal gain; violation of the civil rights of citizens to make arrests or secure convictions; abuse of authority to establish or maintain a personal sense of order. According to the police, the suspect should not have had contraband in the first place; the citizen was a criminal deserving of something less than the full protections of civil rights; and, the juvenile had to be "moved along" to prevent crime and ensure order.

The denial of injury also involves defining situations to help justify victimization. Definitions are constructed to allow deviation and to free the deviant actor from the bonds of the larger normative system.

> Vandalism, for example, may be defined by the delinquent simply as "mischief"—after all, it may be claimed, the persons whose property has been destroyed can well afford it. Similarly, auto theft may be viewed as "borrowing," and gang fighting may be seen as a private quarrel, an agreed upon duel between two willing parties. (Sykes & Matza, 1957, p. 667)

For police, the theft of property from a suspect can be defined as "confiscation"; the padding of overtime records can be labelled "just compensation"—there is no injury because the city can well afford it and fails to pay the police properly for the dangerous job that they do; and perjury is just "embellishing" the facts or recalling previously forgotten information to convict someone who is "guilty anyway" (see Hunt & Manning, 1994).

> Officers also commit falsification to serve what they perceive to be "legitimate" law enforcement ends—and for ends that many honest and corrupt officers stubbornly defend as correct. In their view, regardless of the legality of the arrest, the defendant is in fact guilty and ought to be arrested. . . . [There] is a deep-rooted perception among many officers of all ranks within the Department that nothing is really wrong with compromising facts to fight crime in the real world. Simply put, despite the devastating consequences of police falsifications, there is a persistent belief among many officers that it is necessary and justified, even if unlawful. As one dedicated officer put it, police officers

Police Use False and Misleading Information to Secure Warrant for Military-Style Drug Raid

Washington State Patrol Detective Coral Estes began an investigation into a suspected methamphetamine laboratory on the Hervey property in Tacoma. Estes was working in conjunction with the Tacoma Narcotics Enforcement Team ("TNET"), an intergovernmental task force made up of various local, county and state agencies with authority to investigate suspected drug operations. After completing various information gathering, including speaking to informants, flying over the suspect property, and talking to various officers who had visited the property, Estes signed an affidavit for a search warrant.

The warrant affidavit contained the following facts. Estes met with an anonymous citizen informant who relayed that a second anonymous informant knew of a person who was suspected of manufacturing controlled substances in a clandestine laboratory. The first informant described Michael Hervey's residence and relayed that the second informant had detected strong chemical odors "described as acetone." Estes met with the second informant and confirmed these observations. The second informant also indicated to Estes that: United Parcel Service made frequent deliveries to the residence; Hervey used vehicles to block the driveway; and Hervey possessed a firearm.

Estes flew over the subject property and observed three large drums. In her "experience and training" Estes knew that chemicals used in methamphetamine manufacturing were transported in large drums. Estes also observed vehicles parked in the driveway.

. . . Deputies Riehl and Maye of the Pierce County Sheriff's Office responded to a call from Hervey on an unrelated matter. When they arrived at the property, Deputy Riehl heard a portable generator running. Michael Hervey approached them with "white powder on his lips, in his nostral [sic] hairs, and on his hair." According to Estes' affidavit, Deputy Riehl "could smell an odor of cat urine or P2P (a precursor chemical to the manufacture of methamphetamine) about [Hervey's] person." Deputy Riehl also "noticed an odor of acetone coming from one of the vehicles parked in the driveway." Finally, Deputy Riehl "recognized the odors that are consistent with the manufacturing of methamphetamine based upon his training and experience."

Estes' warrant affidavit described Deputy Riehl's background in law enforcement. Deputy Riehl completed courses in "Narcotics and Dangers Drug [sic] for Law Enforcement" and attended the "Clandestine Laboratory Safety Training." The affidavit also indicated that Deputy Riehl was "certified" as a Narcotics Investigator and in Clandestine Laboratory Investigation. Estes presented the affidavit to Pierce County Superior Court Judge Buckner. . . . Judge Buckner issued a search warrant. . . .

TNET prepared to execute the warrant. . . . A surprise raid was planned largely because of the possible danger involved in executing warrants at clandestine drug laboratories. Deputy Sheriff Thomas Lind, one member of the entry team, described the "standard garb" worn by members of the team: "I had a 9mm sidearm in a holster, and a submachine gun with a suppressed muzzle to decrease the chance of an explosion if it were fired in the volatile atmosphere of a drug lab. I was wearing a black fire-retardant Nomex suit, boots, gloves and hood, and a heavy ballistic-vest over that clothing. I was also wearing a full-face respirator mask which had a speaking diaphragm. . . ."

The participants lured Michael Hervey off the property and entered the property secretly, but the element of surprise quickly vanished. Two children on the property spotted the well-armed, strangely dressed team and began yelling. Deborah Couch, Tim Hervey's fiancee, stepped out of a trailer and also began screaming. Eventually, all occupants on the premises were "assist[ed] . . . to the ground" by members of the TNET entry team. Lynn Hervey objected to the assistance provided to her, contending that Detective Estes used unreasonable force.

No methamphetamine laboratory was discovered on the property. The entry team did, however, discover a small marijuana-growing operation. Michael Hervey was subsequently prosecuted for, and pleaded guilty to, possession of marijuana.

We have no doubt that Hervey has made the required substantial showing that Estes made deliberately false statements or recklessly disregarded the truth in the affidavit. Hervey specified precisely what portions of the affidavit were false and supported his claim with documentation. Hervey presented depositions from Deputy Riehl that he was not "certified" in Narcotics Training or Clandestine Laboratory Investigation, as the affidavit purported. More importantly, Riehl indicated that he did not tell Estes that he smelled "acetone" or "P2P" when he was on the Hervey property; indeed he stated that he had no knowledge of the smell of these chemicals. . . . The affidavit contains uncorroborated anonymous informant information of an "acetone" smell, parcel deliveries to the property, and vehicles blocking a driveway. . . . Estes' testimony that Hervey had three large drums on the property is by itself unremarkable.

Shorn of the false information about what Deputy Riehl smelled and his qualifications to do so, the Deputy's observations while on the property do not establish probable cause, either alone or in combination with the rest of the affidavit. His observations of white powder on Hervey and the operation of a generator are not tied in any way to the manufacture of methamphetamine. Riehl's statement that he smelled cat urine and later "recognized the odors that are consistent with the manufacturing of methamphetamine" are far too vague to support probable cause. The specific "odors" referred to in the initial affidavit, acetone and P2P, were falsehoods, and Deputy Riehl denied even knowing what acetone or P2P smelled like. A neutral magistrate could not possibly credit the Deputy's broad statement that he smelled "odors that you'd find at a methamphetamine lab" without knowing more about what those odors were or why and how Riehl was trained to recognize them.

[W]e cannot help but comment on the importance of the false information contained in this warrant affidavit. Estes' imputing of terms such as "acetone" and "P2P" to Deputy Riehl made the affidavit substantially more plausible to Pierce County Superior Court Judge Buckner. . . . The deliberately false or reckless inclusion of those perceptions is unforgivable . . . . Courts must be exceptionally vigilant when officers fabricate these perceptions. Estes' conduct is even more outrageous in this case, where the warrant issued was used to conduct a full-scale assault on the Hervey's property.

Source: *Hervey v. Estes*, 65 F.3d 784 (9th Cir. 1995).

often view falsification as, to use his words, "doing God's work"—doing whatever it takes to get a suspected criminal off the streets. This attitude is so entrenched, especially in high crime precincts, that . . . one recently arrested officer presented with evidence of perjury asked in disbelief, "What's wrong with that? They're guilty." (Mollen Commission, 1994, p. 41)

Equally important as the preparation for deviance and after-the-fact justifications is the effect that denial of injury has on freeing police from the external and internal norms that guide behavior. Denial of injury provides police with insulation from the labels "thief," "perjurer" or "criminal." Police are able to assert that their deviance

> does not really cause any great harm despite the fact that it runs counter to law. Just as the link between the individual and his acts may be broken by the denial of responsibility, so too may the link between acts and their consequences be broken by the denial of injury. (Sykes & Matza, 1957, p. 668)

Police Denial of the Victim

Another common technique of neutralization is the denial of a victim. This not an assertion that victims do not exist; rather it is characterization of victims and victimization in an attempt to justify deviation. Sykes and Matza (1957) explain that

> the moral indignation of self and others may be neutralized by an insistence that the injury is not wrong in light of the circumstances. The injury, it may be claimed, is really not an injury; rather, it is a form of retaliation or punishment. (p. 668)

The imputed character of the target seemingly justifies any deviation from acceptable behavior.

Consider a situation where a traffic violator decides to run from the police. The offender and the situation can be defined in various ways. The officer can perceive the situation as consisting of a relatively minor violation of the law—someone has committed a traffic offense and has overreacted by selecting a very poor course of action. Alternatively, the officer may define the citizen as a dangerous fleeing felon who has taken a drastic and hazardous course of action. Depending on perception and definition, the citizen may be seen as deserving the full force of law. If the violator is captured and exhibits signs of intoxication, the officer again has choices of characterization. In the perception of the officer, the traffic offender can become either a potentially violent offender in need of forceful control or an incapacitated person requiring little if any use of force. Given both the police view of the world and of citizens and the authority orientation instilled in police officers, offenders are usually perceived as potential assailants who have demonstrated their dangerousness by defying police authority. In fact, when a suspect flees from the police, he or she may have committed "contempt of cop." In these situations, police are prone to exact a pound of flesh (see Alpert, Kenney & Dunham, 1997).

Police reason away their use of force as justifiable punishment for some behaviors. In essence, the officer moves himself or herself into the position of an avenger and the victim is transformed into a wrongdoer. Police learn appropriate and inappropriate targets for the transformation of a victim into a person who deserves injury. Appropriate targets take the form of "symbolic assailants" (Skolnick, 1994)—fictional citizens whose characteristics are predetermined by police ideology and manifested when citizens defy authority.

Police culture and ideology set the stage for characterizing certain persons and acts as constituting threats—those who run from the police, citizens who use illegal drugs, and other acts of defiance of the conformity and authority that police value. These people are predetermined as dangerous and in need of state-sanctioned violence. Whether such characterizations are grounded in reality or are merely a manifestation of police beliefs, they provide officers with the necessary intellectual and often a legally plausible justification to deviate from the external and internal norms thought to restrict police responses in these situations. Denial of the victim frees the police to engage in deviant behavior for a higher good—preserving society from those with no respect for the social order.

Police Condemnation of Condemners

By employing this technique, the deviant effectively "shifts the focus of attention from his own deviant acts to the motives and behaviors of those who disapprove of his violation. His condemners, he may claim are hypocrites, deviants in disguise, or impelled by personal spite" (Sykes & Matza, 1957, p. 668). When applied to police deviance, this technique manifests itself in three general forms.

First, police condemn the edicts of the external and internal normative system when they conflict with police informal norms by imputing motive on those criminal justice personnel who attempt to curtail police autonomy and authority. For instance, the exclusionary rule is used by lawyers who are just out to "make a buck" from the criminal justice system. Those who developed this rule did so just to provide "a loophole" for criminals and to make it more difficult for the police to do their job. Criminal charges the police bring against citizens are reduced in plea bargaining arrangements because judges and prosecutors are "soft on crime." These justifications serve to lessen the bonds police have with the larger normative system by replacing formal norms with police norms.

A second form of this technique is a condemnation of people who bring charges of deviance against the police. While distinct from denial of the victim, condemning the condemners is also used to allege that citizens who bring claims against the police are merely "hostile" toward law enforcement; they are "resentful" for being ticketed or arrested; or they are merely "money grubbing" individuals out to make "a quick buck" by filing a lawsuit against the police.

The third use of this technique is to condemn those persons who pass judgment on police conduct. When police officers are convicted of crimes or held liable in civil proceedings, the condemners of police are often characterized as unable to understand the "realities" of police work or the "dangerousness" of criminals. To the police, these people are merely "armchair quarterbacks" who use 20/20 hindsight to pass judgment on actions they do not understand. Police often feel they are the scapegoats of the criminal justice system in that they are expected to ferret out crime aggressively. When they do (under their interpretation of effective crime control), they are condemned by the very people who implored them to do something about crime. Police rationalize that the system, its demands, and unrealistic expectations of accountability are hypocritical. Consider another statement made by the president of the SLPOA.

> The standard policy amongst most major city police departments is don't chase, don't shoot, don't hit. If you do any of the above, you can bet your pension that there will be a lawyer banging at the door of the police commissioner's office *suing everybody* right down the line.

> The department will naturally deny any liability and leave you hanging in the breeze. Then the city will give in, pay off a big settlement and you've got *another rich guy* waiting to get out of prison to spend his money [italics added]. (Oldani, 1992, p. 2)

These remarks attempt to prepare the actor for deviation from internal departmental norms and external societal norms by condemnation of the department and citizens. The author of this passage has rejected the bonds of the larger social order and replaced them with those of the police subculture. He is therefore free to "chase, shoot and hit."

Condemning the condemners prepares the police for deviant exploits by predetermining that the legal rules of police conduct, the people who may allege deviance, and those who may be called upon to sanction deviance are themselves unjust, corrupt, deviant, or ignorant. Through condemnation, police sever the link between their potential courses of action and the external normative system. Police reject the exclusionary rule before its application, thus freeing themselves to collect evidence in an illegal manner. They reject citizen allegations of police wrongdoing by characterizing complaints as motivated by resentment and hostility. They reject challenges to their authority and autonomy by condemning those who pass judgment on their conduct. They reject the system that attempts to hold them accountable and reject the internal norms established by their department. Police can therefore deviate with a steadfast belief that they are righteous in their actions even if they involve "bending," "sidestepping," or "twisting" the rules of the larger society.

> We are given badges, authority and tools of the trade, and then we are sent out to do a job. As we become more *efficient* at our jobs, complaints start coming in. As complaints start coming in, restrictions are placed on us controlling how we do our job. Pretty soon, we have more *restrictions* than *authority* and we are suddenly put on the *defense* rather than the *offense* [italics added]. (Oldani, 1992, p. 2)

Implicit in these statements are the necessary preparations for deviation. The police role is conceptualized in terms of war; an offensive posture is necessary to control crime effectively. Any attempt by controllers to curtail police autonomy and authority is rejected. Since the controllers have been labeled as uninformed and hypocritical, their attempts to control are invalid. Thus, external control can be rejected without forsaking basic cultural beliefs.

Police Appeal to Higher Loyalties

The most powerful technique of neutralization employed by police is the appeal to higher loyalties. More than any other, this technique is directly linked to police culture and allows police to break the bonds of the larger normative system. According to Sykes and Matza (1957, p. 669), "internal and external social controls may be neutralized by sacrificing the demands of the larger society for the demands of the smaller social groups to which the delinquent belongs. . . ." Police are often faced with the conflict of upholding the external norms of the larger society or violating the informal norms of their subculture. For example, a police officer who sees his or her partner brutalize a citizen may be called upon to give testimony. The officer is forced to make a decision between committing perjury (violating an external norm) or adhering to the police code of secrecy that prohibits "giving up" another cop (informal norm). The officer can testify that he or she saw nothing or that the partner did not engage in brutality, thus escaping the sanction of peers but risking the charge of perjury.

One might suspect that this is a wrenching decision; to protect a partner the officer must violate legal and ethical norms by lying. Quite the contrary, this decision is relatively easy since those who have not subscribed to the norms and values of the police culture have been culled from the system. The situation is processed through the ideology of the police. Protecting a fellow officer is expected and even considered noble—not criminal.

Loyalty, Cover-ups and Police Brutality

"James Niehus was arrested on suspicion of drunk driving and brought to a police station in Berkeley, Illinois, a suburb of Chicago. He got into an argument with the police, and a fight ensued in the course of which—he testified—officers Liberio and Vittorio kicked him in the face, breaking his left cheekbone, as a consequence of which he suffered brain damage. . . .

"At the station house Niehus became obstreperous, in part he says because he was afraid that an arrest for drunk driving would jeopardize his status with his employer and with the army reserves, in which he is a sergeant. The police handcuffed one of his arms to the chair in which they had told him to sit. He demanded to be allowed to call his lawyer and to this end tried to slide his chair across the room to the telephone. The defendant officers tried to stop him. Niehus says that they started hitting him and that he fell on the floor and curled up with the left side of his face on the floor and his right arm over his head to protect him. He says they kicked him between five and fifteen times. . . .

"The judge allowed the plaintiff's lawyer to intimate that the Berkeley police department had engaged in a 'cover up,' and he also gave the jury a 'missing-evidence' instruction. . . . The defendants testified that right after the fight with Niehus in the station house they took mug shots of him, but that when later they looked for the photos in Niehus's file they couldn't find them. They speculate that the camera was broken in the fight. But there was testimony . . . that the same camera was working fine the next day. And right after the fight the officers had talked with their supervisor by phone and the phone conversation had been routinely taped, but the tape was never produced. One employee of the police department testified that the tape was erased routinely, but another testified that the tape recorder was malfunctioning on the day of the fight, and the jury may have thought that this was one excuse too many. A third employee, whose job it was to monitor conversations in the booking room where the fight occurred, gave contradictory testimony about what she heard.

"As far as the cover-up is concerned, the indications that the defendants in concert with other employees of the police department tried to suppress evidence of their use of excessive force against Niehus were sufficiently numerous. . . . Here were the defendants . . . strenuously contradicting Niehus's testimony and yet there was a fair probability that they had engaged in active efforts to prevent that testimony from being corroborated by the mug shots, the tape recording, and the employee who heard the fight over the monitoring system.

"Although the defendants gave plenty of excuses for why they failed to produce the mug shots or the (allegedly) broken camera or the tape recording or the (allegedly) malfunctioning tape recorder, there was enough reason to believe that they could and would have produced this evidence had it been favorable to them to warrant the missing-evidence instruction. The evidence of a cover-up is highly pertinent here. Given the degree of cooperation evident among the employees of the Berkeley Police Department, it is nearly certain that the custodian of the evidence would have made it available to the defendants had it been helpful to them."

Source: *Niehus v. Liberio,* 973 F.2d 526 (7th Cir. 1992).

An officer who commits perjury to protect a fellow officer has demonstrated loyalty and solidarity to the group by placing himself or herself in harm's way for others.

Sykes and Matza (1957) note that "the most important point is that deviation from certain norms may occur not because the norms are rejected but because other norms, held to be more pressing or involving a higher loyalty, are accorded precedence" (p. 669). Police are free to pick and choose among social norms because subcultural norms and justifications operate to lessen the bonds police have with society. The police may choose to observe external norms, or they may redefine situations or persons to justify departure from routinely prescribed behavior.

One must keep in mind that the testifying officer may employ all the techniques of neutralization to help in the decision-making process. The officer called to testify may: deny the partner's responsibility for the transgression; deny the injury by defining the actions as necessary and reasonable force rather than brutality; deny the victim by characterization; and condemn those who seek to pass judgment on the other officer. Additionally, the officer is "protecting"—not committing "perjury." In essence, the officer may be cognizant of the wrongfulness of the act but chooses to be loyal to specifically selected cultural norms.

AUDIENCE ACCEPTANCE OF JUSTIFICATIONS FOR DEVIANCE

Thus far we have left relatively untouched the audience's role in the process by which concrete acts are socially situated and how justification works to make some forms of police deviance socially acceptable. Justifications for deviance are intended not only to bring order and a sense of rationality to the actor's perception of the act, but they can be constructed to make the audience more accepting of the act. For justification to work as a deflective shield against social stigmatization, it must be accepted by those who interpret the appropriateness of the behavior. Police justification of deviance must be nestled in a context understandable and acceptable to a particular social audience.

Police prepare the social audience to accept their justifications by invoking the language of crime and disorder. When the Federal Bureau of Investigation presents its crime statistics to the public and shows that reported numbers of violent crimes are rising—but fails to mention that actual rates of victimization may be declining—they are preparing the audience for later courses of action and setting the stage for justification. We have seen this groundwork laid in the public education lectures on the DARE program, the FBI public briefings on organized crime, and law enforcement public statements concerning gangs and violence. Deceptive intent or intentional manipulation need not be inferred from these presentations. More often than not, the presenter believes the material presented. The net effect is the same in any case—the public is prepared for future police actions. Aggressive police tactics, deception and trickery in investigations, and intrusion upon liberty and privacy become more palatable to a well-prepared audience.

Police may also construct their justifications to match social sentiment developed outside police circles. Characterizations of victimized citizens as "drug users," "deviants," "criminals," and "psychopaths" usually serve this function well. Because society has learned that drug use is dangerous; that drug dealers are well organized and heavily armed; that certain deviant segments of society are less deserving of the full protections of the law; and that undefined "others" present a threat to the social and moral order, casting police actions within the context of fighting these groups makes the concrete actions of police, even deviant ones, more acceptable to the audience. The police cast the victims of their actions in the light of existing social sentiment.

The concrete act can undergo changes in justification depending on the intended audience. A justification that will "play" for one audience may not play for another, because most social groups are intellectually and rationally bounded by their own subculture. In the legal context, the police may reason that violence was "reasonable and necessary" given the potential threat; that police action was in "self-defense"; or that to apply sanctions would render the police institution ineffective as a crime control mechanism. By invoking mitigating or justifying language particular to a social audience, the police hope to escape the attachment of the deviant label to their actions, to avoid legal consequences, and to gain acceptance of the justification that is offered. To bring about acceptance from police peers, an officer need only summon subcultural sentiment by using language—"dirt-bag," "scum-ball," or some other contemporary police status designation—that characterizes the undeserving nature of the victim. For the larger public, the victim of police violence must be cast in terms of dangerousness—violating the "thin blue line" provided by the police to preserve society. The image of brave individuals performing a difficult job on mean streets will usually elicit sufficient sympathy.

NEGOTIATING BOUNDARIES OF THE NORMATIVE SYSTEM

Acceptance or rejection of police justification for deviance serves a larger role in the construction of social order. Social reality is made up of shared communication and social definitions. In the communication process there are two points of transmission—the individual and the audience. Perceptions of both parties interact to negotiate the moral and social order. As Charles Cooley (1902) expressed, "society and individual do not denote separable phenomena, but are simply collective and distributive aspects of the same thing" (p. 37). Members of society act and are acted upon based on the content and interpretation of symbolic communication. An audience's response to a social act conveys to the actor a conception of social-self. Social response then limits and shapes the contours of future social behavior by affecting the worldview, norms, and values of the actor. Nachman Ben-Yehuda captured the interactional nature between the larger social audience and the individual actor by observing that the two

> provide a link between the micro and macro sociological levels of analysis. This two way link materializes within defined situations of symbolic interaction. On the one hand, macro sociological level elements such as institutional values, morality and interests, infiltrate face-to-face interactions, influencing definitions of situations, participants' roles, and interactions' outcomes. On the other hand, new orientations, values, meanings, and moralities that are being constantly generated and negotiated on the face-to-face interactional level can influence values, meanings, and orientations of a whole social system. . . . [Normative boundaries] are basically fluid, negotiated among various societal levels as well as within each level, resulting either in the reinforcement of stability or in change. (Ben-Yehuda, 1990, p. 30)

When police justifications are played out in public forums, they provide the foundation for future individual and societal conceptions (we will return to this topic in chapter 11). If the public rejects the justification offered by the deviant, then that justification no longer serves to deflect labels of deviance. The justification must be modified or the behavior must be changed. If, however, the public accepts the justification, then it will continue to be invoked as a technique that shields the actor, and the concrete behavior can continue. Once a justification has been accepted by the audience, subsequent deviance becomes easier for the actor who now has confidence that either the concrete act was reasonable or the justification was acceptable in deflecting the label of deviant. In either case, the actor is free to continue the course of action until the audience response is modified. In this fashion, the norms and values of the police as well as those of the larger society are negotiated, and modifications are made to the existing social and moral order.

SUMMARY

Police who engage in deviant behaviors are faced with both social and psychological strains. From an internal vantage point, deviant police must be able to justify and rationalize their deviant behaviors. This is important if officers are to maintain a conformist self-image, even in the face of committing deviant acts. Externally, deviant police must also be able to project an orthodox, law-abiding image to the public. To overcome these types of strains, the police subculture provides officers with motives and rationalizations for engaging in deviant acts.

The police culture instructs officers on the use of several "neutralization" techniques to justify their involvement in illicit activities. These techniques provide officers with justifications for breaking societal norms. First, the police may deny responsibility for committing a deviant act. Police might, for example, justify the use of excessive force during an arrest by rationalizing that the arrestee left them with few other options. Second, police may deny that anyone was injured by their deviancy. If an illegal search results in evidence of a crime, who is the injured party? Third, the police may deny that there was a victim. Offenders who show disrespect toward the police may receive "curbside justice." The assaulted citizen is no victim—merely someone who got what he or she deserved. Fourth, police may condemn their condemners in order to justify police deviancy. Police may characterize those who question their actions or tactics as mere criminals who have ulterior motives for attempting to discredit the police. Finally, the police may appeal to higher loyalties. This may occur, for example, where an officer chooses to comply with police subcultural norms (that is, a "higher loyalty") rather than the norms of society.

To maintain their self-image, the police must convince the public to accept their characterizations. One way to prepare the public for possible police deviance is by painting a picture of escalating crime rates, highly organized crime rings, and pervasive violent gangs—regardless of the accuracy of these portrayals. When crime is represented in this fashion, the public is mentally "prepped" to understand the need for aggressive and perhaps questionable police tactics. The police can also influence public sentiments by portraying victims of police deviance in socially unacceptable terms. For example, those who claim they are the victims of police deviance may be characterized by the police as drug addicts, ex-convicts, mentally ill, and/or criminal.

Strategies and justifications used by the police to justify their actions must be constructed so that the public approves. This involves a dynamic and interactive negotiation process that is at least partly shaped by the moral, social, and political order of broader society. As we shall see in the next chapter, this process is complex and affected by many factors.

Chapter Six

POLICE BRUTALITY AND
ABUSE OF AUTHORITY
Making Sense of the Senseless
Beating of Rodney King

> Justice without force is impotent; force without justice is tyranny.
> Blaise Pascal (1623–1662)

P olice brutality, perhaps more than any other form of police deviance, has produced public outrage and calls for police reform. What were once isolated acts of deviance between police and unfortunate citizens have now become media events open to public display and scrutiny. The beating and sodomy of Abner Louima in 1997 by NYPD officers received national attention even without graphic videotape of the attack.

In 1992, public attention was deluged with images of police brutalizing citizens. That year, the actions of half a dozen police officers in Kansas City, Missouri were recorded by television cameras. Police were filmed using a stun gun repeatedly to shock a young man who had failed to stop his vehicle when confronted by police. As the young man was being shocked, other officers beat him with night sticks. In Fort Worth, Texas, a citizen parked along an interstate filmed a police officer beating a handcuffed prisoner who appeared to be offering little in the way of resistance. In Trenton, New Jersey the elderly father of a young African-American man inquired as to the reason his son was being arrested. Police responded by repeatedly slapping him in the face and shoving him against a police cruiser. These and other images of police exceeding the legal limits of their authority solidified public concern over use of force.

Consider two more incidents of police violence.

- Responding to what Philadelphia police officers assumed to be a domestic dispute over a missing child, as many as 20 police officers beat a plainclothes female officer who was in the house at the time. According to the account, the African-American plainclothes police officer was beaten by white officers with flashlights and fists until another African-American officer could intervene. [*Lexington Herald-Leader*, 1/13/95, p. A8]

- Two Hartford police officers were charged with beating a Massachusetts man. The incident was captured on video by members of another police department nearby. Officers attempted to stop the man's vehicle. Instead of stopping, the man drove to the other police department because of concerns over brutality by the Hartford police. The videotape shows no signs of resistance by the man but shows the two officers beating the man on the head with pistols. [*New York Times*, 3/8/97, p. 10]

In the history of policing, perhaps no single episode of police brutality generated as much attention and public reaction as the beating of motorist Rodney G. King at the hands of the Los Angeles Police Department (LAPD). The nation's attention had been focused on the aftermath of the Persian Gulf War when the savage beating of King took place on March 3, 1991 in Los Angeles, California. After reviewing the facts of the incident, we will look closely at the context to analyze how brutality can flourish and even become accepted in some police subcultures.

THE POLICE BEATING OF RODNEY KING

From the balcony of his apartment, amateur video camera enthusiast, George Holliday, shot footage of LAPD officers beating a twenty-five-year-old African-American man following a traffic stop. The event began at about 12:40 A.M. Sunday when California Highway Patrol (CHP) officers Melanie Singer and Timothy Singer, a husband and wife team, detected Rodney King's white Hyundai speeding on the Foothill freeway. King's vehicle apparently approached the CHP car from the rear and ultimately passed it. The CHP cruiser left the interstate, but returned to pace King's vehicle. Two of King's friends, Bryant Allen and Freddie Helms, both African Americans, were passengers in his vehicle. The CHP officers reportedly tried to signal King to stop by activating their emergency equipment, but he failed to stop his vehicle. Instead, King continued to drive for several more miles, allegedly running a stop sign and passing through a red light. King later explained he was fearful that a traffic ticket would result in his probation being revoked. King was on a two-year probationary period for a robbery conviction.

Meanwhile, CHP officials notified the LAPD that they were attempting to stop the vehicle but never mentioned over the police radio that it was traveling at a high rate of speed (Christopher Commission, 1991a). Eventually, a LAPD patrol car assigned to Officers Laurence W. Powell and Timothy Wind, a cruiser assigned to LAPD Officers Theodore J. Briseno and Rolando Solano, and a cruiser from the Los Angeles Unified School District Police (LAUSDP) joined in the pursuit.

Following what CHP officials initially called a high speed pursuit (said to have reached speeds of 110 to 115 miles per hour), King pulled his vehicle curbside at Foothills and Osborne in Lake View Terrace and was ordered out of his car. In the meantime, police from several agencies converged on the scene. According to the Christopher Commission's (1991a) investigation "11 additional LAPD units (including a helicopter) with 21 officers arrived at the end-of-pursuit scene" (p. 5). The two passengers complied with police orders to exit the vehicle and were taken into custody with little resistance (Alpert et al., 1992). The unarmed King initially refused to exit the vehicle. When he did, he was twice shocked with a fifty-thousand-volt Taser by LAPD Sgt. Stacey Koon; savagely hit in the head "baseball style" with nightsticks by Officers Powell and Wind; and repeatedly kicked by Officer Briseno. In all, Rodney King was struck at least fifty-six times by the LAPD officers. At least twenty-one officers (possibly as many as twenty-seven)—including LAPD supervisor Stacey Koon, four uniformed members of the CHP, four LAPD field training officers, and several officers from different law enforcement agencies—watched or participated in the beating (Christopher Commission,

1991a). Two minutes later, Rodney King was lying crumpled on the ground with eleven skull fractures, a broken cheek bone, a fractured eye socket, a broken ankle, missing teeth, kidney damage, external burns and permanent brain damage. He was later jailed for four days until prosecutors determined that there was insufficient evidence to try him for attempting to evade the police.

THE AFTERMATH OF THE BEATING

The next day (March 4, 1991), George Holliday attempted to deliver his videotape of the beating to LAPD officials. Holliday was informed by a desk sergeant that the department was not interested in the tape, and no attempt was made to learn about the beating he had witnessed.

> Confronted with what he viewed as disinterest on the part of the LAPD, Holliday made arrangements with Los Angeles television station KTLA to broadcast the videotape Monday evening. On Tuesday, the tape received national exposure on the Cable News Network; thereafter, the incident was reported widely in the media. (Christopher Commission, 1991a, p. 11)

The tape was played repeatedly by major television networks in the United States and was eventually aired internationally. George Holliday's videotape, its dismissal by the LAPD, and the exposure the video received from the news media enabled the nation to witness one of the worst abuses of police power ever captured on film.

Eleven days after the beating of Rodney King, four of the LAPD officers (Koon, Powell, Wind and Briseno) were indicted (March 14, 1991) by a Los Angeles County grand jury on state assault charges. A change of venue was granted the officers because of a court of appeals ruling that they could not receive a fair trial in Los Angeles County given the publicity surrounding the videotape. The trial site was then moved to Simi Valley in Ventura County, a predominately conservative, middle-class, white community of one hundred thousand. Besides being predominately white, Simi Valley is home to many police officers and firefighters. As one police commander put it, "any panel chosen from there was more likely to identify with the four white officers who had held the nightsticks than the one black man on the ground" (Anthony, 1993, p. 8).

The trial began on March 4, 1992, before a jury of ten whites, one Asian, and one Hispanic. The composition of the jury was perhaps not as telling as their backgrounds.

> The panel included a maintenance worker, a printer, a retired teacher and a retired real estate broker. Three of the jurors had

worked as security guards or patrol officers in the U.S. military. Three others were members of the National Rifle Association. One was the brother of a retired L.A. police sergeant. (Anthony, 1993, p. 8)

By the time the case came to trial, Freddie Helms had died in a traffic accident. The other passenger in the King vehicle, Bryant Allen, could provide little information because he was held by police at gunpoint prone on the ground. On April 29, 1992, after four days of deliberation, the jury acquitted the defendant-officers of all but a single charge against Powell.

Within hours of the jury's decision to acquit the officers, Los Angeles erupted in violence. The riots lasted five days and resulted in more than 40 deaths, 2,382 injuries, 5,200 destroyed or damaged buildings, 40,000 lost jobs, an estimated $1 billion in property damage and more than 5,633 citizens arrested (*Koon v. U.S.*, 1996). Analysis following the riots indicated that

> while there can be little doubt that the anger felt by black people concerning the Rodney King verdict provided the spark that started the riot, there is considerable evidence that by the next day, April 30, the riot had spread well beyond the bounds of race. (Petersilia & Abrahamse, 1994, p. 1)

Not only did the participation in rioting spread into other racial groups, it "quickly spread to other cities including, Atlanta, Seattle and Madison, Wisconsin" (Pope & Ross, 1992, p. 7). President George Bush called out the military to establish order in L.A., and police across the country arrested thousands. The riots were among the most devastating ever experienced.

During the course of the state trial, officials from the Justice Department were conducting an investigation into the possibility that the four officers had violated Rodney King's civil rights. On August 5, 1992 federal prosecutors announced that the officers had been indicted on civil rights charges. Koon, Powell, Wind and Briseno were to stand trial again—this time in federal court. Sergeant Stacey Koon was charged with failing to prevent his officers from assaulting Mr. King; Powell, Wind, and Briseno were charged with the assault. The federal jury consisted of six white men, three white women, an African-American man, an African-American woman, and a Hispanic man. The federal trial began on February 3, 1993 with the officers facing the possibility of ten-year sentences and $250,000 in fines. The jury "spent six weeks listening to 61 witnesses, studying more than 100 exhibits" (Mathews, 1993, p. 23). The day before Easter, the jury began its deliberations. After several days of consideration, it found Koon and Powell guilty of the charges; Wind and Briseno were found not guilty. In August, Koon and Powell were sentenced to thirty months in federal prison—a term that was significantly less than that required under the federal sentencing guidelines. The officers appealed their sentence unsuccessfully, but the Supreme Court affirmed the trial court's departure from the federal sentencing guidelines noting that the officers had been put through two trials, that King had provoked the assault, and that the officers might be subject to harsh treatment in prison because of their occupation (*Koon v. U.S.*, 1996).

The social, cultural, and occupational contexts in which LAPD officers operated created an environment where the intersection of how officers viewed the world and others and their perception of justice and the police role in dispensing it culminated in a savage beating witnessed by more than 20 other officers. The sections that follow discuss that environment drawing on information uncovered by the Christopher Commission's investigation of the LAPD, the facts that surfaced at the state and federal trials of the officers involved, and information gleaned from comments made to news reporters by police officials and from Chief Daryl F. Gates' autobiography.

THE LAPD'S WORKING ENVIRONMENT

Daryl F. Gates had been chief of police for thirteen years at the time of the beating of Rodney King. He had spent more than forty-two years working in the LAPD and had moved up through the ranks to become chief. Clearly, Chief Gates was in a position of power that most modern-day police administrators would envy. He had almost absolute authority over the department, its policies, and its personnel; his position was well insulated by unique civil service protections.

> Although the City Charter assigns the Police Commission ultimate control over Department policies, its authority over the Department and the Chief of Police is illusory. Structural and operational constraints greatly weaken the Police Commission's power to hold the Chief accountable and therefore its ability to perform its management responsibilities, including effective oversight. Real power and authority reside in the Chief. (Christopher Commission, 1991b, p. 15).

The Christopher Commission (1991b) noted that Gates' civil service status protected him from either disciplinary action or discharge by giving him a "substantial property right" in his job and declaring that he could not be suspended or removed except for "good and sufficient cause" (p. 15). Even the actions of the city's Police Commission could be vetoed by the city council or undermined by the chief.

Gates had a colorful career as chief of the LAPD, often bringing national attention to both himself and the police department. During his tenure, Gates was credited with establishing an image of professionalism. More often than not, Gates' brand of professionalization focused on the creation of specialized tactical units, the adoption of technologically advanced military hardware, and the indoctrination of police personnel with aggressive attitudes.

> In 1967, Daryl F. Gates, a rising star in the Los Angeles Police Department, approached his chief with an idea: create an elite squad of officers, specially trained and equipped to respond to hostage situations. He wanted to call it SWAT, or Special Weapons Attack Team. (Woestendiek, 1991, p. A-6)

Since his idea came in the aftermath of the Watts riots, image was important and the suggested name was modified to "Special Weapons and Tactics Team." Under Gates' command, the department changed from .38 caliber revolvers to 9mm weapons to "match the firepower on the streets" (Gates & Shah, 1993, p. 207); helicopters were used for assistance in vehicular and foot pursuits; motorized battering rams (tanks) were purchased to make forcible entries into citizens' homes (Prud'Homme, 1991); and the department began to use elite felony squads dubbed "Death Squads" because of the extraordinary number of suspects they killed. During the 1970s, the LAPD had an "intelligence squad" that regularly spied on L.A. citizens despite the fact that they were not engaged in illegal activities (Rothmiller & Goldman, 1992). Adoption of these technologies and practices led to an avalanche of civil rights litigation and a feeling by many that Gates "set an improper moral tone for the department and sent the message that, when it comes to fighting crime, virtually anything goes" (Woestendiek, 1991, p. A-6). In fact, Lou Reiter, a former deputy chief in the LAPD, said that Gates "definitely had his own set ways . . . If your [sic] not with him, you're against him. There is a form-the-wagons-in-a-circle, siege mentality, but that's always been the case in LAPD" (Woestendiek, 1991, p. A-6).

Although these innovations contributed to an external image of the LAPD as a professional organization, they actually served as a veneer for an aggressive police organization that had rapidly distanced itself from the public. While developing as many specialized units as possible and securing as many military gadgets and tactics as the city would allow, Gates instilled a sense of division between the police and public. Because of his civil service protection, Gates was able to express openly his distorted views on minorities, crime, and proper police practices. On more than one occasion, Gates antagonized certain segments of the community with his comments. In remarks to the press, Gates consistently demonstrated his insensitivity to minority segments of the population.

In 1978, after becoming chief, Gates attended a luncheon of the Coalition of Mexicanos/Latinos Against Defamation and was asked about the

LAPD's failure to employ and promote appropriate numbers of Hispanic officers. Gates replied that Hispanics are "lazy" and told a story to illustrate the point (Gates & Shah, 1993, p. 207). Four years later, when besieged with questions about police use of a controversial choke hold that resulted in the deaths of at least sixteen citizens—most of whom were African American, Gates responded that "the veins or arteries [of African Americans] do not open up as fast as they do on *normal* people" (Prud'Homme, 1991, p. 18). In other episodes, Gates called a female news broadcaster an "Aryan broad"; he accused the Soviet Union of sending "Jewish spies" into the city to disrupt the Olympics; and when questioned on television about his views on homosexuals, he said that he was not biased. In fact, he stated in a *60 Minutes* interview that he "admired the upper-body strength of lesbians." It should be noted that Gates, as chief of police, was responsible for providing police service for a city with a substantial gay population. The city, moreover, was made up of 40 percent Latinos, 37 percent whites, 13 percent African Americans and 10 percent Asians.

Gates' distorted views on crime control and criminal justice were reflected in many of his remarks. In 1990 while addressing the Senate Judiciary Committee on the topic of drug control, Gates told Senator Joseph Biden that "the casual drug user ought to be taken out and shot" (Gates & Shah, 1993, p. 330). In a television documentary about police chiefs, Gates told interviewers that inmates should be given water, a few seeds and shovels, and left in the desert to make it on their own. Desert prisons, according to Gates, should be surrounded with explosive mines.

In another incident that involved a lawsuit against Chief Gates and members of the LAPD arising out of an act of police violence, Gates showed his disdain for the legal system. After testifying in a civil case, Gates was questioned by reporters outside the courtroom. The substance of the interviews appeared in three newspaper articles. The quotations varied minimally and the content of his statements was corroborated by all three newspapers. According to the federal court's records Gates said:

> How much is a broken nose worth? $90,000? I don't think it's worth anything. He's probably lucky that's all he has. Given the circumstances in this case, I don't think it's worth anything. [Larez] is probably lucky that's all he had broken. They [the jurors] see the family there all cleaned up . . . They don't know their background, that there is a gang member on parole. They get very sympathetic. I tell my officers to do something—and we do something and they give them $90,000. (*Larez v. City of Los Angeles*, 1991, p. 630; Patterson, 1992).

Gates' ideology was not just rhetoric; it was manifested in LAPD practices. As the Christopher Commission noted, officers were rewarded for aggressive practices; productivity was measured by the number of calls answered by police and the number of citizens arrested. Officers were promoted and received pay increases for arresting citizens rather than for preventing crime. In the mid-1970s, Gates was involved in the development of the CRASH (Community Program Resources Against Street Hoodlums). It had originally been called TRASH (Total Resources Against Street Hoodlums), but someone apparently noted the problem with that image. In 1988, Gates initiated Operation Hammer—sending waves of over one thousand police officers onto the streets to make arrest sweeps. He later joked with other chiefs that this was a "cultural awareness" program. "We have a motto," said Gates, "Travel is broadening. Just get the hell out of Los Angeles . . ." (Gates & Shah, 1993, pp. 337–338). In all, through both organizational action and public comments, Gates set the stage for police violence by articulating a philosophy of bigotry and police aggression. Gates instilled in his personnel a "siege mentality" that informed officers who the criminals were and how they should be treated.

When Gates' philosophy of aggressive policing was called into question, several common justifications were provided to appease citizens. First, the LAPD was understaffed; there were simply too few police for such a large city. Second, the police were out-manned and out-gunned by a swelling tide of crime and criminals entering Los Angeles. Third, these two factors meant that officers had to do more with less and that they had to take an aggressive approach to control crime. These justifications were also advanced by the Christopher Commission's (1991) uncritical review of statistics.

> While the overall rate of violent crime in the United States increased three and one-half times between 1960 and 1989, the rate in Los Angeles during the same period was more than twice the national average. According to 1986 data recently published by the Police Foundation, the Los Angeles police were the busiest among the officers in the nation's largest six cities. . . . Of the police departments of the six largest United States cities, the LAPD has the fewest officers per resident and the fewest officers per square mile. Yet the LAPD boasts more arrests per officer than other forces. (pp. 2–3)

The facts seem clear: the LAPD had more crime and fewer officers than several major cities in the United States. The important omission in this justification, however, is that Gates was the chief of police for over thirteen years during this crime wave and his aggressive crime control tactics had obviously done little to stem the rising tide of crime. In fact, LAPD officers killed more citizens per officer in 1986 than did police in the other major cities and had the highest rate of citizen arrests (Christopher Commission, 1991b). If the rate of crime is a valid measure of police performance, the LAPD saw over a decade of failure under Chief Gates—even with aggressive patrol tactics. Furthermore, the staffing of the LAPD is not a blind or capricious act, it is a policy decision and function of government. In short, the city chose not to hire more police officers but to provide them with the latest military hardware and to allow them to pursue aggression as their major crime control tactic. Given the number of civil rights claims filed against the LAPD (3,716 non-traffic-related claims in five years); the cost of judgments, settlements, and jury verdicts (over $20 million in four years); and cases of excessive force litigated (over 300 in four years); one can only infer that the city was willing to pay the price of police aggression (Christopher Commission, 1991b).

ABERANT CONDUCT OR SUBCULTURE OF VIOLENCE?

Almost immediately following the viewing of the videotaped beating of Rodney King, Chief Gates said that the incident "sickened" him but that, "Even if we determine the officers were out of line, it's an aberration" (Gates & Shah, 1993, p. 366) and not a routine part of the way LAPD officers police the community. Eventually, Gates made a public apology—in which he apologized for beating up a "criminal." Most facts lead to the conclusion that the Rodney King beating was not a mere aberration as characterized by Gates. As Jerome H. Skolnick and James J. Fyfe (1993) observed, "Two cops can go berserk, but twenty cops embody a subculture of policing" (p. 13). Consider the evidence uncovered by the Christopher Commission (1991b) concerning the LAPD's response to officer brutality:

> There is a significant number of LAPD officers who repetitively misuse force and persistently ignore the written policies and guidelines of the Department regarding force. The evidence obtained by the Commission shows that this group has received inadequate supervisory and management attention. Former Assistant Chief Jesse Brewer testified that this lack of management attention and accountability is the "essence of the excessive force problem. . . . We know who the bad guys are. Reputations become well known, especially to the sergeants and then of course to lieutenants and the captains in the areas . . . But I don't see anyone bring these people up. . . ." Assistant Chief David Dotson testified that "we have failed miserably" to hold supervisors accountable for excessive force by officers under their command. Interviews with a large number of present and former LAPD officers yield similar conclusions. (pp. 3–4)

The Commission's examination of citizen complaints against the police found a remarkable pattern of use of excessive force by a violent subculture within the LAPD.

- Of approximately 1,800 officers against whom an allegation of excessive force or improper tactics was made from 1986 to 1990, more than 1,400 had only one or two allegations. But 183 officers had four or more allegations. Forty-four had six or more, 16 had eight or more, and one had 16 such allegations.

• Of nearly 6,000 officers identified as involved in use of force reports from January 1987 to March 1991, more than 4,000 had fewer than five reports each. But 63 officers had 20 or more reports each. The top 5% of the officers (ranked by number of reports) accounted for more than 20% of all reports. [Christopher Commission, 1991b, pp. 3–4]

Even in the face of such data, top administrators of the LAPD did little to correct the problem. In fact, a review of the personnel records of LAPD officers found that supervisors ignored problem officers and often attempted to characterize performance in the most favorable light. An investigation into the personnel records of the LAPD found that

> of the 44 officers identified from the LAPD database who had six or more allegations of excessive force or improper tactics for the period 1986 through 1990 . . . the picture conveyed was often incomplete and at odds with contemporaneous comments appearing in complaint files. As a general matter, the performance evaluation reports for those problem officers were very positive, documenting every complimentary comment received and expressing optimism about the officer's progress in the Department. (Christopher Commission, 1991b, p. 4)

In fact, Laurence Powell testified that before going on patrol the evening of the King beating, he was "encouraged to be 'more aggressive' with baton blows in situations where such force was used" (Alpert et al., 1992, p. 476). The clear message in such an environment is that excessive use of force against citizens will be recategorized favorably by supervisors.

Considerable evidence also indicated that members of the LAPD internalized the aggressive tendencies of their chief. The Christospher Commission (1991b) examined records from the patrol officers' Mobile Digital Terminals (MDTs). After reviewing 182 days of MDT communications, there were

> hundreds of improper messages, including scores in which officers talked about beating suspects. . . . Officers also used the communications system to express their eagerness to be involved in shooting incidents. The transmissions also make clear that some officers enjoy the excitement of a pursuit and view it as an opportunity for violence against a fleeing suspect. (pp. 4–5)

Consider just a few of the comments made by LAPD officers. The comments reflect the existence of a violent subculture and the acceptance of violence by many within the department.

- "I would love to drive down Slauson with a flame thrower . . . we would have a barbecue."
- "A fem named [C] . . . I will be careful . . . we are out to get 211 susp that have been hitting almost twice a night. 2 m/blks . . . are you busy. . . ."
- "I was for awhile. But now I am going to slooow it down. If you encounter these negroes shoot first and ask questions later."
- "Just clear its buxsy [busy] out hear this hole is picking up, I almost got me a Mexican last nite but he dropped the dam gun to quick, lots of wit"

Racism was expressed openly over the communications system by both line officers and supervisors alike. The Commission's review of MDT transmissions found:

> an appreciable number of disturbing and recurrent racial remarks. Some of the remarks describe minorities through animal analogies. . . . Often made in the context of discussing pursuits or beating suspects. The offensive remarks cover the spectrum of racial and ethnic minorities in the City. . . . The officers typing the MDT messages apparently had little concern that they would be disciplined for making such remarks. (Christopher Commission, 1991b, pp. 4–8)

Consider a few of the comments made by LAPD officers about the race of citizens and appropriate police practices.

- "Well . . . I'm back over here in the projects, pissing off the natives"
- "Sounds like monkey slapping time."
- "Oh always dear . . . what's happening . . . we're huntin wabbits"
  "Actually, muslim wabbits"
  "Just over here on this arson/homicide . . . be careful one of those rabbits don't bite you"
  "Yeah I know . . . Huntin wabbits is dangerous."
- "Wees be reedy n about 5"
- "Wees also bees hungry"
- "Hi . . . just got mexercise for the night"
- "Don't be flirting with all ur cholo girlfriends"
- "Okay people . . . pls . . . don't transfer me any orientals . . . I had two already"
- "Lt says learn Spanish bone head . . . Sgt. [A] says tell them to go back to Mexico . . ."
- "Don't cry Buckwheat. or is it Willie Lunch Meat"
- "U can c the color of the interior of the veh . . . dig."
  "Ya Stop cars with blk interior."
  "Bees they naugahyde."
  "Negrohide."
  "Self tanning no doubt."

These communications clearly contain insensitive and racially biased remarks, but it is important to raise the question of whether these transmissions were merely aberrations or evidence of a subculture of racism and violence permeating the LAPD. Addressing this issue, the Christopher Commission concluded that

> the LAPD has an organizational culture that emphasizes crime control over crime prevention and that isolates the police from the communities and the people they serve. With the full support of many, the LAPD insists on aggressive detection of major crimes and a rapid, seven minute response time to calls for service. Patrol officers are evaluated by statistical measures (for example, the number of calls handled and arrests made) and are rewarded for being "hard-nosed." This style of policing produces results, but it does so at the risk of creating a siege mentality that alienates the officer from the community.
>
> Witness after witness testified to unnecessarily aggressive confrontations between LAPD officers and citizens, particularly members of minority communities. From the statements of these citizens, as well as many present and former senior LAPD officers, it is apparent that too many LAPD patrol officers view citizens with resentment and hostility. (Christopher Commission, 1991b)

Koon, Powell, Wind, and Briseno spent much of their working lives in this subculture of prejudice and violence. They learned how to police the "City of Angels" based on beliefs, values and attitudes embraced by this environment.

DISTURBING BELIEFS, FACTS AND FABRICATIONS

Other shocking details emerged from investigations into the Rodney King incident. Manufacturer tests of vehicles similar to the one driven by Mr. King found that even a newer version of King's car could not travel at the speeds reported by the CHP husband and wife team. In fact, CHP's own investigation confirmed that during the car chase, King was never going more than 65 mph—not the 115 mph CHP officers reported (Baker & Wright, 1991).

The LAPD's official report of the circumstances surrounding the arrest claimed that King was under the influence of PCP—a strong tranquilizer with hallucinogenic qualities—and that he resisted arrest. These claims were repeatedly reported in newspapers, magazines, and television interviews with some of the police involved in the beating. One report even noted that the spot where King stopped his vehicle was known as a drug-dealing haven (Tobar & Colvin, 1991). LAPD officers characterized

King's behavior in terms that invoked a drug-crazed image. Sergeant Stacey Koon described King as "dusted" and "oblivious to pain" (Christopher Commission, 1991a, p. 9). Blood tests conducted by the staff at the hospital where Mr. King was treated following the beating found a moderate amount of alcohol (0.075) and traces of marijuana in his system but failed to detect any PCP or other dangerous drugs (Christopher Commission, 1991a). Medical personnel characterized King as quiet and cooperative, and the attending physician said that he did not feel that King was on PCP (Stewart, 1993b). Furthermore, police failed to recover any drugs from his vehicle or person. In short, it is likely that the police fabricated the violent, drug-crazed image of motorist Rodney King to justify their brutal actions.

Finally, according to police accounts Rodney King was taken by ambulance to Pacific Hospital for treatment following the beating and was later lodged in the jail ward of the county medical center. According to nurses on duty at the time King was checked into the emergency room for treatment, officers repeatedly taunted King using "baseball" analogies. After Powell learned that King worked at Doger Stadium he taunted, "We played a little ball tonight, didn't we Rodney? . . . You know, we played a little ball, we played a little hardball tonight, we hit quite a few home runs. . . . Yes, we played a little ball and you lost and we won" (*Koon v. U.S.*, 1996, p. 2041). The officers "openly joked and bragged about the number of times King had been hit" (Christopher Commission, 1991a, p. 15).

During the officers' federal trial it was learned that two of the officers lied in their log entries and that they did not take King directly to the hospital or medical holding facility. Instead, they took him to a police substation where they went inside and told other police officers about the beating. Officer Laurence Powell subjected King to more ridicule by other police officers at the substation. According to prosecutor Steven Clymer, Officer Laurence Powell "sent police officers out to look . . . while Rodney King was in the back seat waiting for medical attention . . ." (Stewart, 1993a, p. 1A).

Following the beating, this exchange was recorded on the LAPD's communication system.

"Oops, what?"

[From Powell/Wind] "I haven't beaten anyone this bad in a long time."

[From Koon] "[U]nit just had a big time use of force. . . . Tased and beat the suspect of CHP pursuit big time."

"Oh not again . . . why for you do that . . . I thought you agreed to chill out for a while. What did he do?"

[From Powell/Wind] "I think he was dusted . . . many broken bones later after the pursuit," (*Koon v. U.S.*, 1996, p. 2041).

The vehicle's speed of travel (and therefore the legal justification for the detention), the reported drug usage by King (and therefore a potential justification for their aggressiveness), as well as the police conduct following the brutality were at a minimum exaggerations and probably total fabrications. Even more shocking than the beating inflicted (although it was severe), the number of officers involved (many), and the initial misrepresentation of the speed of travel was the officialized version of the incident and the calculated characterization of Mr. King to justify police aggression.

There were other "damage control efforts." They were drawn from the same justifications Gates had used to defend his philosophy of aggressive policing: the police have a hard time fighting the war against crime; the LAPD is understaffed and out-numbered by criminals; police have to be aggressive to fight crime. These justifications always ended with a reminder that King was "high" and had a criminal record. Some police officers have learned that waging a dangerous war on crime calls for aggressive measures, and characterizing citizens as violent drug users and criminals provides some deflection and neutralization of their own violent deviance. The massive public relations campaign accompanying our most recent drug war set the stage for this rationalization. As David Musto (1973) points out, issues of drug use and abuse have traditionally been couched in terms of a "drug fiend" mythology in the United States. The current drug war is no different, with stark and shocking images used by the government and the media to characterize the effects of drug use. The LAPD officers were careful to invoke these images and included these fabrications in their reports.

Officers interviewed by television news reporters after the incident repeatedly claimed that Mr. King acted as if he were under the influence of a controlled substance—specifically naming PCP as the suspected substance. To characterize Mr. King as a PCP user might justify an aggressive police response in the public mind, since the public has come to "know" that people under the influence of drugs are dangerous, violent, and the symbolic enemies of a civilized society. In a similar vein, such a characterization served to neutralize the police self-perception of deviance. If King were "high" on PCP, the public would understand the need for police violence—and the officers could justify their conduct to themselves. Their image as upholders of the law would be insulated from charges of lawless abuse of the authority granted to them to protect society.

TARGETING VICTIMS FOR POLICE VIOLENCE

What brought motorist Rodney King to the attention of the CHP couple? The concept of signification explains the initial contact between

Rodney King and the CHP officers. As David Matza (1969) stated, "signification becomes a specialized and protected function of the modern state. The main substance of that state function is the authorized ordaining of activities and persons as deviant, thus making them suitable objects of surveillance and control" (p. 145). In the case of Rodney King, there had to be some form of signification that initiated police surveillance of the vehicle and later control of the occupants of the vehicle. If the vehicle was not speeding as reported by the CHP officers, what were the factors that led officers to single out Rodney King for suspicion? As Matza points out, "The human selection of persons to be cast in one part or another is not blind, fortuitous or without purpose" (p. 151).

The officers perceived the King vehicle as representing a defiance of police authority. When King passed the CHP cruiser, this act was more than likely interpreted as a blatant defiance of the police. Defiance of police authority was further compounded when King failed to stop his vehicle in a timely manner. Skolnick and Fyfe's (1993) interpretation of such action is insightful.

> Regardless of how relatively minor the violations that lead to their flight, fleeing motorists commit a cardinal sin against the police: instead of submitting immediately, they challenge the police and attempt to escape their pursuer's authority. In doing so, in the eyes of police officers accustomed to motorists and other citizens who do not only submit immediately to police authority but even check their speedometers in the presence of police cars, fleeing motorists become prime candidates for painful lessons at the ends of police nightsticks. (p. 11)

The significance of King's behavior to the police is best understood by considering the interaction between state sponsored signification and police interpretation of authority. John Van Maanen (1995) captured the essence of this relationship:

> In a very real sense, the patrolman-to-citizen exchanges are moral contests in which the authority of the state is either confirmed, denied, or left in doubt. To the patrolman, such contests are not to be taken lightly, for the authority of the state is also his personal authority, and is, of necessity, a matter of some concern to him. To deny or raise doubt about his legitimacy is to shake the very ground upon which his self-image and corresponding views are built. (p. 316)

Adding to the signification of King as a deviant was the fact that the CHP couple saw three African-American youths on the interstate in the early morning hours. Combined with the defiant passing of the police vehicle these factors invited a formal response. In the eyes of the police, Rodney King and his friends were motoring deviants—sufficient cause to embark on a course that justifies, invites or warrants intervention and correction" (Matza, 1969, p. 155). The same situation, however, was probably viewed from a very different perspective from within the King vehicle. Rodney King and his friends were out joy riding "doing nothing especially wrong." Absent a legal justification for the stop and subsequent beating, officers had to construct the facts of the encounter in such a manner that state intervention and violence would be acceptable to a larger audience. This was accomplished, after the fact, by the official characterization of King as a dangerous deviant.

CONSTRUCTING REALITY

As the King case demonstrates, the police as public officials are free to inject speculation if not actual misrepresentation into accounts of police-citizen encounters. These constructions later become part of the official record that a jury or other fact finder uses to determine whether an officer's actions in a particular situation amounted to misconduct, a civil rights violation, or criminal behavior. Social definitions and constructed facts also play a major role in the public perception of police and citizen interactions. Police officers are in unique positions, as compared to victims, to characterize situations, events, and behaviors in such a fashion as to lend "official" credibility to their inferences, speculations or even fabrications. In the conversion from observation or fabrication to official reporting, information takes on new and more authoritative meaning. This characterization is tailored retroactively to match society's signification of deviance. The actual initial behavior of the citizens during the police encounter is replaced with behavior known to evoke a particular public response.

There were several police reasons for the social construction of the King beating. First, police wanted to insulate themselves from detection and to ensure public support for their actions by characterizing King as likely to engage in the deviance they fabricated. Second, they wanted to be able to secure a bargaining position if the charges against King were to come to court. Initially, the officers involved in the beating never conceived that they would stand trial for their abuse. In fact, most of the officers demonstrated astonishment and outright indignation at the prospect of facing a criminal trial. Officer Powell remarked following his Federal indictment that, "I didn't do anything wrong, so I can't believe that they're doing this again to me" (Reinhold, 1992, p. 2A). When Sergeant Koon was questioned about the federal trial he remarked, "Piece of cake, . . . It's just a matter of educating the jury" (Stewart, 1993c, p. 2A). Koon even showed up at federal court during his second trial wearing a Groucho Marx nose and glasses (Mathew, 1993). The beating had to be socially situated so that it could be accepted by peers, the department, and the public.

The construction of the reality of a police-citizen encounter is decidedly skewed in favor of the "officialized" police version of the incident. When police officers characterize brutality victims as drug users they are not required to advise citizens that they are free to have independent laboratory analysis conducted to counterbalance the characterization. Citizens may hear the constructed proofs of their officialized deviance only after it is impossible to refute the assertion and a stigma has already been attached to them.

Brutality victims, on the other hand, have no such "officializing" process. Victims of police brutality, even when litigating a civil rights claim against the police, are seldom allowed to characterize police departments as dangerous, violent or even criminal. It is a near certainty that the King juries did not hear of the alleged "death squad" operating within the LAPD. In the rare cases where assertions of this nature can be made, victims lack access to a source of authority that can transform assertions into official accounts. Even the investigating commission could not access the personnel files of the officers involved in the beating because of a court order which prohibited their examination (Christopher Commission, 1991a). Victims' characterizations, therefore, do not carry the force of an "official-authoritative" accounting of events or behaviors. Victims' characterizations must be developed based upon documented evidence which is more often than not under the control of police departments, collected for police use, and sanitized for police purposes. Remember that the Christopher Commission found the personnel records of the most violent LAPD officers were full of outstanding evaluations, commendations, and compliments by supervisors.

Unfortunately, a citizen must be injured to the extent that they require critical medical attention before they would have tangible evidence to counter any such police characterization. This was the case in the "King beating." Had Rodney King not suffered serious physical injuries that called for immediate medical attention and had the beating not been captured on video (Alpert et al., 1992), the violent drug-user characterization would have been left unchallenged and King would have remained just another inner-city, drug-crazed young man who attacked the police.

Even where police departments document incidents of brutality, complaints that are not sustained by police investigators or that are not markedly similar to the incident under review cannot be used to characterize a police agency as having a propensity toward violence. Police departments are allowed to fight the introduction of any such characterization vigorously, via official documents. There is very little to prevent the introduction of the official police characterization of the victim as a dangerous person, drug user, and criminal—labels that carry with them many previously constructed images (Kappeler, Blumberg & Potter, 1996).

While it is desirable to place police use of force within the context in which it was used, courts are less willing to admit into evidence the previous misconduct of a police officer that does not directly and significantly impact the officer's decision to use force in a given situation (*Robinson v. City of St. Charles, Missouri*, 1992). In fact, most courts will limit the evidence a plaintiff can use to the circumstance that immediately surrounded the officer's use of force and exclude any police wrongdoing that occurs before or after the incident under review (*Hopsin v. Fredericksen*, 1992; *Morgan v. City of Marmaduke, Arkansas*, 1992).

Did this practice affect the case of Rodney King? In August of 1993, following the federal court's sentencing of Koon and Powell, journalists uncovered a confidential internal affairs report that indicated the two officers had been involved in a previous beating. According to the report, Officer Powell had used excessive force in the arrest of Danny Ramos in October of 1990. The document indicated that Powell repeatedly struck the handcuffed suspect with a flashlight and that the use of force constituted "serious misconduct." Ironically, Sergeant Koon was also criticized in the document for failing to question Powell's use of force. During the incident, Koon was said to have used profanity and to have destroyed a piece of paper used by witnesses to record the officers' names (Associated Press, 1993). Unfortunately, the LAPD refrained from formally disciplining the officers until after the first trial concluded. The federal judge, John G. Davies, refused to allow the evidence to be admitted during the trial and characterized it as irrelevant to his sentencing decision. Officer speculation regarding a suspect's clarity of mind and inferences as to their alcohol and drug use (*Fernandez v. Leonard*, 1992; *Turner v. White*, 1992) or previous criminal behavior is often seen as directly relevant to an understanding of the context in which an officer used force—even if the officer had no knowledge of it at the time of the incident (*Gora v. Costa*, 1992; *Hafner v. Brown*, 1992; *Logan v. Drew*, 1992). With this advantage, police officers can characterize the victims of police violence in terms that neutralize claims of police deviance or criminality.

There are other indirect, constructed proofs available to the police to allege a brutality victim's criminality and drug use. What clear-minded citizen would run from the police? The ready conclusion is that anyone who runs from the police must have something to hide and in these situations police are justified in using force. The public rarely assumes the suspect may have been beaten by the police on a previous occasion or that certain segments of the population have learned by experience that police-citizen encounters sometimes result in violence. Resembling a criminal is a dangerous proposition in America. Drug users are violent, and criminals are the dangerous enemy in the war on crime. Police use of force has become an accepted justification for keeping the streets safe for law-abiding citizens.

SUMMARY

When citizens are characterized as drug users, it supports the inference that force was necessary in order to subdue the citizen. The constructed reality of drug use instructs the public that users are dangerous people with a propensity for violence. Characterization of citizens as drug users also tends to discredit the victim's account of the alleged police brutality, since drug use clouds judgment and perception. Social definitions inform us that anyone who would use drugs would also be capable of deceit.

Characterizing police brutality victims as drug users inhibits the ability of "ordinary" citizens to identify with the victim—thus making it less likely that a jury reviewing the incident can mentally put themselves in the place of the brutality victim. Characterizations affect the identification process required for establishing credibility with a white, middle-class, fact finder. The assigned new identity controls and overrides any other perception. Through official characterization, King became America's symbol of violence.

Drug and crime characterizations shift the perception of who was in control of the incident from the police to the victim. Therefore, public attention is shifted from what the police did to what the citizen failed to do. In effect, attention is deflected from police criminality to the victim's state-sponsored characterization. In doing so, attention is deflected from police deviance to questions of the victim's deviance.

Chapter Seven

POLICE PREJUDICE
AND DISCRIMINATION
The Investigation of Jeffrey Dahmer

> Equity suggests to the human mind many ideas that
> would not have occurred to it otherwise, and modifies
> nearly every idea that it already possesses.
> Alexis de Tocqueville (1805–1859)

P olice discrimination is inherently difficult to discuss. The topic is socially, politically, and emotionally charged. Regardless of whether their perceptions are correct, many citizens who feel harmed by the police attribute their difficulties to some form of prejudice or discrimination. Discussions of police discrimination are often tinged by strongly held attitudes and beliefs which have been forged by a person's life experiences.

The incidents of massive civil disorder in Los Angeles and other cities have been attributed in part to citizens' perceptions of unequal treatment by the justice system. A second difficulty in analyzing police discrimination is that many forms of police deviance have discriminatory undertones. The Rodney King case (discussed in the previous chapter), for example, includes many facets of prejudice and discrimination in addition to abuse of force. Elements of discrimination are often intertwined with other forms of deviance. Yet in some of these cases, it is especially difficult to determine whether the police were acting in an inherently discriminatory manner or if their acts merely had the appearance of discrimination. To illustrate, one might ask whether the Buddy Boys (discussed in chapter 8) robbed drug dealers because of their minority status, because they had money and little power to protect themselves, or because of a combination of these and other factors. A third factor that compounds the study of police discrimination is that discrimination is often difficult to prove—on many different levels. While some cases involve conspicuous discrimination, most forms of discrimination are far more subtle. For example, how does a motorist ticketed for a traffic violation prove that race discrimination precipitated the action rather than a violation of the law?

On a broader level, debate continues about whether the criminal justice system is (Georges-Abeyie, 1984; Mann, 1993), or is not (Wilbanks, 1987), discriminatory. Part of the problem in discussing the topic are the terms themselves. "Prejudice" and "discrimination" are used broadly and imprecisely. Police discrimination is not only a sensitive and emotionally laden issue, it is a complex topic with many facets. It is also one of the most important issues facing policing today. We begin our exploration of police discrimination by defining the terms prejudice and discrimination, considering some of the ways that police discrimination might be expressed, and discussing why police prejudice and discrimination are especially timely and important topics.

DIMENSIONS OF POLICE PREJUDICE AND DISCRIMINATION

The term *prejudice* means to "pre-judge." Prejudices, then, are preconceived attitudes, beliefs, or opinions. Conversely, to *discriminate* is to act upon the basis of a prejudice (Wilbanks, 1987). Succinctly stated, prejudice refers to an attitude while discrimination refers to a behavior. Distinguishing between the terms is important for two reasons. First, the distinctions signify that even if a person holds prejudicial attitudes, she or he may not act on those prejudices. Second, it should be noted that one can have both positive and negative prejudices (Carter, 1994a). To believe that teenagers from affluent families are not likely to commit delinquent acts is a positive prejudice. Conversely, to believe that most youths from poverty-stricken backgrounds routinely engage in serious crimes is a negative prejudice. This is not to imply a value, but rather a direction.

Prejudices are often based on characteristics such as color, race, ethnicity and gender. Table 7.1 illustrates that prejudices can be premised on a larger array of elements. For example, police may have prejudices about the type of car one drives (luxury or economy, foreign or domestic), one's address (exclusive upper-class or poverty-stricken ghetto), one's occupation (police or nonpolice), or a combination of these and other factors. Moreover, these prejudices may be positive or negative. These multifaceted aspects make it extremely difficult to assess whether prejudice exists and what remedies to propose.

Table 7.1
Attributes Subject to Police Prejudicial Attitudes

Race	Sexual Orientation
Ethnicity	Type of Crime Committed
Skin Color	Prior Criminal Record
Age	Appearance
Gender	Occupational Background
Religious Background	Physical or Mental Disability
Nationality	Geographic Origin
Social Class	

In policing, prejudices may be expressed in discriminatory acts on many different levels. Table 7.2 shows the major dimensions of discrimination in policing. It also illustrates that discrimination can be passive or active. In passive discrimination, police choose to withhold protection or benefits of the law. This would include, for example, instances

Table 7.2
Dimensions of Police Discrimination

	Expressed Internally	Expressed Externally
By Administrators/ Managers	*Examples* • Refusing to place female officers in "dangerous" assignments • Placing minority employees in undesirable assignments • Promotion decisions made on the basis of race/ethnicity or other factors not related to the ability to perform the job • Refusing to commend officers for exceptional performance on the basis of such factors as race/ethnicity, gender, age, etc. • Segregation in assignment by assigning only African-American officers to work together as partners or Caucasian officers to work together as partners • Failing to take corrective action when subordinates discriminate against co-workers	*Examples* • Making selective arrest decisions on the basis of such factors as race/ethnicity, gender, political, or religious affiliation • Refusing to respond to complaints by minority citizens or neighborhoods predominantly populated by minorities • Using police resources and personnel to harass certain segments of the community (e.g., businesses, community groups) • By practice or custom, failing to provide police services to minority segments of the community (e.g., homosexuals, ethnic groups, religious groups) • Failing to take corrective action when officers discriminate against citizens
By Officers	*Examples* • Intimidating minority officers by threatening not to back them up on calls • Making racist or sexist comments in the presence of minority officers • Writing graffiti or posting offensive pictures on lockers belonging to minority officers • Sexual harassment	*Examples* • Not trying to solve crimes where minorities are victims • Harassing youths, college students, or other groups • Hassling businesses patronized by minorities • Not responding to, or purposefully delaying response to, calls in minority neighborhoods • Use of racial slurs or derogatory language when dealing with Hispanic citizens

where police refuse to investigate assaults against homosexuals believing that they "got what was coming to them." Conversely, police engage in active discrimination when they differentially enforce laws or department policies. Police actively discriminate when they target African-American citizens for traffic stops to discourage them from frequenting certain areas of a city.

Although anyone in a police agency may engage in discriminatory acts, most discrimination can be classified into one of the four categories listed in table 7.2. One dimension of the matrix shows that police administrators or managers may engage in discriminatory behavior. Moreover, discrimination by administrators or managers can take place internally or externally.

- Sublette County, Wyoming Deputy Sheriff Rhonda Griggs won a $7,539 judgment against the Sheriff's Department. Griggs claimed that she and two male deputies were demoted, but only her salary was reduced. [*USA Today*, 8/31/92, p. 8A]
- A Federal Bureau of Investigation agent and his supervisor were suspended for forcing a black lawyer to submit to a footprint. The lawyer had been appointed to a federal judgeship and the agents told the lawyer that it was a part of the normal procedure required of newly appointed judges. Following the incident the agents hung the print on the wall and joked about it. [*USA Today*, 7/20/92, p. 5A]

The case of the Sublette County female deputy illustrates internal discrimination, while the latter case is an example of external supervisory discrimination.

As is the case with supervisors or administrators, police officers may engage in discriminatory acts that are focused either internally or externally. In the last chapter we touched on the issue of racism—which is one form of discrimination—among members of the Los Angeles Police Department (LAPD). In addition to unacceptable levels of racism among the agency's rank and file, the Christopher Commission (1991) also found sexism and homophobia. Many LAPD officers openly expressed negative and stereotypical views about female officers. Examples of internally directed gender bias were abundant.

- "Female police officers don't want to do anything but collect a paycheck."
- "A lot of male officers prefer working with men over women. For me, *it's a question of upper body strength*. The department needs a more stringent height requirement" [Italics added].
- "I know most officers have problems working with female officers and dislike working with them because they believe women don't have the *physical stature* to do the job."

- "Many male officers feel very uncomfortable dealing with a physical situation when a female officer is partnered with them."
- "Female officers generally cannot back up officers."
- "Female officers sometimes exacerbate the situation because they feel the need to assert themselves or escalate the potential for use of force."
- "I clearly won't get involved in some situations if I have a female partner. It's protective. It's not a question of comfort, but of safety. I'm more inclined to lay back and evaluate the situation if I have a woman partner. They're just not as strong." (Christopher Commission 1991b, p. 87)

As table 7.2 indicates, prejudice by police officers may also be directed externally toward members of the community. Many of the comments made by male LAPD officers on the Moble Digitial Terminals MDTs) illustrate a conceptual linkage between sexist attitudes and violence—with officers often expressing a desire to control and abuse female citizens.

- "U won't believe this . . . that female call again said susp returned . . . I'll check it out then I'm going to stick my baton in her."
- "Ohh, I just fuckin love it when you talk sexy."
- "U wanna partake w/me my little love bud."
- "Do you know where your pussy is."
- "No but I left a 14 year old girl handcuffed naked on my chin-up bar wearing nothing but a blind-fold and salad oil . . . I'd like to ck on her."
- ". . . 415 female, huh . . . well, just slap that silly broad senseless."
- "Your getting a new boot from Academy . . . a breathtakin blonde with huge kazoopers"

Some members of the LAPD held strong prejudices toward sexual preferences. Many officers showed an open disdain for citizens with alternative sexual lifestyles. Officers expressed deep resentment that these citizens were invading their occupation. Again, a review of a few of the comments from the computerized communications records noted by the Christopher Commission (1991b) shows the attitudes held by the officers.

- "No. 1600 how many homosexuals did you give orals to today"
- "That's a touchy subject . . . not fit for MDTing . . ."
- "Just finished writing 4 tickets to some poo buts"
- "Did you check your fruits at the park . . . I hope you watered them . . ."
- "I figured how to get rid of them . . . I'm sending in a bunch of naked girls, that will scare them away . . ."
- "I'll c u at the County Jail bun-boy . . ."
- "If I W25 a bun-boy you'd be asking to sleep over my house homo"
- "Houston PD has a new chief Elizabeth Watson 40 yrs old . . ."

• "I bet that's going over reeeeeaaalll good with the troops dude . . . they have some dyke bleeding heart for a mayor . . ." (p. 89)

Prejudice and discrimination in policing take on all the forms of bias found in the larger society. Some have maintained that racial and ethnic prejudices held by the police are no more pervasive than the prejudices found in other social or occupational groups (Carter, 1994a). While this proposition may be correct, understanding police prejudice and the environment in which these sentiments are nurtured is very important. Unlike the members of many other occupations, police hold unique positions of power in society. In addition to the powers they hold, the police are the most visible symbol of the justice system. The distinction between police prejudice and biases found in other, less public occupations is that police can act on their beliefs in their official capacity as representatives of the government. Whether the police hold prejudicial sentiments to a greater extent than other members of society is not as important as the idea that even isolated cases of prejudice have a major impact on public perceptions of police and the justice system. Discriminatory behavior by a few officers can contaminate the reputation of an entire department.

Society has certain expectations about how the police provide law enforcement and social services. The public expects police to enforce the law fairly and impartially and to provide citizens from all walks of life the equal protection and benefit of law. Equally important is the expectation that all citizens will receive equal access to police services. If the police categorize citizens into stereotypic groups, there is often a companion belief that certain segments of the community are less deserving of protection. Essentially, when police act on personal prejudices while performing their jobs, they discriminate in the allocation of either services or enforcement of the law. Discrimination often takes the form of either choosing to enforce the law differentially or to withhold benefits.

While prejudice may have been a contributing factor in the LAPD beating of Rodney G. King, the Milwaukee Police Department's (MPD) investigation in the Jeffrey Dahmer case presents chilling evidence of the tragic consequences of police prejudice. More specifically, the incident illustrates the linkage that often exists between police prejudice, discrimination and deviance. In the remainder of this chapter, we explore one aspect of the case where there is strong evidence to support the allegation that members of the MPD failed to extend the full protection of the law to a citizen because of assumptions police officers made about the citizen's sexual orientation and lifestyle.

INVESTIGATION OF THE SEXUAL ABUSE OF KONERAK SINTHASOMPHONE

Many of the facts of the serial killings of Jeffrey Dahmer have become public knowledge, and much media attention has been given to the bizarre nature of his crimes. Far less attention, however, has been paid to the information that surfaced concerning the behaviors of certain members of the MPD who initially made contact with Dahmer months before he extended his killing spree and was eventually apprehended by the police.

In the spring of 1991, Jeffrey Dahmer (white, thirty-one, working in a chocolate factory) was on probation for molesting and sexually abusing a male child. As a result of his criminal conviction, Dahmer served ten months in a house of corrections and was later released on probation. While still on probation for child sexual abuse, Dahmer lured Konerak Sinthasomphone (Laotian and fourteen years old) to his Milwaukee apartment with the promise of money if he posed for photographs. Once there, Dahmer drugged, tortured, and sexually abused the child. In the early morning hours of May 27, 1991, Dahmer left his apartment to buy beer. Seizing the opportunity, Sinthasomphone escaped onto the streets of Milwaukee looking for help. Drugged, naked, and bleeding from his rectum the child staggered about the streets outside Dahmer's apartment until two young African-American women, Nichole Childress and Sandra Smith, saw Sinthasomphone and called an emergency telephone operator.

To Childress and Smith, it was painfully obvious that Sinthasomphone had been abused by Dahmer. The women communicated the following information to a 911 operator from a phone booth only a block away from Dahmer's apartment.

> I'm on 25th and State, and there is this young man. He's buck naked.
> He has been beaten up . . . He is really hurt . . . He needs help (*Estate*,
> 1992, p. 1345).

The emergency telephone operator dispatched both police and paramedics to the scene. While Nichole Childress and Sandra Smith were waiting for help, Dahmer located Sinthasomphone and attempted to recapture him. Dahmer's attempt was blocked by the two women who intervened long enough for the police to arrive. MPD Officers John Balcerzak, Joseph Gabrish, Richard Porubcan, and a police trainee arrived at the scene and directed the emergency medical personnel to leave the area. After a cursory investigation into the incident, the MPD officers returned Sinthasomphone to Dahmer's apartment. About twenty minutes after the officers had returned the youth to Dahmer, a concerned citizen called police to find out what had been done to help Sinthasomphone. The caller was informed that everything was under control. It was later learned that soon after the officers left the scene, Dahmer killed Sinthasomphone.

Little was apparently done about the Sinthasomphone incident until July 22, 1991 when a hysterical man, wearing a handcuff on one wrist and running down the street, flagged a MPD cruiser. The man, Tracey Edwards, told the officers how he had been held captive and attacked by Dahmer. The two MPD officers went to Dahmer's apartment and detected a foul odor. Investigating further, the officers uncovered evidence of sexual abuse, torture, mutilation, and murder. The evidence included photographs of victims, human body parts, and the body of Sinthasomphone. During the ensuing investigation into Dahmer's killings, officials discovered the incident of two months earlier when the officers had returned Sinthasomphone to the custody of the killer.

While there was local outrage and charges that the incident reflected an established pattern of racist and homophobic behavior by the MPD, the issue was muted at the national level by the sensationalism of the atrocities that Dahmer committed. Sufficient public pressure was brought about, however, to cause Mayor John O. Norquist to appoint a citizen commission to investigate the charges of systematic racism and prejudice in the MPD.

While it is important to understand the factual scenario surrounding the MPD's failure to protect Sinthasomphone, it is equally important to consider the context in which this omission took place. In the sections that follow, consideration is given to the environment in which MPD officers worked by drawing on information uncovered by the citizen commission's investigation of the MPD, the information gleaned from comments made to news reporters, and the issues raised in a civil case brought against the City of Milwaukee as a result of the officers' failure to take measures to protect the child.

THE MPD'S WORKING ENVIRONMENT

When the Dahmer investigation began in 1991, the MPD was headed by Chief Philip Arreola who had been in office for about two years. According to reports, Arreola was an advocate of community-oriented policing and attempted, with substantial resistance, to move the department in that direction. Because of the limited time Chief Arreola had spent in office, his ability to affect the department's environment, personnel, and operations was limited.

Former Chief Harold Breier served in the department from 1940 to 1984; the long tenure had a substantial impact on the department. In fact, the Mayor's Citizen Commission (1991) noted that about three-fourths of the department's personnel, including most of those in command positions, had joined the force while Breier was chief. Breier's philosophy of policing was captured in a comment he made in August of 1991. The chief stated:

> You can take community policing and stick it in your ear. There's no substitute for strong law enforcement. First, a police officer doesn't have the training to take care of all the social ills of the city. And second, he should be so busy maintaining law and order that he doesn't have time for that crap. . . . When I was chief we were relating to the good people, and we were relating to the other people too—we were throwing those people in the can. . . . I always said, "The good people of Milwaukee, they bought what the Department was selling."
> (Mayor's Citizen Commission, 1991, p. 9)

Like LAPD's Chief Gates, Breier was an up-through-the-ranks chief who endorsed a hard-nosed approach to law enforcement and policing. To Chief Breier, people could be classified quite simply as "good" or "bad." Yet as the Mayor's Citizen Commission noted, the good/bad distinction used by officers in the MPD was all too often based on prejudices and resulted in discrimination.

At the time of the Dahmer investigation, the population of the City of Milwaukee was 63 percent white, 30 percent black, 2 percent Asian American and 1 percent Native American. MPD personnel, on the other hand, were 82 percent white, 12 percent African American and about 6 percent Hispanic and Native American (BJS, 1992). This picture of MPD personnel fails to show the dramatic underrepresentation of minorities at command levels in the police department. For example, in 1986, of 47 captains on the police force only 1 was African American; of 49 lieutenants, only 2 were African Americans and one was Native American; of 118 sergeants, only 9 were African American; and of 203 detectives, only 16 were African Americans, 2 were Native Americans, and 3 were Hispanic (Mayor's Citizen Commission, 1991, p. 28). In 1986, not a single female held a ranking position in the department. In 1987, only 8.6 percent of the officers in the entire department were female (Reaves, 1989). While 1991 statistics showed an overall improvement in minority representation as compared with previous years (because of a consent decree), the MPD had not yet reached gender or minority parity with the composition of the city. Even the rate of attrition among female and minority police officers was high, suggesting that the MPD was an undesirable place for women and minorities to work.

The gender and racial composition of a police department can be the product of many factors that are not the result of intentional bias or discrimination. As David Carter (1994) cautions,

> If most officers are white, while the preponderance of citizens in a given geographic area are of a racial or ethnic minority, then interac-

tion between the police and the community may have the appearance
of discrimination . . . police discrimination may largely be perceived
rather than a real phenomenon. (p. 306)

This was clearly not the case in the MPD. The composition of Milwaukee's police force was the result of intentional and systematic discrimination in the selection of police personnel. The Mayor's Citizen Commission (1991) found clear evidence of intentional racial discrimination in
the methods and techniques used to select citizens for police service. The
commission noted that:

> we have heard testimony which suggests that investigators "dig
> deeper" for disqualifying factors when investigating candidates from
> racial minority groups, or disqualified these candidates for factors
> which do not result in disqualification for other candidates. (p. 31)

Discrimination in the selection of police officers was not limited to racial
or ethnic discrimination. The commission also uncovered evidence of discrimination based on sexual preference. Consider the commission's
remarks: "We have heard testimony from employers and pastors who
were asked about a candidate's sexual orientation. We have been told
that candidates are reluctant to complain about these questions because
they fear not being hired if they complain" (Mayor's Citizen Commission,
1991, p. 31). In essence, the MPD manipulated the selection process so
that minorities and citizens who led alternative lifestyles were systematically excluded from employment with the department. Because of discriminatory selection practices, Milwaukee's police force failed to reflect
the diversity of the community it served.

DEFICIENT OVERSIGHT OR SUBCULTURE OF PREJUDICE AND DISCRIMINATION?

Again, failure of a police department to reflect the diversity of the
community served does not automatically mean that officers discriminate
against citizens. It is possible for a police organization to perform its function without discriminating on the basis of such factors as color, race, sex,
or preferences in lifestyle. This, however, was not the case with the MPD.
Information obtained through interviews with Milwaukee citizens
revealed a pattern of externally focused discrimination by both officers
and supervisors. For example, when white citizens living in the inner city
called police to report crimes, they were sometimes told, "Don't call us,
call a moving van" (Mayor's Citizen Commission, 1991, p. 21). Citizens
who were the victims of "gay bashing" were advised by police that the violence directed toward them was their "own fault," a clear implication that

homosexuals should expect to be victimized because they deserved it.

> Victims and witnesses of all races and sexual orientations report examples of police officers as exacerbators of community tension and violence at scenes of incidents, rather than as peace makers. Our police officers seem to need improved and updated training in being peace officers: to resolve conflicts, to calm people who are hostile or distraught; to treat people as individuals, not as stereotypes; and to see members of the community as allies and aides, not as enemies. (Mayor's Citizen Commission, 1991, p. 21)

The commission went on to note that MPD officers often aggravated already tense situations with citizens by their use of insensitive, or outright offensive, remarks. Testimony taken by the commission revealed that officers discriminated against citizens on the basis of race/ethnicity, gender, sexual orientation, age, and social class. Importantly, the commission pointed out that pervasive externally focused discrimination by officers could not take place without either the implicit or explicit approval of other officers and police supervisors. The commission emphasized the need to break the code of silence that prevents officers from reporting errant fellow officers. Perhaps even more significant was the commission's realization that police supervisors must be held accountable for ensuring that discriminatory behavior by officers is corrected and stopped. "There must be a clear message from command staff, reinforced by the organization structure, that misbehavior of this kind will not be tolerated" (Mayor's Citizen Commission, 1991, p. 24).

There was also evidence of internal discrimination. Women and people of color who were working in the MPD were surveyed in a 1991 study sponsored by the Bradley Institute for Democracy and Public Values. The survey revealed that regardless of race or ethnicity, women in the department reported low levels of acceptance by their male colleagues. In some cases, male officers were openly hostile toward female employees. Both factors contributed to the creation of an adverse working environment for female employees. The survey also revealed that even though male and female minority employees said that the department had an official equal opportunity policy and that the testing process itself seemed fair, there were more subtle forms of discrimination at work in the MPD. In particular, both male and female minority employees reported that they had not been appointed to special assignments, nor had they been provided with opportunities to develop experience in various work positions. They believed that both types of job opportunities were important for success and advancement in the MPD.

The commission noted that it made little sense for the MPD to recruit persons for a diverse police force if those who were selected did not remain employed with the department. To rectify internal discrimination, the MPD must create a working environment in which officers are respected for their work and in which race, sex, or sexual orientation are irrelevant. The Chief must declare an unambiguous Departmental policy on valuing diversity among its members, and must enforce discipline against violators of this policy . . . . Testimony we heard supports this concern; we have also been told that gay men and lesbians in the MPD feel that they cannot be open about their sexual orientation because of the attitudes of their coworkers. Chief Arreola must recognize the contributions of gays and lesbians to the Department, as well as the contributions of African Americans, Native Americans, Hispanics, and others. (Mayor's Citizen Commission, 1991, p. 29).

What happened in the Sinthasomphone case does not appear to have been an anomaly where officers either did not interpret the situation correctly or erred in making a decision about how to handle the call. Instead, there is much evidence to characterize the MPD as having a strong subculture of prejudice and discrimination. Investigations of the MPD's working environment revealed that there were several reported incidents where officers discriminated against both citizens and peers. Supervisors and administrators contributed to a situation where prejudice and discrimination were permitted to flourish. Little was done by supervisors, for example, when officers discriminated against members of the public. In addition, administrators failed to hold first-line supervisors accountable for blatant discriminatory acts committed by officers. There were also indications that MPD supervisory personnel subtly discriminated against minority officers by limiting their opportunities to become well-rounded employees and thus strong candidates for promotion or prestigious assignments. In sum, discrimination in the MPD took all of the forms identified in the typology presented earlier in the chapter. Supervisory personnel and officers engaged in discriminatory practices that were directed both internally and externally. This was the existing climate when officers chose to handle the Sinthasomphone case as they did.

DISTURBING FACTS AND OMISSIONS

Several shocking details came to light in the investigation of MPD's handling of the Sinthasomphone case. As discussed earlier, Nichole Childress and Sandra Smith, the two African-American women who had called police, were convinced that something was terribly wrong and delayed Dahmer until police and paramedics could arrive on scene. Sinthasomphone's distressed state was sufficient to alarm the witnesses, but the officers—for whatever reason—told paramedics that they were not needed and dismissed them. Despite having medical personnel available at the scene, police failed to request even a cursory examination to check for injuries.

Childress, Smith, and others tried to tell officers that Sinthasomphone was a juvenile, that they believed he was trying desperately to escape from Dahmer, and that Dahmer had referred to Sinthasomphone using several different names—signifying that the two were neither friends, lovers, nor close associates. Bystanders also attempted to tell the officers that Sinthasomphone was under the influence of drugs or alcohol and that he had been assaulted and sexually abused. Witnesses later recounted that during the entire time MPD officers were at the scene, the child seemed to be fearful of Dahmer. In response, the police allegedly threatened to arrest Childress and Smith if they persisted in trying to provide them information or if they continued to request that the police further investigate the incident. Police also threatened Smith and Childress with arrest if they tried to intervene to help the boy. In essence, police deliberately and intentionally refused to listen to information provided by witnesses at the scene and actively prevented citizens from helping the child.

Dahmer purportedly explained to the police that Sinthasomphone was an adult, that he and Sinthasomphone were homosexual lovers, and that they had simply had an argument. Presented with contradictory stories, officers at the scene could have requested more information from both Dahmer and Sinthasomphone. Had the police tried to verify information provided by Dahmer, they might have found that Dahmer was on probation for sexually abusing Sinthasomphone's younger brother. No inquiry about Dahmer was made by police. Given charges from bystanders that Sinthasomphone was a child, officers also could have sought more information about Sinthasomphone's status. Instead, they apparently accepted Dahmer's version of the situation and "ultimately delivered Sinthasomphone into Dahmer's custody, without obtaining consent from Sinthasomphone or his parents" (*Estate*, 1992, p. 1346). Although officers were inside Dahmer's small apartment, they failed to detect anything out of the ordinary, even though by then Dahmer had killed and dismembered several victims in the apartment. In fact, Dahmer had murdered and dismembered the body of another young boy just two days before officers were in the apartment. Dahmer later revealed that minutes after police left the apartment, he strangled Sinthasomphone, had sex with the body, and took photographs as he dismembered the corpse. As he did in other murders, Dahmer kept Sinthasomphone's skull, allegedly planning to construct some sort of altar in the apartment.

Witnesses who had observed the Sinthasomphone incident, however, were still not convinced that the matter had been properly handled by the police. Glenda Cleveland, the concerned African-American citizen mentioned earlier, called police advising them that she was very worried about the child's safety since police had returned him to Dahmer. In addition, Ms. Cleveland insisted that Sinthasomphone was a child and not an adult as presumed by the police. In response, police gave false assurance to Ms. Cleveland, and other concerned callers, that the situation was under control and that the child was, in fact, an adult. It was later learned that officers joked among themselves about the incident and characterized it as a homosexual lovers' spat.

Tragically, Dahmer murdered at least four other young men after Sinthasomphone. An attorney representing the family of one of the four youths argued that officers didn't fully investigate the Sinthasomphone incident because the victim was Laotian, the complainants were African American, and Dahmer and Sinthasomphone were believed to be homosexuals. "If [Sinthasomphone] had been white there is a high probability there would have been a more thorough investigation and Mr. Dahmer would have been taken off the streets, not left out there to sacrifice people" (Editor, 1991a, p. 5).

Allegations of discrimination in the case were perhaps best summed up in a civil rights lawsuit filed against the City of Milwaukee by the victims' families. Attorneys for the families of the dead youths argued that the MPD had a long history of discriminating against racial minorities and homosexuals. Furthermore, the suit alleged, MPD officers who handled the Sinthasomphone call were products of the department's discriminatory policies.

> This caused them not to perceive that crimes had been committed before their arrival, and were continuing before their eyes on May 27, 1991. It caused them to treat "an obviously serious and grave incident with deliberate indifference, and jocularity, as if it were somehow comical." It caused them to disregard a call from a concerned black citizen, shortly after Sinthasomphone was returned to Dahmer, in which the caller insisted that Sinthasomphone was a child. It caused the police to disregard information that a reported missing person, Konerak Sinthasomphone, was the victim in the May 27 incident. (*Estate*, 1992, p. 1347)

The depth of the influence of the working environment in the MPD was evident in the reaction of the rank-and-file members once details of the Sinthasomphone case became known. They vociferously supported the three officers who had handled the call on May 27, 1991. In a police union survey conducted after Chief Arreola suspended the three officers, 93 percent of the department's officers said they had no confidence in Arreola's ability to run the department. Even more telling was the finding that 98 percent of the officers thought the suspensions were wrong (Editor, 1991b). In another survey of MPD personnel conducted by the *Milwaukee Journal*, officers reported that they felt betrayed by the criticism heaped on the department by the City's citizens (Newspaper Survey, 1991b).

The surveys reveal the apparent inability of MPD personnel to understand that to have public support and respect for the police, the police must first support and respect the community served. The tragedy for Milwaukee officers was also apparent in the newspaper survey. Officers were not only frustrated in their jobs, but they had a host of personal problems:

> 37 percent said they drank excessively; 12 percent admitted having become physically violent with a member of their family; and 16 percent said they had sought counseling . . . ; and 35 percent had become physically ill because of something they witnessed on the job. (Editor, 1991c, p. 5)

SUMMARY

Police prejudice and discrimination may be the most sensitive topics in policing today. Society expects that the police will use their unique positions of power without regard to such factors as race/ethnicity, gender, religious background, and social class. The public expects the police to perform their jobs fairly and impartially. When even a few officers in an agency engage in discriminatory behavior, the reputation of an entire department can be tainted in the eyes of the public.

In general, discrimination in policing can be expressed internally (inside of the department) or externally (toward the public). Both supervisors and officers, moreover, can engage in discriminatory behavior. Discriminatory behavior by officers with an external focus can be passive (where officers withhold benefits or protections of the law) or active (where officers differentially enforce laws or department policies). Few cases illustrate the many facets of police prejudice and discrimination as clearly as the grievous details surrounding the death of Konerak Sinthasomphone.

Chapter Eight

DRUG-RELATED POLICE DEVIANCE
The Buddy Boys Case

We live counterfeit lives in order to resemble
the idea we first had of ourselves.
Andre Gide   (1869–1951)

Few contemporary social issues have generated so much attention as the illicit drug problem. Public opinion polls show that Americans consider illegal drugs to be one of our nation's most pressing problems. Criminologists as well as politicians have repeatedly emphasized a connection between drug usage and criminality, and it is estimated that local and state police expenditures exceed $10 billion annually for the "war on drugs" (Dennis, 1990)—which amounts to more than 20 percent of their total budgets (Nadelman, 1989). Although it is difficult to gauge expenditures on illegal drugs accurately, some estimates suggest that Americans spend anywhere from $40 billion (Wilson, 1990) to $140 billion (Bureau of Justice Statistics, 1992b) each year on illegal drugs. Revenues from the sale of cocaine alone are estimated at about $50 billion each year.

It is clear that enormous profits can be made in illegal drug markets. The immense profits in the illicit drug market, coupled with intensive drug enforcement efforts, have led to the corruption of police and other criminal justice personnel. Virtually every law enforcement agency in the country has been touched by some form of drug corruption (Carter, 1990). Consider this sampling of newspaper reports on drug-related police corruption from across the country:

- Dale Jones, a former Ford Heights, Illinois police officer, was sentenced Friday to 14 years in prison for taking bribes from 3 narcotics dealers to overlook their distribution of crack and cocaine. [*Chicago Tribune*, 10/25/1997, p. 1.]
- A west Texas Sheriff was sentenced to life in prison for assisting drug smugglers in transporting about $48 million worth of cocaine across the Mexican boarder into the United States. [*Chicago Tribune*, 1/5/97, p. 1]
- Washington, D.C. police officer Fonda Moore was indicted and charged with assisting a drug trafficking ring. [*USA Today*, 7/1/92, p. 9A]
- A Floyd County, Kentucky deputy sheriff, Larry Newsome, pled guilty to 5 counts of drug trafficking. The plea was in exchange for dismissing 4 other charges against the deputy. The guilty plea involved the deputy's sale of 261 tablets of a controlled substance. The deputy had served as chairman of the boards of two well-known medical clinics in the area. [*Courier-Journal*, 8/25/92, p. B5]

As these cases illustrate, illegal drugs may be connected to police deviance in several ways. Before discussing drug-related police deviance, it may be helpful to consider a few of the ways that police may be "corrupted" by illicit narcotics. Off-duty police may use drugs for "recreational" purposes. Of the various forms of drug-related police deviance, off-duty recreational drug use may involve the greatest number of officers

(Carter & Stephens, 1994). A second form of drug-related police deviance is on-duty drug use by police officers. Not only are these officers potential safety hazards, they may also be more vulnerable to manipulation and corruption because of their illegal behavior. While little is known about police on-duty drug use, Peter B. Kraska and Victor E. Kappeler (1988) found that about 20 percent of the officers they studied in a medium-sized department used marijuana twice a month or more while on-duty.

A third form of drug-related police deviance occurs in cases where officers violate the rights of defendants by planting evidence in order to make arrests, committing perjury to obtain convictions, or through other means to penalize drug users and sellers. In this form of drug-related deviance, the police pursue ostensibly legitimate goals. In the process, they subvert the constitutional guarantees they are charged with protecting. Officers may attempt to justify this form of deviant behavior by criticizing prohibitively restrictive laws and agency rules.

A fourth broader category of drug-related police deviance is what Carter (1990) refers to as traditionally conceptualized drug corruption. In this form of deviance, officers seek personal gain. Traditional drug corruption may involve a host of illicit activities. Officers might, for instance, permit drug dealers to operate in exchange for payoffs to look the other way. This form of deviance also includes officers who confiscate and keep drugs or money discovered on arrestees (*Brown v. State's Atty.*, 1992) and those who carry out robberies of narcotics traffickers. Officers who steal drugs, cash, or other property from police property rooms (*Cooper v. City of Greenwood, Miss.*, 1990) fall into the classification of traditional drug corruption.

A final category of drug-related police deviance revolves around the police use of violence (Manning & Redlinger, 1977, 1978). This category includes officers who use physical force to extract information from suspects and who threaten the use of violence against drug users or dealers (*Ting v. United States*, 1991). Examples are numerous: officers who beat or torture suspects; threaten them by placing loaded weapons to their heads (*McDonald v. Haskins*, 1992); or wantonly demolish a suspect's residence while ostensibly searching for narcotics.

Clearly drug-related police deviance involves a number of possible activities. Officers may be involved in one or more of these forms of deviance simultaneously. Officers engaged in drug-related deviance are likely to be involved in other forms of corruption and misconduct. The "Buddy Boys," a group of officers working in the New York City Police Department's 77th precinct, offer a notorious example of the many different facets of drug-related police deviance.

THE BUDDY BOYS CASE

The 77th precinct is known as one of New York City's toughest and poorest; it has also developed a reputation for having some of the most corrupt cops. While once considered a prominent part of Brooklyn, the 77th precinct began to experience radical transformation in the 1950s and 1960s. As in other cities, an influx of minorities was followed by a massive exodus of white citizens. At the same time, the economic infrastructure of the area began to deteriorate, as did social cohesion. By the late 1970s, the precinct had become a crime-ridden ghetto known as "Black Brooklyn" (McAlary, 1987). By the mid-1980s, the 77th precinct was one of the biggest centers of drug traffic in New York City. Some dealers operating in the area distributed mimeographed flyers containing the addresses of crack houses, prices, and hours of operation (Smothers, 1986). In 1986, there were 205 uniformed officers and 17 sergeants to deal with these types of problems (Havesi, 1986).

A group of police officers who worked in the 77th precinct from around 1980 to the latter part of 1986 came to be known as the "Buddy Boys." Thirty-eight officers were ultimately disciplined by the department; a few were key players. Officer Henry Winter was one. In 1986 when the Buddy Boys case broke, he had worked six of his nine years as a New York City police officer in the 77th precinct. Winter was an outspoken maverick who was known for his outrageous antics both on and off the job. Winter's partner, Tony Magno, was a seventeen-year veteran who worked as a patrol officer for his entire career. A publicly reticent person who avoided taking credit for arrests because he did not want to have to testify in court, Magno was an "old-time" cop who was liked and respected by other officers in the precinct. Another key player in the Buddy Boys case was Brian O'Regan. O'Regan was an ex-marine who also had about nine years experience with the New York Police Department in 1986. In addition to being a meticulous strategist in planning illegal activities for the Buddy Boys, O'Regan was also called "Space Man" because peers questioned his mental health (McAlary, 1987). The precinct's union representative, William "Junior" Gallagher, was considered by his colleagues to be egotistical, pretentious, and arrogant. He was also deeply involved in corrupt activities in the precinct and was ultimately charged with eighty-six criminal counts (Purdum, 1987). Robert Rathbun worked as an undercover officer in the anti-crime unit; he would be found guilty of 37 criminal offenses for his role in the Buddy Boys case (Buder, 1987c). The Buddy Boys were involved in virtually every form of drug-related police deviance noted above. While impractical to review all of the known illegal activities, we will use the typology of different forms of drug-related police deviance to categorize some of their corrupt acts.

Off- and On-Duty Substance Abuse

There is evidence that officers working in the 77th precinct were involved in both off- and on-duty drug use. McAlary (1987) sketched a general picture of police officer drug use in the precinct.

> Certainly the 77th Precinct had a drug problem. Some officers smoked marijuana in their patrol cars on the late tour and snorted cocaine in the locker room lounge. Many more used drugs off duty, snorting cocaine with girlfriends they had met in the precinct while working. It was not at all unusual for a cop in the 77th Precinct to leave his wife and kids in the suburbs for a prostitute in the slum. (pp. 106–107)

Officer Henry Winter acknowledged that he would occasionally smoke marijuana with friends at social gatherings. Winter also admitted to using more dangerous drugs while on-duty, offering justifications for his illegal behavior.

> I never touched coke until I got to the precinct. And I just wanted to see what the hell it was. I wasn't an addict or anything. It's like—say you're doing an eight-to-four tour, and you wind up going through the four-to-twelve to the midnight-to-eight, then you come back, you work and do another eight-to-four. You're tired. You do some coke. It was a nice feeling. Kept you up, kept you aware, kept you awake. (McAlary, 1987, p. 108)

Later in his career, Winter sampled and used drugs that were confiscated from arrestees, sometimes working parts of his shifts in a haze. Many other officers in the 77th precinct were also engaged in illegal drug use both on- and off-duty. Crystal Spivey, a female officer in the precinct, was allegedly receiving an eighth of a gram of cocaine each week in exchange for protecting a dealer. Ironically, the dealer was Spivey's boyfriend, and he testified against her at her trial for possession of narcotics. Another officer, Peter Heron (nicknamed Peter Heroin by fellow officers), was fired for using heroin while on the job. Thomas Texiera, a veteran officer in the 77th precinct, was terminated following a positive drug test. Texiera was forced to take the test after a man complained that he had seen his wife and Texiera smoking marijuana together (McAlary, 1987).

Drug use was so common in the 77th precinct that on-duty alcohol use barely raised an eyebrow. For example, Johnny Massar, a veteran with thirty-five years experience on the force, routinely drank while on duty. As the precinct's assistant station house officer, "His principle responsibility was to keep a ready supply of cold beer on hand" (McAlary, 1987, p. 99). The precinct's locker room and lounge were regularly used by officers as a makeshift bar. Buddy Boy Tony Magno frequently arrived at the station house at least a couple of hours before his shift in order to socialize and drink beer with other officers. As did other officers, Magno would drink beer while patrolling in his cruiser or in neighborhood bodegas during his shift. Henry Winter admitted that on some shifts, he and Magno would only respond to radio calls that they absolutely had to handle:

> We'd do a job and shoot back to Macho's Bodega . . . for a beer. We sat in the back on milk boxes, drinking bottles of beer and playing with the roaches, betting on the fastest ones. There were times we'd have eight or nine cops in the back of the store, hooting and hollering, arguing about who was going to go out to the refrigerator to get the next round of beers. . . . We got everything we ever needed from the bodega—cigarettes, batteries, sandwiches, and beer. All for free. The store owner and Anthony the numbers man both loved us. We were the right type of cops. (McAlary, 1987, p. 172)

Subjugation of Defendants' Constitutional Protections

There were several instances where police officers used constitutionally impermissible means to "fight crime" in the 77th precinct. It was common practice in the precinct (and in others as well) to falsify arrest reports and to commit perjury in court. For various reasons, officers making a "collar" would frequently not want to be officially credited for the arrest. Thus, it was common for an arresting officer to pass-off an arrestee to another officer for formal processing. The new "arresting" officer would subsequently claim the arrest in a formal police report and, if necessary, provide perjured testimony in court that he or she was the one responsible for apprehending the offender.

Officers also used other means to deal with some offenders. Blaming the inability of the criminal justice system to handle offenders effectively, officer Henry Winter began to mete out street justice to suspected offenders. On one occasion, for example, Winter brought a suspected drug dealer back to the station house. Winter discovered that the dealer was not in possession of any drugs but had $170 in cash. McAlary (1987) described what happened next:

> Henry piled the bills into a small heap and lit a match to them. The dealer began to scream, drawing a small crowd of police officers into the room. As his fellow cops shrieked their approval, he burned all the money, reducing the cash to a pile of cinders. For added dramatic effect, Henry then blew the ashes into the drug dealer's lap. The cops cheered, all of them failing to take action on what amounted to the robbery of a drug dealer by a uniformed police officer in their own station house. (pp. 116–117)

Officer Winter used other similarly spectacular measures to deal with people he policed. Soon after burning the suspected drug dealer's cash, Winter regularly began to force dealers to flush their money and drugs down toilets at the precinct (Wallace, 1988). On one night shift, Winter drove a young mugger far out of the precinct, forced the offender to strip to his shorts, and left him stranded (see also *Klock v. Cain*, 1993; *Ketchum v. City of West Memphis, Ark.*, 1992). At the scene of a dispute, a Jamaican woman holding her baby called Winter a "blood clot." Winter responded to the affront by striking the woman in the head with his flashlight, knocking her unconscious (McAlary, 1987).

Many officers working in the 77th precinct used whatever measures they pleased to deal with suspected offenders. In some cases, this meant that police violated departmental regulations and criminal procedure to make arrests and obtain convictions. In other instances, officers simply delivered their own form of street justice to suspected offenders.

Traditional Forms of Drug-Related Corruption

Although the Buddy Boys were engaged in many illegal and unethical activities, they are perhaps most notorious for their involvement in traditional forms of drug-related corruption. Several officers in the precinct were receiving payoffs from drug dealers. Drug dealers paid police for two reasons: to bribe officers not to interfere with the dealer's business and to protect the dealer's trafficking operation from other police. The amount of money paid to police varied greatly. In some instances, an illegal dealer might slip an officer $10–20 for stopping by to say "hello." In other cases, dealers were paying officers fairly large sums of money for protection. At one point, for example, Officers Junior Gallagher and Brian O'Regan were splitting $1,700 per month for protecting a single drug dealer. Ironically, we'll learn later that the officers had no control over drug investigations and thus could do very little to protect dealers. In the end, it was a dealer cooperating with internal affairs officers that led to the breakup of the Buddy Boys' operation (McAlary, 1987).

Precinct officers were infamous for their involvement in robbing drug dealers. Some of the officers got their start by engaging in "opportunistic" thefts. These types of thefts often involved taking money or other items while at crime scenes. Officers Winter and Magno, for example, "once stepped over a dead man's body, discovered in his apartment on the last day of the month, to seek out and steal his rent money" (McAlary, 1987, p. 167). On another occasion, the two officers found a shoulder bag apparently dropped by a drug dealer they were chasing. The officers split $5,000 of the $5,500 they found inside, before turning the bag in as found property.

Several officers in the precinct became involved in "planned thefts." In nearly every case, this meant that officers would rob dealers selling drugs in the 77th. By 1984, the Buddy Boys had developed a methodical routine for identifying and robbing drug dealers. While performing their patrol duties, the Buddy Boys would look for apartments and other locations in the precinct where drugs were being sold. Talking in code over the police radio, officers would set up a location to meet with other Buddy Boys to plan robberies for the night. With their plans finalized, the Buddy Boys would converge on the identified drug trafficking locations, break in using whatever means were necessary, and grab money, drugs, electronic equipment, and anything else of value. Police would remove drugs and money from dealers and other persons at the raid sites; these people would then conveniently be allowed to "escape" (Wallace, 1988; Buder, 1987a).

With experience, the Buddy Boys became much more systematic in carrying out their robberies. Mike McAlary (1987) describes some of their maneuvers:

> Henry, having nearly broken his foot when he tried to kick down a metal door with his sneakers, bought a pair of steel-tipped boots. Gallagher and O'Regan began carrying a sledge hammer, crowbar, and pinch bar in the trunk of their patrol car. They all packed screwdrivers in their attaché cases along with their paperwork. . . . If the cops wanted to get into a third-floor apartment, they would climb to the roof, tie a rope around an elevator housing and then rappel down the side of the building, crashing feet first into the apartment window. Some Buddy Boys also carried ash cans—small but powerful fireworks—which they would light up and slip through mail slots, literally bombing people out of their apartments. (p. 183)

If the Buddy Boys found themselves lacking equipment to carry out a robbery, it was not uncommon for them to send an officer to a local firehouse to borrow the necessary tools. In at least a few cases, officers stole or borrowed equipment from construction sites or other locations in the precinct to carry out robberies. Although they never proceeded with the idea, a few officers even considered purchasing a van and outfitting it with all of the tools and equipment they might need to rob drug sites. In sum, the Buddy Boys used whatever means necessary to rob drug dealers; they became experts in a specialized form of deviance.

Once they had broken into drug apartments, officers often did more than conduct a cursory inspection for money or drugs. In many cases, they executed painstaking searches, looking for drugs hidden under floorboards, in ceilings, and inside of false walls. Brian O'Regan would carry out meticulous searches, was willing to search behind broken toilets, and once found a bag of drugs under a feces-filled bathtub in an abandoned apartment (McAlary, 1987).

During their robberies, the Buddy Boys would invariably find different quantities of illegal drugs. At first, the Buddy Boys would destroy whatever drugs were found, often flushing them down the toilet, or simply throwing them away. It was not long, however, before officers realized that they were discarding drugs worth hundreds, or even thousands, of dollars. Thus, the Buddy Boys began selling confiscated drugs to traffickers they knew in the precinct. On at least a couple of occasions, the Buddy Boys became street-level dealers:

> It was like we were insane or something. I mean one time we hit this . . . [place] . . . on a late tour. . . . We tossed everybody. While me and Nicky were in the back searching through things, a line of customers formed. Brian started selling them coke through the slot in the door. And it was a good thing he did, too, because we came up with a small amount of money and a large amount of coke. So O'Regan made more money for us. He did it for about an hour. There was this one guy who came up to the door and wanted to sell his sweater. It was a nice, brand-new sweater. But there was a long line so we couldn't open the door. That would have been bad for business. Brian tried to get the guy to slip the sweater under the door, but it wouldn't fit. (McAlary, 1987, pp. 185–186)

Following the robbery of another dealer at the dealer's apartment, Robert Rathbun sold marijuana to customers through a peephole until he had earned enough money for his vacation (Wallace, 1988). The Buddy Boys had become so brazen in stealing and selling drugs that two of the officers returned to this same apartment a couple of days later to try to reopen it for drug sales. "[B]ut they were wearing uniforms and parked in front of the building, scaring off potential customers. They left after making only a few dollars" (McAlary, 1987, p. 221).

At first, some of the Buddy Boys justified their robbery of drug dealers by arguing that it was an effective means for handling criminals and taking drugs off the street. Seemingly oblivious to the consequences of their actions, the Buddy Boys themselves had become major drug traffickers for residents in the 77th precinct. Some officers were so busy breaking into apartments and stealing from drug dealers that they did not care about making arrests or working overtime. "Essentially they were moonlighting as thieves while working in uniform" (McAlary, 1987, p. 108).

THE UNFOLDING OF THE BUDDY BOYS CASE

By the mid-1980s, several reports had surfaced of police officers' illegal activities in the 77th precinct. Some of the Buddy Boys suspected that they were being investigated by members of the department's Internal Affairs Division (IAD). The case broke for IAD officers, however, when a drug dealer from the 77th precinct was arrested for possession of about a pound of cocaine. The dealer, Benny Burwell, claimed to have been paying off corrupt police in the 77th precinct for years. Burwell struck an agreement to work with IAD investigators to catch officers who were accepting payoffs. IAD investigators subsequently videotaped Burwell giving Henry Winter and Tony Magno protection money on several occasions (McAlary, 1987).

On May 23, 1986, IAD investigators took Winter and Magno into custody. Both officers were presented with a deal: to work undercover for IAD to collect evidence on other Buddy Boys and be accorded immunity for crimes they committed, or to be charged and tried for several criminal offenses (Wallace, 1988). Winter and Magno agreed to work with IAD. In doing so, "they would become the first partners in the history of the New York Police Department to turn against an entire precinct" (McAlary, 1987, p. 42).

For the next few months, Winter and Magno continued to work as patrol officers in the 77th precinct as if nothing had happened. There was an important difference, however. Both officers were wearing "wires" and helping IAD investigators amass evidence against their corrupt peers in the precinct (Purdum, 1986b).

Barely four months later, Magno and Winter had obtained enough evidence to warrant the suspension of thirteen of the precinct's officers (Havesi, 1986); another twenty-five would be subjected to the departmental disciplinary process (McAlary, 1987). Criminal indictments were eventually handed down for the arrest of thirteen officers, all of whom were ordered to surrender for arrest on November 6, 1986. Twelve of the officers appeared as ordered. Brian O'Regan failed to show up to be arrested, booked, and arraigned. Instead, O'Regan drove to an isolated motel, wrote a one hundred-page note, and shot himself in the head with a .25 caliber pistol (Purdum, 1986d).

THE NYPD'S WORKING ENVIRONMENT

Since its creation, the New York Police Department (NYPD) has found itself repeatedly mired in corruption. Both historically and today, much police corruption in the city has been related to vice activities. Prostitution, gambling, alcohol, and illegal drugs have all provided incentives for New York City police to violate their oaths. The debacle of the Buddy Boys seems merely another incident in a continuum of corruption scandals (table 8.1 summarizes major investigations of the NYPD).

Table 8.1
Major Investigations of the New York City Police Department

Year	Name of Investigation	Focus of Investigation
1894	Lexow Committee	Corruption from gambling and prostitution operations. Extortion of money from legitimate businesspersons. Collusion with criminals. Intimidation, harassment of citizens.
1913	Curran Committee	Corruption from gambling and prostitution operations.
1932	Seabury Committee	Corruption from the manufacture, distribution, sale and consumption of illegal alcohol. Extortion of money from prostitutes.
1949	Brooklyn Grand Jury	Corruption from gambling payoffs.
1972	Knapp Commission	Corruption from gambling and drugs. Payoffs from citizens, and the operators of legal and illegal businesses.
1994	Mollen Commission	Drug corruption. Robberies and thefts committed by officers. On-duty substance abuse. Excessive use of force. Effectiveness of Internal Affairs in detecting and investigating police wrongdoing.

In 1892, the Reverend Charles Parkhurst, a political activist, kicked off a personal campaign to reform alleged irregularities in the NYPD. Largely due to his efforts, the New York State Senate appointed a special committee in 1894 to investigate charges of corruption. Chaired by Senator Clarence Lexow, the committee subpoenaed nearly seven hundred witnesses. What the Lexow Committee discovered was indeed shocking. Payoffs to police officers were routine in the city. In fact, virtually every policeman in the department believed that payoffs were a perquisite of police work. Witnesses called before the committee told stories of having money extorted from them by police. Legitimate businesses paid police to overlook city ordinance violations. Bookmakers, gambling dens, houses of prostitution, and other illegal businesses also made regular payments to the police. Detectives negotiated deals with pickpockets, thieves, and other criminals and took a percentage of the profits. Since police operations were largely controlled by politicians, it was no surprise to find that the police did whatever they could to influence elections (see chapter 2). The committee learned that appointments and promotions in the department were routinely sold (see chapter 2). Finally, witnesses told the committee of being frequently intimidated, oppressed, and abused by police officers (Fogelson, 1977; Richardson, 1970). In sum, the committee's investigation found that corruption and general misconduct pervaded the department. In response, Theodore Roosevelt was appointed to head the department, but it was only a few years before corruption in the department returned to "normal" (Sherman, 1978, p. xxv).

Seventeen years later, another committee was created, once again, to investigate allegations of corruption in the NYPD. The formation of the Curran Committee was precipitated by the murder of a gambler who had provided the media with information about corruption in the department. The committee found that police were systematically extorting payoffs from illegal gambling and prostitution operations. The Curran Committee blamed the corruption on inefficient management practices. Accordingly, city officials recommended the creation of a separate squad of officers who would be responsible for investigating complaints made against the police (Knapp Commission, 1972; Report of the Special Committee, 1913).

In 1932, the Seabury Committee issued its report on corruption in the NYPD. The Committee reported that police were receiving hundreds of thousands of dollars each year in payoffs from speakeasies, bootleggers, and gambling operations. The committee also reported on the corrupt activities of the vice squad. Members of the squad had falsely framed several women, charging them with prostitution. The officers had worked out an arrangement with bondsmen and lawyers for a cut of the fees that the women would subsequently pay to extricate themselves from the charges (Fogelson, 1977).

The NYPD was again the subject of intense scrutiny in the early 1950s. This time, the inquiry was prompted by a series of newspaper reports that police were protecting a massive bookmaking operation. The Brooklyn Grand Jury was subsequently used to investigate these allegations of corruption. After his arrest, Harry Gross, the head of the bookmaking operation, provided investigators with detailed information about payoffs he had been making to hundreds of police officers. Gross told the grand jury that he had first provided police with payoff money in the 1940s when he started a small bookmaking operation. As his business grew over the years, so did the number of police he paid. The public was shocked to learn that corrupt police in the NYPD were receiving about $1 million each year in cash from Gross alone. In addition, Gross regularly provided police with personal gifts that included televisions, furs, jewelry, and even cars. Police involvement in the scandal extended from the lowest to the highest levels in the department. Among those implicated were the police commissioner and chief inspector. Ultimately the mayor, who was a former policeman himself, was forced to resign (Police Corruption, 1986). About 45 police officers were fired after they were convicted of either criminal or departmental charges. Another 150 officers either retired or resigned from the force during the investigation (Kornblum, 1976; Knapp Commission, 1972).

Following the Brooklyn grand jury investigation, police administrators moved to control corruption by implementing rigid bureaucratic procedures in the department. Documentation through written records was emphasized, particularly for those working in vice control. Administrators, however, sent the message down the hierarchy that while they would punish those flagrantly involved in corrupt practices, they really did not want to know about routinized corruption (Skolnick & Fyfe, 1993; Sherman, 1978). This administrative posture contributed to one of the largest, and most damaging, investigations in the department's brief history.

The Knapp Commission released its report on August 3, 1972, capping a complex story that began six years earlier when a young, persistent patrolman refused to become involved in corrupt practices that had become customary in the department. In January of 1966, newly transferred plainclothes officer Frank Serpico was handed an envelope by another officer containing $300 in cash. Serpico was informed that the money represented his share of monthly payoffs from a local gambler. Serpico subsequently met with Captain Philip Foran of the Department of Investigation squad. The Captain informed Serpico that he had two options: he could keep his mouth shut or he could pursue his complaint and end up at the bottom of the East River. Serpico turned the money over to his sergeant but did nothing else at the time to push his complaint (Knapp Commission, 1972).

In December of 1966, Serpico was transferred to another plainclothes squad. During his first month, Serpico was again offered payoff money and learned that corruption was even more widespread in his new division. Serpico subsequently met three times with First Deputy Commissioner John Walsh, the number two person in the NYPD, advising him of what he had learned about corruption in the department. Nothing was done. Serpico also met confidentially with Jay Kriegel, who was Mayor John Lindsay's personal assistant, informing him of corruption in the department. Several weeks later, Kriegel told Serpico nothing could be done at the time because it was important not to upset the police. Serpico also told Commissioner of Investigation Arnold Fraiman of wrongdoing in the department. Again, nothing was done (Knapp Commission, 1972; Maas, 1973).

Finally, Serpico went to his division commander, informing him of the corruption. This time, Serpico's complaint led to a grand jury investigation, and the indictment of eight of his fellow officers. Serpico was convinced that little had been done to remedy systemic corruption in the department. In February of 1970, Serpico and three other officers approached David Burnham of the *New York Times* with information about corruption in the department. The attention generated by media stories that followed ultimately caused Mayor Lindsay to appoint the Knapp Commission to investigate departmental operations (Maas, 1973; Skolnick & Fyfe, 1993). The Knapp Commission's (1972) report was damning:

> We found corruption to be widespread. It took various forms depend-
> ing on the activity involved, appearing at its most sophisticated
> among plainclothesmen assigned to enforcing gambling laws. In the
> five plainclothes divisions where our investigations were concentrated
> we found a strikingly standardized pattern of corruption. Plain-
> clothesmen, participating in what is known in police parlance as a
> "pad," collected regular bi-weekly or monthly payments amounting to
> as much as $3,500 from each of the gambling establishments in the
> area under their jurisdiction, and divided the take in equal shares.
> The monthly share per man (called the "nut") ranged from $300 and
> $400 in midtown Manhattan to $1,500 in Harlem. When supervisors
> were involved they received a share and a half. A newly assigned
> plainclothesman was not entitled to his share for about two months,
> while he was checked out for reliability, but the earnings lost by the
> delay were made up to him in the form of two months' severance pay
> when he left the division. (p. 1)

The commission found that there was also extensive corruption in narcotics enforcement. Individual narcotics enforcement officers received payoffs called "scores" that frequently amounted to enormous amounts of money. Scores were kept by the officer, but were sometimes shared with a partner or a supervisor. "They ranged from minor shakedowns to many thousands of dollars, the largest narcotics payoff uncovered in our investigation having been $80,000" (Knapp Commission, 1972, p. 2).

The commission found that corruption extended throughout the department. Some sergeants, for example, received payoffs that weren't shared with patrolmen. Uniformed patrol officers, in addition to receiving regular gratuities, received small but regular payments from "construction sites, bars, grocery stores and other business establishments" (Knapp Commission, 1972, p. 2). Patrol officers also received payoffs from motorists, after-hours bars, tow truck operators, cab drivers, parking lot operators, prostitutes, and persons wanting cases "fixed" in court. Patrick V. Murphy, who was appointed Police Commissioner during the Knapp Commission investigation, commented that in 1971 the Mounted Division's 220 horses "were perhaps the only foot soldiers in the N.Y.P.D. that we were absolutely certain were corruption-free!" (Murphy & Pate, 1977, p. 230).

Nor did the Buddy Boys case alter the working environment. The Mollen Commission began to hear testimony in September, 1993. Witnesses reported systematic corruption that was strikingly similar in detail to that in the Buddy Boys case. Michael Dowd, a former officer in the 75th precinct, bluntly described how he and his peers routinely robbed crime victims, drug dealers, and arrestees of money, drugs, and anything else of value. Dowd revealed that many officers were receiving substantial sums for protecting illegal drug operations; Dowd's share amounted to about $4,000 each week. Dowd told of officers routinely using drugs and alcohol while on duty, informing the Commission that he regularly snorted lines of cocaine off the dashboard of his police cruiser (Frankel, 1993). Other witnesses told of extensive use of excessive force culminating in the physical and psychological brutalization of many citizens (Frankel & Stone, 1993). Testimony suggested that corruption was endemic in the 75th and other precincts; it was permitted to flourish because officers were reluctant to transgress against the postulate of never "ratting out" another cop.

TARGETING VICTIMS FOR POLICE RIPOFFS

Of all the forms of police corruption the Buddy Boys might have chosen, why did they primarily concentrate on robbing small-time, street-level drug dealers in a poverty stricken ghetto? Why this form of deviance? In the early 1980s, NYPD patrol officers were virtually eliminated from involvement in drug investigations. This was done to minimize the possibility of having street officers corrupted by the drug trade. Theoretically, uniformed officers were to provide the narcotics division with any information they came across about illicit drug sales; narcotics officers would then handle all such cases. One reason the Buddy Boys did not set up highly organized, more lucrative drug protection rings is because the organizational structure and standard operating procedures of the NYPD restricted their opportunities to do so. As patrol officers, the Buddy Boys could not provide drug dealers with guarantees of protection from the precinct's narcotics division. Thus, in order to tap into profits from the precinct's drug trade, the Buddy Boys resorted to robbing street-level dealers. In essence, what began as an attempt to prevent corruption by curtailing the responsibilities of officers led to an increase in police violence.

The Buddy Boys chose their victims carefully. Although there are geographic clusters of fairly prosperous citizens living in the 77th precinct (Smothers, 1986), the Buddy Boys did not commit planned thefts from these persons. Instead, the Buddy Boys ripped-off drug dealers and users who were living in the most destitute, poverty-stricken areas of the precinct. Since the ripped-off drug dealers had committed a crime originally, they were in no position to complain when they were victimized. Secondly, most victims had criminal records; credibility would have been suspect. Any complaints would likely be received by police with skepticism. It would be the word of a known criminal pitted against that of veteran, decorated officers (Service Records, 1986). Third, given the social and educational backgrounds of those who were victimized, it is reasonable to assume that they were probably unfamiliar with the procedure for reporting police wrongdoings. In addition, victimized dealers probably had genuine fears about what might happen to them if they did inform on the rogue officers. Given the lawlessness of the Buddy Boys, victims had ample reason to worry about their safety if they should become known as informers.

The Buddy Boys chose prime locations and times to commit robberies. Most rip-offs occurred during the graveyard shift when there would be few "respectable" or "credible" witnesses around. The Buddy Boys did not rob dealers in well-traveled public areas. Instead, they scouted out tenement buildings and apartments where they could conduct their affairs out of sight.

In sum, the Buddy Boys targeted a segment of the population with the necessary resources to make corruption viable and with the least ability to protect themselves from police deviance. The Buddy Boys did not rob the precinct's wealthiest residents; instead, they preyed on the precinct's poorest citizens. The victims were "poor" in the sense that they had little credibility, little social and economic power, and little to gain by reporting their victimization to authorities. As marginal members of mainstream society, they were literally "sitting ducks" for the Buddy Boys.

THE TOLERATION AND RATIONALIZATION OF DEVIANT ACTIVITIES

While there are many factors responsible for precipitating and fostering deviant conduct in the Buddy Boys case, two general areas warrant further discussion. First, there are indications that administrators bear some responsibility for the actions that took place in the 77th precinct. Second, based on the theories and observations presented in earlier chapters of the book, we will look at how the Buddy Boys were able to justify their involvement in serious criminal activities.

Administration and Management Factors

Several administrative features of the NYPD's 77th precinct contributed to an environment where corruption was permitted to flourish. For years, the 77th precinct was used as a "dumping ground" for officers who had been labeled as troublesome. McAlary (1987) characterized the 77th as a black-sheep squadron that had some good, honest officers, but also included "drunks, duty shirkers, wife beaters, drug addicts, rule benders, and discipline problems who were not quite bad enough to fire. . . . 'What are you in for, kid,' the veterans would ask new arrivals. 'Murder, rape, or robbery?'" (p. 86). Good officers found themselves working with unmanageable misfits. In addition, with its high crime rate and extensive poverty, the 77th precinct was considered as an undesirable assignment. Labeled as miscreants, many officers in the 77th precinct saw themselves permanently trapped in rotten jobs. With their career aspirations crushed, the stage was set for some officers to try to improve their situations by one of the only means left—engaging in illegal activities.

As noted in chapter 3, most types of corruption require at least some support from others in the police organization. This was clearly the case in the 77th precinct. At least a few sergeants in the precinct were active participants. Sergeant Robert J. Jervas was one of the original thirteen Buddy Boys indicted for crimes in the case (Service Records, 1986). Sergeant William Stinson, a supervisor on the graveyard shift where many drug rip-offs occurred, filled out retirement papers when rumors were circulating about criminal activities on his shift. However, "he rethought his position. . . . telling friends, 'If they're going to let me retire, that means they don't have nothing on me'" (McAlary, 1987, p. 91).

Some supervisors in the precinct, aware that officers were engaging in criminal acts, were simply apathetic and did nothing to try to correct any problems. Officers in the precinct sensed that most supervisors merely wanted to "get their time in and move on before a major scandal broke" (McAlary, 1987, p. 94). Rumors circulated in the community that IAD officers were also a part of the Buddy Boys operation and that if citizens reported misconduct, officers would know and take appropriate retaliatory actions.

Conversely, some supervisory personnel did take steps to address wrongdoings committed by officers. As early as 1982, a precinct captain reported to his superior that he suspected some officers were committing thefts at burglary scenes. No action was taken. The next year, a newly transferred Sergeant, Jerome Schnupp, provided Internal Affairs with a list of officers in the precinct whom he suspected of wrongdoing. One of the Buddy Boys with a friend in Internal Affairs secured a copy of the list and posted it in the precinct locker room. Afterwards, Schnupp found a dead rat with his name on it pinned to a blackboard in the muster room. Within two years, Schnupp was forced out of the precinct. "He spent a lot of his time out in the parking lot after work, changing flat tires on his car" (McAlary, 1987, p. 104).

When Internal Affairs did try to catch corrupt cops in the 77th by setting up "integrity tests" or "stings," the Buddy Boys were tipped to the operations by colleagues in other divisions. Given the apathy of most supervisors in the precinct, and the few bungled attempts to catch crooked officers, the Buddy Boys considered themselves "untouchable," "too street smart" and thus, "bullet proof" (McAlary, 1987, p. 111).

Against this backdrop of management problems in the 77th precinct, it is worth noting that police officers throughout the NYPD questioned the integrity of Police Commissioner Benjamin Ward.

> Ward was an unpopular administrator who was nicknamed "Bubba" by the department's rank and file cops. When he was a deputy commissioner in 1972, he apologized to a group of Muslims after a cop was shot to death in a Harlem mosque. In 1984, Ward's first year as a police commissioner, he faced charges of indulging in a tryst at Rikers Island prison with a woman who wasn't his wife. Ward was also accused of getting drunk at a police union convention and urinating from his helicopter, a craft without a toilet, on the way home. Ward admitted the extramarital affair and apologized for his public drunkenness at a press conference. (McAlary, 1987, pp. 231-232)

A survey of sergeants and lieutenants in the NYPD after the Buddy Boys case broke found that many did not know the names of the officers they were responsible for supervising, nor were they able to name their own commanders (Purdum, 1986f). The results of the survey further called into question the ability of the department's first line supervisors to prevent corruption and misconduct among officers.

Todd Purdum (1986a) echoed the concerns of others when he noted, "the fact that at least 13 people in a precinct of some 200 officers have been accused raises questions about who else in the precinct could, or should, have known of their activities" (p. B4). Police Commissioner Benjamin Ward, also apparently recognizing that something was amiss in the precinct's chain of command, eventually ordered the transfer of every supervisor who was assigned to the 77th precinct (Purdum, 1986c). Yet supervisors were not the only ones who could have known of illegal goings-on in the precinct. Given the visibility and extent of the Buddy Boys' activities, it is reasonable to conclude that most officers in the precinct were also aware, at least peripherally, of their peers' criminality. Accordingly, Commissioner Ward eventually ordered the transfer of all patrol officers in the precinct (Purdum, 1986e).

Rationalizing Deviant Conduct

As a group, the Buddy Boys developed a "we/they" perspective toward the people they were policing. The insularity felt by officers was compounded because most of the Buddy Boys came from social backgrounds that were diametrically opposed to the people who were living in the precinct. For the most part, the Buddy Boys came from white, middle-class, suburban backgrounds; they continued to reside in the suburbs after becoming police officers. (A mayoral report released after the Buddy Boys case was exposed called for broad changes in departmental selection and promotion practices in order to diversify the racial and ethnic composition of the force (Purnick, 1986).) Confronted with the realities of urban poverty, ghetto life, and vast differences in cultural values, officers hardened their emotions and perspectives toward the precinct's residents. Hence, suspects and criminals were commonly referred to as "skells." The 77th precinct was named the "Alamo" by officers who had T-shirts printed with the logo, "77th Precinct. The Alamo. Under Siege" (McAlary, 1987, p. 89). To the Buddy Boys, the shirts and the precinct's nickname represented the idea that they were the thin blue line between anarchy and order. Buddy Boy Brian O'Regan committed suicide while wearing his "Alamo" shirt (Purdum, 1986d).

In courtroom testimony and media interviews that followed the disclosure of the case, the Buddy Boys used virtually every rationalization discussed in chapter 5 to justify their behavior. First, some of the officers charged with criminal offenses denied responsibility for their actions. Henry Winter, for example, tried to justify his robbery of drug dealers by saying that he got tired of arresting drug dealers, only to see them back on the street the next day. Brian O'Regan also suggested that he robbed drug dealers merely to punish them. To both officers, the inefficient, ineffective, and awkward criminal justice system was the real culprit; since the system was a failure, officers had to resort to their own means of dealing with the drug problem. One officer used a different slant to deny responsibility for his actions. At trial, officer Robert Rathbun denied responsibility for his involvement, suggesting that he had been enticed into committing crimes while he was suffering from severe depression. Rathbun claimed that he had given most of the $4,000 he was accused of stealing to church charities (Buder, 1987b). The jury in the case, however, didn't buy Rathbun's argument and found him guilty of all thirty-seven crimes (Buder, 1986c).

Buddy Boys also suggested that no one was really injured by their acts, nor were there any real victims in the robberies they committed. Not long after starting their robberies, officers learned that it was best not to take everything from their victims.

> We always tried to leave the bad guys with a little something. If you go into a place and take everything, they're gonna bitch. They may even come down to the precinct and file a complaint against you. . . . But if you catch guys and let them go with a little money and drugs, they're not going to bitch. They're as happy as a pig in shit. They're thinking, "I'm not going to jail. So I lost a little money. I'll make it up next week." (McAlary, 1987, pp. 169–170)

Once arrested, the Buddy Boys lashed out by attempting to condemn their condemners. Almost immediately following their suspensions from duty, attorneys for the arrested officers claimed their clients had been entrapped by officers Winter and Magno (Purdum, 1986b). As a part of their defense, several of the charged officers alleged that they were "clean" until they were enticed by officers Winter and Magno into committing drug rip-offs. The justification was successful in officer James Day's trial; after he was acquitted, a juror explained that "[the prosecution] had no case. They built it around Magno, and he was lying through his teeth" (Buder, 1987e, p. B4). In other cases, Buddy Boys condemned police administrators and other governmental officials for their predicaments. Brian O'Regan, for example, argued that the entire city government system was corrupt, pointing out various officials who had been indicted or convicted for corrupt activities. O'Regan also chastised police administrators for his troubles, arguing that he began committing crimes only after he was repeatedly exposed to rampant corruption in the precinct (McFadden, 1986). In O'Regan's mind, if administrators had not tolerated corruption in the precinct, he would never have been seduced into committing crimes with other officers.

Finally, some of the Buddy Boys tried to justify their crimes by appealing to higher loyalties. The higher loyalties in this case meant that officers abided by deviant subcultural norms that governed behavior in the precinct. Some of the Buddy Boys suggested, for example, that they either drifted, or were pulled, into deviant activities by their partners. To these officers, it became more important to abide by such edicts as never "ratting out" other officers, or not trusting others unless they had been "checked out," than it was to report irregularities. In essence, officers argued that they were merely following the code of conduct that governed daily life in the precinct.

Once the details of the Buddy Boys' criminal activities became known, few officers expressed remorse even though many citizens were victimized (see, e.g., Buder, 1987d). They expressed no sorrow for having violated the public trust by committing literally hundreds of serious crimes. Instead, officers including Henry Winter expressed the most grief over having broken the "code of silence" by giving up fellow officers (Wallace, 1988). Officers also expressed little remorse over the fact that at least eighty criminal cases were jeopardized because of their illegal activities and suspensions from the force (Nix, 1986). The Buddy Boys had internalized the norms, values, beliefs, and code of conduct of a deviant police subculture.

SUMMARY

The corruption of police by the illicit drug market is a major concern for contemporary law enforcement administrators. While the Buddy Boys case may appear to be an extreme example of drug-related police deviance, other similarly shocking cases involving the police and drugs have been reported across the country (Dombrink, 1994; Sechrest & Burns, 1992).

Drug corruption takes many forms. In the Buddy Boys case, officers used illicit drugs and other substances on- and off-duty; they routinely subjugated the rights of drug suspects; and it was common for them to engage in violence when dealing with drug dealers and users. The Buddy Boys' most shocking offenses involved rip-offs of drug dealers. Officers stole anything of value from small-time, street-level dealers in the precinct.

From a historical perspective, the NYPD has been rocked by similar scandals many times in the past. Since 1894, major misconduct investigations have occurred in the department about every twenty years. Thus, there was a preexisting climate in the department for corruption. Second, it was difficult to catch officers who were stealing from the precinct's drug dealers. The Buddy Boys were "wired in" to the department's "grapevine" and were able to find out when IAD officers were investigating officers in the precinct. Precinct residents who were victimized by the Buddy Boys were unlikely, or unable, to complain about police wrongdoings. In essence, the Buddy Boys purposefully selected victims who were powerless to do anything about what had happened to them. NYPD administration and management practices created an environment where officers were able to do as they pleased. The 77th precinct was used, for example, as a dumping ground for the department's misfits. Supervisory personnel were unwilling or unable to do anything about the misdeeds committed by officers in the 77th precinct. Non-corrupt officers who worked in the precinct and who were probably aware of the illegal activities also did nothing. Presented with an environment conducive to deviance, the absence of effective supervisory oversight, and the availability of an endless stream of powerless victims, the Buddy Boys were consumed by greed in their quest to steal as much as they possibly could.

Chapter Nine

VARIETIES OF
POLICE DEVIANCE
The District of Columbia's
Metropolitan Police

> Vice only wounds people from time to time; by its visible character.
>
> Denis Diderot   (1713–1784)

The nation's capital is steeped in symbolism. In addition to images of democracy and political power, Washington, D.C. has recently become known for more sordid reasons. In the past decade, the District has begun to symbolize the intractable problems facing many urban areas in the country: increasing crime and citizen fear of crime; drug trafficking and the violence that accompanies it; racial and ethnic tensions; and a deepening chasm between the prosperous and the destitute.

Washington is a city of contrasts. The District enjoys the prosperity generated by thousands of government jobs; however, a growing segment of its population is comprised of poor, minority, undereducated, unemployed, and underemployed citizens. Social problems accompanying economic inequalities have been well documented. Most notably, the District has developed the distinction as the nation's murder capital (Hinds, 1992) and perhaps as the nation's crime capital. A few blocks from the White House there are about ninety open-air drug markets; some have charged there are more drug markets than supermarkets in the city. In the eighth ward, where much of the District's crime and drug activities are centered, more than 80 percent of the population is African American, household incomes are well below the national average, and only about 30 percent of the area's students graduate from high school. Journalist Sabra Chartrand (1992) describes the fraying of the ward's economic and social fabric:

> Businesses are so scarce that the area does not have a single restaurant, only fast-food outlets. There are no major department stores and only one major supermarket for 72,000 people. The area does not even have a Little League baseball team. (p. 20)

Washington, D.C. is a place "where charming brick row houses collide with abandoned public housing, where many in government share stoops with people on welfare, where chauffeured limousines negotiate the streets while police helicopters buzz rooftops in search of fugitives" (Hinds, 1992, p. A14).

There have been recurrent rumors of rampant corruption in the city's government (Guskind, 1989). By the end of the 1980s, eleven government officials, including two deputy mayors, had pleaded guilty to charges involving corruption. About the same number left under a cloud of suspicion or were fired. The mayor's right-hand man pleaded guilty to embezzling nearly $200,000 of the city's money (Guskind, 1989). Mayor Marion Barry's activities came under increasing suspicion (Knight, 1983a, 1983b). In 1983 Barry's former wife, Mary Treadwell, was convicted of embezzling from a government fund that she and Barry had run.

Treadwell served time in a federal prison, was re-hired by the city, and pled guilty for yet another theft of city funds in 1997 (Miller & Woodlee, 1997). In 1984, Barry acknowledged that he had a personal relationship with a former city employee who pleaded guilty to distributing cocaine (Guskind, 1989). In his twelfth year as mayor of the District, Barry was convicted for possession of cocaine and served four months in prison (Chartrand, 1992). Despite the criminal record, Barry was re-elected mayor in 1994. The District's social and economic problems became so serious that Congress created a financial control board comprised of private citizens to oversee the operation of several city departments—largely stripping Mayor Barry of his administrative authority. In the past two decades, the District has suffered from critical mismanagement problems, exacerbated by seemingly pervasive corruption.

Allegations of extensive deviance in the District of Columbia's Metropolitan Police Department (DCMPD) have surfaced recently. In a 1993 article, for example, journalist Tucker Carlson leveled several charges: officers were involved in several thefts and the disappearance of evidence and departmental property; lax and inconsistent recruitment and training standards resulted in the hiring and retention of incompetent and corrupt officers; negligent and incompetent supervision resulted in DCMPD officers regularly disregarding their police responsibilities; and the department's disciplinary process was so dysfunctional that officers with serious problems continued to be employed. In sum, Carlson portrayed the DCMPD as a police agency riddled with problems.

Although these are serious charges, there have been few scholarly inquiries into deviance within the DCMPD. Perhaps the most compelling evidence of department-wide serious misconduct is the number of officers facing work-related criminal charges. At the close of May of 1993, 71 officers—or about one of every 60 commissioned police in the DCMPD—were under indictment or awaiting grand jury action for criminal matters (Editor, 1993a).

In this chapter we review evidence of crucial problems in the DCMPD by drawing from extensive news reports, legal cases, a report on departmental operations prepared by the Police Executive Research Forum (PERF), and recommendations for change presented by the Commission on Budget and Financial Priorities of the District of Columbia. In the process, we illustrate several forms of police deviance.

THE DCMPD'S WORKING ENVIRONMENT

From 1981 to 1997, four chiefs served the DCMPD. All four were up-through-the-ranks "insiders." From 1981 to 1989 Maurice Turner served as chief of police for the department. Turner joined the agency in 1953 and worked his way through a succession of supervisory positions before his appointment to the chief's job. With a reputation as a "tough" law enforcement official, Turner was considered a "cop's cop" by other members of the department (Simeon, 1989). Speaking on the issue of corruption in the department, Turner had commented to a news reporter, "Like in everything, there are times when you have a bad apple; you don't throw away the whole bushel, you throw away the bad apple. A dirty cop must be fired. We don't want any stains on . . . this badge" (Folks, 1989, p. G8). When Turner announced his resignation in 1989, Marion Barry characterized Turner's career as "illustrious and distinguished" noting his service to the "finest police department in the country" (D.C. Chief Quitting, 1989, p. 9). The Mayor's comments were ironic since Barry and Turner had reportedly been at odds for several years because of Barry's intervention in police affairs. Despite critical problems facing the DCMPD, Turner proclaimed when he announced his retirement that, "this department will stack up against any department in the country" (Turner Calls It Quits, 1989, p. 5).

Isaac Fulwood served as chief from 1989 to 1992. At the time of his appointment, Fulwood had served twenty-five years with the DCMPD and was characterized as a "blunt talking tough guy" who used an "aggressive" management style (Folks, 1989, p. A13). Fulwood pledged to reduce the city's murder rate, redeploy desk officers to the streets, and not to tolerate "dirty cops" who might tarnish the department's reputation. Notwithstanding these proclamations, the District's murder rate during Fulwood's tenure continued to increase, reports critically questioned personnel management and operating procedures in the department, and the agency continued to suffer from repeated reports of serious police corruption and misconduct. Despite these problems, when Fulwood announced his retirement three years later, he emotionally proclaimed,

> I will retire as the chief of the greatest police force in the world. . . . To the members [of the department] I say this has been a great love affair; this has been a job well done. This city can be proud of you. (McCraw & Reilly, 1992, p. E3)

Fred Thomas replaced Fulwood as the chief of the DCMPD in November of 1992. Thomas was also an insider; he served for twenty years with the department before his retirement in 1985 to head a youth program in the city. He returned to the department after being chosen for the chief's position by Mayor Sharon Pratt Kelly. Tragically, just hours after Thomas' appointment, former Chief Isaac Fulwood's 43-year-old brother was found shot to death and became homicide victim number 402 in the District for 1992 (New Police Chief, 1992).

Marion Barry appointed Larry D. Soulsby chief in 1995. The first caucasian to lead the department in nearly 20 years, Soulsby was also an up-through-the-ranks insider. The federal control board backed his appointement, but he was the subject of substantial criticism by those who questioned his ability to transform the department (Horwitz, 1997). Former New York City police commissioner William Bratton, for example, indicated that the DCMPD's problems appeared to be

> rooted in its culture and leadership, including Chief Larry D. Soulsby. . . . It comes to leadership, and, quite frankly, it's not here in D.C. . . . The reality is that an insider has baggage, and it's a lot harder to reform a police department that way. (Powell, 1997, p. B1)

In addition to concerns about his leadership abilities, there were questions about his level of knowledge of wrongdoing in the department. These concerns are addressed later in this chapter.

As noted above, city officials and former chiefs of the DCMPD have characterized the agency as one of the finest in the nation and the world. Despite these assertions, others have reached far different conclusions about District government and the DCMPD.

With all of its social problems, one would expect to find that the District of Columbia suffers from a lack of adequate resources. By certain measures, such an assumption would be far from accurate. The District employs about 50,000 workers; there is 1 government worker for every 13 residents. In comparison, there is 1 government worker for every 60 citizens in Chicago, and 1 for every 22 in New York City (Guskind, 1989). "The District's $3.2 billion budget comes out to $5,095 per Washingtonian, and the city's taxpayers shoulder a $3,361 per-person tax burden, 50 percent higher than the national average for combined state and local taxes" (Guskind, 1989, p. 129). In relative terms at the citywide level, the District seems to enjoy substantial fiscal resources.

What about resources for the city's police department? Throughout the past decade, politicians, police union officials, and police department administrators have repeatedly called for more officers to address escalating crime in the District. In March of 1989, for example, DCMPD officers were placed on a sixty-hour workweek (Folks, 1989), contributing to an expenditure of $21.7 million for overtime pay for that fiscal year (Commission, 1990). A spokesman for the D.C. Chapter of the Fraternal Order of Police claimed that such a move was clear evidence that the department was understaffed (D.C. Cops Brace, 1989). An additional 300 officers were scheduled to be hired in 1990, and Congress had approved funding for 700 more officers to be hired over a five-year period of time (Folks, 1989). Cries for additional police personnel continue; in 1993 the mayor of the city called for the President to authorize the use of military personnel to supplement police in the District.

Despite being portrayed as a city under siege with few officers to combat crime, studies of DCMPD operations suggest that the department is overstaffed rather than understaffed. In an extensive assessment of the department's personnel operations, PERF (1990) recommended "that the staffing level of the Metropolitan Police Department be reduced by 1608 sworn positions and increased by 78 civilian positions" (p. iv). The PERF report noted that while police staffing levels vary widely in cities across the country, the DCMPD employed significantly more officers per capita than any other comparable department in the United States. Patrick V. Murphy and James Fyfe, two of the country's leading experts on police operations, noted, "The department is grossly overstaffed, with eight officers per 1,000 citizens. Among 12 other comparable cities we studied, Baltimore is the next highest with 3.9 officers per 1,000 population. Philadelphia and New York have 3.6; Detroit 3.3; Los Angeles 2.2" (D.C. Police Department, 1991, p. 3). Murphy and Fyfe also observed that their calculations did not include the 5,000 federal and regional officers who work in the District. If they had been figured into the equation, police strength in the city is between four to ten times higher than in any other major city in the country. Even with the recommended staffing decrease of 1,608 officers, the DCMPD would continue to have the highest ratio of officers to citizens of any comparably sized law enforcement agency in the nation (PERF, 1990).

If police strength is greater in the DCMPD than in virtually any other city in the country, why do department and city officials continue to call for hiring additional personnel? Murphy and Fyfe concluded that the DCMPD is the most bloated police department in the United States and also the most inefficient (D.C. Police Department, 1991). Several inefficiencies in the assignment and deployment of personnel plague the department. Prevailing thought in policing is that about two-thirds of an agency's sworn personnel should be assigned to patrol duties (Gaines, Kappeler & Vaughn, 1996). In the DCMPD, only 44 percent of the department's officers were assigned to uniformed duty. Worse yet, many of those who were on uniformed duty were handling paperwork rather than providing actual police services. Twenty-one officers were assigned full-time tabulating other officers' overtime (D.C. Police Department, 1991).

The PERF report (1990) noted that the department scheduled officers' days off on peak days of the week. The report noted, for instance, that "more personnel are scheduled off during the weekends when call for service demand is the greatest" (p. 19). Despite PERF's suggestion that officers needed to be deployed more intelligently to handle citizen requests for service effectively, most officers in the DCMPD in 1992 were working standard 7 to 3, 3 to 11 and 11 to 7 shifts. One expert who examined the DCMPD's staffing patterns noted, "They don't know how to use data. They don't know how to use mapping to look at patterns of complaints and when they occur, whether it's weekly or seasonally" (Marchak, 1992,

p. G12). A chief of police from another agency noted that "they're about 20 years behind the times" in using means such as staggered shifts to compensate for call loading. The PERF report also noted that several positions in the DCMPD staffed by commissioned personnel should be civilianized. It was recommended that many positions in dispatch, report preparation, employee timekeeping, crime prevention and community education could be filled by civilian personnel rather than fully commissioned officers. Recommendations were made to expand automation in the department and to control overtime by revising operating policies and procedures. The PERF report (1990) concluded that if personnel reductions were implemented and workers were properly reallocated, the number of officers deployed on patrol in the District would remain about the same. By employing all of these basic management techniques, the District would enjoy a projected savings of $334.4 million over a five-year period from fiscal year 1992 through 1996.

Finally, questions were raised about the philosophy of policing endorsed by the DCMPD. Historically, the department judged its success on such traditional measures as the number of arrests made by officers. In 1989, for example, then Chief Maurice Turner argued that the DCMPD was one of the best in the country, noting, "We arrest more people per 1,000 residents than any police department in the country. We have more people incarcerated in this city than any other city or country in the Free World. So I think we're capable of performing our duties" (Turner Calls it Quits, 1991, p. A5). What Turner did not say, however, was that even though the District arrested and incarcerated persons at a higher rate than other cities, violent crime rose by 27 percent from 1985 to 1989, while the murder rate almost tripled (PERF, 1990). The report concluded that:

> while the District is facing a critical drug and crime problem, studies indicate that increasing the number of police officers and making more arrests does little to permanently change criminal activity. This research finding is supported by the District's own experience with Operation Cleansweep which, despite 46,000 arrests, has had little or no effect on drug availability, drug abuse, or drug-related crime and violence. (Commission, 1990, pp. 4–5).

The commission's report further noted the need for the DCMPD to implement community policing, introduce foot patrols in parts of the community, and the importance of enlisting citizens in the effort to suppress crime, maintain order, and assert social control (Commission, 1990). Implicitly, the extensive study by PERF suggested that the DCMPD was grossly mismanaged and that the department was using ineffective, inefficient, and outdated procedures to provide police services.

Despite its conclusions and strong recommendations, the report was perfunctorily dismissed by both the District's political leaders and DCMPD administrators. Mayor-elect Sharon Pratt Dixon flatly rejected the ideas put forth by PERF and the Commission. The chief at that time, Isaac Fulwood, simply denied that the department was overstaffed, proposing that the "study was based on incorrect figures" (D.C. Police Department, 1991, p. 3).

Ineffective organization, management, and administration in any department does not mean that the agency will inevitably experience problems with police wrongdoing. While mismanagement is probably a *necessary cause* for corruption and deviance in a police department, it is not a *sufficient cause* that invariably leads to the same results. Despite this qualification, many preconditions for pervasive police deviance existed in the DCMPD. Although the department attempted to generate an image as a professional, crime-fighting machine, the results of its efforts were negligible. Crime rates in the District continued to increase despite the DCMPD's use of several "professional model" police strategies. Aggressive policing had the effect of distancing the agency from the community it served. Recommendations for improving police operations in the District were rejected by city officials and the department administration. Perhaps most troubling were assertions by DCMPD administrators that the agency was one of the "best" or "finest" in the world—despite consistent reports to the contrary. These environmental elements set the stage for instances of police deviance.

ABUSE OF AUTHORITY

In chapter 1 we noted that police abuse of authority has been defined by David Carter (1994b) as action by a police officer that tends to injure, insult, trespass on human dignity, manifest feelings of inferiority and/or violate an inherent legal right of a member of the police constituency (p. 272). According to the typology developed by Carter, officers may abuse police powers in three ways: (1) by using excessive physical force, (2) by causing emotional or psychological distress through the use of verbal assault, ridicule, or harassment, and (3) by violating citizens' federal or state constitutional rights. This typology provides a framework to examine some of the more disturbing incidents where DCMPD officers abused police powers in the performance of their duties.

In a six-month period in 1985, judgements totalling more than $1.5 million were awarded to plaintiffs in three separate civil cases filed against the DCMPD. In the case resulting in the largest award, David Leach was awarded $950,000 in damages for injuries and psychological trauma suffered following an arrest for driving while intoxicated. Leach testified that when officers stopped his car and discovered he was an attorney, they slammed him against the side of a car and ridiculed him. When officers took him to a hospital for treatment, one of the patrolmen allegedly put a revolver to Leach's forehead and pulled the trigger (D.C. Jury, 1985).

In another case, Stanley Wiggins was awarded $205,000 for injuries he received when officers arrested him for disorderly conduct. Wiggins prevailed on claims that officers violated his constitutional rights by falsely arresting him and using unreasonable force—striking him in the face with a police baton which caused him to be knocked unconscious and to lose four teeth. Wiggins was hospitalized for a week following the arrest. Criminal charges were eventually dropped against Wiggins, and no departmental charges were ever brought against the officers involved in the incident because their supervisors concluded the force was reasonable to effect the arrest and to subdue Wiggins (D.C. Police Beating, 1985).

In the third case, Don Parker claimed that DCMPD officers violated his constitutional rights by using excessive force. Parker was shot and wounded by officers after they went to his home to question his wife concerning his whereabouts. Officers claimed that Parker had tried to elude capture and that he was shot after one officer thought he saw Parker reaching toward his waistband for a gun. No weapon was found following the shooting. Following a two-week trial, Parker was awarded $425,000 (D.C. Police Lose, 1985).

When questioned about the string of awards and their amounts, police union officials characterized the decisions as a "bum rap," stating "I think D.C. has gone so far the other way that if there's a tough one to call, officers . . . [will] . . . avoid tough confrontations" (D.C. Jury, 1985, p. 7). Despite the union rhetoric which attempted to invoke citizen fear that the police would be less aggressive in "tough" cases, two of the incidents were misdemeanors; Leach was driving while intoxicated, while the charge against Wiggins was for disorderly conduct. Union officials further attributed the large verdicts to juror "sympathy for the underdog and a belief in a city where billions of dollars are thrown around every day, that the government has deep pockets to pay a few hundred thousand dollars here and there" (D.C. Jury, 1985, p. 7).

In a 1986 case, two persons alleged that DCMPD police used excessive force and acted recklessly when officers falsely arrested them (*Carter v. District of Columbia*, 1986). The case is instructive because the plaintiffs, Charles Carter and Aleta Parker, alleged a widespread pattern of police misbehavior in the DCMPD. According to Carter and Parker, they were sitting in Carter's vehicle outside of Parker's residence when three men in street clothes brandishing shotguns and pistols approached them and ordered them to "freeze." Fearing a robbery, Parker drove away; the men fired their weapons three times. While heading to a police station, the car was stopped by an unmarked police vehicle using an emergency light. According to Carter and Parker's version of the incident:

> The same men who had confronted plaintiffs in the alley jumped out of the vehicle, pointing a shotgun and pistols. Two of the men pulled Carter from his automobile, threw him to the ground, struck him with the butt of a pistol, put his hands in handcuffs, and kicked and beat him. The third man directed a shotgun at Parker and commanded: "Bitch, get out of the car." Carter, prone on the pavement with hands cuffed behind him, endeavored to ask why . . . [they] . . . were encountering such treatment. One of the men placed a pistol to Carter's head and threatened: "Nigger, shut the fuck up or I'll blow your mother fucking brains out." (*Carter v. District of Columbia*, 1986, p. 119)

The three men, it was later learned, were DCMPD officers. Carter was arrested for assault on a police officer for striking one of the officers with his vehicle when he first attempted to elude them. Parker was held because officers discovered a small quantity of marijuana in her possession, but charges were dropped the next day. A grand jury subsequently refused to issue an indictment against Carter. Carter and Parker brought suit against the officers involved, the DCMPD, and the District of Columbia alleging that they had been arrested without probable cause and that the officers had filed false reports and used unreasonable force.

At trial, Parker and Carter introduced evidence that there was a pervasive pattern of unreasonable force by members of the DCMPD. The evidence included several instances where officers beat, choked, and taunted suspects. In addition, Carter and Parker alleged that DCMPD administrators tacitly endorsed a pattern of police brutality:

> (1) from 1974 to 1979, officers were exonerated in 93% of the misconduct investigations [the DCMPD] conducted; (2) in 1983, the MPD Service Weapon Review Board cited 26 officers for using weapons unjustifiably, but the chief took adverse action against only one of them and merely reprimanded the others; and (3) of 21 cases in which the Civilian Complaint Review Board (CCRB) recommended adverse action against police officers since 1982, the police chief took such action in only five cases. (*Carter v. District of Columbia*, 1986, p. 124)

At trial in the District court, a jury awarded the plaintiffs a total of $114,000. Although the jury's verdict was vacated by the D.C. Circuit Court of Appeals, the information presented in the case outlines a pattern of abusive behavior by DCMPD officers.

In a nationally publicized case in 1991, the eighteen-year-old son of former Atlanta Mayor Andrew Young, alleged that he was beaten by DCMPD officers. Andrew Jackson Young III claimed that as he was slowly driving his car through a crowd of people, an officer ordered him to stop. Young claimed that after stopping his vehicle, he was pulled from the car by police, placed face down on the ground, and beaten by several officers. He was then charged with disorderly conduct (Andrew Young's Son Protests, 1991). Young suffered a broken ankle and cuts and bruises on his head, neck and legs and subsequently filed a formal brutality complaint against the officers (Andrew Young's Son Files, 1991).

In a 1993 case, another citizen alleged that DCMPD officers used excessive force, inflicted emotional duress and violated his Constitutional rights (*Cox v. District of Columbia*, 1993). The plaintiff in the case, James Cox, was awarded a total of $525,000. The *Cox* case is important. It clearly illustrates the three dimensions of abuse of authority discussed by David Carter (1994b), and the District court found that the District of Columbia was deliberately indifferent to a pattern of brutality complaints against DCMPD officers.

Cox was stopped by DCMPD officers Barry Goodwin and William Brady for a traffic infraction. The officers approached Cox's vehicle, asked some basic questions, and then:

> Goodwin reached into the plaintiff's car though the window, turned off the ignition, removed Cox's car keys from the ignition and threw them over his shoulder onto the pavement. Goodwin proceeded to verbally abuse Cox, ordering Cox not to leave the car and at the same time inviting him to exit his car so that the officer could fight him. This verbal abuse culminated in a threat to shoot Cox. Meanwhile Goodwin had kicked Cox's car keys from the pavement onto the grass.
> . . . Goodwin returned to the paddywagon to write Cox a ticket which he threw onto the passenger seat of Cox's car while taunting Cox. At some point during the interchange, Goodwin threw Cox's license into the grass. In order to retrieve his driver's license, Cox exited the car and while he was out of the car, he asked Goodwin for his badge number. . . . Goodwin struck Cox in the head with his night stick and declared Cox under arrest. Next, Goodwin slammed Cox against the paddywagon and other officers present hit and beat Cox, knocking him to the ground. The officers then handcuffed Cox and, once cuffed, rolled him onto his back. One officer . . . told Cox not to look at the officers and then stepped on him, grinding his boot into Cox's face. (*Cox v. District of Columbia*, 1993, p. 4)

Cox was finally placed in a paddywagon. The officers drove around for twenty to thirty minutes. Because Cox's seat belt had not been fastened, "each time the officer driving the paddywagon maneuvered abruptly or suddenly applied the brakes, Cox was tossed against the interior wall of the paddywagon" (*Cox v. District of Columbia*, 1993, p. 4). In essence, officers gave Cox a "screen test" (police jargon for applying the brakes on a police vehicle so that the handcuffed prisoner will be thrown against the metal protective screen between the officer and the prisoner).

At the station house, Cox asked Officer Brady why he had been mis-treated. Brady responded that it was a "slow night" (*Cox v. District of Columbia*, 1993, p. 5). Cox was charged with a turn signal violation and disorderly conduct and posted a $25 bond. Both charges were subsequently dropped because no police officer appeared in court.

At trial in a civil suit, Cox alleged that the District's Civilian Complaint Review Board (CCRB)—which had the responsibility of investigating citizen complaints of police misconduct—was critically negligent in performing its duties. More than 70 percent of the cases filed with the CCRB contain allegations of excessive force. By statute, the District's CCRB is required to schedule a hearing within thirty days of receiving a complaint. Evidence considered by the court, however, showed that it took an average of two years, and sometimes as many as four years, for the CCRB to hear cases brought before it. Cox argued that if the CCRB had handled cases in a timely manner consistent with its obligation, Officer Goodwin would have been terminated during his first year as a probationary employee because of other serious complaints made against him for excessive use of force. Instead, Goodwin, and other officers, were able to complete probationary periods—while continuing to victimize citizens—because of the CCRB's extensive backlog of cases. Importantly, the court found that:

> . . . the District of Columbia's maintenance of a patently inadequate system of investigation of excessive force complaints constitutes a custom or practice of deliberate indifference to the rights of persons who come into contact with District police officers. In this case, the District of Columbia has allowed a "known hazardous risk" of failing to conduct timely investigations of allegations of police excessive use of force to continue over a protracted period of time without taking significant steps to alleviate that known and obvious risk. (*Cox v. District of Columbia*, 1993, p. 13)

In yet another case, Brian Mooar, a reporter from the *Washington Post*, filed a $171 million suit against the District and the DCMPD, alleging he was injured in a scuffle with officers. The suit arose from a December 1993 incident where two DCMPD officers arrested a woman for driving under the influence of alcohol. The woman, wearing a short skirt with no coat on a day when the temperature was 34 degrees, was handcuffed to a mailbox by officers Ehpraim Williams and Edward Ford. Mooar passed by the scene, heard the woman screaming for someone to take her picture, and stopped to take photographs. Mooar alleged he received back injuries when officers physically took his camera and attempted to remove the film. Officers reportedly told Mooar that he was not permitted to take photographs because he did not have the woman's permission and because he was hindering an investigation. Mooar received his camera when a sergeant arrived at the scene and ordered officers to return it. The department subsequently suspended Williams for 30 days and Ford for 20 days for excessive use of force and harassment (Panel, 1995).

Findings in these cases strongly suggest that a subculture of violence existed in the DCMPD. Brutality and police abuse of authority were not, however, the only problems the department has experienced.

MISUSE OF CONFIDENTIAL INFORMATION

Due to the very nature of their jobs, police possess various types of confidential information. The everyday routines of observing and speaking with citizens, conducting investigations, and making contacts with suspects, offenders, other police, and public officials provide police officers the opportunity to acquire information that most members of the public would not encounter. Police engage in deviant or criminal behaviors when they use this information for unethical or illegal purposes. When police release confidential information, the ramifications range from minor to serious. Public confidence in the police may be diminished, ongoing investigations may be jeopardized, and the safety of officers, witnesses, and others may be placed in peril.

The misuse of confidential information is often tied to other forms of police misconduct. Deviant officers might, for example, receive payoffs from illegal business operators in exchange for information about imminent raids or ongoing investigations. This is precisely what happened in a 1987 case involving DCMPD officers working in the fourth district's vice squad. In that case, which was investigated by the Federal Bureau of Investigation, it was learned that at least four or five of the twelve officers assigned to the squad received payoffs in exchange for providing drug dealers with information about drug sweeps and other pending police actions (U.S. Prosecutor, 1987). Officers also allegedly skimmed drugs and money that were confiscated during raids. The results of the officers' deviant conduct were disastrous. Perhaps most importantly, the U.S. Attorney's Office was forced to dismiss nearly four hundred drug-related cases that officers on the squad had handled. Officers who had been indicted, arrested, or were under investigation had lost their credibility and were easy targets for impeachment by defense attorneys. Many of the dismissed cases involved major drug distributors. For example, charges were dropped against one trafficker who had been arrested with cocaine and heroin valued at $250,000 (Drug Cases, 1987).

The release of confidential information affected the city and the DCMPD in other ways. In 1985–86, the DCMPD was involved in "Operation Caribbean Cruise," a sixteen-month investigation engineered to break up a Jamaican crime ring involved in distributing guns and drugs. Information about the investigation and a planned drug sweep was allegedly provided to the crime ring by fourth-district officers. As a result, only a few arrests were made when the sweep was conducted. After the failed raid, the DCMPD conducted an internal investigation, placing blame for its failure on Lieutenant William Goulart, who supervised the operation. The District of Columbia, however, hired a private consulting firm to investigate the internal review that the DCMPD had conducted about the failed raid—in effect, an investigation of the police department's investigation of the operation.

The consulting firm issued a scathing report suggesting that the internal affairs probe conducted by the DCMPD was "horrendous . . . slipshod, if not intentionally slanted" (Consultant, 1989, p. A1). The consulting firm noted that officers taking part in the raid were provided thirty day's advance notice of when it was to occur. In the interim, news about the sweep was leaked to the media and became common knowledge on the street. The head of the consulting firm remarked, "I have been in law enforcement for over 30 years and have studied and written on internal affairs for the greater portion of my career and have never seen [an investigation] as badly conducted" (p. A7). The report noted that the internal affairs probe neglected to investigate inconsistent statements provided by three administrative officials involved in the case—Assistant Chief Isaac Fulwood, Deputy Chief James Shugart, and Captain Claude Beheler. The report concluded that Lieutenant Goulart was made a scapegoat for the failed raid and noted that, if anything, Goulart probably should have been commended for doing an outstanding job under the circumstances. Police administrators were derelict for their failure to properly evaluate the compromised raid. "It would appear that ranking officers of the department were satisfied to take a chance on the success of the operation, then look for 'scapegoats' when it did not meet their specifications" (p. A7).

Plagued by recurring information leaks, the DCMPD implemented policy in 1997 requiring all employees in its homicide unit to sign a "security agreement." The agreement prohibits detectives from discussing cases or related information concerning their work with the public, news media, or other law enforcement agencies. Detectives criticized the non-disclosure pledge, arguing that it prevents them from sharing information on closed or open cases with other law enforcement agencies—and even with fellow DCMPD officers—that could be valuable in solving crimes. Chief Soulsby supported the policy as essential to prevent cases from being compromised by the leakage of crucial investigative theories and information (Thompson & Lewis, 1997).

In one of the most grim cases of police deviance to occur in the DCMPD in recent years, officer Fonda Moore was arrested in 1992 for her part in the contract murder of a nineteen-year-old drug dealer (D.C.

Officer, 1992). The Moore case shows how the release of confidential police information may be connected to other, more serious forms of police deviance. Moore, a seven-year veteran of the DCMPD, was allegedly a member of a major drug gang that was selling about $1.5 million worth of crack cocaine each month in the District of Columbia. She reportedly provided members of the drug gang with a police photograph of a man they wanted eliminated (Reilly, 1992). Billy Ray Tolbert was subsequently kidnapped, tortured, and shot to death. Moore reportedly served as the armed driver for the hit men who murdered Tolbert. After the murder, she provided members of the gang with confidential police files on the investigation of the Tolbert killing. Moore was subsequently charged with first-degree premeditated murder, felony murder, conspiracy to murder, kidnapping, and conspiracy to distribute crack cocaine (Reilly, 1992). She was the twenty-ninth DCMPD officer to be indicted for criminal conduct for the year 1992.

DECEPTION AND DISHONESTY

Thomas Barker and David Carter (1994b) have suggested that lying by police is both accepted and tolerated by most law enforcement agencies. According to Barker and Carter's taxonomy, police sometimes lie to work toward what they perceive as legitimate goals. In certain instances, for example, police may fabricate facts to obtain search warrants or to justify illegal stops. Police justify this type of dishonesty by arguing that it is necessary to apprehend persons whom they regard as criminals. In at least a few cases, DCMPD supervisory personnel condoned deceptive and dishonest practices for such goals.

In 1980, the District passed legislation requiring city employees, including police, to establish residency in the city within 180 days of being hired. Some had criticized the residency requirements for limiting the applicant pool for police positions, thus resulting in less qualified persons being hired as police officers (Carlson, 1993). However, the mayor (Marion Barry at that time) had publicly stated that he favored the residency requirement (Sommers, 1987). In 1987, officers and former employees of the DCMPD testified before a House District Subcommittee that police supervisors routinely altered resignation letters. Supervisors changed letters of resignation by deleting any reference to leaving the department because of the residency stipulation. In other instances, officers who resigned "were told not to cite the city's residency requirement as a reason or they would not get a good referral for their next job, would never be rehired by the department and could have problems getting their severance pay" (Sommers, 1987, p. A14). Supervisors allegedly used coercion and committed forgery because the mayor supported the policy.

Another practice involved a somewhat different form of deception. In 1987, it was revealed that the DCMPD had surreptitiously administered pregnancy tests to female police applicants since 1971. Although women applicants were advised in advance that they would be required to submit to X-ray examinations and drug screens, no mention was made that their urine would be tested to determine if they were pregnant. Police officials justified the tests by suggesting that pregnant applicants were "deferred" from active duty until they gave birth "to avoid jeopardizing [their] health and well-being along with that of the unborn child" (Neufield & Piccoli, 1987, p. G9). After the practice was publicized, then Chief Maurice Turner ordered that all women applicants be advised in advance that they would be given pregnancy tests.

Thomas Barker and David Carter (1994b) have noted that police also use deceptive and dishonest practices for illegitimate reasons. Police may lie, submit false reports or give perjured testimony to cover themselves or other officers when excessive force is used against a suspect. There is evidence that some DCMPD officers used illegal and unethical means to manipulate overtime pay for court appearances. "Officers, for example, tell of others—but never themselves—who routinely rush to crime scenes where they're not needed or figure out ways to insert themselves in criminal investigations, angling for court appearances and likely overtime pay" (Duggan, 1993, p. A7). Other officers were disciplined for submitting fraudulent overtime records. One justification offered for the practice was that DCMPD employees had not received a pay increase since October 1989 (Duggan, 1993). It is unclear just how many officers manipulated the system to receive overtime pay. "In 1989 the average number of overtime hours worked was 190 hours per officer. This equates to an average of $5,000 overtime pay for each officer" (PERF, 1990, p. 36). Although overtime control measures were put into place and the total overtime pay was reduced for fiscal year 1992, court-related overtime pay decreased only slightly (Duggan, 1993).

The manipulation of overtime pay once again became an issue in 1997 when city officials learned that 87 detectives and supervisors working in the homicide unit had accumulated $2.4 million in overtime during the previous year (Thompson & Ordon-ez, 1997). City officials indicated that detectives and supervisors in the unit were collecting thousands of dollars for overtime that they did not work. One sergeant in the unit supplemented his regular annual pay of $48,304.47 with an additional $101,814.54 in overtime. "Eleven others collected from $52,842 to $85,870 in overtime, and 21 officers and supervisors doubled their salaries" (Thompson, 1997b p. A1). After the story broke, William Corboy, a lieutenant formerly assigned to the unit, advised the D.C. Council he had supplied DCMPD administrators with a previous report, but that no action was taken. Corboy "told of detectives putting in for 99 hours of overtime a week, and he said one detective was paid overtime for working 27 hours in a day" (Thompson & Ordon-ez, 1997 p. C1). A captain in the homicide unit argued that it was Chief Soulsby who authorized unlimited overtime for the unit.

> Several law enforcement sources have said the chief cannot escape some of the blame for the woes of the homicide division. He once headed the unit and, as an assistant chief in 1995, was well aware of high overtime in the division. (Keary, 1997 p. A1)

POLITICAL COVER-UPS

Long before his conviction for possession of cocaine, there were allegations that former Mayor Marion Barry was associating with known drug traffickers and was a user of illicit narcotics. In January of 1982 Inspector Fred Raines, head of the DCMPD's intelligence unit, received written reports from department investigators alleging that Mayor Barry had either used cocaine or was present while it was used during a 1981 Christmas party held at a bar featuring nude dancers. The information presented in the reports was vague, and Raines reportedly advised the chief at that time, Maurice Turner, of the allegations.

On March 12, 1982, a detective spoke to three female employees of the nude bar where the alleged cocaine use had occurred. One of the women made the statement that if the mayor could come to the "[bar] for the Christmas party, use Coke [sic] in the open; it was obvious there was no fear of the police" (Knight, 1983b, p. A1). Inspector Raines then met with a justice department employee and informed him of the allegations against the mayor. Raines was subsequently advised by the employee that the department would not investigate the case since it involved allegations of recreational use of cocaine. Raines then allegedly advised Chief Turner of the new information.

In September of 1983, Raines received another intelligence report alleging drug use by Mayor Barry. Raines said that he again met with Chief Turner and advised him of the new report. "According to Raines, Turner said he would pass the information along to the internal affairs division, which also investigates allegations concerning city employees. Turner denied this and said he [knew] nothing about a . . . report" (Knight, 1983b, p. A1). Chief Turner later met with Mayor Barry and informed him of the allegations. Turner justified providing the mayor information about the allegations because, "I don't think he should be seen in places like that" (p. A1). Turner also indicated that he believed the information to be so unsubstantiated that no follow-up investigation was warranted (Knight, 1983a). Raines was chastised by Turner for having gone to the Justice Department without informing his superiors. Turner suggested, "Fred Raines *owes* a *loyalty* to *me* and the *police department*" [emphases added] (Knight, 1983b, p. A1). Raines justified his actions in providing an outside agency with the information by stating his belief that politically sensitive allegations should be checked out thoroughly. For his efforts, Turner subsequently reassigned Raines to a position as a night supervisor, a move perceived as a punishment.

In 1988, Chief Turner again found himself forced to deal with allegations of questionable conduct by Mayor Barry. This time DCMPD police were investigating a drug complaint at a Ramada Inn against Charles Lewis, a friend of Barry's. Police quickly stopped the investigation, however, when it was learned that Mayor Barry was in Lewis' hotel room. Barry purportedly suggested to Turner that he should announce that a departmental inquiry into the matter was concluded. This time, however, Turner handled the matter differently, turning the investigation over to the U.S. Attorney's Office (Simeon, 1989). Lewis, the suspected drug dealer, was later convicted and sentenced to fifteen months for possession and sale of drugs. Lewis also later testified in a grand jury hearing that he had observed Barry using drugs (Johnston, 1990).

According to testimony at his trial, Barry was using illegal drugs openly and regularly during the latter part of his term of office. If this is true, it is likely that DCMPD officers assigned to the mayor's protective service would have observed the illegal behavior. At Barry's trial, two DCMPD officers assigned to the mayor's security detail were called to testify. The officers, James Stays and Warren Goodwine, both denied that they had ever seen Barry using drugs. But information presented by the prosecution questioned the truthfulness of the officers' testimony. Another witness testified that Stays once handed her an envelope from Barry containing money that she was to use to buy drugs. Prosecutors presented evidence that Goodwine had requested a transfer from the mayor's security detail because of reservations about Barry's lifestyle, including his use of drugs (Ayres, 1990).

Allegations of improprieties of DCMPD officers assigned to the mayor's security detail have shadowed Barry's return to office. In April of 1995, a member of the mayor's security detail used an electronic key to enter the D.C. Board of Elections. When questioned by office workers, the officer said he was simply securing an absentee ballot for Barry because the mayor would be out of town for the election. Barry later acknowledged that the officer's actions were inappropriate. In 1996, an unmarked police car assigned to Barry's security detail was observed transporting two voters to a polling place to cast votes—a violation of federal law. The department responded by initiating an internal affairs investigation (Harris & Williams, 1996).

Another senior member of Barry's security detail, Ulysses Wall-tower, was investigated in 1995 after a woman accused him of taking her to a house and threatening her about statements she had made about Barry's wife. The woman had accused Barry's wife of campaign finance misconduct. Walltower was subsequently transferred to the department's gang task force. Two gang task force sergeants filed formal complaints with the FBI that Walltower was being paid for a non-working job. The sergeants also complained to their immediate supervisor; she reportedly told them her hands were tied because of the close relationship between her supervisor, Walltower, and Mayor Barry. The sergeants later told a D.C. Council committee that because of their complaints, they were intimidated, threatened, branded as "rats," and their careers took dramatic downturns. Walltower later resigned from the department rather than fight the departmental charges that had been levied against him (Mooar, 1997).

Finally, a homicide case remains under investigation with alleged ties to a former aide of Mayor Barry. In 1995, Carlton "Zack" Bryant was kidnapped from his home at gunpoint. Although Bryant's family reportedly paid a $50,000 ransom, he was beaten to death and his body discovered a few days later. Captain William Hennessey, former chief of the homicide unit, advised city leaders that an informant told investigators that a "Barry aide" had "masterminded" the kidnap and murder of Bryant. Hennessey also advised officials that after he was transferred from homicide, he examined the case file on Bryant's murder and discovered that information provided by the informant had been removed. Rhozier "Roach" Brown, an ex-convict former aide to Barry, has denied that he was involved in the Bryant killing, but admits that he is a prime suspect in the case (Milloy, 1997). At the time of this writing, the case remains open and unresolved.

In sum, there have been an unsettling series of questionable incidents involving the DCMPD and the District's political leaders. The behaviors of former chief Turner and other members of the DCMPD suggest the department had information about drug use by Marion Barry long before the mayor was arrested and convicted for possession of cocaine in 1990. Since Barry's return to office, there have been additional questions raised about connections between the mayor's office and the DCMPD. It would seem that there continues to be a reluctance to take any action that would damage the political linkages that exist between city government and the DCMPD.

DISTURBING ALLEGATIONS OF MISCONDUCT AND MISMANAGEMENT

The critical problems experienced by the DCMPD noted above are not the only difficulties confronting the department. Serious allegations of thefts by DCMPD officers have been raised. In one case, sixty weapons in police storage were determined "missing" after one of the weapons was used in a murder case (Carlson, 1993). Months later, in the spring of 1992, a handgun was taken from a convicted felon; that weapon was also recorded as in police storage. Journalist Tucker Carlson (1993) revealed what happened next:

> A subsequent police-department audit of the warehouse used to store confiscated weapons and drugs estimated that close to 3,000 seized guns were unaccounted for. The vault in which the guns had been kept had been used by police employees as a kitchen, replete with a refrigerator and a microwave oven. Employees simply put the guns in their coats and walked out after fixing lunch. (p. 27)

In an attempt to assure citizens that confiscated weapons had not been provided to criminals, a DCMPD spokesman attributed the missing guns to poor bookkeeping procedures. Carlson went on to note that thefts plagued the department in other ways since one station reportedly "chains its typewriters to desks to keep them from being taken by officers and police-department personnel" (p. 27).

Police management and control of evidence and property has, if anything, worsened in recent years. A police report issued in 1993 found that a property warehouse where police store evidence had no management controls over security, had no system for tracking evidence, and was administered under an "honor system" for officers. Because of the absence of controls, there were substantial opportunities for the theft of drugs and weapons by DCMPD employees. A 1995 city audit revealed that DCMPD had failed to deposit into bank accounts $1 million in forfeited drug money. Instead, the cash was simply put in boxes which were placed in a police vault (Powell, Horwitz & Thompson, 1997).

In 1997, the firm of Booz-Allen & Hamilton, Inc. reviewed police procedures used to handle and store evidence. Although the reports were intended to be confidential, information leaked about the findings was damning for the DCMPD. Boxes of drugs and cash were found stored in a non-secure drug lab. Unsecured guns and drugs were discovered in a police storage warehouse. DNA evidence for prosecuting rape cases was destroyed after being stored in humid conditions with temperatures exceeding 100 degrees. Alarmed by the report, a D.C. Superior Court judge warned that the mishandling of evidence threatened to undermine thousands of pending criminal cases. Following disclosure of the problems, defense attorneys indicated they would begin using the report as a foundation to challenge the evidentiary value of items seized by police. As one attorney noted, "If their own experts said the process was invalid, then defense attorneys start asking the courts to throw cases out" (Powell & Miller, 1997 p. A1).

The DCMPD has also experienced critical equipment-related problems. Most of these problems could not be attributed to the lack of resources of the District or the department. Instead mismanagement and poor decision making accounted for their deficiency. First, the DCMPD has not maintained an adequate number of operable police vehicles. A *Washington Times* investigation suggested that more than one-half of the department's patrol cars are out of service at any one time (Carlson, 1993). As a result, some districts have had as many as forty calls backed-up; in other instances, older calls have simply been ignored. In some cases, car shortages have meant that detectives have been unable to complete investigations. A department spokesman claimed that new cruisers had been ordered but not delivered (Horwitz, 1990). When asked, one DCMPD sergeant attributed the vehicle shortage to accidents caused by the reckless driving of younger officers (Carlson, 1993). Another likely cause for vehicle shortages was revealed in a consulting firm's analysis of the Fleet Management Division (FMD). That analysis suggested that the FMD suffered from poor employee productivity and an inability to control the quality of employees hired by the division (KPMG, 1990). Whatever the reasons, Mayor Sharon Pratt Kelly publicly criticized Chief Fulwood for the vehicle shortage in August 1992 (McCraw & Reilly, 1992).

Among the other equipment problems experienced by the DCMPD: (1) a shortage of police radios—one squad reportedly had only one radio for the ten officers assigned; (2) a lack of ammunition and books for the police training academy; (3) no bulletproof vests for academy graduates; (4) not enough typewriters, sometimes resulting in conditions where an office of thirty detectives had only one manual typewriter; and (5) other shortages including rubber gloves, film for photographs, tires for police cruisers, and inoperable copy machines (Horwitz, 1990). In addition to equipment problems, many DCMPD buildings and facilities were in a severe state of disrepair. Mismanagement was thus responsible for many officers in the department lacking the fundamental equipment and facilities necessary to perform basic police work.

Grave problems in the DCMPD's homicide unit were brought to light in 1997. In 1996, the Justice Department provided DCMPD officials with a report and analysis of 136 unsolved homicide cases from 1990 to 1994. The report provided recommendations for improving operations, noting that cases were not reviewed, there was lax supervision in the unit, and there were no attempts to improve case management. Justice

Department officials noted that "several hundred files related to homicides that occurred from 1990 to 1994 could not be readily located" (Thomas-Lester & Miller, 1997 p. A1). No changes were implemented in the unit, and the department's homicide case closure rate continued to decline steadily, from 55 percent in 1994 to 43 percent in 1995 and to 42 percent in 1996. The unit's overall closure rate for 1997 was 34 percent in September of that year.

Despite substantial indicators that the homicide unit was in deep trouble, no action was taken until a report was presented to Chief Soulsby by the division's former captain, Alan Dreher. It was revealed that forty-nine detectives in the unit, which is about half of the personnel assigned to investigations, had failed to close even one case assigned to them in the first six months of 1997 (Thomas-Lester & Miller, 1997). Other serious problems were disclosed as well: detectives frequently failed to attend autopsies for cases they were investigating; documentation directly relating to investigations was unable to be located; detectives were flagrantly abusing overtime pay ostensibly for court appearances; some investigations were prematurely discontinued; and detectives were failing to follow the unit's investigative procedures (Thompson, 1997c).

Following disclosure of the problems, Chief Soulsby removed the commander of the homicide unit and 17 supervisors assigned to the division. Soulsby also indicated that he would seek to hire a college-educated homicide commander with a proven track record from outside the agency—a first for the department (Thompson, 1997a). As might be expected, members of the public scathingly criticized Soulsby's failure to properly oversee the division. As one writer noted, "This alarming development is not simply a matter of bureaucratic failure; it pierces . . . this community's already shaky confidence in the police and returns us to the verge of lawlessness" (Gilliam, 1997 p. C1). In remarks to a newspaper, Soulsby promised a sweeping internal probe that would go as high as needed "up to and including the chief himself" (Keary, 1997 p. A1). The day following the comments, however, Soulsby remarked to another reporter, "As chief of police I'm responsible for everything. But what you had was five layers of supervision between me and homicide" (Gilliam, 1997 p. B1).

The DCMPD has also experienced problems with personnel recruitment, training, and retention. In 1986, the department came under fire for a special program it had developed to hire more Hispanic officers. Under that program, forty residents of Puerto Rico were hired, a move calculated to double the number of Hispanics on the force. Hispanic leaders in the District of Columbia criticized the program, arguing that the DCMPD should have focused its efforts on recruiting Hispanics living in Washington (D.C. Police Criticized, 1986).

Since then, the DCMPD has come under fire for other recruitment and training practices. In 1989 alone, the department hired 1,800 officers. In the process of hiring such a massive number of new employees, background checks were either postponed or not completed at all. One former police academy instructor claimed, "We swore in entire classes—hundreds of people—without background checks" (Carlson, 1993, p. 28). The chief at that time, Isaac Fulwood, set the tone for hiring when he reportedly told employees, "Hire them now, we'll fire them later" (p. 28). Many recruits were later found to have criminal backgrounds. Of the 201 officers arrested between 1989 and 1992, about one-half were from the 1989 and 1990 DCMPD recruit classes. Arrested officers were charged with a variety of offenses ranging from shoplifting to rape and murder (Powell, Horwitz & Thompson, 1997).

Coupled with questionable hiring practices are allegations that recruit training was inconsistent and inadequate. Academy curriculum changed every year for the past decade; records of the changes were apparently not kept. In 1988, the academy abolished its comprehensive exam after 40 percent of graduating recruits failed it (Carlson, 1993). A former instructor at the academy indicated, "I've saw [sic] people who were practically illiterate. I've seen people diagnosed as borderline-retarded graduate from the police academy" (p. 30). As noted above, the ramifications of lax recruitment and training procedures are serious. With about one-half of the DCMPD's officers having been hired since 1988 (Editor, 1993b), it is unknown just how many current employees are literal "time bombs." That question was raised following the arrest of a twenty-two-year-old DCMPD officer for allegedly holding his 9mm duty weapon to the head of his ex-girlfriend and forcing her to perform a sex act (Editor, 1993b).

THE CONTINUING QUEST FOR STABILITY IN THE DCMPD

The DCMPD has struggled—albeit largely unsuccessfully—in its attempts to provide viable police services for residents of the District. The serious problems experienced by the agency are the product of years of inattention and mismanagement. Michael Powell and his colleagues (1997) have suggested:

> . . . the department has been on a 20-year descent. Once recognized as a model of fine policing, the force has endured two decades of political interference by Mayor Marion Barry and the D.C. Council, a persistent lack of fiscal controls, bad hiring practices and poor management. (p. A1)

In addition to the categories of deviance already discussed, the DCMPD continues to suffer from ongoing reports of wrongdoing by its officers. A sampling of other issues with which the department finds itself confronted includes:

- In 1996, several DCMPD employees were investigated for purchasing stolen merchandise at discount prices from a secretary with the Bureau of Alcohol, Tobacco and Firearms (ATF). The ATF employee had used agency credit cards to illegally purchase electronic items ranging from laptop computers to portable phones. Assistant Police Chief James B. Sarvis and 18 other DCMPD officers and civilian employees were implicated in the scheme. Eight officers were eventually suspended without pay for their involvement in the scheme. [*Washington Post*, 9/15/97, p. A9]

- In early 1997, two DCMPD patrolmen were arrested for allegedly running a crack cocaine distribution operation. The officers were reportedly involved with the distribution of cocaine worth up to $100,000 over a three-month period. One of the officers used a police station telephone to arrange a meeting with a drug contact. The announcements of the arrests came hours after the chairman of the D.C. Appropriations subcommittee urged Police Chief Soulsby to purge the 3,600-member department of officers with criminal records. [*Lubbock-Avalanche Journal*, 3/7/97]

- In October 1997, the FBI executed a search warrant in the DCMPD's check and fraud unit. Agents seized a computer used to make identification documents. Ironically, the computer equipment had been seized by D.C. police nearly two years prior in an investigation of two college students suspected of making and selling false identification. Records in the investigation have remained sealed, but someone allegedly attempted to extort money from a District government official using false identification made with the computer. After disclosure of the investigation, it was learned that the department's internal affairs unit had issued warnings nearly two years prior that the equipment was ripe for potential illegal misuse. [*Washington Post*, 10/31/97, p. C4]

- The department's civilian review board was disbanded in June of 1995. At the time the board was abolished, it was years behind and left a backlog of 770 unresolved complaints. Concerned that the department is incapable of using internal means to objectively evaluate allegations against officers, the D.C. Council is considering a plan for retired judges and mediators to review complaints and recommend disciplinary action. [*Washington Post*, 9/16/97, p. B3]

- The department is currently attempting to identify officers convicted of domestic violence charges. Under a 1996 federal law, domestic abusers— including police officers—are prohibited from carrying firearms. Department officials are aware of at least 100 officers who have been accused of domestic violence in the past. In 1997, Inspector Adrian Barnes retired after it was learned that he had been convicted of battering his wife. Barnes had been handpicked by Chief Soulsby to oversee a zero-tolerance crime-fighting plan. Although Soulsby said he was unaware of Barnes' previous problems, others in the department said the chief's lack of knowledge was inconceivable since "Everyone on the department knew about Adrian Barnes." [*Washington Post*, 9/11/97, p. A1]

The litany of allegations about what Chief Soulsby knew reached a crescendo in December 1997. Soulsby resigned hours before his friend, Lt. Jeffrey Stowe, was indicted for embezzlement and extortion. Stowe was the commander of the fraud and extortion unit; he controlled three separate police funds. Stowe had a reputation in the department for living beyond his means (Bai, 1997). Soulsby, no longer living with his wife, accepted Stowe's invitation to move into his downtown apartment. The chief claimed to be unaware that Stowe had rented the apartment (at one-third the usual fee of $1800) under pretenses of police surveillance. Stowe alleged that he was innocent of the charges in the indictment and that they were motivated by people targeting Soulsby.

Reform efforts in the DCMPD have been abject failures. Soulsby's resignation was just one more downfall in an endless series. His background as a department insider was a serious impediment. As Lawrence Sherman stated, "Chief Soulsby [wa]s a lifelong product of a department that now needs a major cultural and administrative change" (Powell, 1997, p. B1). Problems have surfaced and resurfaced for so long that their systemic nature will not be easily uprooted. Jamie Raskin commented that the environment in which the District police function is also a contributing factor: "It's not just the police. Agency after agency, commission after commission. Spend five minutes investigating any one of them, and you find the most outrageous things going on" (Bai, p. 42).

REACTIONS TO POLICE DEVIANCE

Undoubtedly there are conscientious DCMPD officers who are not actively involved in deviant or criminal misconduct. The corollary issue is why such officers have not come forward. As we learned in chapter 4, part of the answer lies in the nature of the police subculture: officers are socialized to remain quiet. Testimony before the Mollen Commission (1994) illustrated that loyalty and a misguided notion of nobility can lead officers to accept blame for misconduct to protect their fellow officers.

> [While still a rookie, Hembury and his partner] stopped a motorcycle for a number of traffic violations. Because the driver became irate, Hembury's partner thought he would teach him a lesson by removing a spark plug coil to disable the engine. Eventually charges for damaging the motorcycle were wrongly brought against Hembury, not his partner. But the code of silence compelled Hembury to accept the pun-

ishment—a loss of fifteen vacation days—for something he did not do. (pp. 55–56)

Some DCMPD officers have stepped forward to reveal deviant and criminal acts committed by other police, but the costs of breaking the police code of silence are high. In one case, an officer reported that a fellow cop placed a belt around the neck of a prisoner while taunting and verbally abusing him. The officer who reported the incident later found an envelope attached to his locker containing his police baton, which had been ground into sawdust (*Weber v. District of Columbia*, 1989). Others quickly learn that allegations will be vigorously denied.

In 1989, a DCMPD detective and his wife filed suit against the department. In that case, the detective's wife wrote an anonymous letter to the mayor, alleging "official abuses of authority, favoritism, and misconduct within her husband's command in the department" (*Weber v. District of Columbia*, 1989, p. 829). When DCMPD officers discovered who had written the letter, they allegedly began a campaign to harass and intimidate the detective and his wife, who subsequently filed suit alleging that the harassment caused them to experience "extreme emotional distress" leading to the detective's involuntary resignation from the department and the dissolution of the marriage.

In 1983, a thirty-four-year-old DCMPD officer charged with distributing cocaine spoke with the media and alleged that there was widespread drug use by officers in the department. He claimed that he and many other officers used drugs while on duty. Maurice Turner, then chief, flatly denied that drug use was widespread, stating that all allegations of drug use were thoroughly investigated by the department (Officer Alleges, 1983). Seven years later, however, the department implemented a random, mandatory drug testing program for all DCMPD officers (Gonzales & Fields, 1990).

Non-corrupt, non-deviant officers in the DCMPD have four options to choose from in order to cope with the critical problems facing the department. First, some officers will join their corrupt peers and become involved in deviant activities. Second, others may choose to become whistle-blowers and risk censure from their colleagues. Third, many officers will remain with the DCMPD, coping in whatever ways they can and continuing to work in a dysfunctional environment. Finally, many officers, disgusted with job conditions and the work environment, will either quit or retire from the DCMPD. The last option may be the choice of many; estimates suggest about 2,400 officers are eligible for retirement from the DCMPD (Gonzales, 1990).

SUMMARY

As the seat of the nation's capital, there have been intense pressures to resolve the District's crime problem—especially drug trafficking and the homicide rate. The city has had little success in responding to public demands to "do something about crime." City administrators and police officials followed the standard response and blamed the problems on a lack of manpower—ignoring the fact that the number of police officers serving a city has little to do with its crime rate but much to do with political posturing.

The reality is that the district has suffered from corruption, mismanagement in city government, and serious incidents of misconduct by police officers. A report by a city commission questioned staffing patterns—not numbers—in the DCMPD, recommending hundreds of police positions be eliminated and that officers be redeployed to patrol duties.

Police engage in deviant behavior when they use confidential police information for unethical or illegal purposes. In the DCMPD, officers have received payoffs in exchange for providing criminals with information about drug raids, criminal investigations, and confidential police documents. The results have been serious: investigations have been jeopardized; hundreds of criminal cases were dismissed; and, in one instance, a contract murder was reportedly facilitated. Several other forms of deviant conduct by DCMPD personnel have surfaced. Administrators and officers used deceptive and dishonest practices; information about alleged criminal conduct was overlooked, ignored, or mishandled; and there were serious allegations raised of the theft of hundreds of weapons from police evidence.

Numerous citizens have raised excessive force complaints against DCMPD officers. Information presented in these allegations suggests a persistent pattern of police abuse of power. One mechanism for controlling police abuse of authority, which we will discuss in the next chapter, is the civilian complaint review board. In Washington D.C., the board was ineffective. Police executives and city officials routinely failed to mete out discipline to officers the citizen's board had found guilty of serious misconduct. Complaints by citizens were delayed for years. The public officials responsible for providing adequate resources and personnel for the investigation of complaints failed to do so; the department often actively obstructed the investigative process. The pattern of reported instances of police wrongdoing among a significant number of officers in the DCMPD indicates the need for the internal and external controls discussed in chapter 10.

Chapter Ten

INFLUENCING POLICE DEVIANCE AND CORRUPTION
Internal and External Controls

The inadequate is productive.
J. W. von Goethe   (1749–1832)

Police power and authority serve as a double-edged sword. On the one edge is the authority and power necessary to protect life and do "justice." On the other edge is the ability to abuse power and authority, to injure individuals, to damage the community, and to affect the social order negatively. This dilemma reflects a constant and recurring theme in policing: the need to assure citizens' safety and the need to control abuses of police powers. Also important is a clean and positive public image of the police, since they are the symbolic representatives of our justice system and our government. The effective control of police deviance requires both internal analysis and discipline of officers and external review of their behavior. While it is impossible to control police deviance totally from either the inside or the outside, a combination of efforts yields the best results. That is, police power and authority must be governed by organizational design, administrative supervision, and attention to the elements of the subculture as well as by laws, civilian oversight, and professional standards. Likewise, attention must be paid to the effects police interactions with the community have on both the perception of the police and actual participation in deviance.

Traditionally, internal control of the police has focused on increasing the formalization and specification of rules and procedures. This has been considered the best method to control police abuses of power and to curtail deviance. History, however, has demonstrated that this internal and formal approach will affect some police behavior but will not control all types of deviance. As discussed in chapters 2 and 8, the New York City Police Department adopted policy statements earlier in its history, but it has still experienced a high level of police deviance and corruption. This may in part be due to the failure of police officials to enforce established standards routinely and effectively. Many departments which have modernized and strengthened their policies and directives have experienced significant improvements, but there is still a great need to improve the internal controls over police personnel. In this chapter, we will review the internal and external methods used by law enforcement agencies to control deviance and corruption by addressing both formal and informal methods of control. Throughout the discussion, we will identify critical points of control and highlight some of the many influences on police deviance and corruption.

FORMAL METHODS OF INTERNAL CONTROL

Any effective system for controlling deviance by internal means must be based on quality personnel operating with policies which provide a clear definition of proper and improper conduct; mechanisms for detecting and sanctioning improper conduct; and techniques for rewarding exemplary conduct. As discussed in chapter 4, police selection and training techniques are key elements in creating an organization responsive to community needs, in making the police institution representative of the communities served, and in developing capable personnel. First, officers must be selected who possess qualities conducive to becoming capable police officers. Second, the type of training officers receive is vital to their preparation for police work. Third, the content and language of the policies which guide officers' behavior are critical. Fourth, the seriousness with which the guidelines are communicated, enforced, and systematically applied will direct police behavior. Fifth, the methods by which deviant officers are supervised and sanctioned are crucial in molding behavior patterns. Finally, the ways in which officers are held accountable for their actions can help keep behavior within appropriate boundaries.

While there is no foolproof method to screen applicants for police work that predicts whether a person will become and remain a competent officer, police officials must begin to look beyond the ability of applicants to perform basic tasks. Personnel selection decisions should encompass values, respect for human life, and sensitivity to cultural diversity. The United States Department of Justice (1987) suggests that police officials consider the following principles when selecting personnel:

- A police department should recruit and select a ratio of minority-group employees in proportion to the community it serves.
- Emphasis should be placed on bringing people with a college background into law enforcement.
- Individuals should be psychologically suited to handle the requirements of police work. (pp. 1–25)

Enhanced selection techniques alone, however, will not eradicate police deviance and corruption. Political pressures and the language of disorder can drastically influence the police selection process.

> With more cops on the beat, there are bound to be more confrontations. And cops who've been ordered to take back the streets can get the wrong idea about what that means. . . . It's also possible that in the rush to saturate the streets with cops, cities have hired officers who might not have made the cut otherwise." (Beals & Bai, 1997, p. 53)

As part of the crime bill passed in 1994, the federal government has funded the addition of more than 60,000 officers nationwide. Washington, D.C. hired 50 new officers without having completed the usual background checks. Pittsburgh added more than 400 cops in the last five years. Deputy Chief Charles Moffatt remarked, "We had to turn them out quickly, and we couldn't give them as much closely supervised field training as we'd like to" (p. 53).

The International Association of Chiefs of Police (IACP) conducted research on ethics and integrity and warned (1989):

> There is no guarantee that an individual of good character, hired by a police department, will remain honest. There are a variety of factors . . . which can erode an officer's commitment to integrity. Many officers face temptation every day. . . . Management has the capacity and control to reinforce high integrity, detect corruption, and limit the opportunity for wrongdoing. (p. 53)

This research emphasized the importance of management and supervision of police officers. The results of the research indicated that officers who engage in corrupt activities are also likely to be involved in other forms of deviance (an important point examined later). Further, the IACP suggests that supervisors can compromise, by both actions and inactions, the integrity of their officers. They note that supervisors must enforce agency policies; cannot overlook irregularities, misconduct or early indications of problems; and cannot be influenced by personal relationships with subordinates. The IACP (1989) cautions that "supervisors who fail to audit the activities of personnel fail to perform their jobs, a fact which must be accepted by the officers as well as the supervisors" (p. 57). Beyond auditing officers' actions, supervisors must take action against those who do not meet the appropriate standards set by the department. Similarly, they must reward those who go beyond ordinary tasks and serve the department and community in an exemplary fashion. The methods for assessing behavior should be clearly communicated in the department's policies, in verbal communication, and in action.

The Development of Guidelines

The communication of organizational expectations by police officials informs officers what conduct will be accepted and what will not be tolerated. These expectations are established through the development of policy, procedure, and rules. A *policy* is a statement of guiding principles which must be followed in activities that fall within either specific organizational objectives or the overall police mission. A policy is a guide to thinking based on an organization's orientation to achieving its goals. A *procedure* is the method of performing a task or a manner of proceeding with a course of action. It differs from policy in that it specifies action in a particular situation to perform a task within the guidelines of policy. A procedure is a guide to action. A *rule* is a mandate which either requires or prohibits specified behavior. A rule is a mandate to action. These various control mechanisms are designed to address a multitude of needs, including the need for regulation and uniformity of police activities. Although this process is much more formal, the three elements bear a resemblance to the cultural themes, ethos, and postulates we discussed in chapter 4. Those three elements contribute to the ideology of policing at the sub-cultural level. Policies, procedures, and rules create the formal organizational culture of the police. If the formal framework is constructed with a knowledge of the influence of the informal organization, the prospects for eliminating undesirable undercurrents and conflicts are greatly improved.

The National Advisory Commission on Criminal Justice Standards and Goals (1973) report on the police provides an excellent discussion of the differences among written policies, procedures and rules.

> Policy is different from rules and procedures. Policy should be stated in broad terms to guide employees. It sets limits of discretion. A policy statement deals with the principles and values that guide the performance of activities directed toward the achievement of agency objectives. A procedure is a way of proceeding—a routine—to achieve an objective. Rules significantly reduce or eliminate discretion by specifically stating what must and must not be done. (p. 54)

These directives, in varying degrees, establish parameters for officers to perform day-to-day operations in a manner consistent with the philosophy and values of the organization. Collectively, rules serve to control behavioral choices by limiting alternative courses of action and steering officers toward decisions that fall within pre-established boundaries.

Law enforcement agencies must have guidelines to control the broad powers of their officers. However, as officers are confronted daily with a variety of complex situations, discretion is necessary. Discretion must be guided by legal strictures and administrative philosophy rather than by personal feelings, individual prejudices, or notions of street justice. Written and enforced directives are necessary for the proper control of law enforcement functions because of the structural, personal, and situational factors that affect behavioral choices. These directives are formulated by determining objectives and identifying the principles or ideas which will best guide the officer in achieving them (Alpert & Smith, 1993).

Gary Cordner (1989) has questioned the wisdom of departmental management by extensive directives: "The question of most importance is whether extensive written directives make police organizations more effective. Do rules and regulations improve the quality of police service? Do they contribute to police goal attainment?" (p. 18). The question is particularly relevant in the context of providing police services; it is based on the criterion of efficiency in attaining that goal.

In terms of controlling deviance, the criterion of goal attainment is less persuasive. Many of the measures that can directly affect the level of deviance or corruption in a police organization may not be the most effective measures for furthering the organization's overall goals. Policy should not be developed solely on its ability to increase efficiency but must incorporate the ability to shape acceptable behavioral bounds for achieving goals. While it might be an efficient and effective practice for law enforcement officers to use coercion to extract information from criminal suspects, it is nonetheless outside the bounds of legal behavior and should be against departmental policy. In this illustration, the policy may not contribute to the goal of law enforcement, but it serves to structure the means by which that goal will be achieved. Departmental policies should be constructed so that they reflect the values of the organization and the society in which it operates. The United States Department of Justice (1987) suggests the following actions as some of the most important values a police department can incorporate.

- Preserve and advance the principles of democracy
- Place the highest value on protecting human life
- Prevent crime; the number one operational priority
- Involve the community in delivering police services
- Believe in accountability to the community served
- Commit to professionalism in all aspects of operations
- Maintain the highest standards of integrity. (pp. 1–25)

Written polices and directives are not panaceas for controlling deviance and corruption. Howard S. Cohen and Michael Feldberg (1991) suggest that written directives may be necessary, but used alone they are not sufficient to control police personnel. Although New York, Los Angeles, and Washington, D.C. have extensive policies and procedures manuals, they have all experienced serious problems with deviance and corruption. Cohen and Feldberg have identified three factors which provide police with sufficient information to operate successfully in a law-enforcement agency.

> The practical ingredients an individual needs . . . in matters of professional conduct are an understanding of the values that inform his or her profession, the intention to live up to the values, and an environment that supports those values and discourages behavior that is contrary to them. (pp. 148–149)

Appropriate departmental policies are the first step in creating an environment conducive to good decision making. They provide a statement of organizational values, structure discretion, and channel the use of power. If an officer is properly trained and internalizes those values and guidelines, he or she will be able to use discretion properly. Training and understanding set the stage for appropriate behavioral choices.

Training and Education

Training is almost universally regarded as one of the most critical needs of a police department. Police training, however, must move beyond the traditional "nuts and bolts" of "how to do" police work. Too many officers have received hundreds of hours of training—learning only what others have done in the past, what is expected of them by their immediate supervisors, and how to follow orders without questioning them. Such practices cater to and reinforce existing values and practices while stifling change. In organizations inundated with deviance and corruption, this type of training does little more than transmit values conducive to furthering deviance. This creates generations of officers who, at best, can only react to their existing environment. Police training must help officers to *think* as well as to react and respond (Alpert & Dunham, 1997). This means the police must not only be trained, they must be educated. Police training must teach critical thinking and problem-solving techniques.

Some police agencies are requiring more than one thousand hours of pre-service training and quarterly in-service training for the discussion of new ideas and the renewal of deteriorating skills. These requirements provide an opportunity to prepare officers to employ infrequently used skills and to keep them current with laws and enforcement techniques. However, this preparation only provides the officer with the *ability* to perform his or her job well. As Cohen and Feldberg (1991) remind us, the officer must *want* to do what is right. One method of assisting police officers in the development of attitudes appropriate for responsive policing is to incorporate values education into police training programs. The United States Justice Department (1987) suggests that police departments consider these questions when training recruits and selecting training officers:

- Should field training officers for police cadets have demonstrated conformity to department values?
- What type of officer is appointed as a field training officer—those with a high or low tolerance for violence?
- Is that officer a "negotiator" or "confrontationalist"?
- Are field training officers trained in methods of negotiation, problem resolution, and other "alternative" police responses?
- Do field training officers receive informal as well as formal rewards for their services to the department?
- Does the formal training process for officers include classroom time devoted to community relations and other alternative responses?
- Which received greater emphasis in the training curriculum—firearms instruction and self-defense or group and interpersonal interaction skills? (pp. 1–25)

Strong guidelines and thorough training in state-of-the-art procedures may support proper law enforcement, but they do not guarantee the control of deviance. High-visibility incidents of police wrongdoing can have dramatic effects on police training. "The enduring image of the Los Angeles Police Department—cops whaling away with nightsticks at a prostrate victim—was engraved on the nation's retina by the Rodney King beating in 1991" (Cray, 1997, p. 30). After the stinging criticism sparked by the brutality, the LAPD took action to prevent future incidents.

Greg Dossey, a 25-year veteran, was charged with massive retraining of the rank and file. He converted 8,000 use-of-force reports into a statistical database which he used to create prototypical police altercations. His research showed that in two-thirds of the altercations, the officer and suspect were eventually wrestling on the ground. Previous training methods had focused on upright resistance. A flexible "C grip"—a loose grab that does not provoke an angry response—is now taught. Officers are instructed to wait for backup and team takedowns to apprehend a suspect. If those methods fail, chemical sprays or shotguns that fire beanbags are used. Interviews after the King incident revealed the unsettling news that departmental members had diverse opinions as to whether or not the officers involved in the beating were following official procedures. Only eight instructors now teach use of force. Department Commander Charles Binse says, "The idea is to teach from the same book" (Cray, 1997, pg. 30). Each week, 100 officers are retrained; every 18 months, they are required to attend a two-day refresher course. Dossey characterizes the program as "the most ambitious arrest-control training program you'll find" (p. 30).

The Role of Supervision

Supervision entails the direction of individual police officers in their day-to-day activities. Specifically, supervisors must make sure that subordinates are aware of the agency mission, its policies, and procedures. Further, the supervisor is responsible for ensuring that officers are acting properly and conforming to the rules and regulations on a day-to-day basis. The supervisor's first loyalty must be to the organization.

Because supervisors are promoted through the ranks, they have often attended the academy with subordinates or have known them for a long time, often as equals. It may be difficult for supervisors to exercise control over their former peers because they shared the same socialization and culturalization experiences (Gaines et al., 1997). However, a minor breach of authority can create serious problems for a new supervisor who chooses to accommodate his or her former equal over control responsibilities. Supervisors must establish a style that is acceptable to subordinates but also creates a working atmosphere that is healthy, productive, and conforms to acceptable values.

Methods of rewarding officers for jobs well done are essential (Alpert & Dunham, 1997). While supervisors must sanction deviance, they must also provide incentives for officers to comply with organizational values. In some police organizations, officers are more likely to be awarded a departmental commendation for shooting a criminal suspect than for saving a life. These types of mixed signals can contribute to misconduct.

Effective supervisors should be the first to learn about an officer's deviance or problem because they should be monitoring behavior. Supervisors must learn about their officers and have a good understanding about their strengths and weaknesses. There is little excuse for supervisors not wanting to know or not caring about the activities of their subordinates. There must be established procedures for addressing incidents of suspected deviance. If a supervisor hears about deviance, some action must be taken. Whether a face-to-face confrontation, an investigation of the incident, or a memo to the personnel file, some action must be taken to document and to correct the misconduct. Supervisors who look the other way or pretend misconduct does not exist are failing themselves, their responsibility, their subordinates, and the public. In a real sense, they are promoting deviance.

Specific methods have been devised to manage these issues. Performance evaluations can provide appropriate information concerning an officer's strengths and weaknesses. Complaints filed against an officer can also provide some information about his or her behavior. Attendance problems, tardiness, use of force, number of arrests and tickets, as well as other behavioral indicators can help the supervisor assess, control, and discipline those under his or her command.

Accountability and Discipline

Officers and supervisors must be held accountable for their actions. Officers who make contact with citizens are usually asked to take notes on the meeting to preserve any information that was provided. Officers involved in automobile accidents must complete an accident reporting form. Officers who are in possession of controlled substances for undercover operations must provide documentation of the circumstances surrounding the possession. Officers who seize property must record the transactions and are accountable for the property. Officers who use force to control suspects should be responsible for completing a "control of persons," or a "use of force" report. If deadly force is used, an officer must complete a form describing and explaining the "why, where and how" of that force. Police departments should require officers to complete critiques which include recent sleeping habits, off-duty employment, and other personal information which might relate to or help explain the event (Alpert & Fridell, 1992).

It is important to establish an accountability system for any officer who has been involved in some low-risk and all high-risk activities. Writing a critique is the first step. This process serves several purposes: (1) an analysis of the information contained in a critique can help determine if the action was necessary and conducted within departmental policy; (2) critiques will help determine if specific training is needed; (3) critiques will help determine if a change in policy is needed; and (4) an analysis of the aggregate data generated in these reports will reveal trends and demonstrate specific risk factors. As an additional step, the agency must assign supervisory personnel to evaluate these reports and to determine if a violation has occurred and to suggest disciplinary action if necessary.

An agency's disciplinary system is a critical reinforcer of its values, policies, and rules. Discipline sends a serious message to anyone who has violated an order. This message can range from a verbal warning or re-training to suspension or termination of employment. Another important function of the disciplinary action is the message that is sent to others when an officer is disciplined—or when he or she is *not* disciplined—for a policy violation. The mere existence of extensive policies and rules without appropriate supervision, evaluation, and reinforcement is only a hollow veneer of responsible policing. As discussed in the first three chapters of the book, the informal values, practices, and customs of the police often differ dramatically from formal statements of the organization. If enforcement of policy violations is lax or nonexistent that becomes the "unstated" policy of the organization and can actually promote deviance.

All officers must understand the importance of the rules and regulations—and the consequences for violating them. For example, if an officer is involved in a preventable motor vehicle accident, it is important to have a disciplinary scheme established. The first violation may result in a written reprimand, while a second violation may require counseling or remedial training. A third violation may result in a change of duty so the individual does not have an opportunity to use a motor vehicle. At some point, a department will have to take more drastic action, and those steps must also be public reminders of responsibilities. Failure to take disciplinary action may be seen as condoning deviance, and subordinates may begin to respond not to the stated rules of the organization but to the actual enforcement practices of supervisors. This concept has been summarized by The United States Commission on Civil Rights (1981) which found that ". . . disciplinary sanctions commensurate with the seriousness of the offense that are imposed fairly, swiftly, and consistently will most clearly reflect the commitment of the department to oppose police misconduct" (p. 158).

It is, however, equally important that the police department recognize personnel who conform to the policies, procedures, and values of the organization. Recognition of exemplary behavior reinforces the policies and values of the agency. The United States Department of Justice (1987) suggests that police officials consider the following questions concerning the reinforcement of values.

- Which officers receive the most sought after special assignments and better regular duty assignments—negotiators or confrontationalists?
- Does the department most frequently commend officers who use force—or who avoid using it—in achieving department objectives?
- When was the last occasion the department recognized, formally or informally, an officer for the ability to avoid using force?
- Most departments have an item of uniform apparel which recognizes firearms proficiency. Does yours have one for force-avoidance skills? (pp. 1–25)

The St. Petersburg, Florida police department incorporates its statement on values and discipline into its policy manual. We have reprinted it as an example of how to create an appropriate atmosphere for police officers by delineating the values of the organization, discussing the police mission, and setting expectations for officers in the department.

Centralized Administration

Although administrative tasks vary considerably depending on the type and size of law enforcement agencies, the general principles used and the form of administration are similar. For example, *administration* involves a focus on the overall organization and its mission, while *management* is involved in the day-to-day operations of the various units within the organization.

Administrations may be centralized or decentralized. Decentralized administrations delegate authority by geographic areas and/or type of activity to officers or members of the command staff. For example, a police department could have several districts which are self-contained and operate as mini police agencies. Alternatively, these districts could be responsible only for traffic, patrol, and emergencies; major crimes, investigations and planning could be handled by the main office. There are multiple methods by which to organize an agency.

What impact do these various organizational frameworks have on police deviance? A centralized administration may keep closer control over officers and their behavior, but the officers will suffer a loss of independence and the ability to adapt to the various communities they serve

---

Discipline Philosophy

St. Petersburg Police Department

Tensions and hostility are a part of policing. Police officers must, as part of their job, issue orders to people, catch them in violation of laws, deprive them of their freedom, and bring charges that may lead to the imposition of severe punishment. Contacts between officers and citizens are often initiated under conditions that are emotionally charged, such as immediately after a fight or other disturbance, or following the commission of a crime. Even the person getting a traffic ticket frequently becomes indignant. However scrupulous the police may be in carrying out their responsibilities, they are bound to incur the wrath of some of those against whom they must proceed. This hostility manifests itself in various forms—sometimes immediately, by verbal abuse or physical resistance to the police; sometimes later by alleging that the officer's actions were improper or illegal. Under such circumstances an officer must be able to count on support for actions taken in the line of duty. . . . the police officer expects and indeed needs some insulation from the community being served. But insulation can serve as a shield for the officer who is not so scrupulous—who in fact acts improperly (Goldstein, 1977).

The adversarial nature of policing is one of the key factors noted by Herman Goldstein that complicates the control and review of police actions and behavior. The public grants the police considerable authority to act on its behalf in the effort to create an environment as free of crime, the fear of crime, drug abuse, violence and disorder as possible. Although in almost all encounters with the public, police officers and nonsworn employees use this authority appropriately, there are times when citizens have legitimate questions about how this authority has been used. Unfortunately there are also times when that authority has been abused. Therefore, it is critical that a system of discipline be established that contributes to minimizing abuse of authority and promotes the department's reputation for professionalism.

The most effective disciplinary system is one that combines the reinforcement of the right set of values in all employees with behavioral standards that are established in clear policies, procedures and rules that are consistently and fairly applied. Each employee of the St. Petersburg Police Department must understand and be guided by the standards that have been established in the department (and city) General Orders, rules, regulations and procedures.

Employees of the St. Petersburg Police Department are expected to conduct themselves, both in interactions with each other and with the public, in a manner that conveys respect, honesty, integrity, and dedication to public service. In turn, employees of the department can expect to be treated fairly, honestly and respectfully, by their peers and other employees of the department who hold positions of greater or lesser organizational authority.

It is recognized and understood that employees of the department will make judgmental errors from time to time in carrying out their responsibilities. (In fact, employees who never make any mistakes may be doing very little to try to improve the performance of the department.) While each error in judgement offers an opportunity for the department and the individual to learn, it is also realized some errors will have greater consequences than others for the public, the department and the employee. The department has an obligation to make its expectations as clear as possible to employees. The department has an equal obligation to make the consequences for failing to meet those expectations clear as well. While both of these obligations are difficult to meet, the latter is obviously more complex. There are often circumstances that may have contributed to errors of judgement or poor decisions that need to be considered when determining the appropriate consequences for behavior found improper.

In trying to define fair and consistent treatment in disciplinary matters in the abstract, employees often say they would like the department to give them a list of the prohibited behaviors along with the consequences for engaging in those behaviors. Experience tells us though, when employees are directly involved in the disciplinary process—either as the subject of the process or in a review capacity to recommend or decide on the consequences—most will want to consider the consequences in light of the circumstances that might have contributed to the violation. This of course is a critical aspect of the application of discipline in a consistent and fair manner. For some employees consistency is seen as the same treatment for the same behavior in every case; it is thought if this is done, the consequences will be fair to everyone. For the St. Petersburg Police Department **consistency** is defined as holding everyone equally accountable for unacceptable behavior and **fairness** is understanding the circumstances that contributed to the behavior while applying the consequences in a way that reflects this understanding. In order to ensure that employees are treated in a consistent and fair manner, the application of consequences for behaviors that are not in keeping with the expectations of the department will be based upon a balanced consideration of several factors.

A number of factors that are considered in the application of discipline are identified and discussed below. All of the factors may not be considered in every case because some will not apply to the particular set of circumstances. Also, there may be a tendency to isolate one factor and give it greater importance than another. These factors should generally be thought of as being interactive and having equal weight, unless there are particular circumstances associated with an incident that would give a factor greater or lesser weight. The factors which will be considered in disciplinary matters include:

Employee Motivation. The police department exists to serve the public. One factor in examining an employee's conduct will be whether or not the employee was operating in the public interest. An employee who violates a policy in an effort to accomplish a legitimate police purpose that demonstrates an understanding of the broader public interest inherent in the situation will be given more positive consideration in the determination of consequences than one who was motivated by personal interest. Obviously there will be difficulty from time to time in determining what is in the public interest. For example, would it be acceptable for an employee to knowingly violate an individual's First Amendment right to the freedom of speech to rid the public of what some might call a nuisance? Or is it acceptable as being in the public interest to knowingly violate a Fourth Amendment right against an unlawful search to arrest a dangerous criminal? Although it would clearly not be acceptable in either case for an employee to knowingly violate a Constitutional right, these are very complex issues that officers are asked to address. The police have a sworn duty to uphold the Constitution. It is in the **greater public interest** to protect those Constitutional guarantees in carrying out that responsibility even though it might be argued the public interest was being better served in the individual case. But if an employee attempts to devise an innovative, nontraditional solution for a persistent crime or service problem and unintentionally runs afoul of minor procedures; the desire to encourage creativity in our efforts at producing public safety will carry significant weight in dealing with any discipline that might result.

The Degree of Harm. The degree of harm an error causes is also an important aspect in deciding the consequences of an employee's behavior. Harm can be measured in a variety of ways. It can be measured in terms of the monetary cost to the department and community. An error that causes significant damage to a vehicle for example, could be examined in light of the repair costs. Harm can also be measured in terms of the personal injury the error causes such as the consequences of an unnecessary use of force. Another way in which harm can be measured is the impact of the error on public confidence. An employee who engages in criminal behavior—selling drugs for example—could affect the public confidence in the police if the consequences do not send a clear, unmistakable message that this behavior will not be tolerated.

Employee Experience. The experience of the employee will be taken into consideration as well. A relatively new employee (or a more experienced employee in an unfamiliar assignment) will be given greater consideration when judgmental errors are made. In the same vein, employees who make judgmental errors that would not be expected of one who has a significant amount of experience may expect to receive more serious sanctions.

Intentional/Unintentional Errors. Employees will make errors that could be classified as intentional and unintentional. An **unintentional** error is an action or decision that turns out to be wrong, but at the time it was taken, seemed to be in compliance with policy and the most appropriate course based on the information available. A supervisor for example, might give permission for a vehicle pursuit to continue on the basis the vehicle and occupants met the general description of one involved in an armed robbery. The pursuit ends in a serious accident and it is learned the driver was fleeing because his drivers license was expired. Under these circumstances, the supervisor's decision would be supported because it was within the policy at the time it was made. Unintentional errors also include those momentary lapses of judgement or acts of carelessness that result in minimal harm (backing a police cruiser into a pole for example, failing to turn in a report, etc.). Employees will be held accountable for those errors but the consequences will be more corrective than punitive unless the same or similar errors persist.

An **intentional** error is an action or a decision that an employee makes that is known (or should have been known) to be in conflict with law, policy, procedures or rules, at the time it is taken. Generally, intentional errors will be treated more seriously and carry greater consequences. Within the framework of intentional errors there are certain behaviors that are entirely inconsistent with the responsibilities of police employees. These include lying, theft, or physical abuse of citizens and other equally serious breaches of the trust placed in members of the policing profession. The nature of the police responsibility requires that police officers be truthful. It is recognized however, that it is sometimes difficult to determine if one is being untruthful. The department will terminate an employee's employment when it is clear the employee is intentionally engaging in an effort to be untruthful. Every effort will also be made to separate individuals from the department found to have engaged in theft or serious physical abuse of citizens.

Employee's Past Record. To the extent allowed by law, policy and contractual obligations and the employee's past record will be taken into consideration in determining the consequences of a failure to meet the department's expectations. An employee who continually makes errors can expect the consequences of this behavior to become progressively more punitive. An employee who has a record of few or no errors can expect less stringent consequences. Also, an employee whose past reflects hard work and dedication to the community and department will be given every consideration in the determination of any disciplinary action.

Following the careful consideration of all applicable factors in any disciplinary review, every effort will be made to determine consequences that fit each specific incident in a consistent and fair manner. The rationale for disciplinary decisions will be explained as clearly as possible.

The St. Petersburg Police Department has a well established tradition of serving the community with integrity and in a professional manner. It is among the finest police organizations of this nation. To maintain that tradition and continue improving the quality of service the department provides to the community, each and every employee must accept the responsibility for their role in maintaining integrity, quality and high professional standards.

Darrel W. Stephens
Chief of Police
May 23, 1993

---

compared to decentralized administration. The decentralized administration will be more independent and better able to understand and serve communities, but there will be significantly less control over the officers and their behavior than with centralized administration.

If police officials were concerned solely with controlling deviance, having officers comply with the rule of law, and making officers accountable, they would operate under highly centralized management. While a centralized scheme of organization offers the best structure for controlling deviance and corruption, it conflicts with recent trends in policing and may hinder the ability of the police to be responsive to community needs (Kappeler, 1997).

Because the trend toward community-oriented and problem-solving policing is so dominant in the 1990s, decentralization has become a very popular management design. While this allows officers to spend time with community members and to adapt policing strategies to particular problems, it lacks many controls over discretion and renegade behavior (Bracey, 1992). As decentralization reduces traditional controls of the centralized agencies, leadership must be analyzed and enhanced (leadership as a strategy of control will be discussed below). When leadership and supervision prove inadequate, deviance can occur. If police officials become aware of deviance, or merely claims of misconduct, the internal security division or internal affairs office is summoned. This operation is basically a police department within a police department.

Internal Affairs

The Internal Affairs (IA) unit is the mechanism for internal accountability that receives, processes and investigates complaints against police officers—whether for violations of criminal law or breaches of policies and procedures. Actions taken by this division can include: investigating citizens' complaints; reviewing incident reports filed by police officers (such as discharge of weapons or police pursuits); or departmental investigations of possible officer misconduct.

Sam Walker (1992) has noted that IA units can be strong or weak and that "the key variable is the attitude of the chief executive" (p. 290). Beyond a good attitude, the administration must provide support—including resources and freedom—to the professional compliance division. The IA commander must have unlimited and direct access to the chief and not be responsible to anyone else. Support, access, and authority are essential preconditions for a strong internal affairs division, but they are not guarantees.

The functions of internal affairs units vary. Some units respond only to complaints filed; others actively search for deviance and corruption within a department. Once a complaint is received or there is an allegation of corruption, the tenacity and thoroughness of the investigation can vary from agency to agency. For example, some units will interview only people named in a complaint or those who can be identified easily. Other units will canvas door-to-door, attempting to locate witnesses using the same methods they would use if investigating a murder or rape. Differences also occur when agencies terminate an investigation. Some units will terminate an investigation after a complaint is withdrawn or if a complainant refuses to cooperate. Other units will continue to investigate regardless of the complainant's wishes. Similarly, some units will only investigate those specific allegations mentioned in a complaint, while other units will widen the scope of an investigation if information about deviance or corruption is uncovered.

The emphasis placed on internal affairs by police officials will have a strong influence on the behavior and morale of employee officers. On the one hand, if an IA division is merely a mask to approve all police behavior, whether appropriate or not, then it provides little or no deterrence to officers who engage in misconduct (Kappeler & Kraska, 1994). On the other hand, if sufficient resources and an open structure encourage officers or citizens to bring grievances or to file complaints and the complaints are investigated fairly, then the division may discourage officers from deviancy. Another key to the success of these units is the selection of staff. The chief and IA commander must select officers who are willing to conduct thorough, objective, and ethical evaluations of other officers' behavior.

Another integral function of an IA unit is police-community relations. One of the most serious complaints about internal investigations is that they merely cover up any police misconduct and help the accused officers justify and rationalize their behavior. One of the problems in any investigation is determining whether the alleged complaint is accurate. IA units classify complaints into categories that correspond to the following (see Christopher, 1991):

1. Unfounded—there was no evidence uncovered that can substantiate the complaint;
2. Not Sustained—the evidence uncovered was not sufficient to clearly prove or disprove the complaint;
3. Exonerated—the actions noted in the complaint occurred but they were justified and proper; or
4. Sustained—the officer engaged in the behavior which was specified in the complaint. (p. 155)

Traditionally, most citizen complaints are dismissed as unsubstantiated or not sustained, which leads to the popular belief that the police refuse to discipline themselves.

Victor E. Kappeler and Peter B. Kraska (1994) report that:

> While differences in complaint systems abound, many police departments have adopted tactics that effectively block a large proportion of potential citizen complaints. These tactics have generally included: requiring citizens to file complaints in person rather than anonymously; requiring citizens to file complaints at station houses; restricting access to the complaint system (either through location or language barriers); requiring citizens to sign written formal state-

ments (often accompanied by warnings of criminal prosecution for falsely reporting); requiring citizens to take polygraph tests before beginning an investigation; and limiting complaints to only those behaviors recognized by police as falling within their self-defined areas of accountability. Finally, and hopefully to a lessor extent, police have used some draconian measures to prevent citizen complaints. Some of these measures have included: making citizens wait at station houses for hours (hoping they will forego complaining); threatening minority citizens with notification of the immigration and naturalization service; making it known that police will run warrant checks on anyone filing a complaint; and, threatening citizens with defamation lawsuits. (p. 77)

As with failure to enforce violations of departmental policy, failure to respect the citizen's complaint process and/or to utilize and control its IA unit, the internal affairs division instructs officers that deviance is permissible. If police do not police themselves—or if the public perceives that the police are not policing themselves—there will be calls for other methods of controlling police. For example, from 1993 to 1995, the Chicago Police Department's Office of Professional Standards looked into 8,620 citizen complaints of excessive force. Of those, 707 (8 percent) were sustained; 20 percent were ruled unfounded; the remaining 72 percent were classified as "not sustained" (Zorn, 1997a). In the federal consent decree with Pittsburgh (see chapter 11), the term "not resolved" has been substituted for "not sustained"—a symbolic element which at least more accurately describes the situation (Zorn, 1997b). Over that same period, the Chicago Police Board ruled that 13 officers were guilty of brutality and should be fired. None of those terminations resulted in criminal battery charges. A spokesman for the State's Attorney's office said that the police almost never bring brutality cases to the attention of prosecutors. "Generally the police conduct an internal review and administer their own discipline" (p. 1).

The Office of Professional Standards does not consider past complaints against officers. As a result, incriminating patterns of behavior are not considered. OPS rules on citizen complaints with no knowledge of an officer's history. A former director of the Office of Professional Standards, David Fogel, wrote in a 1987 internal memo to the mayor that the system "operates to immunize police from internal discipline and gives the appearance of formal justice, but actually helps to institutionalize subterfuge and injustice" (Zorn, 1997a, p. 1). As Edward T. Stein, an attorney who represents plaintiffs in police-related civil suits, stated,

When you see numerous complaints about the same officer or out of the same district alleging the same MO, and these complaints come from individuals who don't know each other, common sense tells you something is going on. But the review process is not set up to catch that. (p. 1)

The effectiveness of IA investigations depends on how officers in the unit respond to citizen and police complaints. If IA officers assume that any complaint made by a civilian is an attack on policing or a personal attack on their department, they may shield the individual officer and discourage the civilian from pursuing the complaint (Kappeler & Kraska, 1994). In such an environment, the process of safeguarding individual rights fails. If the officers evaluate each complaint honestly on its own merits, the process will succeed. When internal controls over police operate properly, potential deviance can be deterred before it develops into more serious activities. If the process simply masks the problems and keeps important information from officials and the public, then the behavior will continue and perhaps worsen. Our discussion of the LAPD's (chapter 6) approach to the investigation of police misconduct provides an excellent example of a failed system.

Early Warning Systems

One innovation increasingly being used to control police misconduct is called an Early Warning System (EWS). The EWS tracks all citizen and departmental complaints, whether substantiated or not. A system can be devised to track the kinds of behavior mentioned or complaints by type, seriousness, location, or any number of variables. If a specified number of problems or issues are noted during a period of time, an officer's file will be reviewed for indications of problems (see Alpert & Dunham, 1997). For example, an officer could have received numerous unsubstantiated or minor complaints that trigger a review and interview. After meeting with the officer, it may be learned that he or she had been assigned to a high-crime area and had been tough on crime and alleged criminals. This alone is not a sufficient reason to exonerate the officer from possible misconduct. If, however, subsequent investigation reveals the complaints were an attempt to have the officer transferred out of the area precisely because his or her police work was effective, it would be clear the officer was targeted unjustifiably. Alternatively, investigators could conclude that the officer is experiencing problems at home or has an alcohol problem that affected his or her police work. The IA division and EWS program can pinpoint difficult areas and provide help to officers before a problem gets too serious.

NYPD's System Of Monitoring Abusive Officers

[A bus driver, Vann, was driving his regular route in Brooklyn, New York.] Defendant Raul Morrison was an off-duty city policeman driving his own automobile. As Morrison attempted to execute a U-turn, his car collided with Vann's bus. Morrison, who was not in uniform, got out of his car, identified himself as a police officer, drew his service revolver, and told Vann, "I should shoot you nigger and make sure you never drive a bus." Morrison proceeded to hit Vann in the head and face several times, threw him against a wall and against the bus several times, and handcuffed him. Morrison placed Vann under arrest and took him to the police station, where the precinct commander voided the arrest. As a result of Morrison's use of force, Vann was treated at a hospital for injuries to the head, face, and body. The injuries forced Vann to miss work for some seven weeks.

. . . The record showed that Morrison had been the subject of numerous complaints, lodged by both colleagues and civilians; that he had been disciplined several times, psychologically evaluated, and placed on restricted duty; and that he had been returned to active duty, following which he was involved in several additional incidents before assaulting Vann. Between 1982 and 1983 Morrison was involved in at least nine incidents where he used improper force and abusive language against citizens.

In March 1984, in light of the numerous complaints, Morrison's then-precinct commander, Captain Anthony Lamattina, referred Morrison to the Department's Early Intervention Unit (EIU). One of EIU's functions was to encourage officers with personal problems to seek help before their problems affected their work performance. EIU interviewed Morrison, who repeatedly expressed the view that he was not accorded the proper "respect." EIU concluded that Morrison had an "attitude" and that most of the civilian complaints against him stemmed from incidents that should not have occurred. Shortly after that interview, Morrison was the subject of yet another complaint. In the wake of the new complaint, whose details and resolution are not revealed in the record, Captain Lamattina referred Morrison to the Department's Psychological Services Unit (PSU). [This unit of the Department's Health Services Division evaluates employees suspected of experiencing psychological problems to determine the officer's psychological fitness for duty.]

On April 6, 1984, PSU psychologist Dr. Arthur Knour commenced an interview of Morrison but suspended it because he did not have the details of the civilian complaints against Morrison. The interview was not resumed until April 30. In the meantime, on April 27, Morrison referred himself to PSU, stating in an interview with Detective Richard Kleiner and PSU psychologist Dr. Eloise Archibald that he was depressed because of a recent break-up with his girlfriend. He also stated, "When I get aggravated, I get easily ticked off, and then I get the civilian complaints." As a result, Morrison was officially relieved of his firearms and was placed on restricted duty pending psychological evaluation. On April 30, 1984, Knour resumed his interview of Morrison. He found Morrison to be a very rigid, defensive, somewhat passive aggressive individual who had a great deal of difficulty adequately handling and expressing his feelings of anger and resentment and, as a result, his behavior could, on occasion, lead to the escalation of initially minor situations.

In a July 13, 1984 interview with Knour, Morrison stated that he was no longer depressed and that he wanted to return to full duty. . . . Morrison was not at that time returned to full-duty status, however, because of problems in his performance on his restricted duty assignment, which was in the Department's Health Services Division. On August 1, 1984, Knour was asked to interview Morrison again because Morrison had repeatedly been late returning to work from his meal break and was having difficulty getting along with his coworkers. These complaints led to the referral of Morrison to psychiatrist Dr. Abe Pinsky for an independent evaluation. Dr. Pinsky found no signs of psychiatric illness and recommended that Morrison be returned to full-duty status with firearms.

Knour nonetheless did not recommend a return to full-duty status because Morrison continued to have conflicts with his coworkers. During the summer of 1984, three of Morrison's supervisors at the Health Services Division informed Knour that Morrison was a source of problems, failing to do his share of the work and not getting along with others, uniformed or civilian. For example, Morrison was involved in at least one physical conflict with a police aide. Knour stated that Morrison repeatedly denied the facts presented with respect to his conflicts and confrontations and that he refused to accept any responsibility for any of the incidents, usually blaming the other individuals involved. Noting that Morrison had initially been referred to PSU because of his full-duty conflicts with civilians, Knour observed that Morrison's confrontations had continued in the context of the non-stressful restricted duty assignment, thereby "rais[ing] questions about whether counseling had really been effective in bringing changes in this officer's mode of interaction with others and whether he could function without undue problems as a full-duty police officer."

In December 1984, Morrison received a negative psychological evaluation. He was rated substandard in impartiality, human relations, communication skills, work analysis, self-image, stability/flexibility, police ethics, decisionmaking, and judgment. His supervisor also gave him a below-standard overall evaluation, noting Morrison's several altercations with his coworkers. In January 1985, Morrison physically assaulted a female police aide. When the aide attempted to close a window that Morrison had opened, Morrison shoved her and put his hand to her neck.

In the meantime, in November 1984, departmental charges had been brought against Morrison for lateness, failure to comply with an order, and displays of discourtesy and disrespect toward a senior officer. In December 1985, Morrison was found guilty and was docked 30 days' vacation pay, ordered to cooperate in any programs PSU recommended for him, and placed on disciplinary probation from December 22, 1985, to December 21, 1986. The ruling also stated that any further violation of rules and regulations would entitle the Department to order Morrison's dismissal.

In February 1986, following approximately a year without any incident of which Knour was aware, Knour recommended that Morrison be restored to full-duty status with firearms. Knour noted that in 1985, Morrison had received positive evaluations from three supervisors. One stated, "After being the subject of disciplinary proceedings, disposition of which is pending, [Morrison] has done an about face and now is performing a vital role for this command. He deals with fellow officers in a manner that is without incident. His sick record for this year is exceptional and [he] appears motivated to advance in this department." Knour expressed surprise at the favorable evaluations in light of Morrison's earlier attitude and behavior, but he concluded that Morrison apparently had changed "as a result of administrative sanctions." Knour concluded that, although "Morrison has always been somewhat rigid, and it is possible that back on the street his rigidity might reassert itself, . . . deserves a chance. . . ." Knour ended his February 1986 report by noting that Morrison was still on probation and stating that "should new problems surface he could be administratively terminated. . . ."

Morrison's firearms were returned to him on May 28, 1986, and he was reinstated to full-duty status on June 6, 1986. He was assigned a patrol function, which placed him in direct contact with the public. Less than two months later, on August 3, 1986, a civilian complaint was filed with the Civilian Complaint Review Board (CCRB), alleging that Morrison had unnecessarily used force, injuring a civilian by ramming him in the stomach with a nightstick. One week later, another civilian complaint was filed with the CCRB alleging that Morrison had verbally abused, and unnecessarily threatened, the complainant, saying that he was going to "beat the shit out" of him. . . .

On April 13, 1987, he was the subject of another civilian complaint filed with the CCRB. The complaint alleged that, while off duty and driving a vehicle, Morrison had become involved in an altercation with another driver and the driver's wife, during which Morrison assaulted, menaced, and pointed his gun at the complainant. In the wake of this complaint, Morrison was placed on modified assignment and prohibited from carrying firearms. On August 17, 1987, an investigation resulted in the conclusion that the complaint was unsubstantiated; he was returned to full-duty status with firearms. On February 1, 1988, Morrison assaulted Vann.

The evidence . . . suggests that the defendant City of New York's monitoring system is woefully inadequate to monitor and supervise officers with the kind of behavioral history like Morrison. For example, any system that allocates 1.25 persons to monitor 200 officers on disciplinary probation . . . is no system at all. Any system where the monitors perform only "clerical functions" is no system at all. . . . This evidence strongly supports the conclusion that the system of monitoring officers like Morrison is, in fact, not a system at all.

Vann presented evidence of the Department's general methods of dealing with problem police and of its responses to past incidents involving Morrison. . . . The deposition testimony indicated that, after a problem officer was restored to full-duty status, the Department's supervisory units paid virtually no attention to the filing of new complaints against such officers even though such filings should have been red flag warnings of possibly renewed and future misconduct. . . .

PSU psychologists had early noted Morrison's personality disorder; they had noted thereafter that he did not respond productively to counseling and that he altered his attitude and behavior only in response to administrative discipline; they foresaw that if restored to full duty his problems might recur; and they suggested that if he engaged in further misconduct, he should be dismissed. Yet even while Morrison was on disciplinary probation, there was no mechanism for ensuring that . . . PSU was alerted . . . [to] new complaints of his physical abuse of civilians. We note that appellees' contention that the Department's treatment of the three postreinstatement complaints against Morrison did not bespeak indifference because the complaints were "unsubstantiated" is a matter for argument to the jury, given the Department's apparent inclusion of conciliated complaints in that category and the fact that at least one of the earlier conciliated complaints against Morrison resulted in his being disciplined.

Morrison was acting in accordance with his established, and departmentally well-known, tendency to escalate confrontations inappropriately, to the point where he used force. In light of the Department's "systemic failure" to alert the supervisory units of the filing of new complaints against problem officers, and in the absence of any significant administrative response to Morrison's resumption of his abusive misconduct upon reinstatement, it was entirely foreseeable that Morrison would engage in misconduct yet again.

In sum, a rational jury could find that, where an officer had been identified by the police department as a "violent-prone" individual who had a personality disorder manifested by frequent quick-tempered demands for "respect," escalating into physical confrontations for which he always disavowed responsibility, the need to be alert for new civilian complaints filed after his reinstatement to full-duty status was obvious. The jury could also rationally find that the Department's election to staff DAO [the department monitoring officers on disciplinary probation] with the equivalent of just 1.25 employees to monitor 200 problem officers, together with the systematic lack of communication to the supervisory divisions of information with regard to new civilian complaints—including PSU's routine failure, despite its expertise, to instruct commanders to relay that information—reflected a deliberate indifference on the part of the municipal defendants to the dangers posed by problem police who had been restored to full-duty service.

Vann v. City of New York, 72 F.3d 1040 (2nd Cir., 1995)

Some of the most important factors police officials should consider when reviewing an officer's performance for purposes of assessing potential deviance include:

- The number and nature of use of force reports filed.
- The number of civilian complaints filed against the officer.
- The outcome of investigations into citizen complaints against the officer.
- The number of departmentally generated complaints for policy violations relative to the time the officer has served in the department.
- The outcome of investigations into departmentally generated complaints for policy violations against the officer.
- The existence of a pattern of similar conduct based on both citizen and departmentally generated complaints.
- Departmental intelligence reports on the officer's conduct, control of per-

sons reports, the frequency of the officer's use of charges of resisting arrest or assault against the police.

- The demographic characteristics of citizens and departmental personnel filing complaints against the officer.
- The demographic characteristics of persons arrested by the officer and the types of charges filed against these citizens.
- The officer's assignments in terms of operational aspects, geographic location, partners, and supervisors.
- The officer's record of discipline and performance evaluations in relation to the above mentioned indicators.
- The officer's training record, including academy training, field training and in-service training.
- The officer's prior commendations and citations for performance.
- The officer's use or abuse of sick leave and punctuality in reporting for assignments.
- The officer's general attitude toward work, fellow officers, and citizens.
- The officer's off-duty behaviors as well as unique personal problems or stressors the officer might be experiencing.

Chicago has instituted an innovative yet controversial attempt to control police misconduct. The Internal Affairs Division in Chicago uses a commercially available neural network program to sort through the files of every officer in the department. Robert Geinosky purchased BrainMaker Professional two years ago. The neural network arrived as a clean slate; Geinosky trained it by entering data from the files of 190 officers fired by the department and information on a control group of 380 officers with exemplary records. The software identifies patterns; as those patterns are repeated, the connections are strengthened. Four times a year, the program identifies 50–100 officers whose records suggest they're "drinking too much, shaking down store owners, pocketing evidence or otherwise screwing up" (Grescoe, 1996, p. 19).

Geinosky points out that bureaucracies are flooded with statistics and figures. "We have millions of pieces of information: figures on years on the job, absent without permission, insubordination, excessive force, public complaints, medical history, summary punishments" (p. 19). The software reads 13,185 files in minutes. In one quarterly session, 91 officers were identified. Of those named, 47 turned out to have been identified previously by supervisors for behavior problems. Allegations of misconduct had been made against half of the others. The computer identified 22 officers who had not yet been questioned. Internal Affairs believes it would take an annual budget of a million dollars and a staff of 30 investigators to get the same results as the software, which cost $795.

The police union objects to the use of "a cut-rate crystal ball" (p. 19). Ironically, the union's dissatisfaction with the arbitrary/subjective criteria used by human supervisors had instigated the search for a different system. Internal Affairs thought the computer solution was ideal—it answered the union's objections and eliminated any biased, perhaps even corrupt, human element. The union, however, complained about a mechanical Big Brother. The union alleges that most complaints against officers are motivated by revenge or are totally unfounded.

Despite union objections, the software is fair. No complaint is entered unless it has been sustained by a disciplinary panel. The union argues that traffic accidents should not be included as a variable in the program, but experience would suggest that someone with a record of repeated accidents probably is not focused on patrol work. Raymond Risley, former superintendent of Internal Affairs, claims that

> What the police officers say to each other in the locker room and what they may feel about it in the privacy of their own home may be entirely different. A tremendous amount of our anonymous complaints about serious, corruption-related police misconduct comes from other police officers who make us pledge that we will not identify them. (p. 20)

The formal nature of IA and other control features of the police can be effective, but informal actions are, at a minimum, equally significant. Formally, police organizations operate under a paramilitary structure. However, it is rare that an organization will function solely according to formal strictures. Organizational reality is often guided by what is commonly known as "office politics" (Rubinstein, 1973). Dorothy Guyot (1977) has noted that "within police departments, as in any formal organization, there are subdivisions, hierarchies, status groupings, and other formal arrangements. There are also informal relationships, cliques, friendship patterns, and temporary collaborations" (p. 109).

As was evident in previous chapters, these informal influences have important and significant consequences which often conflict with formal statements of policy.

INFORMAL INFLUENCES—
ORGANIZATIONAL AND SUBCULTURAL

Leadership skills are critical for police and other organizational managers. The ability to lead, supervise, and motivate are perhaps the most important managerial skills for an administrator to possess. Earning the respect of subordinates and developing a good rapport with them is the real test of a good leader. These leadership skills include the ability to motivate subordinates and to resolve conflicts. Leadership in law enforcement requires ". . . a blend of several different, yet related skills. Human relation skills, conceptual skills, and technical skills are three major requirements for good leadership" (Alpert & Dunham, 1997, p. 97). A strong leader will positively influence his or her subordinates with instruction and direction to achieve the police mission (within socially and legally acceptable bounds) effectively and efficiently. This task is achieved through authority and power.

Authority and power, while related to leadership, are different concepts. Authority can be understood as the control conferred or granted to a position by the organization. That is, authority is the basis on which an individual in a particular position can command or require a subordinate to act. Power is the force behind the authority. For example, if a person in a position of authority commands a subordinate to act and he or she refuses, the person in authority can exercise power to enforce the command. This is described by Max Weber as the rational-legal type of authority.

A leader's strength also comes from his or her abilities to persuade someone to want to do something voluntarily; Weber used the term charismatic to describe leaders who inspire voluntary compliance. The dedication, energies, and traits of the leader will likely be reproduced or mirrored by the subordinates. The leader's informal actions—including style, perceived strengths and weaknesses—will all have a significant influence on the operation of a police agency and the behavior of its officers (Alpert & Dunham, 1992). Police departments with supervisory officers who tolerate deviance or who do nothing to reduce and eliminate it will experience more incidents of deviance and corruption than those departments which organize against it.

Organizing Against Deviance

Administrators and supervisors should develop methods to control current problems and minimize future ones. Planning should include the identification and analysis of the opportunities for participation in deviance in a particular community. For example, some agencies may focus on drug-related deviance. Other agencies may have to guard against financial opportunities, including rackets or extortion. Still other agencies may have to be concerned with sexual issues, including the particular problems associated with prostitution, the exploitation of crime victims, and the abuse of criminal suspects. While some agencies may experience these specific, identifiable concerns, most agencies will have to focus on more general and widely diverse forms of police deviance. These agencies will have to develop organizational strategies to detect, analyze, and control an extensive variety of deviant acts.

There are numerous ways to lead properly, but nearly all include earning the trust and confidence of subordinates and acquiring information on what is happening on the street between the police and the public. One method which will assist police officials in gaining this information is to set an example for officers by becoming involved in their activities. By working the street or riding with officers, an official gains a first-hand sense of the problems and issues facing departmental personnel. Token appearances or staged arrivals for publicity will be detected and resented. The willingness to work the street and to show support must be genuine. It will pay off in a more complete understanding of what officers face—including opportunities for deviance.

In addition to the valuable hands-on experience of working the streets, police officials can raise their level of information with informal and formal discussions with officers, an analysis of complaints and lawsuits, and with surveys. Vertical staff meetings (with officers of several ranks and assignments attending) can be held to discuss the many issues pertinent to police deviance. Surveys can be conducted with members of the community to determine their concerns and evaluation of police activities, including deviance and corruption. Surveys can elicit information on the community members' impressions or perceptions of the crime problem, issues of victimization, and police activities. Information from this process can assist in planning and checking on the actions of officers who respond to calls for service. By surveying a sampling of consumers of police service, officials will be able to determine if citizens are satisfied with the officers who respond to their calls (Alpert & Dunham, 1988; Furstenberg & Wellford, 1973). This information will provide officials with information to compare what the police *are* doing in the communities to what *should* be happening in the community. If differences are determined, a plan to create appropriate activities or behavior can be designed. This affirmative action will help establish an organizational culture that will guard against deviance and corruption.

As police agencies make the transition into community-oriented, problem-solving policing, participatory management will become institutionalized. Until that process of communication and information sharing is common, it may be instructive to have study or focus groups discuss the potential for police deviance. The splintering of police officers into groups or subcultures can encourage deviance. It is critical to discuss issues and to solve problems as a unified force rather than as multiple subcultures. While harmony may not be easy to achieve, it is a goal which must not be abandoned. Similarly, different factions or subcultural groups may lobby for different priorities or assignments. The understanding and control of the subcultural influences becomes a crucial aspect of controlling deviance and corruption.

Subcultural Influences

We have reviewed the powerful influence the police subculture has over the behavior of officers. While all social groups have some means of teaching new members the norms, values, and attitudes that are highly valued by the group, this influence is exceptional in the police environment. The academy experience begins the formal socialization process to separate the recruit from the society at large. On-the-job experiences while performing duties and acting out the role of a police officer provide the continued socialization that often pulls the officer into a very distinct and powerful subculture. Members of this subculture often view the outside world suspiciously as opposing their best interests or activities. This occurs as members of a police subculture are set off from the general society and even the administration. As John Van Maanen has noted (1997):

> The main result of training is that the recruit soon learns it is his peer group rather than the "brass" which will support him and which he, in turn, must support. For example, the newcomers adopt covering tactics to become proficient at construing consensual ad hoc explanations of a fellow-recruit's mistakes. Furthermore, the long hours, new friends and ordeal aspects of the recruit school serve to detach the newcomer from his old acquaintances. In short, the academy impresses upon the recruit that he must now identify with a new group: his fellow officers. (pp. 94–95)

Many officers are not aware of the strong influences of the police subculture or how the norms affect their lives and careers. Many do not realize that companionship in the group influences how they view the world and, more specifically, how they view and act toward citizens outside of the police subculture. To function properly in the police role, it is often believed that officers must conform to the theme of solidarity and the ethos of secrecy.

The influence of the police subculture has the potential to create enormous problems, as we saw in the discussion of the Buddy Boys. The cultural themes of isolation and solidarity reinforce the code of secrecy among the members of the subculture; those tendencies must be channeled in a productive way. There are a number of measures that police departments can take to mitigate the negative effects of the police occupational culture. These measures begin with the selection, training, and assignment of police personnel.

First, police organizations can select employees who have demonstrated a commitment to cultural diversity and sensitivity. As more tolerant police personnel are brought into the department, abuses that stem from prejudice would decline. The department can then use training academies to shape the values of the police subculture by introducing new ideas and approaches that broaden the police vision of the world. By training police officers in social and departmental values that are conducive to good community relations, much of the alienation felt by the police may begin to diminish. The police may begin to view the public not as enemies but as partners in the community. Third, police organizations can attempt to break the transmission of negative cultural influence from one generation of officers to the next by the careful assignment of new officers and the careful selection of training officers. Reducing a new police officer's exposure to deviant and corrupt subcultures within a police department will allow departments to create their organizational culture rather than allowing it to perpetuate tired stereotypes.

A second set of measures that can have a positive impact on police culture and ultimately deviance involve shaping the nature of police-citizen interactions. First, police departments must encourage officers to develop and maintain interests outside the police province. Police administrators can actively establish tasks for officers to perform that remove them from their traditional police roles. There have been some experiments to place officers in civilian clothes and to integrate them naturally into society. These programs have experienced relative success (Walker, 1992b). Second, police administrators must provide specific opportunities for officers to become integrated into the neighborhood they serve and to have positive experiences with those outside the world of law enforcement. Officers must experience the positive elements of a neighborhood or community and must want to do more than merely put in their duty time. Third, officers must want to go beyond the "us versus them" dichotomy. There has to be more to police work than chasing after and arresting criminal suspects. While no one would expect a police agency to tell its officers not to associate with their fellow officers, it may be helpful for police training to include the potential dangers of maintaining only police friends and the positive benefits that can come from associations with others.

> Cooperative efforts between administrators and employees result in an officer who truly likes people and the opportunity to serve them, who enjoys a successful career, both personally and in terms of positive feedback from the community. Of all the traits needed to be successful in law enforcement, the single-most important one is the need for social intelligence—the ability to enjoy and to interact effectively with people. (Alpert & Dunham, 1997, p. 106)

EXTERNAL CONTROLS AND INFLUENCES

Criminal and civil laws establish the parameters of policies and procedures for the police. Police officers can be held criminally responsible, as can any citizen, for a violation of the penal code. State codes contain the well-known or "common" criminal offenses such as assault, robbery, and homicide. States also have statutory provisions in their criminal codes which can be directed specifically at police officers and include such behavior as "official misconduct." Title 18 of the federal criminal code has several sections that can be attached to police work (see del Carmen, 1993). These include Section 242 (Criminal Liability for Deprivation of Civil Rights) and Section 245 (Violation of Federally-Protected Activities).

Chapter 6 discussed the most celebrated case of criminal charges against the police. The beating of Rodney King resulted in both state and federal charges being brought against the officers and separate jury trials for each jurisdiction. In the 1980s, criminal charges were also brought against several Miami police officers, including Luis Alvarez and William Lozano. Alvarez was tried for the shooting death of a young African-American male in a video game room. Riots in Miami were attributed to both the shooting and the acquittal of Alvarez. Lozano was charged with manslaughter when he shot a suspect involved in a high-speed chase. Civil disturbances were blamed on this shooting, but further problems were averted when he was convicted. On appeal, officer Lozano was acquitted by a jury; fortunately, no disturbances took place. These cases received enormous publicity, but criminal charges against the police are relatively rare. Nonetheless, criminal law determines the legal boundaries for acts committed in the line of duty. Police officers who violate those boundaries face the possibility of criminal charges.

Similarly, civil law establishes parameters for the police. Officers who violate civil laws cannot be sentenced to jail or prison, but they can be disciplined (for violating policy) or held financially responsible for their actions. Civil laws protect private interests of individuals or their property. Persons who suffer private interest harms can bring legal actions against the party inflicting the harm or damage (the officers), their supervisors, and the governmental agency for which they work. In the situations reviewed above, the police behavior violated both criminal and civil law. In each case, civil lawsuits were brought against the officer and municipality for which he worked. Depending on the nature of the accused behavior, an aggrieved or injured party can file suit under state and/or federal civil law.

State Liability Actions

There are two types of torts which affect police officers under state law: intentional tort and negligence tort. Although strict liability torts are available, they rarely affect the police (Kappeler, 1997). Intentional torts are those behaviors, committed intentionally, that are very likely or highly probable to result in unreasonable harm. Each state has different legal standards, but the behaviors that are associated with intentional torts are similar. These include wrongful death, false arrest, false imprisonment, and assault and battery.

Negligence torts are those behaviors that include the following four elements: (1) legal duty; (2) a breach of that duty; (3) proximate cause; and (4) damage or injury. In other words, to determine negligence, it must be asked whether an officer's action was based on a duty owed to an individual, whether the officer violated the duty owed to the individual, and whether the officer's breach of that duty caused harm to the individual. Even if all the elements of negligence are met, police officers and their agencies have legal defenses to liability. These include claims of self-defense, immunity, and proximate causation, among others (del Carmen, 1994; Kappeler, 1997).

Federal Liability Actions

The federal civil laws which can be applied to police officers and agencies include Title 42 Sections 1985, 1983, and 1981. Sections 1981 and 1985 are used far less frequently than Section 1983. Section 1981 refers to violations of equal rights under the law and Section 1985 refers to actions which conspire to deprive a person of his or her civil rights. United States Code, Title 42, Section 1983 refers to the deprivation of civil rights and is known as The Civil Rights Act of 1871.

The Civil Rights Act has a rich and colorful history. It was originally passed to serve those damaged or wronged by members of the Ku Klux Klan. In 1871, Congress passed the law intending that no government official acting under the color of state law can violate an individual's civil rights. Conduct which can be redressed under Section 1983 is limited to federally protected rights or violations of the United States Constitution. The various federal circuits across the country have different interpretations of the standards used to determine a violation and therefore liability under Section 1983. These standards vary in degree, and successful lawsuits must establish that the agency was "in conscious disregard," "deliberately indifferent," or "shocked the conscience." Examples of police action often questioned as "1983" violations, include: failure to train; failure to supervise; failure to have a departmental policy; negligent retention; negligent hiring; failure to discipline; and negligent entrustment. As with state tort actions, the police have a variety of defenses against Section 1983 claims, even when all the elements of the action are met. These defenses include absolute, qualified and good-faith immunity, and proximate cause (Alpert et al., 1997, Kappeler, 1997).

While it is true that police liability, both criminal and civil, has its costs, it can also serve as a benefit. "[S]uits against the police that prove inadequate administrative controls, deficient policies, or customs or practices that are improper or illegal, can force the department to correct its deficiencies and review all policies, practices and customs" (Alpert & Dunham, 1997, p. 244). The filing of lawsuits alerts officials to problems with certain officers or types of conduct; they can then serve their departments and communities by analyzing department-wide behavior patterns. As discussed in chapter 5, police may blame irate citizens or "liberal" courts for the filing of lawsuits or adverse decisions rather than taking a dispassionate look at what caused the problem. Sometimes local politicians will side with the police and blame the "indignant and ungrateful" citizen or the "misguided" judge who has ruled against the department. When this happens, politics become a liability to good and proper policing, and officers have another basis for rationalizing their deviance.

Political Influence

Politics has had a long and sordid history with law enforcement. The origins of police were based on political patronage, and jobs were provided on the basis of loyalty and allegiance. The political machine used police departments to maintain control over a neighborhood or a whole city (Harring, 1983; Uchida, 1997). Unfortunately, the political patronage system still survives in many police departments. Although this phenomenon is difficult to study systematically, two examples are presented to illustrate the devastating impact local politics can have on the operation of police departments.

James Ahern (1972), former chief of police in New Haven, Connecticut, wrote about this issue in the 1970s:

> There is nothing more degrading or demoralizing to a police department than the knowledge that every favor or promotion within it is controlled by hack politicians and outright criminals. And there is nothing more universal. Five years ago, anyone with the most superficial knowledge of the workings of the New Haven Police Department could point to the political power behind every captain on the force. Every cop who wanted to get ahead had his 'hook'—or as they say in New York, his 'rabbi.' Everyone owed his success to a politician—from the Town Chairman on down—or to an influential underworld figure. Needless to say, in a situation like this there was no chance whatever of the department functioning in the public interest. (pp. 96–97)

More recently, the Miami police department has suffered from a handicap of political interference. Journalist John Dorschner (1993) described the scene of a 1987 football game between the two major police departments in Miami (the Miami City department and the Metro-Dade department):

> What's most interesting about the Metro side of the field is what's missing: politicians. . . . Now, look over on the Miami police side. . . . Here the politicians are obvious, and it is here the knowledgeable ones in the stands are watching carefully, much the way the observers in Moscow look at the positioning of the top pols on the Red Square podium. (pp. 262–263)

Dorschner describes the various associations and connections he observes on the field—who is talking with whom and what the implications may mean for the internal operations of the police. He continues his portrait:

> Meanwhile, up in the stands, old J. L. Plummer is holding court. Here's the city commissioner who loves being an amateur cop, patrolling with the cops at night, and who's sitting up there with him? . . . The knowledgeable spectators in the stands are watching all this, because they know how much politics influences the Miami Police Department, and to them the political choreography on the sidelines becomes much more important than the game. . . . There's too much interference from City Hall and too many police officers who try to play politics.

This symbolic scene at the football game was another indication that the politicians and police officers were going to manipulate each other regardless of the consequences. Just a few years earlier, a citizen panel studying police practices after several civil disturbances warned: "The actual or perceived use or misuse of political power and the manipulation of minority-group conflicts contribute to racial unrest in Miami" (Overtown Blue Ribbon Committee, 1984, p. 169).

It is discouraging that police officers and politicians must rely on each other to such a great extent. Certainly, there is a necessary oversight function that politicians must perform. There must be financial responsibility, and there must be oversight of the chief and his or her administrative function. However, daily interference in the hiring, promoting, assignment, and deployment of police officers is a political function that has no place in modern-day policing. As suggested by the New Haven and Miami examples, such interference dooms the appropriate functioning of a police agency to failure and sacrifices the ability of the agency to do justice in the community it serves. One method which can guide agencies out of a political abyss is self-assessment or accreditation.

Accreditation

In the 1960s and 1970s, segments of the law enforcement community were concerned with the lack of standards that existed in the policing profession. Those interested in resolving the issue turned to other professions for a model of governance and oversight. Comparisons were made between policing and education, the law, and a variety of other professions (Greenberg, 1989). In the early 1970s, representatives from the major police professional associations, including the International Association of Chiefs of Police (IACP), National Organization of Black Law Enforcement Officers (NOBLE), the National Sheriffs' Association (NSA), and the Police Executive Research Forum (PERF) gathered to establish minimum standards for police agencies of various sizes. A private corporation named the Commission on Accreditation for Law Enforcement Agencies (CALEA) was created to provide assistance to agencies desiring accreditation and to bestow their seal of approval if the agencies met all the accreditation criteria. There are approximately 440 standards in 40 chapters. Many of these standards are required for large agencies and some are recommended but optional for accreditation of smaller departments (Commission on Accreditation for Law Enforcement Agencies, 1994).

On the one hand, many professional law enforcement administrators advocate accreditation as an essential element of professionalism and stand by its process. Generally, their point is that self-regulation is preferable to external controls, and accreditation will remove unacceptable policies, procedures, and practices. On the other hand, some police professionals maintain that accreditation only addresses the formal, written aspects of police agencies and has no effect on compliance with those standards (Eastman, 1985). Some critics note that the minimum standards set by the commission are likely to become the level at which a department will remain. That is, once a minimum standard is met, there is little reason to go beyond it.

Accreditation, for all its costs (and it is very expensive to become accredited), does provide an important process for law enforcement agencies (see Rachlin, 1996). At a minimum, the process includes an assessment of the department's written directives. This helps to ensure that departmental polices and practices do not actively contribute to deviance by providing an appropriate set of guidelines from which officers operate. There are model policies and procedures manuals available, and a department can perform the assessment without the help of CALEA (Greenberg, 1989). It is the process of assessment that is critical as opposed to the certificate provided by CALEA. As we have discussed earlier, departments must have appropriate selection, policies, training, supervision and accountability systems in place and functioning if they are to control deviance. CALEA assists departments in developing standards to accomplish these objectives. However, these are necessary but not sufficient conditions for a police department that wants to control deviance and corruption. One other external method of control over the police is the civilian review or oversight board.

Citizen Oversight

As discussed, the Internal Affairs (IA) division of a police department traditionally was the primary investigator of complaints concerning police officers. Unfortunately, these investigations were conducted under a double cloak of secrecy; IA files were confidential and unavailable for public analysis. The alternative to police investigating their own officers is to integrate others into the process. The concept of civilian review of the police involves civilians receiving, reviewing, and analyzing complaints of alleged police misconduct. Sam Walker and Betsy Kreisel have recently analyzed citizen review and police accountability issues (1997). They report some conceptual differences and similarities between this external function and the internal investigations conducted by the department.

> The idea that citizen review is more independent and effective than internal review involves four closely linked propositions: that citizen involvement in the complaint process will produce (1) more objective and more thorough investigations; (2) a higher rate of sustained complaints and more disciplinary actions against guilty officers; (3) a greater deterrence of police misconduct (through both general and specific deterrence); (4) higher levels of satisfaction on the part of both individual complainants and the general public. (p. 322)

The researchers point out that these important questions have never been answered, and the linkages among them and their effects have never been studied. However, there is a general belief that creating civilian oversight will produce or promote desired results. Although serious research results are lacking, it is conventional wisdom that oversight boards can help make police abuses and corruption visible to the public, provide a vehicle to review police policies and procedures, and influence the proper punishment of deviant officers. However, there are questions concerning the way in which a civilian review board can best be designed. In other words, what is the best way to design and implement an oversight board to perform these duties to the satisfaction of both the police and the public?

Wagner and Decker (1997) have looked at the citizen review process in its broader organizational framework. They note that police, in general, have been unable to address properly the problems posed by citizen complaints and citizen review. "Absent in the operation of the complaint process has been a procedure, a well-defined mechanism for dealing with such allegations in a way that guarantees both due process for officers and accountability to the public" (p. 316).

Although there is a lack of experimentation to determine the impact of various forms of civilian review, the typical review or oversight board usually includes a representative cross section of the community and is independent of the police department. The members are often selected by the mayor or some other political figure. This method of appointment has been criticized by members of the minority communities as one more way to ensure that no action against the police will take place (United States Commission on Civil Rights, 1981). Many patrol officers and police administrators also complain about the composition of the boards; they believe that politicians are attempting to maintain control over police behavior. In essence, detractors argue that non-police cannot appreciate or understand the complexities of performing police work.

The traditional hostility of the police toward civilian oversight is based on their opinion of reformers being soft on crime, not understanding police work, and viewing the oversight process as another instance of coddling criminals. A common reason given by the police for opposing civilian oversight is that effective policing requires secrecy. Civilian oversight interferes with this secrecy and compromises police operations. Another reason for police opposition is the claim that one cannot evaluate police behavior and operations fairly without having been personally involved in crime control.

In spite of police opposition, civilian oversight remains an important issue of control (Wagner & Decker, 1997, Walker & Kreisel, 1997, West, 1993). The boards are viewed by many as important vehicles for making the police more democratic and accountable. Although some boards have achieved a measure of success, many of the efforts at civilian oversight have met with failure.

Police researchers have blamed this failure on the fact that the boards serve only in an advisory capacity. They have no subpoena power or ability to decide cases and impose punishment. It is also argued that traditionally and legally only the police chief has the power to make decisions concerning the discipline of his or her subordinates. Another reason given for the failure of citizen oversight boards is a general lack of resources and insufficient investigative staffs. Perhaps more importantly, police have created the appearance of impartial review by using "civilian boards." While the New York board was intended to be composed entirely of civilians, a majority of its members are former law-enforcement officials, prosecutors, and lawyers (Lacayo, 1997). In short, the ineffectiveness of many citizen oversight boards was ensured by the way they were created. The police feel that they can do a better job of controlling police deviance and corruption with their own internal investigation divisions, without compromising their ability to maintain order and control crime (Walker, 1992b). Yet, efforts to establish effective civilian oversight persist.

The renewed interest in civilian oversight of government has created a second generation of oversight boards with interests broader than just law enforcement. For example, some jurisdictions are establishing panels that will hear complaints about all government workers. They conduct an investigation against a public works employee in the same way they conduct an investigation against a police officer. Some of these panels are being given broad powers, but others are very limited in their scope of investigatory and enforcement powers (Alpert & Dunham, 1997, Wagner & Decker, 1997, Walker & Kreisel, 1997).

If outside oversight is determined to be appropriate, different communities may adopt different structures. The civilian oversight board may have broad or limited powers, depending on the tasks to be conducted. A structure with both civilians and police officers working together may resolve some of the criticisms discussed earlier. This design fits well under the umbrella of community policing. The scope of complaints heard by a civilian review board would be limited. Violations of the law subject to criminal penalties would be the province of prosecutors in the District Attorney's office.

SUMMARY

Effective internal discipline and external monitoring of police activities are in the best interests of the police department and the community. It is essential to the control of deviance and to officer morale that these activities be understood by all officers and administrators. Further, it is central to the department's public image to have a system of control that is known and trusted by community members. The public must have confidence in the willingness and ability of the police to police themselves.

It is ineffective to focus excessive attention on negative discipline as a means of controlling police deviance and corruption. The word "discipline" does not refer only to reprimands and punishments. It is derived from the same Latin root as disciple—follower or pupil. The concept refers to following a leader or someone in authority because of agreement with common principles, not because of the fear of punishment.

There are three important aspects to the development of an effective system of discipline. First, a department must have a well-formulated and consistent set of policies, procedures, and rules. They must be internally consistent and must reflect the moral constraints that are accepted in our society—particularly in the community being served by the police. Second, the rules and procedures must be communicated fully and effectively to officers at all levels of the organization through proper training. A third factor important in establishing an internal system of discipline is proper supervision and leadership within the department to ensure conformity to the rules and to maintain a working environment conducive to following the rules.

The problem of police deviance and corruption will never be completely solved, just as the police will never be able to solve the crime problem in our society. The role and functions of a police officer are such that numerous opportunities exist for deviant and corrupt behavior. As long as these opportunities exist, some deviance and corruption will take place, despite our best efforts to end it. The police subculture helps officers cope with the ambiguity and uncertainties inherent in the police role. If the socialization effects of the police subculture can be channeled to enhance and expand the officers' views of the community and their role in it, the subculture can be a powerful tool in the prevention of police deviance.

Chapter Eleven

PROSPECTS FOR CONTROLLING DEVIANCE
Forging the Boundaries of Police Behavior

We are all caught in an inescapable network of mutuality
Martin L. King   (1924–1968)

Police deviance presents a paradox for both law enforcement and society. On the one hand, deviance disturbs our image of the police and contradicts society's formal norms. Police deviance interrupts the efficient operation of the criminal justice system. It undermines justice because it inhibits the performance of police duties, usurps judicial authority, and often involves selective law enforcement and discriminatory patterns in the provision of police services. Therefore, deviance can be viewed as disruptive to the institution of policing, the criminal justice system, and society. At a minimum, incidents of police deviance erode public trust and confidence in the justice system and in the police institution. Surely, the Rodney Kings of society have learned that police are a formidable and sometimes violent instrument of social control. Certainly, the citizens of Milwaukee have learned the tragic effects of withholding valuable police services. Undoubtedly, residents of New York City have seen the line between cop and criminal blurred.

On the other hand, police deviance also serves functional roles for society. Police misconduct often supports existing social stratification, social relations, and the distribution of power in society. Police deviance reinforces in the minds of many citizens the primacy of the police as the enforcers of the social order. Differential victimization of citizens at the hands of police officers calls into question the equity of the social order that directs the activities of law enforcement. The police, however, are not merely passive actors responding to the influences of social structure. As Peter K. Manning (1995b) remarked, police are "engaged in dramatic marking and arranging of the vertical and horizontal order, and in defending, in a variety of ways, the status quo" (p. 359). In short, the police are both actors and pawns in the existing social structure.

Combining these views suggests that while deviance is disruptive it can also shape, support, and advance the social and moral order. These concepts are so abstract and their influences so latent that few citizens give them much thought. The public tends to think of police deviance and corruption as the isolated incidents which are occasionally exposed. The reason for this is twofold. First, since the public rarely recognizes the influence of social structure and its resultant moral order, the police role in shaping them is similarly overlooked. Second, most acts of police deviance come to public attention only when they outrage citizens, distort our view of society, critically hinder the operation of the criminal justice system, or violate our most basic concepts of normative behavior. Less sensational abuses by the police often go unnoticed.

Police corruption and deviance in our nation's major cities is played out in public forums, but far less attention is paid to police abuses that contribute to the police mandate to control crime and enforce the moral order. Police have historically used deviant means or what some have termed "street justice" to supplement existing forms of social control, to help establish order, or to maintain peace—as those concepts are interpreted by the police institution. The public seems oblivious to daily abuses by the law enforcement community. This chapter considers the social function and utility of deviance; it then turns to a consideration of how normative bounds of police behavior are shaped and negotiated in public forums by the construction of messages. Finally, the social organization of police deviance is considered, followed by the prospects for controlling deviance and corruption in the future.

FUNCTIONS OF DEVIANCE

Deviance reinforces the boundaries of acceptable moral behavior in a society and provides concrete examples of the consequences of normative violations (Durkheim, 1938).

> The deviant is a person whose activities have moved outside the margins of the group, and when the community calls him to account . . . it is making a statement about the nature and placement of its boundaries. It is declaring how much variability and diversity can be tolerated . . . before it begins to lose its distinctive shape, its unique identity. (Erikson, 1966, p. 11)

From the functionalist perspective, deviance serves a positive social purpose. The reaction of the police to deviant activities within their ranks is the process by which images of conformity are shaped. Theoretically, calling attention to deviant cops as examples of nonconformity makes an occupational statement about the bounds of acceptable behavior. Hence, by uncovering acts of police deviance and by sanctioning officers, the police and society attempt to establish boundaries of behavior for the entire police institution.

In a sense, deviance lends unity to our image of the fundamental fairness of the existing social order by reinforcing cohesiveness while maintaining the boundaries of moral behavior. However, this social function becomes distorted. A favorable public image of the police is created by branding blatant deviant behaviors as aberrations that are not part of an institutional problem. Thus, the public image of the police as loyal social control agents acting within the bounds of the formal normative system is maintained. Police deviance is classified as the misconduct of a few aberrant cops working under incredible pressures.

The public trusts this image and relies on the police to police themselves and to employ fail-safe controls on the abuse of power. Looking beyond the imagery, police deviance suggests that the police are unable to control even the most extreme behaviors that they publicly acknowledge as being serious breaches of the normative system—much less the more latent and routine abuses that are generally accepted in police circles.

The surfacing of an act of police deviance illustrates the inherent conflict between society's normative statements and the norms of the police. In essence, society's formal norms help create a law-abiding image of the police while advancing a conception of the law as providing rigid, well delineated, and definite boundaries that officers rarely cross. Police officials contribute to this misunderstanding by managing the images of police deviance. Police occupational policies, procedures, and rules promote an image of uniformity and consistency between society's formal norms and actual police practices and customs. Police policy is perceived as a rigid boundary of behavior congruent with society's accepted norms. This veneer of singularity, uniformity, and consistency masks a disjuncture; it hides fluidity and conceals the plurality of actual behavioral bounds from which many police officers operate.

As discussed in chapters 1 and 5, the normative system that shapes police conduct is composed of three general groupings of behavioral guidelines: the formal normative statements of society, normative statements made by the police institution, and norms derived from police culture. This results in a multidimensional system of behavioral boundaries. These boundaries are permeable, allowing behavior to occur based on different contexts, situations, occupational interpretations, and reactions. Boundaries of behavior derived from the police subculture overlay society's formal norms as well as department policies. The existence of occupationally and culturally accepted deviation results in the modification of formal bounds of conduct and provides the basis for rationalizing departures from social and policy-generated expectations. In short, police are able to move across our imaginary boundaries of formal normative conduct. They are free to deviate because they superimpose a subculturally derived system of values over those of society and even those of their own institution.

From this discussion, it should be clear that the police are not merely passive actors subject to previously constructed formal, occupational, and cultural norms. They are active participants in creating an alternative normative system that allows them to interact with and transcend society's expectations. The police routinely test the boundaries of the formal normative system by engaging in acts of deviance and corruption. This view of police deviance, however, is still too narrow to explain the interaction between police and society as it shapes the entire normative system.

NEGOTIATING THE BOUNDS OF BEHAVIOR

The envelope of the normative system that influences police behavior is constantly changing due to the interaction of police and society. The stage for this interaction is set by the assumptions that police and society hold about the nature of crime, disorder, and the role that law enforcement plays in addressing these problems. One way of understanding the negotiated nature of the normative system as it affects police conduct is to examine the messages sent to the police by various participants in the negotiation process. While there are a multitude of events, acts, and participants that can contribute to the construction of the normative system, we will focus on four of the most significant message sources: political officials, police officials, the judiciary, and the law. These messengers influence to varying degrees the shape of the normative system, the degree to which police adhere to that system, and the emphasis that police place on each level of the system.

Messages from Politicians

Politicians routinely negate or modify the effectiveness of the formal normative boundary by encouraging aggressive police practices and attributing a warlike orientation to crime control. When crime is politicized and community leaders and police officials generate and capitalize on citizens' fear of crime, they encourage officers to exceed the bounds of legal behavior in an effort to control crime.

A telling example of the link between politics, fear of crime, and the war ethos was the request from the mayor of the District of Columbia for the use of the National Guard to help control crime in the nation's capital. Responding to an unprecedented level of community fear of violent crime, Sharon Pratt Kelly called for President Clinton to authorize the use of the National Guard to police the city. Although the request was denied, it solidified citizens' fear of crime by ratifying the "war solution" as an effective means of controlling crime. Consider a few of the examples Peter Kraska (1994) used to illustrate the growing militarization of policing in the United States.

- After the L.A. riots, California Governor Wilson and President George Bush called on the National Guard, and active duty Marine and Army troops, to police the streets of Los Angeles.
- The National Guard of Puerto Rico in 1994 took over domestic law enforcement functions. Even though Puerto Rico operates under the United States Constitution, supporters claim that only the military could do something tangible about their serious "social problems."
- An example of the federal police operating militarily, and poorly at that,

was the incident in Waco, Texas. The disastrous military-style assault on the Branch Davidians raised serious questions about the ATF's myopia in pursuing martial solutions to complex law enforcement problems. Interestingly, the FBI eventually called in the Texas National Guard, even though it clearly violated the *posse comitatus* law. The United States Justice Department circumvented this prohibition by using a newly created exception to the law which allows the use of the military if it involves "drug interdiction." The FBI claimed that the Branch Davidians might have been manufacturing methamphetamine. (p. 1)

Citizen fear of crime and political cries for law and order result in formal modification of the laws that bind police. This, in turn, allows the police to legitimately engage in behaviors that once were considered deviant. Drug forfeiture laws and the growing list of exceptions to Fourth Amendment protections offer clear evidence of the negotiated nature of formal legal bounds placed on the police. As society panics over crime, it negotiates away civil liberties in hopes that the police will stem the tide of crime and disorder. This trend is frequently played out in the political arena. In the fall elections of 1993, many citizens voted to remove political officials in favor of candidates who ran on hard-core, law-and-order platforms, including governors in Virginia and New York and Rudolf Giuliani, a former prosecutor, as mayor of New York. In Pennsylvania, citizens elected at least three mayors with law enforcement backgrounds. In the same year, Congress passed the Brady Bill to control the sale of handguns; enacted legislation to place 100,000 more law enforcement officers on the nation's streets; and passed a crime bill that expanded the use of the death penalty.

Joseph D. McNamara (1997), former police chief of San Jose, California, commented on the dangers of politicians pandering to the public's fear of crime.

> Small groups of police officers share a fermenting contempt for the people they encounter. Rogue cops band together and cover one another's crimes. . . . this wouldn't happen if some cops didn't believe they had a mandate for such behavior. . . . Many of the current brutality cases show officers in an almost maniacal rage. The message of politicians to police that they are soldiers in a war may be driving these angry and violent expressions of contempt. It is common in war to dehumanize the enemy. And all wars produce atrocities. (pp. 28–29)

While political leaders generate concern over crime and effective law enforcement, police officials actively participate in setting the stage for negating the controls placed upon them. Police officials have historically supported and capitalized on the crime-fighting image of law enforcement and have advanced the misconception that they can effectively control crime (Manning, 1997). In essence, police have conveyed the message that all that is needed is more resources and greater autonomy from legal regulation. This is particularly true for relaxation of the controls placed on the police related to drug enforcement. What often results when the public accepts a reduction of civil liberties because of fear is an increase in police deviance associated with the retraction of those rights.

Messages from Police Officials

Further veiling our understanding of police deviance is the behavior of police officials. These officials tend to confront issues of deviance in a manner that cultivates a positive image for the police institution. When an act undermines popular conceptions of the institution, when it challenges our notions of the fairness of the justice system, or when it serves police interests, it is more likely to be publicly acknowledged and sanctioned. In other words, when serious police deviance becomes public knowledge, officials are quick to characterize the deviance as an aberration; they immediately employ rhetoric exhibiting a commitment to control.

As discussed in chapter 8, the New York Police Department (NYPD) has periodically aired its dirty laundry publicly—but only after media reports and the actions of other governmental agencies have brought massive corruption to the public's attention. In 1992, New York City Police Commissioner Raymond Kelly attempted to paint the department's corruption problem in the most favorable light by stating, "There's certainly some. But it's not systemic" (Frankel, 1992, p. 2A). The accuracy of this statement is suspect since the U.S. district attorney in Manhattan was investigating corruption in at least ten of the department's precincts (Gottlieb, 1992). Since Kelly was an up-through-the-ranks commissioner who spent more than twenty-nine years in the NYPD, the statement cannot be attributed to a lack of knowledge about departmental history or the agency's tendency toward corruption.

In many incidents, police officials actively encourage departures from the normative controls placed on officers by defining and rewarding deviance as "good" police work when it results in the achievement of institutional and political goals. Police officials often rely on the "unstated" organizational customs of meting out punishment situationally—subordinating the formal normative order to that of political and institutional objectives.

> During my years as a police chief, I found that police misconduct often had its roots in subtle indications by supervisors to officers that the sort of "extralegal" tactics common to quality-of-life policing were acceptable. Cops in minority neighborhoods would detain, question and push around people on the street without reason. If a young man asserted his legal right to leave, cops "kicked ass." Inevitably a num-

ber of officers felt justified in using illegal and at times fatal force. (McNamara, 1997, p. 29)

All the while, police officials actively promote a public conception of the police that differs drastically from their actual practices and customs. The power of administrators to sanction and reward places police officers in a position where they are forced to interpret law and policy situationally. Content is less relevant than administrative custom and practice (Manning, 1978). According to many police officers, the same enforcement practice can result in either discipline or reward, depending on the political climate and police officials' perceptions of the institutional consequences surrounding the behavior.

Anthony Miranda, head of the Latino Officers Association in New York, discusses the reversed direction of policing in that city after Giuliani's election.

> For years the police department has allowed crime to concentrate and flourish in certain areas, and overnight that has changed. We now have aggressive enforcement without any understanding of neighborhoods or history. We have gone from a tolerance of crime in certain areas to zero tolerance without any concern for how the neighborhoods might react. As a result, there are more serious incidents and an escalation of police aggressiveness that leads to what local areas see as harassment and escalates into brutality. (Farley, 1997, p. 38)

Police officials often undermine attempts by citizens and political leaders to develop adequate accountability systems that would make the police subject to citizen inspection and public disclosure of police conduct. As a candidate in 1993, Giuliani addressed a demonstration of 10,000 off-duty officers who had assembled outside city hall to protest Mayor David Dinkins' decision to establish a civilian review board. He communicated his support for their position and emphasized his law-and-order, pro-police platform. After his election, critics claimed Giuliani was slow to hire investigators for the board; in 1996, he tried to reduce the investigative staff by one-fourth but was overruled by the city council.

The department had reason to be concerned about citizen participation in the handling of complaints against the police. Testimony before the Mollen Commission characterized the NYPD as "disorganized, incompetent and so ineffective that honest police officers feared reporting their crooked colleagues" (Meyers, 1993, p. A4). Commander Robert McKenna, a nineteen-year veteran of the NYPD, told the commission that the department had "an ingrained unwillingness to confront corruption that allowed corrupt officers to stay on the force as supervisors ignored or denied their crimes. . . ." (Meyers, 1993, p. A4).

Messages from the Judiciary

The legal community promotes police deviance by failing to adequately sanction police misconduct. Failure to find police officers liable for constitutional violations, failure to impose penalties for criminal conduct, or imposing token punishments or damage awards all contribute to deviance and corruption. Inaction by the justice system facilitates police use of deviant means to accomplish politically generated crime control goals. The United States Department of Justice reported that between 1985 and 1990 it received 15,279 citizen complaints of official misconduct by the nation's police. Yet, of the 15,000-plus cases, the Justice Department brought legal action in only 42 cases. Even those cases that find their way into the courtroom are most often decided in favor of the police. Only about 8 percent of all the federal civil liability claims against law enforcement officers ever result in a verdict against the police (Kappeler, 1997). Moreover, federal criminal convictions of police officers, while seemingly on the increase, are even more rare.

This does not, however, mean that a few cases cannot have a dramatic impact on the police. The judgment of the federal jury in the Rodney King case illustrates this point. The jury's verdict can be interpreted as condoning some illegal police violence, but subsequent jury verdicts suggest that society will draw a line when police abuses become too extreme. For example, two police officers were convicted for the murder of Malice Green, a black man, in southwest Detroit. Green died at the hands of seven police officers—six white, one black—who beat him to death with metal flashlights. Green was dropping a friend off in a "drug riddled" neighborhood; he was said to be in possession of "crack." The tangible evidence of police brutality presented at the Detroit officers' trial paled in comparison to the evidence available in the King trial. Yet, the Green jury found two of the officers guilty of murder and meted out terms of imprisonment between eight and twenty-five years.

The King and Green jury verdicts are reconcilable only when one recognizes the negotiated nature of police deviance. The normative order as it affects police officers had been negotiated in the King trial. Society had expressed its tolerance of police abuse yet refused to tolerate only the most extreme abuse. The boundary of police behavior had been modified by public response to police deviance. Conversely, since the Green case resulted in a citizen's death, the officers' actions could only be interpreted as an extreme abuse that went beyond the bounds of abuse negotiated in the King trial. It is noteworthy that prosecutors in the Green case had little trouble coming up with a viable criminal charge to file against the Detroit officers whereas prosecutors in Los Angeles spent considerable time debating the applicability of criminal statutes to the police.

Two inferences can be made from these observations. First, prosecutors in the King case needed the public debate over criminal charges to test whether or not society expected a negotiation of the normative order. Had there been little public support for the indictments, it is doubtful they would have taken place. The second inference that can be drawn from the comparison of these two cases is that only the most extreme incidents of police deviance have the ability to modify the normative system on a grand scale. The lack of debate in the subsequent Green case suggests that the normative system had been effectively, possibly permanently, negotiated by the King case. Even when police misconduct is detected and sanctioned, the Supreme Court has chosen to view police officers as less deserving of punishment than their civilian criminal counterparts (*Koon v. U.S.*, 1996). The ultimate message negotiated in the King and Green cases may inform police officers that police abuse will be tolerated to control "problem" segments of society—so long as it is not extreme.

Another outcome negotiated by egregious cases of misconduct is the intervention of the Justice Department. A recently enacted provision (42 U.S.C. Sec. 14141) permits the federal government to bring suit against a law enforcement agency which has engaged in unconstitutional patterns or practices. In February 1997, the Justice Department filed a lawsuit for declaratory and injunctive relief against the Pittsburgh Bureau of Police (PBP). A brief review of previous conduct of the PBP explains the context which brought federal attention.

By the late 1980s, police were out of control. ACLU attorney Timothy O'Brien stated, "They were taking people off the street with absolutely no due process and throwing them in jail" (Lacayo, 1997, p. 28). Almost every complaint to internal affairs was dismissed. In 1995, Jonny Gammage, 31-year old cousin of Ray Seals (then defensive end for the Pittsburgh Steelers) was driving Seals' Jaguar through a primarily white suburban neighborhood. He was stopped by the police, allegedly for driving erratically. After one officer knocked a cellular phone from Gammage's hand, others pinned his face on the pavement. He later died of suffocation. Three of the five officers present were arrested. One was acquitted of involuntary homicide by an all-white jury; the case against the other two was declared a mistrial.

In the complaint filed by the Civil Rights Division, the government alleged that the PBP had engaged in unconstitutional practices which included use of force; false arrests; and improper stops, searches, and seizures since 1990. Ordinary encounters with citizens routinely escalated into violent confrontations. False arrests included those of citizens attempting to report police misconduct or who challenged the authority of PBP officers. The government also alleged that the PBP acquiesced to the unconstitutional acts of its officers by failing to provide adequate training, supervision, monitoring, and discipline.

On April 16, 1997 Pittsburgh resolved the case by entering into a consent decree with the government. The police department agreed to: develop a use-of-force policy and to restrict sharply the use of strip searches; implement an early warning system to identify problem officers by establishing a database of all arrests (by location, race, and violation), traffic stops, searches and seizures by each officer plus all citizens' complaints, all transfers, and disciplinary actions; strict documentation of the use of force; extensive training; and appointment of an outside auditor with access to police disciplinary records. Despite the detailed federal settlement and over the objections of the mayor, Pittsburgh residents voted in May to create a Citizen Police Review Board with the power to investigate and subpoena witnesses.

Legal End Runs

The ambiguity in the criminal law further advances police deviance by allowing the police broad discretion on when and how to invoke the force of criminal law. This ambiguity is compounded by the judiciary's willingness to accept, often without question, police interpretation of situations that led to forceful use of police power. Society grants the police extraordinary discretion to choose when and how to enforce ambiguous laws—without simultaneously imposing mechanisms that would require adequate accountability (Kappeler & Kraska, 1994).

Society has allowed the police to be the primary investigators into their own misconduct and has taken at face value their renditions of situation and necessity. Police play on the images of crime and criminals. These images often excuse police misconduct by signifying victims of deviance as villains. The officialized police version usually prevails. The Pittsburgh consent decree may signal a chink in this protective armor. The decree calls for the elimination of the practice of automatically assigning an officer's statement greater credibility than the statement of the complainant (Zorn, 1997b). This practice often removes responsibility from the police for their deviance and shifts blame to victims. Such imagery and its attendant excusing mechanisms are created in political forums that are constantly negotiated.

In several cases, the judiciary has issued rulings intended to restrict the ability of the police to abridge citizens' Constitutional rights. Yet at the same time, the courts have created various exceptions to these landmark rulings. These exceptions have inevitably led police to use deviant means to obtain confessions, seize evidence, and make arrests. In the landmark *Miranda v. Arizona* (1966) case, for example, the U.S. Supreme Court held that prior to custodial interrogation, suspects must be advised of their rights. When the Court's decision in *Miranda* was announced, police across the country voiced their objections to the new rule, arguing that the requirement would impede their ability to perform police work effectively.

In the more than one-quarter of a century since the decision in *Miranda*, however, the courts have carved out various exceptions to the rule. In *Illinois v. Perkins* (1990), for example, an undercover police officer was placed in a cell with a suspect who had reportedly been involved in a murder. The inmate, Lloyd Perkins, subsequently revealed to the officer that he had committed the murder. The U.S. Supreme Court ruled that undercover police are not required to give the *Miranda* warning to incarcerated suspects before eliciting incriminating statements. Michael S. Vaughn (1992) has noted that since the decision in *Perkins*, other lower court rulings have held that the police may use various forms of trickery and psychological deception to obtain confessions from suspects. Various lower court decisions have held, for example, that "accomplices, relatives, friends, and even crime victims can cajole, trick and deceive an unsuspecting defendant into bragging or admitting involvement in criminal activity" (p. 81). Ironically, exceptions made by the courts appear "to condone precisely the psychological deception and trickery that the 1966 *Miranda* Court was attempting to forbid" (p. 90).

The police have employed other strategies to deliberately circumvent the probable cause requirement for the issuance of search warrants mandated under the Fourth Amendment. These deviant strategies are often implicitly endorsed by at least some members of the judiciary. In one study, L. Paul Sutton (1991) discussed major strategies used by police to "get around" the probable cause requirement for obtaining search warrants from judges. A common strategy is for officers to use subtle coercion to obtain "consent" from persons to search property. In order to avoid having to secure a search warrant, some officers "time" arrests so that a subject is arrested in his or her vehicle, for instance, so that officers can subsequently impound the car and perform an "inventory" search of its contents.

African Americans have a name for one version of this technique: "driving while black." David Harris (1997), a professor at the University of Toledo College of Law, comments on the police use of traffic infractions as legal excuses for stops.

> Since traffic laws include not only simple "moving violations" but also a dizzying array of arcane driving and equipment rules (distance for which drivers must signal, brightness of lights, depth of tire tread and required stickers, to name a few), police know that they can pull over anyone, any time, by following the driver for a short distance. And the law allows this, whatever the real reasons for the stops are. (p. 19)

Harris provides this illustration of one African-American family who experienced differential interpretations of the law.

> In Maryland, police stopped Robert Wilkins and his family, who were returning from a funeral in Chicago. Wilkins, an attorney, requested that he and his family be allowed to leave as soon as police had written the warning they said they were going to give. Instead, when the family refused to allow a search of the car, they were detained and made to stand in the rain while a police dog searched the vehicle. When Wilkins filed a class-action lawsuit, the police quickly settled and agreed to some statistical monitoring of stops. (p. 19)

The data gathered after the suit showed that 75 percent of those stopped and searched by the state police were black, although only 17 percent of drivers are black.

Sutton (1991) noted that officers often "judge-shopped," by routinely seeking out magistrates who had reputations for not carefully scrutinizing applications for search warrants. In some cases, judges were complicitors in sanctioning illegal searches. "Consider the precautionary words to a police officer of one magistrate we interviewed, as the magistrate signed a warrant that he himself conceded—at the time he issued the warrant—was based on less than probable cause: 'This is an illegal warrant, so don't shoot nobody; don't kill nobody; just get the . . . [drugs] . . . off the street!'" (Sutton, 1991, p. 439).

In sum, case law rarely provides definitive guidelines to the police about what they can or cannot do in applying the law. Although the courts typically issue broad rulings on the legality of certain law enforcement practices, the police are left with considerable discretion in deciding when and how to employ the full force of the law. In some cases, the judiciary issues conflicting messages to the police indicating, for example, that while involuntary confessions are inadmissible, some tricks or deceptive practices may be used to elicit information from suspects. In other instances, judges implicitly and explicitly condone unconstitutional police practices by "looking the other way" when police use deviant strategies to circumvent legal requirements.

The Social Organization of Police Deviance

The prospects for controlling police deviance and corruption are undermined by our very conception of deviance. Virtually all citizens and most writers on the subject view police deviance as isolated, very limited, and distributed among a very small percentage of the police population. This conception of deviance, however, runs contrary to what is known about the nature of occupational deviance in other professions. Deviance is a social event; as such, it requires social interaction and organization.

An example of socialized deviance came to light in 1997 when the spotlight of public attention was focused on abuses by the Internal Revenue Service. The unpopular mission of collecting tax revenue creates an "inbred 'us vs. them' bunker mentality" (Hirsch, 1997a, p. 31). "IRS collection agents are a close fraternity. They're bound together by the intense pressure of their jobs, which includes a daily dose of screaming from angry taxpayers" (Hirsch, 1997b, p. 39). In testimony before the Senate Finance Committee, abuses were portrayed as "the product of a badly dysfunctional agency, a seemingly totalitarian financial regime where bullying personalities can find a place to exercise unbridled power over people's lives" (p. 34). A parade of witnesses painted a "chilling portrait: government agency as thug" (Widder, 1997, p. 1). The testimony revealed the agency as a "mismanaged bureaucracy arrogantly accountable to no one. Its culture appears to verge on a police state mentality, suspiciously viewing average citizens as cheats who deserve punishment" (p. 1). The parallels to police deviance are striking, particularly given the powers held by both organizations. Socialization takes place in every organization, but the public is not often exposed to the patterns or the consequences.

Joel Best and David F. Luckenbill (1982), in their book *Organizing Deviance,* suggest that most deviance is an organized behavior which is related to the networking of individuals in and outside the contexts of organization. They employ four conceptual tools that explain why deviance has organizational and interactive aspects. These tools include association, transaction, position, and role.

Association is defined as a "network of relations between a number of individuals who form some sort of group" (Best & Luckenbill, 1982, p. 14). These associations may be formal or informal. In the case of the police, a formal association would include all members of the police agency or a specialized unit within the agency. A formal association has all the rules and regulations normally associated with an organization or agency. A collection of police officers from different locations within the organization who come together to carry out an act of corruption or deviance would constitute an informal association. Informal associations often spread beyond the bounds of a single agency and are most often regulated by mutual understandings that develop between associates over time, rather than by written rules and regulations. Consider the case of a police officer who steals drugs from the evidence room of a large police department. The officer would need to have access to the room, a source to distribute the drugs, and some way to launder the proceeds. These factors suggest the development of at least loose associations, if not highly organized structures, to carry out deviant acts.

In the NYPD these associations were referred to as "crews." According to investigators crews are akin to street gangs: small loyal, flexible, fast moving, and often hard hitting. They establish areas to plan and discuss their operations. They often structure their legitimate police work to generate the leads they need to locate promising targets. They use the police radio network, and code names, to force entry. They manipulate fellow officers, their supervisors, and the courts to their advantage. And they fuel each other's corruption through their eagerness to prove their loyalty and toughness to one another. . . . Engaging in open criminality safely requires an agreement among the officers involved. Having such an agreement was critical to their corrupt conduct because it was a way to doubly insure that fellow officers witnessing their crimes would not report them. (Mollen Commission, 1994, p. 18)

A *transaction* is defined as a "network of relations between two or more individuals in a common activity, whether or not they belong to the same association" (Best & Luckenbill, 1982, p. 14). Transactions are the exchanges that take place between individuals that shape the nature of the associations. In the case of police corruption, this would include the transmission of techniques by which to engage in corruption as well as the role that each officer plays in carrying out the activities needed to achieve that objective. To take a simple example, testimony before the Mollen Commission in New York City revealed that rookie officers were given the "Dowd test" to determine their willingness to participate in illegal activities. The "Dowd test" amounted to requiring rookie officers to enter a store or restaurant and to take food or beer without paying for it. This test was not only a screening mechanism, it was a learning exercise that instructed new officers that if they listened to their corrupt mentors and abided by the rules of the subculture, they also could be the recipients of the proceeds from illegal activities.

Position was defined as "a category of membership whose incumbent is expected to act in a specified way" (Best & Luckenbill, 1982, p. 15). Positions, like associations, may be either formal or informal. In the case of police organizations, an officer's rank is the person's official designation of position. In an informal group, a person's position may be labeled by the function that individual serves in the association. In the Mollen Commission investigation of police corruption, for example, it was learned that one of the corrupt NYPD officers was called the "mechanic" because his role in the corrupt association was to use brutality to "fine tune" citizens for the association.

Finally, Best and Luckenbill (1982) defined a *role* as the dynamic side of position—those activities that are actually performed for the benefit of an association. Extortion, brutality, theft, and the sale of narcotics are all roles that a corrupt police officer might play in a deviant association. Similarly, other members of the organization might provide indirect support for the corrupt activities by supplying information about internal investigations, destroying or altering evidence, or doctoring official documents. While these officers might not be directly involved in corruption, their role facilitates and advances the activities of those who are.

As previously mentioned, there are few acts of police deviance or corruption that are carried out in total isolation. More often than not, a single act of police deviance is indicative of a larger and more extensive problem of wrongdoing within a police organization. Similarly, the uncovering of an act of police brutality or the unmasking of an extensive brutality problem within a police organization does not mean that the organization's problems are limited to mere brutality. To the contrary, because police deviance is organized like any other social activity and because it usually involves associations and transactions, the uncovering of a specific form of deviance is often indicative of the presence of other forms of deviance. Since deviance involves transactions, it is unlikely that only a single actor is involved in the behavior. A police officer who uses excessive force frequently requires the support of his or her peers at a minimum and, at the other extreme, the active assistance of supervisors to conceal the activities of the officer from detection.

While behaviors can be isolated and classified into specific categories of deviance—like brutality, discrimination, sexual exploitation, corruption, and drug trafficking—the individuals involved in these activities often have membership in other deviant groups and hold different positions in these groups. An association of officers who engage in excessive force may also contain fringe members who use illegal, controlled substances. These officers may be more central members of another association of officers who are routinely involved in stealing drugs from suspects and crime scenes; this association may, in turn, have fringe members who sell drugs for profits. Because of the configuration of associations, transactions, and the various forms of police deviance, it is a complex undertaking to introduce any change to an organization that is literally gridlocked with deviance and corruption.

Police organizations and their cultures are highly adaptive, but they resist fundamental change tenaciously. Structural and organizational arrangements can be modified to manage public appearances so that deviance can continue and even flourish in an organization. While this might seem contradictory, police cultures and organizations have a remarkable ability to retain their cultural essence and to continue their activities. The LAPD is no exception to this observation. In the spring of 1996, about five years after the beating of Rodney King and the release of the Christopher Commission report, a new commission released its findings on the progress made by the LAPD in implementing the reforms. Unlike the disbanded Christopher Commission, which attempted to identify problems with the department and its culture, the new commission (composed of four lawyers) was concerned with evaluating the progress of the department and making recommendations to the new office of inspector general.

One area which experienced change in the aftermath of the Rodney King beating was the personnel responsible for monitoring and supervising the operation of the LAPD. Richard Riordan was elected mayor, the Police Commission was replaced, and the City Council gained several new members. Perhaps most importantly, Daryl Gates was replaced as chief of police.

The commission remarked that the LAPD has made substantial progress toward improving many of the critical problem areas identified by the Christopher Commission. According to the new commission,

> The use of force has declined in absolute numbers, although not as a percentage of arrests; the severity of force used has decreased with the deployment of chemical spray, which has all but eliminated the use of the baton; diversity is improving overall, although far too slowly in the upper ranks; and the increased role of Internal Affairs has enhanced the quality of disciplinary investigations. Ugly incidents have diminished and, although arrests are down, the reductions in serious injury to suspects have not been accompanied by feared increases in the crime rate or by significant increases in the numbers of officers injured (Bobb et al., 1996: v).

The commission reported that between 1990 and 1995 use of force incidents dropped dramatically in the LAPD. According to the commission there was a 36 percent reduction in use of force incidents during this time period (Bobb et al., 1996). The commission found that the number of use of force incidents dropped from 3,403 in 1990 to 2,187 in 1995. On its face this would represent a remarkable turnaround in the LAPD. The commission, however, never mentioned that the most dramatic decline in reported use of force incidents came in the very year that Rodney King was beaten and before the Christopher Commission released its findings and recommendations for reform. In fact, 81 percent of the 36 percent reduction occurred in 1991. According to the commission, since 1991, the number of reported use of force incidents remained relatively stable. This, however, is only part of the story about change in the LAPD.

When the number of arrests made by LAPD officers is taken into account, the rate of arrests involving force actually increased between 1990 and 1995. This fact, however, was only acknowledged by the task force in a footnote. Perhaps the most dramatic decline in the use of force by the LAPD was found in officers' use of batons. From 1990 to 1995 use of batons declined from 500 reported incidents in 1990 to only 43 in 1995. Once again the commission failed to note that the most drastic reduction in use of the police baton occurred in 1991. In fact, reported use of the baton that year dropped from 500 incidents to 167 incidents. This trend, however, was also met with an increase in the use of chemical agents like pepper spray. Between 1990 and 1994, the number of reported uses of chemical agents by LAPD officers rose from 21 to 835. If the commission had compared the number of incidents in which LAPD officers reported the use of either a baton or a chemical agent in 1990 (521) to the use of either of those two instruments of force in 1994 (878), they would have found a 68 percent increase in officer use of force. Since the number of arrests made by the LAPD decreased 61 percent, the rate of increase was notable. In essence the use of force by the LAPD has increased as much as their arrests have decreased.

Although the commission noted that racism and sexism contribute to excessive force (Bobb et al., 1996) it remained silent on the characteristics of the citizens exposed to the use of force by the LAPD. Demographic variables like race, gender, sexual orientation, and nature of the offense were not included. The commission remarked, "In this way the LAPD is at the nation's forefront of reducing the level of force used by officers" (Bobb et al., 1996, 8). The assessment of a department's level of change depends on the variables measured. We learned in chapter 10 that the LAPD targeted use of force as an area needing improvement. As seen here, redefining what constitutes force leads to one conclusion. From another perspective, the opposite is true. The power to decide what to measure dictates the results.

THE IMPROBABILITY OF CONTROLLING POLICE DEVIANCE

Several "celebrated" and highly publicized police deviance cases have been brought to light in law enforcement agencies across the country in the past few years. One would hope that police agencies which suffered through such debacles would have taken steps to rectify organizational deviance. Yet at least some of the agencies reviewed earlier in the text have experienced a resurgence of deviance—often reflecting mirror images of past police wrongdoings.

In 1986, the Buddy Boys scandal (discussed in chapter 8) rocked the NYPD. In 1992 following the arrest of officer Michael Dowd, the NYPD once again maintained that Dowd was merely a rotten apple in an otherwise clean barrel. He was "an aberration and corruption was limited to a few 'rogue cops.'" Police corruption was said to be a matter of isolated and sporadic opportunities, rather than planned or organized group efforts. It was said to be motivated solely by greed, nothing more. The Commission found that the lone officer and rotten apple notions of police corruption were "wrong and vastly underestimate the serious nature of present-day corruption" (Mollen Commission, 1994, p. 10).

There are striking similarities between deviance unveiled in the Buddy Boys case and the deviant activities of officers working in the city's 73rd precinct. Officers working in the 73rd precinct formed into gangs who ripped-off drug dealers for money and illicit narcotics. Testimony before the Mollen Commission suggests that the 73rd precinct was used by the NYPD as a "dumping ground," where trouble-prone officers with "checkered pasts" were assigned as a punishment; one officer testified that "officers would leave the precinct unpatrolled while they rolled off in squad cars, in 'caravans,' to rob drug houses" (Quindlen, 1993, p. A19). Officers working in the precinct held backyard barbecues, replete with cocaine. On one occasion, officers raided a brothel, raping prostitutes working there.

Even the Mollen Commission chose to ignore the historical corruption that has permeated the NYPD by characterizing it as something new or different than previous corruption. According to the commission,

> Today's corruption is far more criminal, violent and premeditated than traditional notions of police corruption suggest and far more invidious than corruption of a generation ago. Testimony and field investigations demonstrated that its most salient forms include groups of officers protecting and assisting drug traffickers for often sizable profits—stealing drugs, guns and money—and often selling the stolen drugs and guns to or through criminal associates; committing burglary and robbery; conducting unlawful searches of apartments, cars and people; committing perjury and falsifying statements; and sometimes using excessive force, often in connection with corruption. (Mollen Commission, 1994, p. 10)

Throughout this text we have tried to uncover meanings beneath surface appearances—whether the police image projected to the public or the hidden aspects of deviance as a reflection of society. The intersection of political ploys, institutional goals, citizen expectations and demands, and individual behavior can result in a euphoric sense of cooperative accomplishment at one extreme or a horrific case of wanton brutality at the other. As evidenced by the beating of Rodney King, nothing is as instantly fixating as a vicious assault. But will the fixation result in comprehensive change, or will it rechannel sub-rosa behavior in another direction?

The context of a beating which shocked the nation in 1997 provides another opportunity to look beyond seemingly concrete details. The reputation of New York City had suffered a free fall for a number of years by any measure—economic, social, or political. The crime rate was one of the most noticeable factors affecting both residents and potential visitors to the city. Between 1993 and 1997, the crime rate decreased 54 percent. The reasons for the decrease were complex: several mayoral administrations focused on rebuilding housing and putting 2,000 new officers on the street; an influx of immigrants who could not afford housing elsewhere moved into rundown neighborhoods and reclaimed them; eleven thousand community organizations operated in the five boroughs, undertaking activities from environmental efforts to anti-crime patrols (Marks, 1997). The most public acclaim for the decrease centered on an aggressive policing strategy that abandoned arrests as a measure of success and embraced a "broken-windows" strategy. The foundation of the strategy was the belief that eliminating minor infractions (loitering, panhandling, public drinking, loud music, graffiti, etc.) will serve as an early intervention against more serious offenses.

Many of the issues discussed in this text were contributing factors to a gruesome assault. On Saturday, August 9, Abner Luima (30-year-old security guard; immigrated from Haiti in 1991; married father) went to a Flatbush, Brooklyn music club. As patrons left the Club Rendez-Vous at closing time (3:30 A.M.), a fight broke out between two women. Officers from Brooklyn's 70th precinct responded to the disturbance. Louima was arrested by officers Justin Volpe and Thomas Bruder on charges of assault, resisting arrest, disorderly conduct, and obstructing justice. Prosecutors later surmised that Louima was targeted and assaulted because officers thought he was the black man who sucker-punched Volpe while police tried to break up the fight. Louima was handcuffed and put in a patrol car driven by Thomas Wiese and Charles Schwarz. When he protested, officers kicked him and beat him with police radios on the way to the station house.

Volpe reportedly announced at the precinct, "He hit me, this collar is mine." (Barry, 1997a). In the public lobby of the station house, Louima was stripped naked from the waist down and brought in handcuffs to the bathroom where Volpe, wearing gloves borrowed from another officer, shoved a wooden stick (possibly from a plunger) into Louima's rectum and then into his mouth, breaking his front teeth. During the assault, the officers taunted him with "That's your s___, nigger"; "We're going to teach niggers to respect police officers"; and "This is Giuliani time, not Dinkins time." After the attack, Volpe was seen carrying the stick and returned the stained gloves to the owner (Barry, 1997b). At 6:00 A.M. an ambulance was called. Although it arrived at 6:25, it did not leave the station until 7:58 because paramedics are required to wait for police officers to escort them. Louima was taken to Coney Island Hospital where doctors performed surgery to repair a ripped bladder and punctured lower intestine. On August 15 Louima was transferred to an intensive care unit at the Brooklyn Hospital Center.

Mayor Giuliani visited Louima in the hospital on August 13 and vowed justice would be served. He called for six months of community forums between city residents and members of the police force; all 38,000 police officers would be required to attend one meeting (*Chicago Tribune* 1997b). A task force of 28 people with a budget of $15 million was formed to investigate police and community relations (Firestone, 1997). That evening Giuliani and Police Commissioner Safir met with the leaders of the Haitian community and other civic leaders to reassure them that their concerns and anger over police brutality would be addressed. On August 19, Safir announced that Haitian-American officers who were in Haiti to help the police force there restrict brutality incidents would be called back to work in the 70th precinct (Kifner, 1997a).

Police regulations require officers to fill out form PD 244-150 which lists injuries to prisoners and accompanies them through the system. Louima's form listed "trauma to rectum" but nothing was entered in the "Remarks" section. The department's patrol guide clearly specifies that serious injuries are to be reported up the chain of command, up to and including internal affairs (Kifner, 1997b). Until Louima's family reported the attack to internal affairs at 3:55 P.M. on Sunday (36 hours after it happened), none of the police officers who were present offered any information (Cooper, 1997).

Days later, it was revealed that a phone call was placed by nurse Magalie Laurent from Coney Island Hospital to Internal Affairs between 9 and 10 P.M. on August 9 to report the beating. Commissioner Safir acknowledged the call and that the tip was handled improperly (Kifner, 1997c). Prosecutors have frequently criticized IA for concealing corruption and brutality complaints. The Mollen Commission in 1995 had specifically mentioned the failure of the Internal Affairs Action Desk in fielding calls from informers. Department guidelines require any allegation of brutality or corruption to receive a log number; those numbers are sent to the appropriate district attorney's office daily. Allegations of criminal brutality are to be reported immediately (Kifner, 1997c). Instead, the official notification was logged at 3:55 Sunday, and the Brooklyn district attorney's office was notified at 10 A.M. Monday.

Three weeks after two officers had stepped forward to cooperate, investigators had learned almost nothing from 100 officers (almost one-third of those assigned to the 70th precinct) granted immunity and questioned. Investigators believe that the "blue wall of silence was bolstered by the initial mishandling" (Barry, 1997c). The 36-hour delay may have given officers sufficient time to develop cover stories and to dispose of evidence. Volpe's locker had been cleaned out by the time investigators arrived. The stick was not recovered; Volpe confided to colleagues that he had thrown it down a sewer.

On August 12, Volpe and Schwarz were placed on modified duty; their guns were taken and desk jobs were assigned while the case was investigated. Charges against Louima were dropped August 13. That same day, Volpe was arrested and suspended. Schwarz was indicted on

August 15. On August 18, Wiese and Bruder were charged with 2nd degree assault—pummeling Louima with fists and car radios. All four were later charged with attacking Louima because of his race. By August 14, two top commanders were transferred, a desk sergeant suspended, and 11 other officers pulled off active duty—all were in the stationhouse the night of the incident (Cooper, 1997).

On August 17, it was announced Louima would sue the city for $55 million. Louima planned to hire Johnnie Cochran, Jr. to argue the lawsuit against the city; he will also seek $465 million in punitive damages (*Chicago Tribune* 1997c). The U.S. Justice department began a federal civil rights investigation. U.S. Attorney Zachary W. Carter characterized the behavior as "an act of almost incomprehensible depravity. . . . The boldness of the action [within a police precinct] suggests a mind-set that they could get away with this extraordinarily heinous offense. There might be some reason for them to believe they could" (Barry, 1997b).

As the story unfolded over several weeks, these particulars about the major figures in the incident emerged. Justin Volpe, a 25-year-old son of a retired police detective, had received six commendations in his 4 years on the force. There had been three complaints against him, none substantiated. He was released on $100,000 bond. After his arrest, he floated allegations that Louima was injured during homosexual sex in the nightclub (Associated Press, 1997). Charles Schwarz, partner to Thomas Wiese, allegedly held Louima down for the attack. The 31-year-old, 6-year veteran was suspended for 15 days in 1992 for "striking someone in the face" (Barry, 1997a). He was released on $100,000 bond.

Thomas Wiese was the second officer to provide information to investigators. On August 17, the 33-year old, 8-year veteran claimed that Volpe attacked Louima alone and that Schwarz was not present. He claimed that he and Schwarz spend the morning near the desk sergeant doing paperwork and playing with a puppy which eventually wandered down the hall causing Wiese to find Volpe alone with Louima in the bathroom (Cooper, 1997). He was released on $25,000 bail. Thomas Bruder, a former transit officer, had received four commendations and was "Cop of the Month" in 1995 when he helped break up a robbery spree. The three complaints against the 31-year-old, 3-year veteran were not substantiated. He was Volpe's partner and claimed he removed Louima's handcuffs in the holding cell after the assault (Barry, 1997b). He was released on $25,000 bail. State civil service laws require that the salaries of the arrested officers be reinstated after 30 days. Police Commissioner Safir directed that although the salaries would be reinstated in compliance with the law, the officers would remain suspended with no shield and no weapon (*Chicago Tribune*, 1997d).

Eric Turetzky, 26, was the first officer to step forward with information. He returned from the disturbance at the nightclub shortly before 5

A.M. and saw Schwarz leading the handcuffed Louima, pants down, to the first floor bathroom; 15 minutes later saw he saw Volpe leading Louima back and holding a stick (Cooper, 1997). Giuliani said, "He put decency and the law and concern for other human beings above misplaced loyalty. We are taking steps to protect him" (Barry, 1997a). Interestingly, Guiliani characterized Turetzky's testimony as "putting the lie" to the *myth* of the blue wall of silence. Yet, as noted above, later interviews yielded no new evidence, and the mayor clearly believed that Turetsky was in danger. Mark Schofield, a 4-year veteran, called internal affairs to tell them about the gloves used in the attack. The morning of the attack, Schofield lent his gloves to Volpe and complained when they were returned dirty. Volpe said, "So, wash them off." Schofield did and put them on top of the locker to dry (Barry, 1997c). When he learned about the brutality investigation, he asked another officer to secure the gloves as evidence (Kifner, 1997a).

On August 16, approximately 4,000 protestors marched from the Club Rendez-Vous to the 70th precinct two miles away. "KKK must go!" was chanted as demonstrators waved plungers. In September several hundred protestors marched to the Justice Department in Washington, D.C. to urge an investigation of police misconduct nationwide and the creation of a federal data bank to track brutality allegations (*Chicago Tribune*, 1997d). Louima left Brooklyn Hospital Center on October 10, 1997—nine weeks after the beating.

The aggressive street level tactics credited with the reduction in the crime rate may encourage prejudice—the dark side of allowing institutional goals to take precedence over civil liberties. "All but career criminals are happy with the nationwide drop in such crimes as murder, rape and assault. But the Louima attack, which is also an assault, has citizens wondering whether one kind of public order has been achieved at the cost of another." (Lacayo, 1997, p. 27) Norm Siegel, director of the New York Civil Liberties Union, helped draft the civilian review board ordinance. He says,

> the crackdown that reduced crime had a dark side. It led to a feeling by some police officers that they could do whatever necessary to get the bad guys—including, if necessary, violating their civil rights. The problem is that the political leaders don't take the allegations seriously enough. It's a denial syndrome. They always claim it is just a few bad apples. (Goozner, 1997, p. 1)

The police work at the junction where many social issues converge. What negotiations of boundaries will ensue from this incident? Will the public identify with Abner Louima more than it did with the victims of the Buddy Boys or the victimization recorded by the Mollen Commissio There are endlessly possible permutations of reactions to excesses, op tunities, and perceptions. It is impossible to predict the connections that will be traced and the inferences drawn from an incident or a sequence of incidents—or the consequences that will result from any action taken. Will Justin Volpe replace Michael Dowd as another name in a ceaseless succession of names? New York is hardly alone; there is no shortage of examples.

Other agencies also continue to experience a litany of critical deviance problems. In terms of discriminatory practices, two police officers in Minneapolis, Minnesota, were suspended after reportedly transporting an intoxicated Native American to the hospital in the trunk of their police cruiser (Minneapolis, 1993). In Portland, Oregon, two officers were reprimanded after admitting they imitated tribal drumming while dancing around a Native American who had been detained for drinking (Portland, 1993). Drug-related deviance also continues to plague many agencies. In El Paso, Texas, two officers were arrested after they allegedly bought cocaine from undercover FBI agents (Deputies, 1993); another undercover officer in the city was arrested for conspiring to possess and distribute 110 pounds of marijuana (Two Charged, 1993). In Long Island, New York, a Federal Drug Enforcement Administration agent was found dead in his home of a heroin overdose (DEA Agent Dies, 1989). In a separate case, another DEA agent was charged with drug trafficking following his arrest for possession of 62 pounds of cocaine (DEA Agent Arrested, 1989). In Atlanta, Georgia, three police officers were arrested for murdering a nightclub owner, while two other officers were taken into custody for armed robbery. All of the officers were reportedly members of a robbery and burglary ring that targeted stores and nightclubs featuring nude dancers (Georgia Officers, 1993). In Philadelphia, a police lieutenant and his wife were charged with running a major prostitution ring that fronted as an escort service (Cop Arrested, 1992). In New York, at least five state police officers were being investigated for fabricating evidence in order to obtain criminal convictions in several cases. As late as 1997 New York state police were still investigating the fabrication of evidence by troopers. After a four-year investigation, special prosecutors concluded that at least 36 cases involving 6 troopers were based on fabricated evidence and another 10 cases were tainted by the troopers' conduct (*New York Times*, 1997).

This text has reviewed problems in Los Angeles, Milwaukee, New York, Washington, D.C., Chicago, Pittsburgh, and New Orleans. It has mentioned incidents in a number of other locales. As also noted, federal agencies are included in the ranks of troubled organizations. Frederic Whitehurst, a bomb residue expert, reported that he and his colleagues at the FBI laboratory were skewing results to bolster prosecutors' cases. In testimony before a Senate Judiciary subcommittee hearing in September 1997, current and former agents claimed that the laboratory was a haven of favoritism where reports are altered, truth-tellers are punished, and wrongdoers promoted. Senator Charles Grassley blasted the lab and the bureau as suffering from a "cultural disease" that puts too much emphasis on slamming defendants. "It appears to be a culture that rewards public image-building over discovering the truth. Those who engage in image-building, though they may do wrong, are rewarded. Those who challenge image builders, though they may speak the truth, are punished" (Bendavid, 1997, p. 6). Collectively, these and other reported cases of police wrongdoing indicate an underlying theme of deviance in the police occupation. If this is true, what are the prospects for controlling police deviance and corruption?

SUMMARY

If any conclusion may be drawn, it is that police deviance is a complex, multifaceted, and multidimensional enigma. Thus, there are no simplistic, quick-fix, cookbook solutions for the problems of police wrongdoing. Despite these cautionary notes, a complex, interrelated web of remedies are suggested. At the simplest level, the opportunity structure inherent in the nature of policing presents officers with virtually unlimited chances to engage in deviant activity. Hiring well qualified and capable employees, providing appropriate training and education programs, mandating that supervisors hold officers accountable for their behavior, and centralizing administrative control are all simple means to thwart deviance in the police organization. Other control mechanisms are suggested as well. Included among them are the development and endorsement of agency guidelines that are clear, practical, reasonable, and workable. Progressive and consistently applied disciplinary schemes in the police institution are critical. Internal affairs units and review boards, if they are able to function with integrity and handle complaints objectively, can also be used as checks and balances to minimize organizational deviance.

Although all of these factors are important in the control of police deviance, they alone cannot ensure the control or elimination of deviance in the police occupation. In fact, there are agencies that use many or all of these mechanisms, yet continue to suffer from problems of organizational deviance. In order to effect significant change in the police occupation, deeper, more fundamental modifications to the existing social order and police normative structure are indicated.

Police deviance serves functional roles for society and the police culture. Thus, society has two options. One is to acknowledge the role of deviance in maintaining the culture of the police and the existing social order.

Although not a remedy for deviance, recognition of the functional aspects of police deviance is a foundation from which society can begin to understand the realities of both policing and police wrongdoing. Public acknowledgment of the parameters of police misconduct would help to dispel myths such as the rotten-apple theory of misconduct, and portrayals of police as loyal social control agents supportive of the expressed moral order. Unfortunately, this would permit and even encourage corruption.

A second, more radical approach would entail modifying the bounds of both society's normative system and the police normative structure. Attaining congruity between the two would obviously be a formidable challenge. Public officials would need to refrain from politicizing crime, capitalizing on citizen fear of crime, imputing a warlike mentality for crime control, and advancing the misconception that the police can effectively control social disorder and crime itself. The judiciary must send a clear and constant message that police deviance will not be tolerated. Ambiguities in the criminal law must be resolved by both the legal and law enforcement communities. This means, among other things, that equitable and ethical approaches to attaining justice must be emphasized, while backdoor approaches used to circumvent legal requirements must be discontinued. Administrative customs and practices in the police institution must conform with both the stated law and agency policy. In essence, the radical approach suggests restructuring the law, reordering the social structure, and reinventing police culture.

In the final analysis, society must confront the most fundamental question of all: How much social change should be made in an attempt to control deviance and corruption in the police system? While not an answer to the question, we are reminded that any society may have as much crime and deviance as it deserves. It remains unclear whether or not it is impossible to control police deviance. Without substantial social change, however, it seems clear that attainment of this goal will be improbable at best.

REFERENCES

Adlam, K. R. (1982). The police personality: Psychological consequences of becoming a police officer. *The Journal of Police Science and Administration, 10*(3), 347–348.

Adler, F., Mueller, G. O. W., & Laufer, W. S. (1995). *Criminology* (2nd ed.). New York: McGraw-Hill.

Adorno, T. W. (1950). *The authoritarian personality.* New York: Harper.

Ahern, J. (1972). *Police in trouble.* New York: Hawthorn Books.

Albrecht, S. L., & Green, M. (1977). Attitudes toward the police and the larger attitude complex: Implications for police-community relationships. *Criminology, 15*(1), 67–86.

Alpert, G. P. (1993). The role of psychological testing in law enforcement. In R. G. Dunham & G. P. Alpert (Eds.), *Critical issues in policing: Contemporary readings* (2nd ed., pp. 96–105). Prospect Heights, IL: Waveland Press.

Alpert, G. P., & Dunham, R. G. (1988). *Policing multi-ethnic neighborhoods.* Westport, CT: Greenwood Press.

Alpert, G. P., & Dunham, R. G. (1997). *Policing urban America* (3rd ed.). Prospect Heights, IL: Waveland Press.

Alpert, G. P., & Fridell, L. (1992). *Police vehicles and firearms: Instruments of deadly force.* Prospect Heights, IL: Waveland Press.

Alpert, G. P., Kenney, K. J. & Dunham, R. G. (1977). Police pusuits and the use of force: Reorganizing and managing "The Pucker Factor"—A research note. *Justice Quarterly, 14*(2), 371–385.

Alpert, G. P., & Smith, W. C. (1993). Developing police policy: An evaluation of the control principle. In R. G. Dunham & G. P. Alpert (Eds.), *Critical issues in policing: Contemporary readings* (2nd ed., pp. 237–251). Prospect Heights, IL: Waveland Press.

Alpert, G. P., Smith, W. C., & Watters, D. (1992). Implications of the Rodney King beating. *Criminal Law Bulletin, 28*(5), 469–478.

279

ABA (1976). *Comparative analysis of standards and goals of the national advisory commission on criminal justice standards for criminal justice for the American Bar Association*. Washington, DC: American Bar Association.

Amnesty International (1992). *Amnesty international USA: Police brutality in Los Angeles, California, United States of America*. London, England: Amnesty International.

Andrew Young's son files complaint against police who allegedly beat him. (1991, October 7). *Jet*, 18.

Andrew Young's son protests his reported beating by D.C. cops. (1991, September 30). *Jet*, 5.

Angell, J. E. (1977). Toward an alternative to the classical police organizational arrangements: A democratic model. In L. K. Gaines & T. A. Ricks (Eds.), *Managing the police organization*. St. Paul, MN: West.

Anthony, S. (1993). *Nights of fire*. Las Vegas: Las Vegas Metropolitan Police Department.

Apple, N., & O'Brien, D. J. (1983). Neighborhood racial composition and residents' evaluation of police performance. *Journal of Police Science and Administration, 11*(1), 76–83.

Argyris, C. (1957, June). The individual and organization: Some problems of mutual adjustment. *Administrative Science Quarterly*, 1–24.

Associated Press (1993, August 16). Earlier reprimand for LA officer. *Kansas City Star*, p. A7.

Associated Press (1997, August 23). *Chicago Tribune*, Sec. 1, p. 8.

Ayres, B. D. (1990, July 20). Barry's bodyguards testify that they never saw him using drugs. *New York Times*, p. A9.

Bahn, C. (1984). Police socialization in the eighties: Strains in the forging of an occupational identity. *Journal of Police Science and Administration, 12*(4), 390–394.

Bai, M. (1997, December 8). A chief's fall from grace. *Newsweek*, 42.

Baker, J. N., & Wright, L. (1991, April 1). Los Angeles aftershocks. *Newsweek*, 18–19.

Balch, R. W. (1972). The police personality: Fact or fiction. *Journal of Criminal Law, Criminology and Police Science, 63*(1), 106–119.

Baldwin, J. (1962). *Nobody knows my name*. New York: Dell.

Banton, M. (1964). *The policeman in the community*. New York: Basic Books.

Barker, T. (1990). Peer group support for police occupational deviance. In T. Barker & D. L. Carter (Eds.), *Police deviance* (2nd ed.). Cincinnati: Anderson.

Barker, T., & Carter, D. L. (Eds.) (1994). *Police deviance* (3rd ed.). Cincinnati: Anderson.

Barry, D. (1997a, August 16). Officer charged in torture in Brooklyn station house. *New York Times*.

Barry, D. (1997b, August 19). Two more police officers charged with attack on Haitian. *New York Times*.

Barry, D. (1997c, September 5). Officers' silence still thwarting torture inquiry. *New York Times*.

Bayley, D. H. (1976). *Forces of order: Police behavior in Japan and the United States*. Berkeley: University of California Press.

Bayley, D. H., & Bittner, E. (1997). Learning the skills of policing. In R. G. Dunham & G. P. Alpert (Eds.), *Critical issues in policing: Contemporary readings* (3rd ed., pp. 114–138). Prospect Heights, IL: Waveland Press.

Bayley, D. H., & Mendelsohn, G, (1969). *Minorities and the police: Confrontation in America.* New York: The Free Press.

Beals, G. & Bai, M. (1997, September 1). The thin blue line. *Newsweek,* 52–53.

Becker, H. S. (1963). *Outsiders.* New York: The Free Press.

Beigel, H. (1978). *The closed fraternity of police and the development of the corrupt attitude.* New York: John Jay Press.

Bell, D. (1960). *The end of ideology: On the exhaustion of political ideas in the fifties.* New York: The Free Press.

Bendavid, N. (1997, September 30)."Four testify FBI lab data altered, favoritism rife." *Chicago Tribune,* Sec. 1, p. 6.

Benedict, R. (1934). *Patterns of culture.* Boston: Houghton Mifflin.

Bennett, R. R. (1984). Becoming blue: A longitudinal study of police recruit occupational socialization. *Journal of Police Science and Administration, 12*(1), 47–57.

Ben-Yehuda, N. (1990). *The politics and morality of deviance.* Albany: State University of New York Press.

Berg, B. L. (1992). *Law enforcement: An introduction to police in society.* Boston: Allyn and Bacon.

Berg, B. L., Gertz, M. G., & True, E. J. (1984). Police-community relations and alienation. *Police Chief, 51*(11), 20–23.

Best, J., & Luckenbill, D. F. (1994). *Organizing deviance* (2nd ed.). Englewood Cliffs, NJ: Prentice Hall.

Bittner, E. (1995a) The capacity to use force as the core of the police role. In V. E. Kappeler (Ed.), *The police & society: Touchstone readings* (pp. 127–137). Propsect Heights, IL: Waveland Press.

Bittner, E. (1995b). The quasi-military organization of the police. In V. E. Kappeler (Ed.), *The police & society: Touchstone readings* (pp. 173–183). Prospect Heights, IL: Waveland Press.

Black, D. (1970). Production of crime rates. *American Sociological Review, 35,* 733–748.

Black, D. (1976). *The behavior of law.* New York: Academic Press.

Black, D., & Reiss, A. J. (1970). Police control of juveniles. *American Sociological Review, 35,* 63–77.

Blum, A. F., & McHugh, P. (1971). The social ascription of motives. *American Sociological Review, 36,* 98–109.

Bobb, M. J., Epstein, M. H., Miller, N. H., & Abascall, M. A. (1996). Five years later: A report to the Los Angeles Police Commission on the Los Angeles Police Department's implementation of independent commission recommendations. Los Angeles: City of Los Angeles.

Bopp, W. J., & Schultz, D. O. (1972). *A short history of American law enforcement.* Springfield, IL: Charles C. Thomas.

Bordua, D. J. & Reiss, A. J., Jr. (1967). Law enforcement. In P. Lazarsfeld, W. Sewell, & H. Wilensky (Eds.), *The uses of sociology.* New York: Basic Books.

Bordua, D. J., & Tift, L. L. (1971). Citizen interviews, organizational feedback, and police community relations decisions. *Law and Society Review, 6,* 155–182.

Bracey, D. (1989). Police corruption. In W. G. Bailey (Ed.), *The encyclopedia of police science.* New York: Garland.

Bracey, D. (1992). Police corruption and community relations: Community policing. *Police Studies, 15*(4), 179–183.

Broderick, J. J. (1987). *Police in a time of change* (2nd ed.). Prospect Heights, IL: Waveland Press.

Brodeur, J. (1981). Legitimizing police deviance. In C. D. Shearing (Ed.), *Organizational police deviance.* Toronto, Canada: Butterworths.

Brodeur, J. (1992). Undercover policing in Canada: Wanting what is wrong. *Crime, Law and Social Change, 18,* 105–136.

Brown v. State's Atty., 783 F. Supp. 1149 (N.D. Ill. 1992).

Brown, L. (1997). Law enforcement execution on the integrity and ethics challenge facing the profession, In S. J. Gaffigan & P. P. McDonald (Eds.), *Police Integrity.* Washington, D.C.: U.S. Department of Justice, National Institute of Justice.

Brown, M. K. (1981). *Working the street: Police discretion and the dilemmas of reform.* New York: Russell Sage.

Buder, L. (1987a, May 2). Code signaled police thefts, witnesses say. *New York Times,* pp. A29, A30.

Buder, L. (1987b, May 14). Corruption-trial jury is told Brooklyn officer is a "victim." *New York Times,* p. B4.

Buder, L. (1987c, May 15). Policeman is convicted of graft. *New York Times,* pp. B1, B8.

Buder, L.. (1987d, June 30). 77th precinct "ringleader" draws a prison term. *New York Times,* pp. B1, B7.

Buder, L.. (1987e, July 9). Officer cleared of taking graft in the 77th precinct. *New York Times,* p. B4.

Burbeck, E., & Furnham, A. (1985). Police officer selection: A critical review of the literature. *Journal of Police Science and Administration, 13*(1), 58–69.

Bureau of Justice Statistics (1992a). *Law enforcement management and administrative statistics, 1990: Data for individual state and local agencies with 100 or more officers.* Washington, DC: U.S. Department of Justice.

Bureau of Justice Statistics. (1992b). *A National Report: Drugs, Crime, and the Justice System* (NCJ–133652). Washington, DC: U.S. Department of Justice, Bureau of Justice Statistics.

Burger, W. (1964). Who will watch the watchmen? *American Law Review, 14,* 11–12.

Cain, M. E. (1973). *Society and the policeman's role.* London, England: Routledge and Kegan Paul.

Carlson, T. (1993). D.C. blues: The rap sheet on the Washington police. *Policy Review, 63,* 26–33.

Carpenter, B. N., & Raza, S. M. (1987). Personality characteristics of police applicants: Comparisons across subgroups and with other populations. *Journal of Police Science and Administration 15*(1), 10–17.

Carter v. District of Columbia, 795 F.2d 116 (D.C. Cir. 1986).

Carter, D. L. (1985). Police brutality: A model for definition, perspective, and control. In A. S. Blumberg & E. Neiderhoffer (Eds.), *The ambivalent force.* New York: Holt, Rinehart and Winston.

Carter, D. L. (1990). Drug related corruption of police officers: A contemporary typology. *Journal of Criminal Justice, 18,* 85–98.

Carter, D. L. (1994a). A taxonomy of prejudice and discrimination by police officers. In T. Barker & D. L. Carter (Eds.), *Police deviance* (3rd ed.). Cincinnati: Anderson.

Carter, D. L. (1994b). Theoretical dimensions in the abuse of authority by police officers. In T. Barker & D. L. Carter (Eds.), *Police deviance* (3rd ed.). Cincinnati: Anderson.

Carter, D. L., & Stephens, D. W. (1994). An overview of issues concerning police officer drug use. In T. Barker & D. L. Carter (Eds.), *Police deviance* (3rd ed.). Cincinnati: Anderson.

Chackerian, R. (1974). Police professionalism and citizen evaluations: A preliminary look. *Public Administration Review, 34,* 141–148.

Chafee, Z., Pollak, W. H., & Stern, C. S. (1969). *Mass violence in America: The third degree.* New York: Anno Press and *The New York Times.*

Chambliss, W. J., & Seidman, R. B. (1971). *Law, order and power.* Reading, MA: Addison-Wesley.

Chartrand, S. (1992, October 8). A Washington district that's a world apart. *New York Times,* p. A20.

Chicago Tribune (1997a, August 15, 1997), Sec. 1, p. 16.

Chicago Tribune (1997b, August 19, 1997), Sec. 1, p. 6.

Chicago Tribune (1997c, August 29, 1997), Sec. 1, p. 20.

Chicago Tribune (1997d, September 9, 1997), Sec. 1, p. 9.

Christopher, W. (1991a). *Report of the independent commission on the Los Angeles Police Department.* Los Angeles: City of Los Angeles.

Christopher, W. (1991b). *Summary: Report of the independent commission on the Los Angeles Police Department.* Los Angeles: City of Los Angeles.

Clark, J. P. (1965). Isolation of the police: A comparison of the British and American situations. *Journal of Criminal Law, Criminology and Police Science, 56,* 307–319.

Clear, T. R., & Cole, G. F. (1997). *American corrections* (4th ed.). Belmont, CA: Wadsworth.

Clemente, G., & Stevens, K. (1987). *The cops are robbers.* Boston: Quinlan Press.

Clinard, M. B., & Meier, R. B. (1995). *Sociology of deviant behavior* (9th ed.). Ft. Worth, TX: Harcourt Brace.

Cohen, H. S., & Feldberg, M. (1991). *Power and restraint: The moral dimension of police work.* New York: Praeger.

Commission on accreditation for law enforcement agencies (1993). *Standards.* Fairfax, VA: CLEA.

Commission on Budget and Financial Priorities of the District of Columbia (1990). *Financing the nation's capital.* Washington, DC: Balmar Printing and Graphics.

Consultant pans D.C. probe of botched drug sweep. (1989, March 31). *Law Enforcement News,* pp. A1, A7.

Cooley, C. H. (1902). *Human nature and the social order.* New York: Charles Scribner's Sons.

Cooper, M. (1997, August 18). Second officer gives account of sex assault of Haitian. *New York Times.*

Cooper v. City of Greenwood, Miss., 904 F.2d 302 (5th Cir. 1990).

Cop arrested for operating a sex ring. (1992, August 24). *Crime Control Digest,* p. 9.

Cordner, G. (1989). Written rules and regulations: Are they necessary? *FBI Law Enforcement Bulletin, 58*(7), 17–21.

Cox v. District of Columbia, 821 F. Supp. 1 (D. D.C. 1993).

Cox, T. C., Crabtree, A., Joslin, D., & Millet, A. (1987). A theoretical examination of police entry-level uncorrected visual standards. *American Journal of Criminal Justice, 11*(2), 199–208.

Crank, J. P. (1998). *Understanding police culture.* Cincinnati, OH: Anderson.

Crawford, P. J., & Crawford, T. J. (1983). Police attitudes toward the judicial system. *Journal of Police Science and Administration, 11*(3), 290–295.

Cray, D. (1997, September 1). Good cop, bad cop. *Time,* 30.

Critchley, T. A. (1985). Constables and justices of the peace. In W. C. Terry (Ed.), *Policing society: An occupational view.* New York: John Wiley.

Cullen, F. T., Link, B. G., Travis, L. F., & Lemming, T. (1983). Paradox in policing: A note on perceptions of danger. *Journal of Police Science and Administration, 11*(4), 457–462.

Daley, R. (1978). *Prince of the city: The true story of a cop who knew too much.* Boston: Houghton Mifflin.

D.C. jury awards $950,000 on police brutality charge. (1985). *Crime Control Digest, 19*(48), 1, 7.

D.C. police beating case. (1985). *Crime Control Digest, 19*(20), 8–9.

D.C. police lose $425,000. (1985). *Crime Control Digest, 19*(41), 10.

D.C. police criticized for recruiting in Puerto Rico. (1986). *Criminal Justice Newsletter, 17*(2), 3.

D.C. chief quitting. (1989). *Crime Control Digest, 23*(7), 9.

D.C. cops brace for prospect of mandatory 60 hour work week. (1989, September 30). *Law Enforcement News,* p. A1.

D.C. police department called nation's most inefficient. (1991). *Criminal Justice Newsletter, 22,* 3.

D.C. officer is arraigned on murder, drug charges. (1992). *Narcotics Control Digest, 22*(15), 7.

D.C.'s Fulwood retires after 3-year tenure plagued by record homicide rates. (1992, September 30). *Law Enforcement News,* pp. A3, A8.

DEA agent dies of heroin overdose—First for agency. (1989, August 16). *Narcotics Control Digest,* pp. 8–9.

DEA agent arrested in cocaine trafficking sting. (1989, August 30). *Narcotics Control Digest,* pp. 9–10.

Decker, S. H. (1981). Citizen attitudes toward the police: A review of past findings and suggestions for future policy. *Journal of Police Science and Administration, 9*(1), 80–87.

Delattre, E. J. (1989). *Character and cops: Ethics in policing.* Washington, DC: American Enterprise Institute for Public Policy Research.

del Carmen, R. V. (1991). *Civil liabilities in American policing: A text for law enforcement personnel.* Englewood Cliffs, NJ: Brady.

del Carmen, R. V., & Smith, M. (1997). Police, civil liability and the law. In R. G. Dunham & G. P. Alpert (Eds.), *Critical issues in policing: Contemporary readings* (3rd ed., pp. 225–242). Prospect Heights, IL: Waveland Press.

Dennis, R. J. (1990). The economics of legalizing drugs. *Atlantic Monthly, 266*(5), 126–132.

Dombrink, J. (1988). The touchables: Vice and police corruption in the 1990s. *Law and Contemporary Problems, 51*, 201–232.

Dombrink, J. (1994). The touchables: Vice and police corruption in the 1980s. In T. Barker and Carter D. L. (Eds.), *Police deviance* (3rd ed.). Cincinnati: Anderson.

Dorschner, J. (1993). The dark side of the force. In R. G. Dunham & G. P. Alpert (Eds.), *Critical issues in policing: Contemporary readings* (2nd ed., pp. 254–274). Prospect Heights, IL: Waveland Press.

Douglas, J. D. (1970). Deviance and order in a pluralistic society. In J. C. McKinney & E. A. Tiryakian (Eds.), *Theoretical sociology.* New York: Meredith.

Drug cases face dismissal in D.C. in wake of probe. (1987, October 13). *Law Enforcement News,* p. A3.

Duggan, P. (1993, April 5). In D.C.'s overtime pit: Where officers wait to testify at $30 an hour. *Washington Post.* Reported in Newsbank, at LAW 37, p. A6.

Durkheim, É. (1938/1982). *Rules of sociological method.* New York: The Free Press.

Eastman, W. E. (1985). National accreditation: A costly, unneeded make-work scheme. In J. Fyfe (Ed.), *Police management today.* Washington, DC: International City Managers Association.

Editor. (1991a). Milwaukee police give chief a "no confidence" vote: Mother of one victim sues. *Crime Control Digest, 25*(31), 5–6.

Editor. (1991b). Three Milwaukee officers file written responses on Dahmer incident charges. *Crime Control Digest, 25*(33), 10.

Editor. (1991c). Milwaukee officers say they feel betrayed by public. *Crime Control Digest, 25*(39), 5–6.

Editor. (1993a, May 29). Shaping up D.C.'s finest. *Washington Post,* p. A30.

Editor. (1993b, June 5). Police on trial. *Washington Post,* p. A20.

Emsley, C. (1987). *Crime and society in England, 1750–1900.* London: Longman.

Erez, E. (1994). Self-defined desert and citizen's assessment of police. *Journal of Criminal Law and Criminology, 75,* 1276–1299.

Ericson, R. V. (1981). Rules for police deviance. In C. D. Shearing (Ed.), *Organizational police deviance.* Toronto, Canada: Butterworths.

Erikson, K. T. (1962). Notes on the sociology of deviance. *Social Problems, 9,* 307–314.

Erikson, K. T. (1966). *Wayward puritans.* New York: John Wiley.

Ermann, M. D., & Lundman, R. J. (1992). *Corporate and governmental deviance.* New York: Oxford University Press.

Estate of Sinthasomphone v. City of Milwaukee, 785 F. Supp. 1343 (E.D. Wis. 1992).

Farley, C. (1997, August 25). A beating in Brooklyn. *Time,* 38.

Federal Bureau of Investigation (1997). *Law enforcement officers killed and assaulted*. Washington, DC: U.S. Government Printing Office.

Federal Bureau of Investigation (1996). *Uniform Crime Reports, 1995*. Washington, DC: U.S. Government Printing Office.

Ferdinand, T. H. (1980). Police attitudes and police organization: Some interdepartmental and cross-cultural comparisons. *Police Studies, 3,* 46–60.

Fernandez v. Leonard, 963 F.2d 459 (1st Cir. 1992).

Firestone, D. (1997, August 21, 1997). Giuliani's panel on police shows strains already. *New York Times*.

Flanagan, T. J., & Vaughn, M. S. (1995). Public opinion about police abuse of force. In W. A. Geller & H. Toch (Eds.), *Police use of excessive force and its control: Key issues facing the nation*. Washington, DC: Police Executive Research Forum/National Institute of Justice.

Fogelson, R. M. (1977). *Big-city police*. Cambridge: Harvard University Press.

Folks, M. (1989, June 14). Fulwood strategy built on recruiting. *Washington Times*. Reported in Newsbank, at LAW 77, p. G7.

Fosdick, R. B. (1920). *Crime in America and the police*. New York: Century.

Frank, J., Brandl, S. G., Cullen, F. T. & Stichman, A. (1966). Reassessing the impact of race on citizen's attitudes toward the police: A research note. *Justice Quarterly, 13*(2), 321–334.

Frankel, B. (1993, September 28). Ex-NYC officer tells stark tale of cops gone bad. *USA Today*, p. A3.

Frankel, B., & Stone, A. (1993, September 30). "You'll be in the fold" by breaking the law. *USA Today*, pp. A1, A2.

Furstenberg, F., & Wellford, C. (1973). Calling the police: The evaluation of police service. *Law and Society Review, 7,* 393–406.

Fyfe, J. J. (1997). The split-second syndrome and other determinates of police violence. In R. G. Dunham & G. P. Alpert (Eds.), *Critical issues in policing: Contemporary readings* (3rd ed., pp. 531–546). Prospect Heights, IL: Waveland Press.

Gaines, L. K., Costello, P., & Crabtree, A. (1989). Police selection testing: Balancing legal requirements and employer needs. *American Journal of Police, 8*(1), 137–152.

Gaines, L. K., Falkenberg, S., & Gambino, J. A. (1994). Police physical agility testing: A historical and legal analysis. *American Journal of Police, 7*(4), 47–66.

Gaines, L. K., Kappeler, V. E., & Vaughn, J. B. (1997). *Policing in America* (2nd ed.). Cincinnati: Anderson.

Gaines, L. K., Southerland, M. D., & Angell, J. E. (1991). *Police administration*. New York: McGraw-Hill.

Garfinkel, H. (1967). *Studies in ethnomethodology*. Englewood Cliffs, NJ: Prentice Hall.

Garofalo, J. (1977). *The police and public opinion: An analysis of victimization and attitude data from 13 American cities*. Washington, DC: U.S. Government Printing Office.

Gates, D. F., & Shah, D. K. (1993). *Chief: My life in the LAPD*. New York: Bantam Books.

Georges-Abeyie, D. (Ed.). (1984). *The criminal justice system and blacks.* New York: Clark Boardman.

Georgia officers charged in killing and robberies. (1993, March 9). *New York Times,* p. A9.

Germann, A. C., Day, F. D., & Gallati, R. R. J. (1985). *Introduction to law enforcement and criminal justice.* Springfield, IL: Charles C. Thomas.

Gerth, H., & Mills, C. W. (1953). *Character and social structure.* New York: Harcourt Brace.

Giacopassi, D. J., & Sparger, J. R. (1991). Cognitive dissonance in vice enforcement. *American Journal of Police, 10*(2), 39–51.

Gilliam, D. (1997, October 4). Homicide unit's failure costing D.C. dearly. *Washington Post,* p. C1.

Goldstein, H. (1975). *Police corruption: A perspective on its nature and control.* Washington, DC: Police Foundation.

Goldstein, H. (1977) *Policing a free society.* Cambridge, MA: Ballinger.

Gonzales, E. J. (1990, August 28). D.C.'s fed-up cops looking to exit through retirement. *Washington Times.* Reported in Newsbank, at LAW 100, p. E9.

Gonzales, E. J., & Fields, G. (1990, September 27). Police begin drug testing. *Washington Times.* Reported in Newsbank, at LAW 100, p. E3.

Goozner, M. (1997, August 16). NYC cut in crime has a brutish side. *Chicago Tribune,* Sec. 1., p. 1.

Gora v. Costa, 971 F.2d 1325 (7th Cir. 1992).

Gottlieb, M. (1992, July 25). Dinkins wants civilians on police review panel. *New York Times,* p. A20.

Greenberg, S. (1989). Police accreditation. In D. J. Kenney (Ed.), *Police and policing: Contemporary issues.* New York: Praeger.

Grescoe, T. (1996, June 30). The brain and the badge. *Chicago Tribune Magazine,* pp. 19–22.

Guskind, R. (1989). Bush's capital, Barry's city. *National Journal, 21,* 126–131.

Guyot, D. (1977). Police departments under social science scrutiny. *Journal of Criminal Justice, 5,* 68–81.

Hafner v. Brown, 983 F.2d 570 (4th Cir. 1992).

Hale, D. C. (1989). Ideology of police misbehavior: Analysis and recommendations. *Quarterly Journal of Ideology, 13*(2), 59–85.

Haller, M. H. (1992). Historical roots of police behavior: Chicago, 1890–1925. In E. H. Monkkonen (Ed.), *Policing and crime control.* New York: K. G. Sauer.

Hannewicz, W. B. (1978). Police personality: A Jungian perspective. *Crime and Delinquency, 24*(2), 152–172.

Harring, S. L. (1981). Policing a class society: The expansion of the urban police in the late nineteenth and early twentieth centuries. In D. F. Greenburg (Ed.), *Crime and capitalism.* Palo Alto, CA: Mayfield.

Harring, S. L. (1983). *Policing a class society.* New Brunswick, NJ: Rutgers University Press.

Harring, S. L. (1992). Class conflict and the suppression of tramps in Buffalo, 1892–1894. In E. H. Monkkonen (Ed.), *Policing and crime control.* New York: K. G. Sauer.

Harring, S. L., & McMullin, L. M. (1992). The Buffalo police 1872–1900: Labor unrest, political power and the creation of the police institution. In E. H. Monkkonen (Ed.), *Policing and crime control*. New York: K. G. Sauer.

Harris, D. A. (1967, March 11). Driving while black: Unequal protection under the law. *Chicago Tribune*, Sec. 1, p. 19.

Harris, H. R., & Williams, V. (1996, September 11). D.C. mayor's police escort taxis voters. *Washington Post*, p. A1.

Harris, R. (1973). *The police academy: An insider's view.* New York: John Wiley.

Havesi, D. (1986, September 24). Police suspend 13 over drug inquiry in Brooklyn unit. *New York Times,* pp. A1, A25.

Herbert, S. (1996). Morality in law enforcement: Chasing "bad guys" with the Los Angeles Police Department. *Law & Society Review, 30*(4), 799–818.

Hernandez, J., Jr. (1989). *The Custer Syndrome.* Salem, WI: Sheffield.

Hewitt, J. P., & Stokes, R. (1975). Disclaimers. *American Sociological Review, 40,* 1–11.

Hinds, M. D. (1992, March 18). Crime's effect in a symbol-rich area. *New York Times,* p. A14.

Hirsch, M. (1997a, October 6). Behind the IRS curtain. *Newsweek*, pp. 28–32.

Hirsch, M. (1997b, October 13). Infernal revenue disservice. *Newsweek*, pp. 33–39.

Holden, R. (1984). Vision standards for law enforcement: A descriptive study. *Journal of Police Science and Administration, 12*(2), 125–129.

Holden, R. N. (1992). *Law enforcement: An introduction.* Englewood Cliffs, NJ: Prentice Hall.

Holden, R. N. (1993). Profit and the police motive: A new look at asset forfeiture. *ACJS Today, 12*(2), 1, 3, 24–25.

Hopsin v. Fredericksen, 961 F.2d 1374 (8th Cir. 1992).

Horwitz, S. (1990, March 10). Shortages tying hands of D.C. police. *Washington Post*. Reported in Newsbank, at LAW, p. B2.

Horwitz, S. (1997, May 19). For D.C. police chief, a second chance. *Washington Post*, p. A1.

Hunt, J. (1985). Police accounts of normal force. *Urban Life, 13*(4), 315–341.

Hunt, J. C. (1990). The logic of sexism among police. *Women and Criminal Justice, 1*(2), 3–30.

Hunt, J., & Manning, P. K. (1994). The social context of police lying. In P. A. Adler & P. Adler (Eds.), *Constructions of deviance.* Belmont, CA: Wadsworth.

Illinois v. Perkins, 110 S. Ct. 2394 (1990).

International Association of Chiefs of Police (1989). *Building Integrity and Reducing Drug Corruption in Police Departments.* Arlington, VA: International Association of Chiefs of Police.

Jacob, H. (1971). Black and white perceptions of justice in the city. *Law and Society Review, 5,* 69–89.

Jarriel, T. (1997, October 24). Betrayed by the badge: Sexual predators, rapists, hiding behind a badge. *20/20 transcripts*, pp. 1–10.

Jenkins, P. (1986). From gallows to prison? The execution rate in early modern England. *Criminal Justice History: An International Annual, 7,* 51–71.

Johnson, D. R. (1981). *American law enforcement: A history.* St. Louis: Forum Press.

Johnson, H. A. (1988). *A history of criminal justice.* Cincinnati: Anderson.

Johnston, D. (1990, January 26). Capital inquiry calls some Barry security guards. *New York Times*, p. A16.

Kappeler, V. E. (1989). St. Louis police department. In W. G. Bailey (Ed.), *The encyclopedia of police science*. New York: Garland.

Kappeler, V. E. (1996). Making police history in light of modernity: A sign of the times? *Police Forum, 6*(3), 1–6.

Kappeler, V. E. (1997). *Critical issues in police civil liability* (2nd ed.). Prospect Heights, IL: Waveland Press.

Kappeler, V. E., Blumberg, M., & Potter, G. W. (1996). *The mythology of crime and criminal justice* (2nd ed.). Prospect Heights, IL: Waveland Press.

Kappeler, V. E., & Kraska, P. B. (1994). Citizen complaints in the new police order. In W. G. Bailey (Ed.), *The encyclopedia of police science* (2nd ed.). New York: Garland.

Kappeler, V. E. & Kraska, P. B. (1998). A textual critique of community policing: Police adaption to high modernity. *Policing*, In press.

Kappeler, V. E., & Potter, G. W. (1993). Deflecting police deviance: A comment on the characterization of brutality victims. *Police Forum, 3*(1), 7–10.

Kappeler, V. E., & Vaughn, M. S. (1997). When pursuit becomes criminal: Municipal liability for police sexual violence. *Criminal Law Bulletin, 33*(4), 467–488.

Keary, J. (1997, October 3). Investigating homicide: No one is off limits. *Washington Times*: Available http:\\wastimes.com:80\metro\metro1.html.

Kelling, G. L. (1997, August 28). The assault on effective policing. *The Wall Street Journal*, p. 13.

Kelling, G. L., & Moore, M. H. (1995). The evolving strategy of policing. In V. E. Kappeler (Ed.), *The police & society: Touchstone readings* (pp. 3–27). Prospect Heights, IL: Waveland Press.

Kelly, M. A. (1985). Citizen survival in ancient Rome. *Police Studies, 11*, 195–201.

Kemper, V. (1993, March). A tough cop on the trail of hope. *Utne Reader,* p. 70–76.

Ketchum v. City of West Memphis, Ark., 974 F.2d 81 (8th Cir. 1992).

Kifner, J. (1997a, August 20). Police to put more black officers in tainted precinct. *New York Times*.

Kifner, J. (1997b, August 21). Investigators expand inquiry of police abuse incident. *New York Times*.

Kifner, J. (1997c, August 23). Early tip in torture case mishandled, police say. *New York Times*.

Kirby, J. (1996, June 7). Big Easy gets tough on crime and crooked cops. *Chicago Tribune*, Sec. 1, p. 24.

Kitsuse, J. I. (1962). Societal reaction to deviant behavior. *Social Problems, 9*, 247–256.

Kitsuse, J. I. (1972). Deviance, deviant behavior, and deviants: Some conceptual problems. In W. J. Filstead (Ed.), *An introduction to deviance: Readings in the process of making deviants.* Chicago: Markham.

Kleiman, M. A. (1992). *Against excess: Drug policy for results.* New York: Basic Books.

Kleinig, J., & Zhang, Y. (1993). *Professional law enforcement codes: A documentary collection.* Westport, CT: Greenwood Press.

Klock v. Cain, 813 F. Supp. 1430 (C.D. Cal. 1993).

Klockars, C. (1995). The legacy of conservative ideology and police. In V. E. Kappeler (Ed.), *The police & society: Touchstone readings* (pp. 349–355). Prospect Heights, IL: Waveland Press.

Knapp Commission report on police corruption. (1972). New York: George Braziller.

Knight, A. (1983a, March 13). Police handling of allegations stirs dispute. *Washington Post*, p. A1.

Knight, A. (1983b, March 19). District chief assigns Raines to night duty. *Washington Post*, p. A1.

Kolts, J. G. (1992). *The Los Angeles county sheriff's department.* A report by special counsel.

Koon v. U.S., 116 S. Ct. 2035 (1996).

Kornblum, A. K. (1976) *The moral hazards: Police strategies for honesty and ethical behavior.* Lexington, MA: D.C. Heath.

KPMG Peat Marwick. (1990, May 15). *Fleet management division, metropolitan police department, productivity enhancement.* Unpublished report.

Kraska, P. B. (1994). The police and the military in the post-cold war era: Streamlining the state's use of force entities in the drug war. *Police Forum, 4*(1), 1–12.

Kraska, P. B., & Kappeler, V. E. (1988). Police on-duty drug use: A theoretical and descriptive examination. *American Journal of Police, 7*(1), 1–28.

Kraska, P. B., & Kappeler, V. E. (1995). To serve and pursue: Police sexual violence against women. *Justice Quarterly, 12*(1), 85–111.

Kraska, P. B., & Kappeler, V. E. (1997). Militarizing American police: The rise and normalization of paramilitary units. *Social Problems, 44*(1), 1–18.

Kraska, P. B. & Paulsen, D. J. (1997). Grounded research into U.S. paramilitary policing: Forging the iron fist inside the velvet glove. *Police and Society, 7,* 253–270.

Kuykendall, J., & Burns, D. (1980). The black police officer: An historical perspective. *Journal of Contemporary Criminal Justice, 1*(4), 103–113.

Lacayo, R. (1997, September 1). Good cop, bad cop. *Time,* 26–30.

Larez v. City of Los Angeles, 946 F.2d 630 (9th Cir. 1991).

Lemert, E. M. (1997). *The trouble with evil.* Albany, New York: SUNY Press.

Logan v. Drew, 790 F. Supp. 181 (N.D. Ill. 1992).

Louis, P. (1989). New York police department. In W. G. Bailey (Ed.), *The encyclopedia of police science.* New York: Garland.

Lynch, M. J., & Groves, W. B. (1989). *A primer in radical criminology.* New York: Harrow and Heston.

Maas, P. (1973). *Serpico: The cop who defied the system.* New York: Viking.

Maguire, K., Pastore, A. L., & Flanagan, T. J. (Eds.). (1996). *Sourcebook of criminal justice statistics, 1995.* Washington, DC: U.S. Government Printing Office.

Maher, P. T. (1988). Police physical agility tests: Can they ever be valid? *Public Personnel Management Journal, 17,* 173–183.

Mann, C. R. (1993). *Unequal justice: A question of color.* Bloomington: Indiana University Press.

Manning, P. K. (1978). Rules, colleagues, and situationally justified actions. In P. K. Manning & J. Van Maanen (Eds.), *Policing: A view from the street*. Santa Monica, CA: Goodyear.

Manning, P. K. (1995a). The police: Mandate, strategies and appearances. In V. E. Kappeler (Ed.), *The police & society: Touchstone readings* (pp. 97–125). Prospect Heights, IL: Waveland Press.

Manning, P. K. (1995b). Violence and symbolic violence. In V. E. Kappeler (Ed.), *The police & society: Touchstone readings* (pp. 357–363). Prospect Heights, IL: Waveland Press.

Manning, P. K. (1997). *Police work: The social organization of policing* (2nd ed.). Prospect Heights, IL: Waveland Press.

Manning, P. K., & Redlinger, L. J. (1977). Invitational edges of corruption: Some consequences of narcotic law enforcement. In J. D. Douglas & J. M. Johnson (Eds.), *Readings in malfeasance, misfeasance, and other forms of corruption*. Philadelphia: J. B. Lippincott.

Manning, P. K., & Redlinger, L. J. (1978). Working bases for corruption: Organizational ambiguities and narcotics law enforcement. In A. S. Trebach (Ed.), *Drugs, crime, and politics*. New York: Praeger.

Marchak, E. A. (1992, March 22). Police fit their time to the crime. *Washington Times*. Reported in Newsbank, at LAW 28, p. G12.

Marks, J. (1997, September 29). New York, New York. *U.S. News & World Report*, 47–52.

Marquart, J. (1986). Doing research in prison: The strengths and weaknesses of full participation as a guard. *Justice Quarterly, 3*(1), 20–32.

Marx, G. T. (1992). When the guards guard themselves: Undercover tactics turned inward. *Policing and Society, 2*(3), 151–172.

Mathew, T. (1993, April 26). Looking past the verdict. *Newsweek*, 20–28.

Matza, D. (1969). *Becoming deviant* . Englewood Cliffs, NJ: Prentice-Hall.

Mayor's Citizen Commission (1991). *A report to Mayor John O. Norquist and the board of fire and police commissioners*. Milwaukee: City of Milwaukee.

McAlary, M. (1987). *Buddy boys: When good cops turn bad*. New York: G.P. Putnam's Sons.

McCaghy, C. H., & Cernkovich, S. A. (1987). *Crime in American society* (2nd ed.). New York: Macmillan.

McCraw, V., & Reilly, B. (1992, September 9). "He was a good, tough cop": Fulwood takes hint, bows out. *Washington Times*. Reported in Newsbank, at NIN 211, p. E3.

McDonald v. Haskins, 966 F.2d 292 (7th Cir. 1992).

McFadden, R. D. (1986, November 8). For O'Regan, the double life of an officer led to despair. *New York Times*, p. A36.

McMullan, M. (1961). A theory of corruption. *Sociological Review, 9*(2), 181–201.

McNamara, J. D. (1997, September 1). A veteran chief: Too many cops think it's a war. *Time*, 28–29.

McNamara, J. H. (1967). Uncertainties in police work: The relevance of police recruits' backgrounds and training. In D. J. Bordua (Ed.), *The police: Six sociological essays*. New York: John Wiley.

Meier, R. F. (1989). Deviance and differentiation. In S. F. Messner, M. D. Krohn, & A. E. Liska (Eds.), *Theoretical integration in the study of deviance and crime: Problems and prospects.* Albany: State University of New York Press.

Meyers, S. L. (1993, October 8). Officers describe police watchdog agency as ineffectual. *New York Times,* p. A4.

Miller, B., & Woodlee, Y. (1997, October 23). Treadwell pleads guilty to theft: Longtime D.C. employee convicted in fraud in stolen city funds. *Washington Post,* p. D1.

Miller, W. R. (1977). *Cops and bobbies: Police authority in New York and London, 1830–1870.* Chicago: University of Chicago Press.

Milloy, C. (1997, November 5). Defending his name on the street. *Washington Post,* p. B1.

Mills, C. W. (1940). Situated actions and vocabularies of motives. *American Sociological Review, 5,* 904–913.

Minneapolis. (1993, April 28). *Houston Chronicle,* p. A10.

Miranda v. Arizona, 384 U.S. 436 (1966).

Model Penal Code, Section 1.1014(1).

Mollen Commission. 1994. *The City of New York Commission to Investigate Allegations of Police Corruption and the Anti-Corruption Procedures of the Police Department: Commission Report.* New York: City of New York.

Mooar, B. (1997, September 26). 2 D.C. officers say whistleblowing backfired: Sergeants tell Council committee that accusing friend led to threats, intimidation. *Washington Post,* p. B5.

Moore, M. H., & Kelling G. L. (1976). To serve and protect: Learning from police history. In A. S. Blumberg & E. Niederhoffer (Eds.), *The ambivalent force.* New York: Holt, Rinehart and Winston.

Moore, M. H., & Trojanowicz, R. (1988). *Corporate stratagies for policing.* Washington, D.C.: U.S. Department of Justice.

Morgan v. City of Marmaduke, Arkansas, 958 F.2d 207 (8th Cir. 1992).

Murano, V., with Hoffer, W. (1990). *Cop hunter.* New York: Pocket Books.

Murphy, P. V., & Caplan, D. G. (1993). Fostering integrity. In R. G. Dunham & G. P. Alpert (Eds.), *Critical issues in policing: Contemporary readings* (2nd ed., pp. 304–324) Prospect Heights, IL: Waveland Press.

Murphy, P. V., & Pate, T. (1977). *Commissioner: A view from the top of American law enforcement.* New York: Simon and Schuster.

Musto, D. (1973). *The American disease: Origins of narcotic control.* New Haven, CT: Yale University Press.

Nadelman, E. A. (1989). Drug prohibition in the United States: Costs, consequences, and alternatives. *Science, 245,* 939–947.

Nasser, H. E. (1993, February 11). Gulf separates races in dealings with police: Poll finds sharply different views of law enforcement. *USA Today,* pp. 1A, 11A.

National Advisory Commission on Criminal Justice Standards and Goals (1973). *Police.* Washington, DC: U.S. Government Printing Office.

National Commission on Law Observance and Enforcement. (1931). *Report on the police.* Washington, DC: U.S. Government Printing Office.

Neufield, M., & Piccoli, S. (1987, November 6). Police to tell applicants of test for pregnancy. *Washington Times.* Reported in Newsbank, at LAW 114, p. G9.

New police chief gets early lesson. (1992, November 20). *New York Times,* p. A19.

Newspaper survey. (1991, August 12). *Milwaukee Journal.*

Niederhoffer, A. (1967). *Behind the shield: The police in urban society.* Garden City, NY: Anchor Books.

Nix, C. (1986, October 2). Suspension of 13 officers puts 80 criminal cases in jeopardy. *New York Times,* p. B3.

Oaks, D. (1970). Studying the exclusionary rule in search and seizure. *University of Chicago Law Review, 37,* 665–757.

Officer alleges "widespread" use of drugs among D.C. police force. (1983, June 27). *Law Enforcement News,* p. 3.

Oldani, R. (1992, September). From the President. *Gendarme,* pp. 2–3.

Opler, M. E. (1945). Themes as dynamic forces in culture. *The American Journal of Sociology, 51,* 198–206.

Overtown Blue Ribbon Committee (1984). *Final report.* Miami: City of Miami.

Paley, R. (1989). An imperfect, inadequate and wretched system? Policing London before Peel. *Criminal Justice History: An International Annual, 10,* 95–130.

Panel recommends suspension for officers who confiscated camera. (1995). News Media Update. Available http:\\www.rcfp.org\NMU\951120d.html.

Patterson, A. (1992, Spring). Comments made by LAPD chief become focus of appeal. *Police Liability Review, 4,* 6–7.

Paynes, J., & Bernardin, H. J. (1992). Entry-level police selection: The assessment center is an alternative. *Journal of Criminal Justice, 20,* 41–52.

Petersilia, J., & Abrahamse, A. (1994). The Los Angeles riot of Spring, 1992: A profile of those arrested. *Police Forum, 3*(4), 1–10.

Piliavin, I., & Briar, S. (1964). Police encounters with juveniles. *American Journal of Sociology, 70,* 206–214.

Pogrebin, M. R., & Poole, E. D. (1991). Police and tragic events: The management of emotions. *Journal of Criminal Justice, 19,* 395–403.

Police Executive Research Forum. (1990). *Issues Paper: Metropolitan Police Department.* Unpublished manuscript.

Pope, C. E., & Ross, L. E. (1992). Race, crime and justice: The aftermath of Rodney King. *The Criminologist, 17*(6), 1, 7–10.

Portland. (1993, May 3). *Houston Chronicle,* p. A11.

Powell, M. (1997, October 21). D.C. police changes should start at top, specialists say. *Washington Post,* p. B1.

Powell, M., & Miller, B. (1997, October 15). D.C. crime evidence in doubt: Judge says reports of improper handling threatens cases. *Washington Post,* p. A1.

Powell, M., Horwitz S., & Thompson, C. W. (1997, October 12). Problems in D.C. police department festered for decades. *Washington Post,* p. A1.

Pringle, P. (n.d.). *Hue and cry: The story of Henry and John Fielding and their Bow Street Runners.* Bangay, Suffolk, Great Britain: Richard Clay.

Prud'Homme, A. (1991, March 25). Police brutality! *Time,* 16–19.

Purdum, T. S. (1986a, September 24). Suspensions stir accountability issue. *New York Times,* p. B4.

Purdum, T. S. (1986b, September 25). 2 Brooklyn officers said to suggest extortion to 13. *New York Times,* pp. A1, B4.

Purdum, T. S. (1986c, November 1). Police transfer of 27 supervisors amid inquiry at 77th precinct. *New York Times*, pp. A1, A36.

Purdum, T. S. (1986d, November 8). Missing indicted officer found dead in motel. *New York Times*, pp. A1, A36.

Purdum, T. S. (1986e, December 10). 90 patrol officers in 77th precinct are shifted elsewhere in Brooklyn. *New York Times*, p. B2.

Purdum, T. S. (1986f, December 11). Police supervisors in survey fail to identify their bosses. *New York Times*, pp. A1, B14.

Purdum, T. S. (1987, March 11). Officer admits guilt in sale of cocaine. *New York Times*, pp. B1, B8.

Purnick, J. (1986, November 11). Broad changes in police urged by Koch panel. *New York Times*, pp. A1, B4.

Puro, S., Goldman, R., & Smith, W. (in press). Police decertification: Changing patterns among the states, 1985–1995. *Policing: An International Journal of Police Strategies and Management*.

Putti, J., Aryee, S., & Kang, T. S. (1988). Personal values of recruits and officers in a law enforcement agency: An exploratory study. *Journal of Police Science and Administration*, *16*(4), 249–265.

Quindlen, A. (1993, October 5). Good cops don't grow in Brooklyn, which needs them. *Chicago Tribune*, p. A19.

Quinney, R. (1977). *Class, state, and crime*. New York: Longman.

Rachlin, H. (1996, January). Accreditation: The complete story. *Law and Order*, pp. 312–327.

Reaves, B. A. (1989). *Police departments in large cities, 1987*. Washington, DC: Bureau of Justice Statistics, U.S. Department of Justice.

Redfield, R. (1952). *The primitive worldview*. Proceedings of the American Philosophical Society, *96*, 30–36.

Redfield, R. (1953). *The primitive world and its transformations*. Ithaca, NY: Cornell University Press.

Reichel, P. L. (1992). The misplaced emphasis on urbanization in police development. *Policing and Society*, *3*, 1–12.

Reilly, B. (1992, June 27). 7-year police veteran held as gang member. *Washington Times*. Reported in Newsbank, at NIN 146, p. C12.

Reinhold, R. (1992, August 6). U.S. jury indicts 4 police officers in King beating. *New York Times*, pp. A1, A12.

Reiss, A. J. (1971). *The police and the public*. New Haven: Yale University Press.

Reiss, A. J., & Bordua, D. J. (1967). Environment and organization: A perspective on the police. In D. J. Bordua (Ed.), *The police: Six sociological essays*. New York: John Wiley.

Report of the national advisory commission on civil disorders. (1968). New York: Bantam Books.

Report of the special committee of board of aldermen of the City of New York appointed August 5, 1912 to investigate the police department. (1913). New York: Authors.

Reuss-Ianni, E. (1983). *Two cultures of policing*. New Brunswick, NJ: Transaction Books.

Reuss-Ianni, E., & Ianni, F. A. J. (1983). Street cops and management cops: The two cultures of policing. In M. Punch (Ed.), *Control in the police organization.* Cambridge: MIT Press.

Reuter, P., & Kleiman, M. A. R. (1991). The dismal economics of the war on drugs. In C. B. Klockars & S. D. Mastrofski (Eds.), *Thinking about police.* New York: McGraw Hill.

Richardson, J. F. (1970). *The New York police.* New York: Oxford University Press.

Richardson, J. F. (1974). *Urban Police in the United States.* Port Washington, NY: National University, Kennikat Press.

Robinson v. City of St. Charles, Missouri, 972 F.2d 974 (8th Cir. 1992).

Robinson, C. D., Scaglion, R., & Olivero, J. M. (1994). *Police in contradiction: The evolution of the police function in society.* Westport, CT: Greenwood Press.

Rokeach, M., Miller, M. G., & Snyder, J. S. (1971). The value gap between the police and the policed. *Journal of Social Issues, 27*(2), 155–177.

Rothmiller, M., & Goldman, I. G. (1992). *L.A. secret police: Inside the LAPD elite spy network.* New York: Pocket Books.

Rubinstein, J. (1973). *City police.* New York: Farrar, Straus and Giroux.

Salopek, P. (1997, January 5). Going crooked: Cops as thugs. *Chicago Tribune,* Sec. 1, p. 1.

Samaha, J. (1974). *Law and order in historical perspective.* New York: Academic Press.

Sapp, A. D. (1994). Sexual misconduct by police officers. In T. Barker & D. L. Carter (Eds.), *Police deviance* (3rd ed.). Cincinnati: Anderson.

Savitz, L. (1971). The dimensions of police loyalty. In H. Hahn (Ed.), *Police in urban society.* Beverly Hills: Sage.

Schur, E. (1971). *Labeling deviant behavior.* New York: Harper and Row.

Schur, E. (1980). *The politics of deviance: Stigma contests and the uses of power.* Englewood Cliffs, NJ: Prentice-Hall.

Scott, M. B., & Lyman, S. (1968). Accounts. *American Sociological Review, 33,* 46–62.

Sechrest, D. K., & Burns, P. (1992). Police corruption: The Miami case. *Criminal Justice and Behavior, 19,* 294–313.

Service records of the officers suspended in the 77th precinct. (1986, September 25). *New York Times,* p. B4.

Sherman, L. W. (1974). *Police corruption: A sociological perspective.* Garden City, NY: Doubleday Anchor Books.

Sherman, L. W. (1977). *City politics, police administrators, and corruption control.* New York: John Jay Press.

Sherman, L. W. (1978). *Scandal and reform: Controlling police corruption.* Berkeley: University of California Press.

Sherman, L. W. (1982). Learning police ethics. *Criminal Justice Ethics, 1*(1), 10–19.

Simeon, E. F. (1989). A hail of problems to the chief. *Washington Times.* Reported in Newsbank, at NIN 126, p. B11.

Simpson, A. E. (1977). *The literature of police corruption, volume 1: A guide to bibliography and theory.* New York: John Jay Press.

Skogan, W. (1991). The impact of routine encounters with police. Paper presented at the annual meeting of the American Society of Criminology, San Francisco.

Skolnick, J. H. (1966). *Justice without trial: Law enforcement in a democratic society.* New York: John Wiley.

Skolnick, J. H. (1994). *Justice without trial: Law enforcement in a democratic society* (3rd ed.). New York: Macmillan.

Skolnick, J. H., & Fyfe, J. J. (1993). *Above the law: Police and the excessive use of force.* New York: The Free Press.

Smith, P. T. (1985). *Policing victorian London.* Westport, CT: Greenwood Press.

Smith, W. C., & Alpert, G. P. (1993). Policing the defective centurion: Decertification and beyond. *Criminal Law Bulletin, 29*(2), 147–157.

Smothers, R. (1986, September 25). In drug-wracked 77th precinct, police suspensions draw varied reactions. *New York Times*, p. B4.

Snyder, H., & Sickmund, M. (1996). *Juvenile offenders and victims: A national report.* Washington, DC, U.S. Dept. of Justice.

Sommers, A. (1988, May 27). City police training program questioned. *Washington Times.* Reported in Newsbank, at LAW 70, p. B3.

Sparger, J. R., & Giacopassi, D. J. (1992). Memphis revisited: A reexamination of police shootings after the Garner decision. *Justice Quarterly, 9,* 211–225.

Spitzer, S. (1975). Toward a Marxian theory of deviance. *Social Problems, 22*(5), 638–651.

Stead, P. J. (1985). *The Police of Britain.* New York: Macmillan.

Stewart, S. A. (1993a, February 26). Prosecutor: King was put on display. *USA Today,* p. 1A.

Stewart, S. A. (1993b, March 9). L.A. trial's "human" face expected today. *USA Today,* p. 3A.

Stewart, S. A. (1993c, March 16). Defense's turn in King Case: "Educating the jury" is key for police officers on trial. *USA Today,* p. 2A.

Stoddard, E. R. (1995). The informal code of police deviancy: A group approach to blue-collar crime. In V. E. Kappeler (Ed.), *The police & society: Touchstone readings* (pp. 185–206). Prospect Heights, IL: Waveland Press.

Strecher, V. G. (1995). Revising the histories and futures of policing. In V. E. Kappeler (Ed.), *The police & society: Touchstone readings* (pp. 69–82). Prospect Heights, IL: Waveland Press.

Sullivan, P. S. (1989). Minority officers: Current issues. In R. G. Dunham & G. P. Alpert (Eds.), *Critical issues in policing: Contemporary readings* (pp. 331–345). Prospect Heights, IL: Waveland Press.

Sullivan, P. S., Dunham, R. G., & Alpert, G. P. (1987). Attitude structures of different ethnic and age groups concerning police. *Journal of Criminal Law and Criminology, 78,* 177–196.

Sutherland, E. H. (1940). White-collar criminality. *American Sociological Review, 5,* 1–12.

Sutton, L. P. (1991). Getting around the fourth amendment. In C. B. Klockars & S. D. Mastrofski (Eds.), *Thinking about police: Contemporary readings* (2nd ed.). New York: McGraw-Hill.

Swanson, C., Territo, L., & Taylor, R. (1993). *Police administration* (3rd ed.). New York: Macmillan.

Swanton, B. (1981). Social isolation of police: Structural determinants and remedies. *Police Studies, 3,* 14–21.

Sykes, G. (1995). Street justice: A moral defense of order maintenance policing. In *Police & society: Touchstone readings* (pp. 139–154). Prospect Heights, IL: Waveland Press.

Sykes, G. M., & Matza, D. (1957). Techniques of neutralization. *American Sociological Review, 22,* 664–670.

Task force report: The police. (1967). Washington, DC: U.S. Government Printing Office.

Thomas-Lester, A., & Miller, B. (1997, September 19). 49 in homicide unit failed to solve any '97 cases, official says. *Washington Post,* p. A1.

Thompson, C. W. (1997a, September 18). 17 supervisors removed from D.C. homicide unit. *Washington Post,* p. A1.

Thompson, C. W. (1997b, September 21). D.C. officials suspect police overtime "scam": $6 million in homicide unit's pay scrutinized. *Washington Post,* p. A1.

Thompson, C. W., & Lewis, N. (1997, September 20). D.C. homicide detectives must sign secrecy pledge: Rules limit information on even closed cases. *Washington Post,* p. C1.

Thompson, C., & Ordon-ez, J. (1997a, October 11). Police captain faults Soulsby on overtime: Council told that Control Board also knew of issue months ago. *Washington Post,* p. C1.

Ting v. United States, 927 F.2d 1504 (9th Cir. 1991).

Tobar, H., & Colvin, R. L. (1991, March 6). Witnesses depict relentless beating. *Los Angeles Times,* p. B1.

Tobias, J. J. (1979). *Crime and police in England, 1700–1900.* Dublin: McMillan.

Turk, A. T. (1969). *Criminality and legal order.* Chicago: Rand McNally.

Turk, A. T. (1976). Law as a weapon in social conflict. *Social Problems, 23*(3), 276–291.

Turk, A. T. (1977). Class, conflict, and criminalization, *Sociological Focus, 10*(3), 209–220.

Turner calls it quits. (1989, May 31). *Law Enforcement News,* pp. A1, A5.

Turner v. White, 980 F.2d. 1180 (8th Cir. 1992).

Two charged in drug case. (1993, March 5). *Houston Chronicle,* p. A30.

U.S. Prosecutor dismisses all drug cases made by unit of D.C. police in wake of scandal. (1987). *Crime Control Digest, 21*(39), 5.

Uchida, C. (1997). The development of the American police. In R. G. Dunham & G. P. Alpert (Eds.), *Critical issues in policing: Contemporary readings* (3rd ed., pp. 18–35). Prospect Heights, IL: Waveland Press.

United States Commission on Civil Rights (1981). *Who is guarding the guardians?* Washington, DC: U.S. Government Printing Office.

United States Department of Justice (1987). *Community relations service.* Washington, DC: U.S. Government Printing Office.

Van Maanen, J. (1995). The asshole. In V. E. Kappeler (Ed.), *The police & society: Touchstone readings* (pp. 307–328). Prospect Heights, IL: Waveland Press.

Van Maanen, J. (1997). Observations on the making of policemen. In R. G. Culbertson & R. A. Weisheit (Eds.), *"Order under law": Readings in criminal justice* (5th ed., pp. 87–107). Prospect Heights, IL: Waveland Press.

Vaughn, M. S. (1992). The parameters of trickery as an acceptable police practice. *American Journal of Police, 11*(4), 71–95.

Wacholz, S., & Mullaly, R. (1993). Policing the deinstitutionalized mentally ill: Toward an understanding of its function. *Crime, Law and Social Change, 19*(3), 281–300.

Waddington, P. A. J., & Braddock, Q. (1991). "Guardians" or "bullies"? Perceptions of the police amongst adolescent black, white and Asian boys. *Policing and Society , 2*(1), 31–45.

Wagner, A. E., & Decker, S. (1997). Evaluating citizen complaints against the police. In R. G. Dunham & G. P. Alpert (Eds.), *Critical issues in policing: Contemporary readings* (3rd ed., pp. 302–318). Prospect Heights, IL: Waveland Press.

Walker, S. (1977). *A critical history of police reform*. Lexington, MA: Lexington Books.

Walker, S. (1992a). The origins of the American police-community relations movement: The 1940s. In E. H. Monkkonen (Ed.), *Policing and crime control, part III*. New York: K. G. Saur.

Walker, S. (1992b). *The police in America: An introduction* (2nd ed). New York: McGraw-Hill.

Walker, S., & Kreisel, B. (1997). Varieties of citizen review: The relationship of mission, structure, and procedures to police accountability. In R. G. Dunham & G. P. Alpert (Eds.), *Critical issues in policing: Contemporary readings* (3rd ed., pp. 319–336). Prospect Heights, IL: Waveland Press.

Wallace, M. (News Reporter). (1988, February). Buddy Boys. *60 Minutes.* New York: CBS.

Weber v. District of Columbia, 723 F. Supp. 829 (D.D.C. 1989).

Wellford, C. (1975). Labeling theory and criminology: An assessment. *Social Problems, 22*, 375.

West, P. (1994). Investigation and review of complaints against police officers: An overview of issues and philosophies. In T. Barker & D. Carter (Eds.), *Police deviance* (3rd ed.). Cincinnati: Anderson.

Westley, W. A. (1953). Violence and the police. *American Journal of Sociology, 59*, 34–41.

Westley, W. A. (1956). Secrecy and the police. *Social Forces, 34*(3), 254–257.

Westley, W. A. (1970). *Violence and the police: A Sociological study of law, custom and morality.* Cambridge: MIT Press.

Westley, W. A. (1995). *Violence and the police.* In V. E. Kappeler (Ed.), *The police & society: Touchstone readings* (pp. 293–305). Prospect Heights, IL: Waveland Press.

White, B. P. (1997, January 13). Police integrity on trial with community. *Chicago Tribune*, Sec. 1, p. 1.

Widder, P. (1997, September 28). Fairness & abuse: A delicate balance. *Chicago Tribune*, Sec. 3, pp. 1, 4.

Wilbanks, W. (1987). *The myth of a racist criminal justice system.* Monterey, CA: Brooks/Cole.

Williams, F. P., & Wagner, C. P. (1995). Making the police proactive: An impossible task for improbable reasons. In V. E. Kappeler (Ed.), *The police & society: Touchstone readings* (pp. 365–374). Prospect Heights, IL: Waveland Press.

Williams, H. (1997). The impact of police culture, leadership, and organization on integrity. In S. J. Gaffigan & P. P. McDonald (Eds.), *Police Integrity.* Washington D.C.: U.S. Department of Justice, National Institute of Justice.

Williams, H., & Murphy, P. V. (1995). Revising the histories and futures of policing. In Kappeler, V. E. (Ed.), *The police & society: Touchstone readings* (pp. 29–52). Prospect Heights, IL: Waveland Press.

Williams, J. R., Redlinger, L. J., & Manning, P. K. (1979). *Police narcotics control: Patterns and strategies.* Washington, DC: U.S. Government Printing Office.

Wilson, J. Q. (1990). Drugs and crime. In M. Tonry & J. Q. Wilson (Eds.), *Drugs and crime* (Vol. 13). Chicago: University of Chicago Press.

Wisotsky, S. (1990). *Beyond the war on drugs: Overcoming a failed public policy.* Buffalo: Prometheus Books.

Woestendiek, J. (1991, April 8). National uproar not the first Gates controversy in LA. *Kansas City Star*, p. A-6.

Zorn, E. (1997, October 2). Police brutality alleged; bring on the internal review. *Chicago Tribune*, Sec. 2, p. 1.

Zorn, E. (1997, October 6). Police terminology clouds unresolved brutality cases. *Chicago Tribune*, Sec. 2, p. 1.

INDEX